STO1

PERSONAL VER

STORM

PERSONAL VERSION 3.0

Quantitative Modeling
for Decision Support

HAMILTON EMMONS
Weatherhead School of Management
Case Western Reserve University

A. DALE FLOWERS
Weatherhead School of Management
Case Western Reserve University

CHANDRASHEKHAR M. KHOT
Storm Software, Inc.

KAMLESH MATHUR
Weatherhead School of Management
Case Western Reserve University

Prentice Hall/Allyn & Bacon
Simon & Schuster Higher Education Group
Prentice Hall Building, Englewood Cliffs, NJ 07632

Acquisition Editor: Valerie Ashton
Production Editor: Joanne Palmer
Cover Designer: Patricia McGowan
Prepress Buyer: Trudy Pisciotti
Manufacturing Buyer: Bob Anderson
Editorial Assistant: AnnMarie Dunn

Designed and developed by:
Storm Software, Inc.
P.O. Box 22658
Cleveland, OH 44122-9998

Published by:
Prentice Hall/Allyn & Bacon
Simon and Schuster Higher Education Group
Prentice Hall Building
Englewood Cliffs, NJ 07632

Printed in the United States of America

10 9 8 7 6

ISBN 0-13-847450-8

PRENTICE-HALL INTERNATIONAL (UK) LIMITED, *London*
PRENTICE-HALL OF AUSTRALIA PTY. LIMITED, *Sydney*
PRENTICE-HALL CANADA INC., *Toronto*
PRENTICE-HALL HISPANOAMERICANA, S.A., *Mexico*
PRENTICE-HALL OF INDIA PRIVATE LIMITED, *New Delhi*
PRENTICE-HALL OF JAPAN, INC., *Tokyo*
SIMON & SCHUSTER ASIA PTE. LTD., *Singapore*
EDITORA PRENTICE-HALL DO BRASIL, LTDA., *Rio de Janeiro*

PREFACE &
ACKNOWLEDGMENTS

Since the first release of Personal STORM in early 1986, we have received a lot of feedback and suggestions for possible enhancements and additions to the software. The release of version 2 in 1989 was our first big step in the direction. The response to version 2 has been very enthusiastic indeed, and has encouraged us to develop version 3.

In this version, we have added the much requested Decision Analysis capability. We trust you will find it up to the standards you have come to expect from STORM. After much consideration, we have decided to introduce the capability in the form of two separate modules on the Main Menu, viz. Decision Analysis: Single Level and Decision Trees. Although many of you may prefer to think of these two modules collectively as Decision Analysis, we found it best to distinguish them from each other for convenience in use, since the data layout for the two modules is quite different.

Recognizing the need to introduce students to meaningful, and therefore moderately large, cases and problems, we had increased the problems sizes in all of the modules in version 2. However, judging by your response, we felt that we had not gone far enough. Accordingly, in version 3, you will find the problem sizes increased significantly.

We have also added the ability to import and export ASCII files from the Data Editor. These new capabilities are available as block operations and can provide a bridge between STORM and popular spreadsheets and database systems. These operations can also come in handy when blocks of input data can be downloaded from a mainframe, thus saving reentry of the data and eliminating a source of errors.

Unlike version 2, this release is completely compatible with your existing data sets. In other words, there are no changes in data layouts in the existing modules, so there will be no need to convert existing data sets to this version. We hope to minimize data layout changes in future releases as well; however, should they become necessary, the import/export facility should come in handy.

We would like to recognize the contributions made by three individuals to this release. Milind Tamaskar participated heavily in the development process, making many suggestions for improvements along the way. He was also dedicated and persevering in the testing phase of the software. Chris Mizer was an asset when it came to the preparation of the user's manual, always remaining enthusiastic through the laborious and painstaking process. Mary Eva took over from Chris and successfully took the manuscript through a series of changes, necessitated by hardware and software upgrades. While working under the pressure of imminent deadlines, she remained cheerful and dedicated.

We appreciate the efforts made by Valerie Ashton, Executive Editor at Prentice Hall, and Rich Wohl, Executive Editor at Allyn & Bacon, to ensure a smooth transition from our previous publisher, and to bring about an expeditious publication of Version 3.

Finally, we wish to express our deepest and sincerest gratitude to our wives - Lin Emmons, Gwen Flowers, and Anita Khot. Without their unfailing support, we could not have persevered.

Hamilton Emmons
A. Dale Flowers
Chandrashekhar M. Khot
Kamlesh Mathur

Cleveland, Ohio

TABLE OF CONTENTS

x

xvi

Chapter 20
STATISTICAL PROCESS CONTROL 337

Chapter 21
STATISTICS 373

STORM

PERSONAL VERSION 3.0

Chapter 1

INTRODUCTION
AND INSTALLATION

1. What is STORM?

STORM is an integrated software package consisting of the most frequently used quantitative modeling techniques for business and engineering problems. It is menu driven for convenience and flexibility, and consists of:

- a flexible and easy-to-use Editor for data input and modification
- eighteen computational modules
- a variety of user-selected outputs for displaying the results of computations

The mathematical models included in STORM are drawn from operations research/ management science, operations management/ industrial engineering, and statistics. The specific modules are:

1) Linear & Integer Programming
2) Assignment
3) Transportation
4) Distance Networks: Paths, Tours, Trees
5) Flow Networks: Max Flow, Transshipment
6) Project Management: PERT/CPM
7) Queueing Analysis
8) Inventory Management
9) Facility Layout
10) Assembly Line Balancing
11) Investment Analysis
12) Forecasting
13) Production Scheduling
14) Material Requirements Planning
15) Statistical Process Control
16) Statistics
17) Decision Analysis: Single Level
18) Decision Trees

STORM makes quantitative modeling easier to do on the computer than has heretofore been possible. It represents a significant improvement in ease of use, and incorporates state-of-the-art software development techniques and computational algorithms.

2. Assumptions About Our Users

It is important that you understand what STORM will and will not do for you, and what type of user we expect to make productive use of STORM. We hope that you are reasonably familiar with using a microcomputer, though we do give you some basic pointers in Appendix A. We also assume that you have some basic understanding of the methodologies being applied by STORM. Neither the software nor this manual attempts to teach the methods being used. Instead, we focus on using STORM to apply the methods to your particular problem. We do try to offer as many helpful hints as possible, and each chapter which describes a module provides a quick review of the problem being addressed.

The types of individuals who should find STORM of use in their business and/or educational pursuits include anyone who needs to perform a good deal of business or engineering analysis.

3. System Requirements

STORM will run on IBM-PC, IBM-XT, IBM-AT, PS2 and 100% IBM compatible microcomputers. The minimal amount of *net* memory required is 320K bytes. That is, you need enough memory to hold DOS and any other programs you wish to run in the background, and still have 320K bytes left for STORM. STORM can be used on a system with just one floppy disk drive, although two floppy drives or a fixed disk is recommended. STORM will operate with any of the standard monitors and printers currently used with the microcomputers identified above. DOS 2.0 or higher is required.

4. Installing STORM

Before you do anything else, you should make a copy of STORM from your original distribution diskettes. This copy should be used to run STORM, and the original diskettes should be stored in a safe place. STORM comes on either three 5.25" low density diskettes or two 3.5" low density diskettes. In the discussions below, we shall assume that if you are not installing STORM on a fixed disk, you are installing it on the same size diskette as your originals. That is, you would use 5.25" diskette originals to make 5.25" diskette copies, and similarly for the 3.5" size.

4.1 Installing STORM to a Fixed Disk

You will need the original STORM diskettes to accomplish this task. You will probably want to create a directory on your fixed disk for STORM (we call it STORM on our machines), and then connect to this directory. We assume that disk drive A: is where you will load the original diskettes for copying in this procedure. Then you would place each of the original STORM diskettes in turn in drive A:, close the door and type:

        copy a:*.*/v

and press enter. When you are done, STORM and all its sample problem data files have been installed in your directory. When you are in that directory, you simply type *STORM* and press Enter to start the program.

4.2 Installing STORM to 5.25" Diskettes

You will need your original STORM diskettes of this size, plus three blank formatted diskettes (consult your DOS manual for information on formatting diskettes, if needed). We assume that disk drive A: is where you will load the original diskettes for copying in this procedure. You will need an A> prompt on your monitor to proceed with this installation. If any other prompt appears, type *A:* and press enter and then continue with the process. Next type *Diskcopy* and press enter. DOS will prompt you to place the source diskette in the drive and press any key to continue. Put the original STORM1 diskette in the drive and press any key. After some time, DOS will prompt you to place the destination diskette in the drive. Place the first of the three blank diskettes in the drive and press any key. You may have to repeat this step to complete copying the disk; if so, DOS will prompt you to that effect. DOS will eventually tell you that the copy is complete and ask if you want to copy another one. At this time, remove the *destination* diskette which now contains your working copy of STORM1, and put a label on it identifying it as the STORM1 diskette (STORM will ask for its diskettes by number when you run it from floppy diskettes, so labeling is important). Then answer *y* for *yes* and repeat the above procedure for the STORM2 and STORM3 diskettes. Remember to label them accordingly. To run your copy of STORM, insert the STORM1 diskette in the A: drive and, with the A> prompt on your monitor, type STORM to start the program.

4.3 Installing STORM to 3.5" Diskettes

You will need your original STORM diskettes of this size, plus two blank formatted diskettes (consult your DOS manual for information on formatting diskettes, if needed). We assume that disk drive A: is where you will load the original diskettes for copying in this procedure. You will need an A> prompt on your monitor to proceed with this installation. If any other prompt appears, type *A:* and press enter and then continue with the process. Next type *Diskcopy* and press enter. DOS will prompt you to place the source diskette in the drive and press any key to continue. Put the original STORM1 diskette in the drive and press any key. After some time, DOS will prompt you to place the destination diskette in the drive. Place the first of the two blank diskettes in the drive and press any key. You may have to repeat this step to complete copying the disk; if so, DOS will prompt you to that effect. DOS will eventually tell you that the copy is complete and ask if you want to copy another one. At this time, remove the *destination* diskette which now contains your working copy of STORM1, and put a label on it identifying it as the STORM1 diskette (STORM will ask for its diskettes by number when you run it from diskettes, so labeling is important). Then answer *y* for *yes* and repeat the above procedure for the STORM2 diskette. Remember to label it accordingly. To run your copy of STORM, insert the STORM1 diskette in the A: drive and, with the A> prompt on your monitor, type STORM to start the program.

5. How to Use This Manual

Before you begin using STORM, you should read Appendix A and Chapters 2, 3, and 4 of this manual. Appendix A introduces you to running STORM on your computer, whether you have a single diskette drive, two diskette drives, or a fixed disk system. Chapter 2, *Getting Started* walks you through a tutorial example to illustrate the basics of using STORM. Chapter 3 covers the *Common Features* of STORM used widely by the modules. Chapter 4 discusses the *STORM Editor* which is used for data entry in all modules. These introductory chapters should definitely be read before using STORM for serious work. You will find that, because much of the material is action oriented, you are gaining hands-on experience while you read.

Chapters 5 through 23 contain detailed descriptions of each of the eighteen computational modules. These chapters are independent of each other; you need only read the one that deals with the module you wish to use. Each of these chapters has the following basic organization:

- An overview of the capabilities of the module
- A brief introductory section
- A section dealing with the solution algorithm being employed by that module
- A sample problem
- Data entry for the sample problem using STORM
- Execution of the module for the sample data
- Tips for using that module
- Instructions for changing the problem sizes for existing data sets

The first page of each chapter contains the module overview and two additional items of information. The first is the maximal problem sizes which can be solved with different versions of STORM. The second is the name of the file wherein the sample problem for that chapter is stored on the STORM diskettes. You may read in this sample file and solve the problem to quickly get a feel for the module. The names of all these files are listed in Appendix B for your convenience.

Appendix C provides a general explanation of our file layouts. Using this explanation, you may create data files using other software which may be submitted to STORM for solution. We use simple ASCII files to facilitate this process.

A remark about the figures in the ensuing chapters is in order. Many of them show you the displays that you will see on your monitor. In Chapter 2 (the tutorial chapter), each such display has been reproduced faithfully, except that large blank areas have been compressed. Reverse video portions of the screen have been boxed in, and the help messages and instructions to the user that appear at the bottom of most screens have been included. In later chapters, these features have been left off the figures as unnecessary extras that would only distract you from the essential content of the screen.

We hope you have no difficulty using STORM, and thoroughly enjoy your experience with it. In case you encounter any problems due to faulty manufacture, damaged diskettes, or anything related to production or distribution, we recommend you return it to your place of purchase.

If you have trouble running the STORM software, first try to solve your own problem by looking for key words in the Index or the Table of Contents of the manual. If you cannot find the information you need, write to us at:

Storm Software, Inc.
Attn: Customer Service Department
P. O. Box 22658
Cleveland, Ohio 44122-9998

Please provide as much detail as possible concerning the exact conditions under which the problem arose, and the various actions you took to try to solve it. Every effort will be made to provide a prompt resolution.

Chapter 2

GETTING STARTED

1. Using STORM: An Example

Before you attempt the exercise described in this chapter, we assume you have:

- Read Chapter 1
- Installed or made a backup copy of STORM
- Reviewed Appendix A to get a better idea as to how STORM will actually run on your computer

If you have not done one or more of the above steps, please take a few moments to do so at this time, and then return to this chapter. We assume you have activated STORM and pressed a key to proceed from the logo to the Main Menu screen. The following example starts from that point.

This sample problem is designed to let you quickly complete an exercise with STORM. It by no means explores all its features, but serves as an introduction to Chapters 3 and 4 where many more features are explained. The exercise should take about 30-40 minutes to complete. If at any time in the example you make an incorrect entry, you may use the Escape (Esc) key to prevent the entry from being recorded if you catch the mistake before it is entered. Otherwise, you will have to make a correcting entry to continue, or simply exit STORM and restart the example.

The example we have chosen makes use of the Transportation module. Do not be concerned if you are not familiar with this procedure, as you will not need a complete understanding of it to work the example. In this problem we have four production plants which make a particular product, which is then shipped to four warehouses for ultimate distribution to customers. If we add the unit cost of production to the unit shipping cost, we will have the total cost of producing and shipping one unit from a particular plant to a particular warehouse. Assuming all such costs are known, along with the plant capacities and warehouse demands, our objective is to compute the lowest cost production and shipping plan.

The data for this problem are in Table 1. The entries in the body of Table 1 are the per unit costs of producing and shipping one unit of the product from the plant identified by the row to the warehouse identified by the column. For example, it costs $4 to produce and ship one unit from Plant 1 to Warehouse 1, $5 to produce and ship one unit from Plant 1 to Warehouse 2 (or Plant 2 to Warehouse 1), $6 for Plant 1 to Warehouse 3, etc. The column headed Supply shows the capacities for each plant for this product to be 100 units. The row labeled Demand shows the need for the product at each of the four warehouses for the coming planning period. We shall answer the question "What is the most economical distribution plan?" by applying the STORM Transportation module to this problem.

| | | Warehouse | | | | |
		1	2	3	4	Supply
P	1	4	5	6	7	100
l	2	5	6	7	4	100
a						
n	3	6	7	4	5	100
t	4	7	4	5	6	100
	Demand	123	97	105	71	

Table 1: Plant/Warehouse Distribution Problem Data

2. The STORM Main Menu

The STORM Main Menu allows you to select which of the computational procedures available in STORM you wish to use. It is shown in Figure 1 as it appears on your screen. Since we wish to use the Transportation module and it is number 3 on the menu, press the 3 in the top row of keys on your keyboard and then press the Enter key. When you have completed this entry, the Input menu shown in Figure 2 will be displayed on your monitor. If you made a mistake and selected some module other than the Transportation module, press the F9 Function key to get back to the Main Menu to reselect, or press the Escape key to return to the previous menu. The other function keys used by STORM are discussed in Chapters 3 and 4. We will use only one other function key in this example, and it is explained later in this chapter.

```
             STORM : MAIN MENU

    1)    Linear & Integer Programming
    2)    Assignment
    3)    Transportation
    4)    Distance Networks (Paths, Tours, Trees)
    5)    Flow Networks (Transshipment, Max Flow)
    6)    Project Management (PERT/CPM)
    7)    Queueing Analysis
    8)    Inventory Management
    9)    Facility Layout
   10)    Assembly Line Balancing
   11)    Investment Analysis
   12)    Forecasting
   13)    Production Scheduling
   14)    Material Requirements Planning
   15)    Statistical Process Control
   16)    Statistics
   17)    Decision Analysis (Single Level)
   18)    Decision Trees (Multiple Levels)

          Select option     1

Use ▾/▴ to change option; Enter to select; Esc to return

F6 Config    F7          F8         F9          F10 Exit STORM   KB:
```

Figure 1: The STORM Main Menu

```
          TRANSPORTATION : INPUT

    1)   Read an existing data file
    2)   Create a new data set

          Select option     1

Use ▾/▴ to change option; Enter to select; Esc to return

F6 Config    F7          F8         F9 Modules  F10 Exit STORM   KB:
```

Figure 2: Transportation Module: Input Menu

3. The "Beep" Sound in STORM

From time to time as you use STORM, you may hear a beeping noise when you attempt some entry. This will perhaps annoy you, but its purpose is to signal that the program could not interpret the entry you attempted. For example, since menu items are identified by number, any alphabetic character would be unacceptable as a response to a menu. Try to type in the letter "A" and see what happens. The beep is to alert you that a simple mistake was made and that the program took no action. For more subtle and complex situations, STORM will provide you with a message on the screen (in addition to the beep) to help you remedy the situation.

4. The Keyboard Status Indicator, KB

In the lower right corner of any menu or Editor screen (the Editor is discussed later) will be the letters *KB:*, possibly followed by the letter *C* or *N* or both. This display informs you of the status of your Caps Lock key and your Num Lock key. If the *C* is displayed, it means you have your Caps Lock key "on," and all alphabetic entries will be displayed as capital letters. If the letter *N* is displayed, the Num Lock key is "on." This means that the numbers 0 through 9 which appear in the Numeric Keypad area are to be interpreted as numbers instead of the alternate symbols shown on those same keys. If no *N* appears, you may assume that the keys' alternate symbols will be used. For example, the upper left key contains the number *7* and the word *Home*. If the *N* is not displayed, pressing this key causes the *Home* interpretation to be given to this key. You should be sure that the *N* is *not* displayed at this time. If it is, press the Num Lock key and it will disappear. Similarly, if the Caps Lock status is not what you desire, press the Caps Lock key to change it.

5. Selecting Items from Menus

Two methods are available for selecting items from any menu in STORM. The first is to use the Up and/or Down Arrow keys located in the Numeric Keypad area. The Up Arrow shares a key with the number 8 while the Down Arrow shares with the number 2. At this time press the Down Arrow key and observe what happens. Before you pressed the key, the first item on the Input menu appeared in reverse video (light background, dark characters). After you pressed the Down Arrow, the reverse video effect moved to the second item on the menu. This reverse video box is called the *Current Location Pointer* in STORM, although we will usually call it simply the Pointer. Its function is to identify the active area of the screen for you. Now press the Down Arrow again. The Pointer moves back to item one on the menu. In general, if you are at the bottom of a menu and you press the Down Arrow, you will be moved to the top. If you are at the top and you press the Up Arrow, you will be moved to the bottom of the menu. Press the Up Arrow at this time to observe this latter effect. Once you have the Pointer on the item you want from the menu, you merely press the Enter key to make that selection (don't press it yet, though).

Alternatively, you may type in the number of the menu item you wish to select. This may be done using the row of numbers at the top of the keyboard or the numbers to the right in the Numeric Keypad area. However, if the Numeric Keypad area numbers are used, the Keyboard Status Indicator (KB:) must have the letter *N* appearing after it (see Section 4 of this chapter).

We want to create a new problem data set, so you should select item two from the Transportation Input menu shown in Figure 2. Select it by using either of the methods described above, and the result will be the screen reproduced as Figure 3.

6. Entering Problem Information: The STORM Editor

Chapter 3 contains a full description of the features and functions available in the Editor. We shall be content to simply explain the general data layout that the Editor uses and how to enter our sample problem data. In Figure 3, several areas or items have been identified and assigned numbers. Each item is explained by number in the following sentences:

1. *The Problem Description Area.* Basic parameters that define the problem size and type are entered here.

2. *The Problem Data Area.* This is a matrix or tabular layout, designed and dimensioned according to the information from the Problem Description area, for entering the problem data. This area will be blank on your screen until all entries in the Problem Description area have been completed.

3. *The Current Location Pointer.* The location of this reverse video box indicates where the next entry will appear.

4. *The Entry Box.* All entries other than the problem title are first typed into this box and then transferred to the position indicated by the Current Location Pointer.

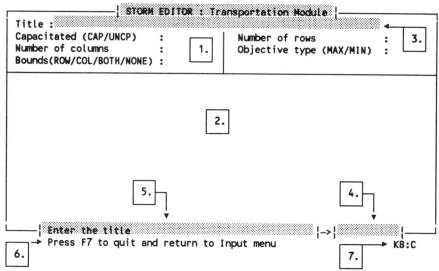

Figure 3: The Editor Screen Layout for Problem Description Entries

5. *The Prompt Line.* Messages to assist you in making the current entry appear here.

6. *The Help Line.* This line tells you how to go on to the next stage and how to make or correct the current entry.

7. *The Keyboard Status Indicator.* This was previously explained in Section 4.

6.1 Entering the Problem Description

We begin by entering the title for our problem. In this case we have called it "PLANT/WAREHOUSE DISTRIBUTION PROBLEM." This is the only item that is entered at its display area on the screen, and the only place where upper and lower case letters are distinguished. All other entries are made in the Entry box (described above) and then moved to their display location. An exception is made for the title since we allow it to be a long string of characters. We elected to turn on the Caps Lock key and enter the title as all caps. At this time type in the title and press the Enter key. The display will now appear as in Figure 4. If you make a mistake you may correct it by using the Backspace key (top right portion of keyboard) and re-entering. If you do not catch the mistake until after you've already pressed the Enter key, you will be given another chance later to correct it.

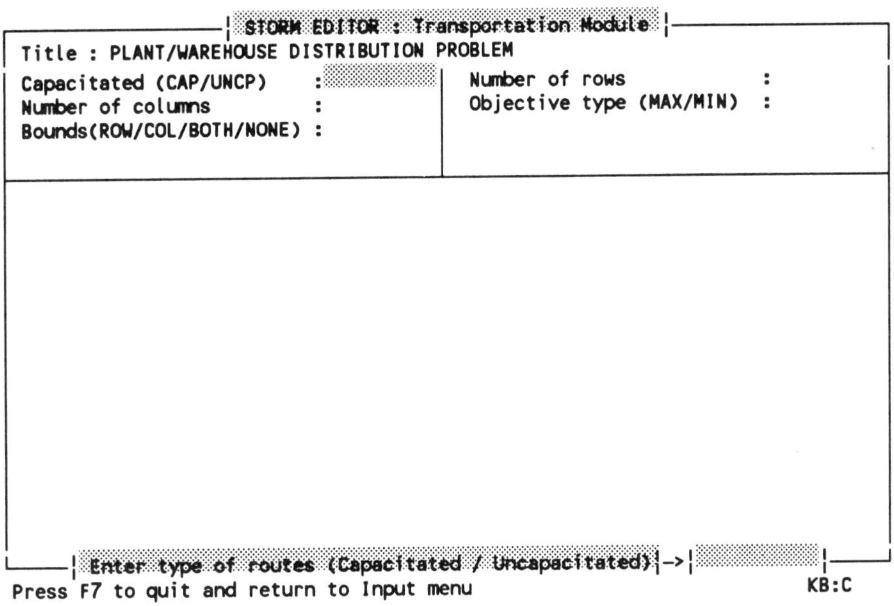

Figure 4: The Display after the Title is Entered

The next entry to be made indicates whether you are solving a capacitated or uncapacitated version of the transportation problem (this is explained in Chapter 8). Our problem is uncapacitated so simply type a *U* (or *u*) and press the Enter key. In general, you only have to enter enough letters to distinguish your choice in situations like this one. Thus, the *U* is enough to differentiate the UNCP from the CAP entry. The display should now appear as in Figure 5.

The next problem description entry requests the number of rows in your problem data (the number of plants for us). Type the number 4 and press the Enter key. Remember that if you make an error, you will have a chance to correct it at the end of the problem description entry process. However, it is not possible to go back immediately to correct it. Next we are asked for the number of columns (warehouses) in our problem, so again we type in the number 4 and press the Enter key.

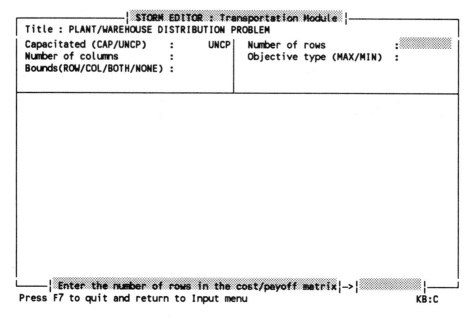

Figure 5: The Display after the Capacitated/Uncapacitated Entry is Made

The next prompt asks us to specify whether we seek to maximize or minimize the objective function. Since our objective function is the sum of production and shipping costs, the appropriate response to this prompt is *MI*. Notice we must use two letters to distinguish between the MAX and MIN options. Type in *MI* and press the Enter key.

The final problem description item does not apply to our problem, so you should type in *N* for NONE and press the Enter key. For the interested reader, bounds are explained in Chapter 8, which deals with the Transportation module. Our final problem description display is shown in Figure 6. Notice that the prompt line in the figure reads *Ready to go on to detailed data ? (y/n)*. The default answer of *Y* for *Yes* appears in the Entry box. If everything is correct, press Enter. Otherwise, if any mistakes were made in any of the previous entries, this is the time to correct them. Simply type *n* (or *N*) and press Enter to be returned to the title area. Then use the Arrow keys to get to the entry where the error was made and make a new entry. When all entries are correct, press the Down Arrow key until the display changes to that shown in Figure 7.

```
┌─────────────────┤ STORM EDITOR : Transportation Module ├─────────────────┐
│ Title : PLANT/WAREHOUSE DISTRIBUTION PROBLEM                              │
│ Capacitated (CAP/UNCP)     :    UNCP │ Number of rows        :        4   │
│ Number of columns          :       4 │ Objective type (MAX/MIN) :    MIN  │
│ Bounds(ROW/COL/BOTH/NONE)  :    NONE                                      │
│                                                                          │
│                                                                          │
│                                                                          │
│                                                                          │
│                                                                          │
└──┤ Ready to go on to detailed data ? (y/n)        ├─>│y         ├────────┘
                                                                      KB:C
```

Figure 6: The Display after the Bounds Decision is Made

```
┌─────────────────┤ STORM EDITOR : Transportation Module ├─────────────────┐
│ Title : PLANT/WAREHOUSE DISTRIBUTION PROBLEM                              │
│ Capacitated (CAP/UNCP)     :    UNCP │ Number of rows        :        4   │
│ Number of columns          :       4 │ Objective type (MAX/MIN) :    MIN  │
│ Bounds(ROW/COL/BOTH/NONE)  :    NONE                                      │
│                                                                          │
│ R1  : C1   COLUMN  1 COLUMN  2 COLUMN  3 COLUMN  4   DUMMY   SUPPLY │
│ ROW   1        .        .        .        .            │         0  │
│ ROW   2        .        .        .        .            │         0  │
│ ROW   3        .        .        .        .            │         0  │
│ ROW   4        .        .        .        .            │         0  │
│ DUMMY       ----     ----     ----     ----     ----    │  ----     │
│ DEMAND        0        0        0        0            │      XXXX  │
│                                                                          │
└──┤ Unit cost (. if route is prohibited)           ├─>│          ├────────┘
  F1 Block  F2 GoTo  F3 InsR  F4 DelR  F5 InsC  F6 DelC  F7 Done  F8 Help KB:C
```

Figure 7: The Display after We Proceed to the Problem Data Area

6.2 Entering the Problem Data

STORM always starts in the upper left corner of the Problem Data area. Notice that COLUMN 1, ROW 1 and the dot are all in reverse video. The cell occupied by the dot is the position of the Current Location Pointer. The reverse video on the phrase COLUMN 1 is the Column Pointer while that on ROW 1 is the Row Pointer. These latter two help you keep track of exactly which entry you are making. This is especially helpful when you are down several rows and off to the right side of the screen. Also notice that in the upper left corner a row and column number are displayed (R1 : C1). These are the numbers of the cell to which the Pointer is currently positioned. Take a second and simply use the Arrow keys (Up, Down, Right, Left) to move the Pointer around and watch how the Row and Column Pointers move to keep pace. Finally, move the Pointer back to the upper left corner so that we may proceed with data entry.

We will enter the numbers into the data area exactly as they appear in Table 1. Thus, the first cost value for distributing from plant 1 to warehouse 1 is $4, so we type in 4 and press the Enter key. The Pointer moves down to the next row and the "4." appears in its old location. If you wanted to enter the data across the row from left to right, you could have used the Right Arrow key to signal the end of the entry instead of the Enter key. In fact, you may use any of the arrows to complete an entry (provided, of course, that you do not have the Num Lock key *on*) and then move the Pointer in the direction of the arrow. You may also use the End key (it also has the number 1 on it and is located in the Numeric Keypad area of the keyboard) to signal the end of an entry if you wish to leave this column and go to the top of the next one.

The second row, first column cost value is 5 so type in 5 and press the Enter key. The next entry is a cost value of 6, so type that in and press the Enter key, then type in 7 and press the Enter key for the next entry.

Notice that after this entry the Prompt line contains the message *No entry*. This is because STORM leaves a blank row (and a blank column to the right of the matrix) so it can equalize the supply and demand in the transportation matrix if your problem does not already have total supply equal to total demand. Thus, you simply skip over this entry by pressing a Down Arrow.

The final entry in the column is the demand for warehouse 1 which has a value of 123. Type in this number and press Enter and observe where the Pointer goes next. It moves to the top of the next column on the assumption that you will want to continue data entry at that point. If this is not so, you can control the direction of movement with the arrow keys as indicated above. The display will now appear as in Figure 8.

```
                      ┌─| STORM EDITOR : Transportation Module |─┐
  Title : PLANT/WAREHOUSE DISTRIBUTION PROBLEM
  Capacitated (CAP/UNCP)     :        UNCP│ Number of rows            :        4
  Number of columns          :           4│ Objective type (MAX/MIN)  :      MIN
  Bounds(ROW/COL/BOTH/NONE) :        NONE  │


  R1   : C2   COLUMN    1 COLUMN    2 COLUMN    3 COLUMN    4      DUMMY      SUPPLY │
  ROW     1             4.          .          .          .          │           0
  ROW     2             5.          .          .          .          │           0
  ROW     3             6.          .          .          .          │           0
  ROW     4             7.          .          .          .          │           0
  DUMMY             ----        ----       ----       ----       ----       ----
  DEMAND             123           0          0          0          │         XXXX




         ┌─| Unit cost (. if route is prohibited)            |─>|          |─┐
  F1 Block   F2 GoTo   F3 InsR   F4 DelR   F5 InsC   F6 DelC   F7 Done   F8 Help KB:C
```

Figure 8: The Display after Entering the First Column

Complete the data entry for the sample problem by completing the other columns in the matrix. Notice that when you get to column 5, the DUMMY column, you should just press a Right Arrow once and then resume data entry with the SUPPLY column (this contains the plant capacities for our problem). When you have completed the last entry in the supply column, the display will appear as in Figure 9.

6.3 Changing the Row and Column Labels

STORM provides you with default row and column labels in each module. If these are acceptable to you, they may be left alone and used for subsequent reporting purposes. However, you may want to edit these to make them specific to the problem at hand. Since these labels are used for the reports which present the results, such editing can contribute significantly to the understanding of the reports.

```
┌──────────────────────| STORM EDITOR : Transportation Module |──────────────┐
│ Title : PLANT/WAREHOUSE DISTRIBUTION PROBLEM                                │
│ Capacitated (CAP/UNCP)      :     UNCP| Number of rows          :        4  │
│ Number of columns           :        4| Objective type (MAX/MIN) :      MIN │
│ Bounds(ROW/COL/BOTH/NONE) :       NONE                                      │
├────────────────────────────────────────────────────────────────────────────┤
│  R5  : C6   COLUMN   1 COLUMN   2 COLUMN   3 COLUMN   4    DUMMY   SUPPLY    │
│  ROW   1         4.        5.        6.        7.        |          100      │
│  ROW   2         5.        6.        7.        4.        |          100      │
│  ROW   3         6.        7.        4.        5.        |          100      │
│  ROW   4         7.        4.        5.        6.        |          100      │
│  DUMMY         ----      ----      ----      ----      ----       ----       │
│  DEMAND         123        97       105        71        |         XXXX      │
│                                                                             │
│                                                                             │
│                                                                             │
│                                                                             │
│                                                                             │
│                                                                             │
│                                                                             │
│                                                                             │
└────| No entry                                             |->|          |──┘
     F1 Block  F2 GoTo  F3 InsR  F4 DelR  F5 InsC  F6 DelC  F7 Done  F8 Help KB:C
```

Figure 9: The Display after All Problem Data are Entered

Let's begin by changing the column labels at the top of the display. Use the arrow keys to move the Pointer to the cell which contains COLUMN 1. Notice that the Row and Column Pointers disappear since we are not making an entry in the data area. Now type in *W 1* (for Warehouse 1) and press the Enter key. The label for column 1 has now been changed, and the Pointer has moved horizontally to the label for column 2. Continue to type the labels *W 2, W 3,* and *W 4* and press the Enter key each time until all these labels have been changed.

Now move the Pointer to the cell containing the label ROW 1. Type in *P 1* (for Plant 1) and press Enter. This time the Pointer moves vertically down after changing the label where it was previously located. Continue to type in *P 2, P 3,* and *P 4* until all these row labels have been changed. Now the display should appear as in Figure 10.

```
                     ┌─| STORM EDITOR : Transportation Module |─────────┐
                     │ Title : PLANT/WAREHOUSE DISTRIBUTION PROBLEM
                     │ Capacitated (CAP/UNCP)    :     UNCP│ Number of rows           :        4
                     │ Number of columns         :        4│ Objective type (MAX/MIN) :      MIN
                     │ Bounds(ROW/COL/BOTH/NONE) :     NONE │
                     │
                     │ R4   : C1          W 1       W 2       W 3       W 4      DUMMY    SUPPLY
                     │ P 1               4.        5.        6.        7.         │        100
                     │ P 2               5.        6.        7.        4.         │        100
                     │ P 3               6.        7.        4.        5.         │        100
                     │ P 4               7.        4.        5.        6.         │        100
                     │ DUMMY             ----      ----      ----      ----       ----     ----
                     │ DEMAND            123        97       105        71         │       XXXX
                     │
                     │
                     └──| Enter a new Row Label (optional)              |→|            |──┘
                       F1 Block  F2 GoTo  F3 InsR  F4 DelR  F5 InsC  F6 DelC  F7 Done  F8 Help KB:C
```

Figure 10: The Display after Labels are Edited

6.4 Ending the Edit Session

We have now completed data entry for our sample problem and are ready to solve it. To do so, press the F7 Function key. This brings you out of the Editor and displays the Process menu to allow you to proceed.

7. Solving the Example Problem: Execution

Figure 11 illustrates the Process menu, which is common to all STORM modules. Notice that the Pointer is located on item 4: *Execute the module with the current data set.* This is because STORM thinks this choice is the most likely one you would want to make once you've finished editing. In fact, this subtle feature is prevalent throughout STORM. As you enter any menu, the Pointer will be indicating the option we think you will want to choose. Of course, we will not always be right, but we try! To the extent that we guess right, you will simply keep pressing the Enter key.

```
            TRANSPORTATION : PROCESS

    1)   Edit the current data set
    2)   Save the current data set
    3)   Print the current data set
    4)   Execute the module with the current data set

            Select option    4

    Use ▾/▴ to change option; Enter to select; Esc to return

F6 Config      F7            F8 Input   F9 Modules   F10 Exit STORM   KB:C
```

Figure 11: The Process Menu

Now press the Enter key to begin execution, and the display in Figure 12 will appear. This shows you the available options for solving your problem. For simplicity, let's pick the first by pressing Enter. The result is the menu shown in Figure 13.

```
            TRANSPORTATION : ITERATION 0

    1)   Go to the optimal solution
    2)   Show all iterations

            Select option    1

    Use ▾/▴ to change option; Enter to select; Esc to return

F6 Config     F7 Edit/Save    F8 Input   F9 Modules   F10 Exit STORM   KB:C
```

Figure 12: Solution Options Menu

```
              TRANSPORTATION : OPTIMAL SOLUTION

      1)   View current solution in tableau format on monitor
      2)   Summary Report for the current solution
      3)   Detailed Report for the current solution

                    Select option    1
      Use ▾/▴ to change option; Enter to select; Esc to return

F6 Config      F7 Edit/Save    F8 Input    F9 Modules    F10 Exit STORM    KB:C
```

Figure 13: Transportation Output Menu

8. Reviewing the Solution Results: The Output Menu

Choose the first option from the menu in Figure 13 and you will obtain the display in Figure 14. This is a format commonly called the Tableau format for the transportation method. We will not delve into an explanation of this output for the reader who is unfamiliar with this method, but

```
           PLANT/WAREHOUSE DISTRIBUTION PROBLEM
        TRANSPORTATION - OPTIMAL SOLUTION - TABLEAU OUTPUT

       COLUMN 1  COLUMN 2  COLUMN 3  COLUMN 4   Dummy    U(I)\SUPPLY
       +---------+---------+---------+---------+---------+
ROW 1  |4.000    |5.000    |6.000    |7.000    |0.000    |0.000
       |    100  |  0.000  |  0.000  |  4.000  |  1.000  |    100
       +---------+---------+---------+---------+---------+
ROW 2  |5.000    |6.000    |7.000    |4.000    |0.000    |1.000
       |     23  |  0.000  |      2  |     71  |     4   |    100
       +---------+---------+---------+---------+---------+
ROW 3  |6.000    |7.000    |4.000    |5.000    |0.000    |-2.000
       |  4.000  |  4.000  |    100  |  4.000  |  3.000  |    100
       +---------+---------+---------+---------+---------+
ROW 4  |7.000    |4.000    |5.000    |6.000    |0.000    |-1.000
       |  4.000  |     97  |      3  |  4.000  |  2.000  |    100
       +---------+---------+---------+---------+---------+
V(J)    4.000     5.000     6.000     3.000    -1.000
DEMAND    123        97       105        71        4
```

```
           Total cost = 1616.0000
```

```
           Press any key when ready
```

Figure 14: The Tableau Format Solution

instead proceed to consider another form of the output. We also should point out that this particular format is available only for small problems that will fit on one screen; otherwise, it simply does not appear as an option on the menu. Press any key to continue.

Notice that since you have already seen the Tableau report, the default (Pointer) selection this time is the next item on the Output menu, called a Summary Report. This, too, is a common feature of STORM. After an item you select from the Output menu has been listed for you, you are returned to the menu with the Pointer on the next logical item on the list. If you do not wish to view this item, simply push the Down Arrow key to skip over it to some other report you do wish to see. Let's select item 2 from the menu at this time by pressing the Enter key.

The result is the report shown in Figure 15, which indicates for each plant the amount (if any) to be shipped to each warehouse, the unit cost and the total cost associated with each cell. Also shown are the cost subtotal for the plant, the total cost of the entire distribution plan, and the number of iterations required by the transportation method to arrive at this answer. We will not go into the detailed report at this time, although you should feel free to look at it if you'd like. Don't forget to proceed to the next section, however.

```
               PLANT/WAREHOUSE DISTRIBUTION PROBLEM
          TRANSPORTATION - OPTIMAL SOLUTION - SUMMARY REPORT
          ------- Cell  ------              Unit       Cell
          Row             Column    Amount  Cost       Cost
          P 1               W 1        100  4.0000   400.0000
          P 1 Subtotal = 400.0000

          P 2               W 1         23  5.0000   115.0000
          P 2               W 3          2  7.0000    14.0000
          P 2               W 4         71  4.0000   284.0000
          P 2               Dummy        4  0.0000     0.0000
          P 2 Subtotal = 413.0000

          P 3               W 3        100  4.0000   400.0000
          P 3 Subtotal = 400.0000

          P 4               W 2         97  4.0000   388.0000
          P 4               W 3          3  5.0000    15.0000
          P 4 Subtotal = 403.0000

          Total Cost = 1616.00
          Number of iterations = 2
```

Press any key when ready

Figure 15: Transportation Summary Report

9. Exiting STORM

By now you will have noticed that in both the STORM Editor and the various menus, there are several function keys whose purpose is stated in abbreviated form at the bottom of each screen. One of these, the F10 key, is used to exit STORM, which would typically put you back to DOS. The other function keys are explained in detail in Chapters 3 (for the menus) and 4 (for the Editor), so we will not discuss them further at this time. Since this concludes our exercise, class dismissed! Press the F10 key to exit STORM.

Whoops! The message on your screen suggests that we forgot a feature of STORM which has saved us countless hours of data entry time. It works as follows. Suppose you have used the Editor to create or modify a data base, and are now about to sign off.

New data will be lost if you do not save it. You may want to lose it, but perhaps you have simply forgotten to store it. At such a time, STORM will ask you if you would like to save it. If so, you should press the Enter key to accept the default *y* for *yes*. You would then be prompted for a filename. Let's not save the example data and simply answer *no* (*N* or *n*) to this question and really be dismissed this time. This concludes our introductory example, and we hope it has helped you get ready to go work up a storm. Good luck!

Chapter 3

COMMON FEATURES OF STORM

There are several facilities which STORM provides which are used extensively in many modules. To avoid frequent repetition, we will give a complete description of them in this chapter. We will not discuss functions performed by the STORM Data Editor, since that is the focus for Chapter 4.

1. Selecting from a Menu

Figure 4 later in this chapter shows the Configuration Options menu, which is similar to many menus used by STORM. There are two ways to indicate your selection from such a menu. First, you may use the Arrow keys to move the Pointer (reverse video box) up or down the list of menu items until it points to the one you want. Then press the Enter key to complete the selection. Alternatively, you may type in the number of the selection (a value from 1 to 5 for Figure 4) and press the Enter key to complete the selection.

2. The Candidate Selection Form

In many of the modules, you will be asked to choose one or a few items from a larger set to serve an immediate need. For example, in the Forecasting module a large number of time series may be present in the input data base. Suppose you now want to analyze one of these to determine whether any trend or seasonality is present. You must specify which one you wish to analyze.

In such a case, the list of possibilities may be quite long. Each item has its own name, which you entered while creating your data set. In the Forecasting module, each variable occupies a column, and the headers initially read SERIES 1, SERIES 2, and so on. You may have replaced these general-purpose labels with names that are more meaningful in context. Suppose you want to study a time series which measures sales in units of a particular product. What name did you choose? SALES? SALES UNIT? SALESUNITS? Unless you jotted down all the variable names, there could be an awkward pause at this point.

The STORM procedure for item selection solves this problem by providing you with a list of all the candidate items. You do not even have to type out the name. There are two cases to consider, each treated slightly differently. The first involves selecting a single item from the list, while the second selects an arbitrary number of items (one or more). We will illustrate both procedures using the Forecasting module.

2.1 Choosing One Item

Suppose you are using the Forecasting module to forecast the future values of one or more time series, based on the given historical data. You may have many different series in the data base. Among your options is to do a detailed analysis of one series. If you choose this alternative, you will be presented with a screen like that in Figure 1. At the right, the names of all the series are listed. In the illustration, there are five series in the data base, and their default labels have not been modified. A Pointer (reverse video box) indicates the first series. By pressing the Up and Down Arrows, the Pointer can be moved to any series in the list. To select the one you wish to analyze, simply position the Pointer and press the Enter key.

```
SELECTION OF A TIME SERIES FOR ANALYSIS          CANDIDATES

                                                 SERIES   1
                                                 SERIES   2
                                                 SERIES   3
                                                 SERIES   4
                                                 SERIES   5
```

Figure 1: Selection Procedure for One Item

2.2 Choosing Several Items

The Forecasting module also allows you to study several time series at once, and obtain reports of the analyses. Choice of this alternative will produce the display illustrated in Figure 2. You must now communicate to STORM which of the candidates are to be included. Again, use the Arrows to move up and down the list. Position the Pointer at each chosen series and mark it with an asterisk. To make it even easier, the Space bar can be used to mark your selection (the Asterisk key works, too). If you change your mind, the space bar will toggle the asterisk off and on repeatedly. As you see, in Figure 2 we are asking for reports on Series 1, 2 and 4.

```
SELECTION OF TIME SERIES                    CANDIDATES

Select time series for reports             *  SERIES   1
                                           *  SERIES   2
Note : * marks selected series                SERIES   3
                                           *  SERIES   4
                                              SERIES   5
```

Figure 2: Selection Procedure for Several Items

There are some other choices which you may make with Figure 2 by using function keys which will appear with the display (not shown in Figure 2). The F1 Function key *selects all* the items in the list, regardless of any selections you might have made before pressing it. The F2 Function key *clears all* selections, regardless of any you might have made before pressing it. The F3 Function key *toggles all* selections, just as though you had gone down the whole list and changed each item to the opposite choice. If we pressed this key for Figure 2, it would result in SERIES 3 and SERIES 5 being marked with an asterisk(*), and the other series being cleared. When you have completed all selections, press the F7 Function key to exit this screen and move on.

2.3 Limitation of Lists to Feasible Alternatives Only

In the above examples, every possible candidate for selection has appeared on the list. However, in some situations certain items are not appropriate, so STORM will not present them. Consider the example of multiple regression and assume the input data file contains ten variables. You will first be asked to choose the dependent variable from the set of 10 candidates. That variable will then be removed from the list, and you will choose the independent variables from the remaining nine. Suppose you pick six of them for the current run. Later, as the regression proceeds, you may wish to choose the next variable to enter the model. If two of the six are currently in the model, only the other four will be listed.

The same sort of thing occurs in other modules. STORM always tries to minimize the effort required and the chances of making a mistake.

2.4 Moving Over Long Lists

When STORM presents you with a list to choose from, there is room on the screen for twenty candidates. In case the list is longer than that, the Down Arrow will cause the list to scroll one item at a time if it is pressed when at the bottom of the screen. To move more rapidly over a very long list, the Page Up and Page Down keys will scroll a screen at a time. Incidentally, in a one-page list, the wraparound feature is available: moving up from the top brings you to the bottom and vice versa.

3. The STORM Form

There are times, in the functioning of certain modules, when you will have to make a whole set of choices to let STORM know how you want it to proceed. There are three types of responses you may be asked for: answering a question "yes" or "no," specifying an alphanumeric or numeric value for a parameter, and selecting from a list of items as discussed above. Often several of these responses are required on the same form. When such an occasion arises, a STORM form will be provided to make it easy to complete the entries.

The use of the *Parametric Analysis* facility in the Linear Programming module (discussed in detail in that chapter) is an example of such a situation. Suppose you wish to determine the way in which the optimal solution varies as a function of one of the right-hand side values. You have four constraints, called DEPT. 1, DEPT. 2, DEPT. 3, DEPT. 4, already in your data base. Having chosen the parametric analysis option, the STORM form shown in Figure 3 appears on the screen, except that the list of candidates will not be shown there at first. Note that default entries have been provided where possible.

You will soon discover that the Up and Down Arrows move the Pointer, so that entries can be made in any order. Default values that are acceptable can be skipped over, and you can go back and revise an entry if you notice a mistake or change your mind. Let us now take Figure 3 from the top.

3.1 Choosing from a List

The first entry requires the name of a constraint, in our case DEPT. 1. If you remember the name in question, you may type it in. If you are not sure, the item selection procedure (see Section 2.1) can be invoked by the F8 Candidates key and the list of all the candidates will appear on the right side of the screen. Now, the Arrows will act to move the Pointer (the reverse video box at right). Having positioned it, press Enter to transfer your choice into the reverse video box at left, whereupon the list will disappear. Finally, if you try to type in your selection and enter a nonexistent constraint (easy enough to do if the constraint names are longer), you will be informed that the constraint is not recognizable and directed to press F8 to obtain the candidate list. You may now use the Pointer to make your selection.

```
       PARAMETRIC ANALYSIS OF RIGHT-HAND SIDE VALUE          CANDIDATES

    Specify range of parametric analysis (. for default)     DEPT. 1
                                                             DEPT. 2
                                                             DEPT. 3
    Constraint name                     : _____          DEPT. 4

    Lower limit (default -Infinity)     : .
    Upper limit (default  Infinity)     : .
```

Figure 3: An Example of a STORM Form

3.2 Specifying a Numeric Value

After selecting the constraint as requested at the top of Figure 3, we come to two numerical entries: the range of values over which the right-hand side may vary (default range: minus infinity to plus infinity). You merely type in the numbers you want to use, and move on down the form. As always, illegal characters (such as alphabetic data in a numeric field) are screened out immediately, and impossible strings (such as numbers with two decimal points) are rejected when you try to advance after entering them. The cursor will be returned to the start of the offending string and you will be asked to try again. Incidentally, when you start to overwrite an entry in a STORM form, the rest of the characters will be wiped away, but they can be retrieved by pressing the Escape key.

3.3 Specifying an Alphanumeric Value

There are situations where STORM may require an alphanumeric response, other than a row or a column label that you may have already created in your data set. Wherever possible, STORM will suggest a suitable default value. If you desire some other value for the parameter, simply type it in to replace the default entry. In most instances, STORM will indicate the acceptable responses on the screen. Occasionally, it may also make the list of responses available to you through the F8 Candidates key. However, you will not have to guess as to the availability of a candidates list. If and when such a list is available, the word "Candidates" will appear in a highlighted box next to the letters F8 at the bottom of the screen. Otherwise, that space will be blank.

3.4 Answering a Yes-or-No Question

The final type of response called for on STORM forms is the yes-or-no question, which is not illustrated in the example we have chosen. It will always have a default value given, and will require a one-character entry only: *y* or *n*. The space bar generally toggles such selections, so you do not have to hunt around on your keyboard for the letters.

3.5 Using Lower or Upper Case Letters

In all STORM form entries, lower or upper case letters may be used interchangeably. Thus, the variable names COST, Cost and cost are not differentiated by STORM. Again, the answer *yes* can be given with a *Y* or a *y*.

3.6 Detecting and Correcting Mistakes

Each type of entry in a STORM form calls for its own kind of data, and meaningless characters or strings will be rejected sooner or later. Another kind of infeasibility is a number that is outside its permissible range. For example, smoothing constants in a forecasting model must lie between zero and one. Such errors will not be trapped until the end, when you attempt to leave the STORM form. At that time, an error message will appear and the Form Pointer will be placed at the unacceptable entry.

3.7 Use of the Enter Key

Generally, pressing the Enter key is interpreted as the signal to move on, whenever a single entry is to be made. However, for STORM forms with multiple entries, we have seen that the Enter key has special functions. First, if you consult the list of candidates, it transfers your selection from there to its proper location on the form. Second, if you have typed an entry directly into the form, pressing Enter will advance the Pointer one position down. Thus, when you have finally completed all parts of the form and are ready to move on, the Enter key cannot be used to terminate this phase. Instead, the F7 key serves this function. In case you find all this hard to remember, instructions appear at the bottom of each screen to remind you how to proceed.

3.8 Use of the Escape Key

As we have already mentioned, the Escape key has several different uses. If you are in the middle of typing an entry and change your mind, Escape will restore the entry that was previously there. If you are in the Candidates list and decide not to use it, Escape will return you to your current location on the form. Generally in STORM the Escape key lets you quit whatever you are doing and return to the previous status.

In keeping with this philosophy, you can also use the Escape key to leave a STORM form at any time and return to the previous menu. You may observe that, with this additional function, there will be times when the Escape key will have two different purposes simultaneously. When this occurs, pressing Escape will have the less dramatic effect first. If you wish to leave the form and return to the previous menu, simply press Esc a second time.

If you keep pressing the Escape key, you will eventually wind up at the Main Menu, after which one more Escape causes you to Exit STORM!

4. Using the Function Keys

Several separate sets of function keys are available to you at different times. Whenever a certain function key is operative, it will be listed and briefly defined at the bottom of your screen. One set, the Editor function keys, is used only when you are editing data. These eight keys, F1 through F8, appear on the Editor screen and are discussed in Chapter 4. Different sets are used with STORM forms and with Candidate Selection forms for multiple selections, as already discussed in this chapter.

Another set of function keys is defined when you are at any of the various menus that STORM uses. There are five of these Menu function keys, namely F6 through F10. As you can see in many of the figures of Chapter 2, they appear at the bottom of menu screens with a brief explanatory word in reverse video to remind you of their purpose. In some menus, certain of the keys are not operative. This is indicated by omitting the reverse video message.

Three of the Menu function keys are used in other sets. Although we have kept their usage as consistent as possible, they have different uses under different conditions. This should not create confusion, since on-screen reminders are always present.

Generally speaking, the purpose of the Menu function keys is to interrupt the straightforward sequence of steps as you select a module and proceed through successive stages of processing. This allows you to stop whatever you are doing, either to make a preliminary adjustment before resuming or to terminate work on the current problem. The order of the keys may appear arbitrary, but each successive key provides a more drastic interruption, taking you a larger number of *steps backward* from your current position. We will now discuss each Menu function key in turn.

5. Configuration Key: F6 (Config)

Pressing the F6 function key, which will be labeled simply *Config* on the screen, results in the menu shown in Figure 4. The last option on this figure will only appear if you do have a graphics adapter card (as opposed to monochrome adapter). Since the function you will most often perform with this key is *Select output devices for reports* (option 3), that is the default selection when you first receive this menu. For continuity, however, we will discuss the choices from top to bottom of Figure 4.

```
              CONFIGURATION OPTIONS

        1)   Save current configuration on disk
        2)   Select disk defaults
        3)   Select output devices for reports
        4)   Set report parameters
        5)   Set display attributes
```

Figure 4: The Configuration Options Menu

5.1 Save Current Configuration on Disk

Choices that you make in options 2, 4, and 5 in Figure 4 may be saved on disk so that they will be the default choices any time you use your copy of STORM. These choices will be saved in a file called *Storm.cfg,* where the *cfg* refers to *configuration.* Choices made with option 3 will not be saved to disk, as these are clearly temporary choices good only for one session of work (or less!). If you choose option 1 from Figure 4 and you are using diskettes to run STORM, you must not have a *write protect tab,* or STORM cannot save your choices. If all goes well, STORM will inform you that your configuration was saved.

5.2 Select Disk Defaults

Figure 5 shows the short STORM form used for this purpose. As you can see, there are two defaults to specify. The first is the default drive and directory for your input data files, while the second is for your output report files. If running from hard disk, you will find drives and directories initially set to the ones you are currently in. If running from a diskette in drive A or B, the opposite of the two drives will be specified. Both drive/directory specifications may be set arbitrarily. Your new entries may be the same or different. The directory names do not have to exist when you enter them on this form, but must exist when you try to use them.

Once you have entered your choices and saved your configuration to disk, these choices will show up as the default choices any time your initiate the STORM program. If you change one or both of them during a session, the new values will remain the default choices for that session *only,* unless you once again save a new configuration.

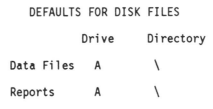

```
          DEFAULTS FOR DISK FILES

               Drive     Directory

Data Files      A           \

Reports         A           \
```

Figure 5: Selecting Disk Defaults

5.3 Select Output Devices for Reports

When you use a STORM module to perform some analysis, you will usually want to make a series of *what if* runs, and review the results on your monitor. During this brainstorming phase, most users expressly do *not* want to create volumes of paper output, nor file after file on a disk. Thus, STORM always defaults to *monitor only* for listing output reports when you first start the program. However, Figure 6 reveals that it is a simple matter to choose *any combination* of monitor, printer and disk file output. Move the Pointer to any of the three lines in the display and press the space bar to toggle the selection to *y* or *n*.

```
              SELECTION OF DEVICES FOR OUTPUT REPORTS


              Send Reports to Monitor ?      : y

              Send Reports to Disk File ?    : n

              Send Reports to Printer ?      : n
```

Figure 6: Output Device Selection Form

If you specify that the reports are to be saved in a disk file, you will be provided a *File Specification Form* (described later in this chapter) with which to list a drive, directory, filename and extension for the disk file. Once a report file has been opened, it will remain active and all subsequent output will be written to it until you indicate otherwise by again pressing F6 and choosing option 3 to specify a combination of devices that does not include disk, or to supply a different file name. Unless you close the file in one of these ways, all reports will continue to be stored there even if you go on to another problem or another module. Only when you sign off STORM will the file be automatically closed.

Note that, with reports going to the printer, the output presentation will be slowed down to match the speed of the printer, which may or may not be a problem. If the printer does not respond for any one of a variety of reasons (perhaps it runs out of paper), you will be informed and given a chance to rectify the problem. *STORM sends all printed output to the parallel port. If your printer is connected to the serial port, then it will be necessary to redirect the output using the MODE command in DOS.*

When you have completed all necessary entries associated with output reports, you will be returned to the *original menu* from which you chose the F6 Config key.

5.4 Selection of Report Parameters

Figure 7 contains the STORM form you will receive if you choose option 4 from Figure 4. We will list and explain each of these entries below.

Printer page length (lines)

This is the number of lines per page which your printer allows. We default it to the standard 66 lines per page common to most printers. If you desire some other value, you may enter it here to replace this default. An example of using this facility is if you wish to import a STORM report into a word processor file, and do not want *hard page breaks* in the STORM file. You could specify a very large value for this entry (say, 9999) so that your entire report would be less than one "page." Then when you import it into your word processor file, the word processor will determine the page breaks.

```
           SELECTION OF REPORT PARAMETERS

      Printer page length (lines)            : 66

      Top margin (lines)                     : 0

      Bottom margin (lines)                  : 12

      Printer left margin offset             : 0

      Issue form feeds (y/n) ?               : y

      Pause between pages (y/n) ?            : n

      Strip control characters (y/n) ?       : n

      New page for each report (y/n) ?       : y
```

Figure 7: Selecting Report Parameters

Top margin (lines)

From the place on the paper where your print head is normally positioned, this is the number of blank lines you desire before printing begins. Since for many printers there is already some such space allowed, we have defaulted this entry to zero as shown.

Bottom margin (lines)

This is the analogous value for the bottom margin on the page. For standard printers with 66 lines per page, our default value of 12 leaves a one-inch bottom margin. If you desire more or less, you should change this entry accordingly.

Printer left margin offset

From the place on the paper where your print head is normally positioned and on which printing would normally begin, this is the number of additional spaces in the left margin which you desire. This feature is generally useful for printers which will print more than ten characters per inch. If you are not sure about this entry, read in one of the sample files that come with STORM and execute the module which uses it. Send one or more of the reports to your printer and see how they line up on the page. If they are not centered horizontally on the page, play with this value until you are satisfied. Then you will want to save it to the *Storm.cfg* file mentioned earlier in this chapter so that it will be correct for future use.

Issue form feeds (y/n) ?

If you leave this at its default answer of *yes,* STORM will send a *top of form* indicator to your printer when it has sent all the lines desired for a particular printed page. If you change this entry to *n* for *no,* it will send blank lines to the printer until the printer page length specified above is reached. Some word processors do not like the *top of form* indicator, so this option is provided to avoid its use, if needed.

Pause between pages (y/n) ?

Some printers support only single feed sheets rather than continuous feeds. If your printer is one of these, you will have to change this from the default choice of *n* for *no,* so that you will be able to load the next sheet into your printer before STORM resumes printing. After loading, you will press any key to signal STORM to resume.

Strip control characters (y/n) ?

When you initially receive STORM, the routines that send output reports to the printer or to disk files cause the report headers to be printed in bold type for most printers. This is done by sending certain control characters to your printer, and will cause your reports to look nicer than they would otherwise appear. If, however, you wish to import these files into a word processor for further processing, you should change the default selection from *n* to *y*. Then you can add your own printing effects in the word processor as you see fit.

New page for each report (y/n) ?

STORM's default procedure is to start every new report you request on a new page during printing. If your data sets are small or the reports you are requesting are short, this may result in a lot of wasted space (and paper). To prevent that from occurring, change the default choice from *y* to *n*. Such a change will cause STORM to add a report to the current page if it will fit. Otherwise, it will skip to a new page to begin a new report.

5.5 Selection of Display Attributes

As we indicated earlier, this option will appear only if you have a graphics adapter card on your computer. If so, and you select this option, Figure 8 will appear on your monitor. It will be in color, even though we have reproduced it in black and white for the manual. Using the display from the figure, you may select your own foreground and background colors for three types of screen displays used by STORM.

The first of these is the normal display. This is used throughout STORM for menu screens, STORM forms and reporting screens. The default choices shown are for a blue background with white lettering (foreground).

Highlighted I is used in the Editor (described in Chapter 4) and on many menus when video effects beyond the normal display are needed. For example, the Pointer and Function key definitions use Highlighted I display attributes. The defaults for these are the reverse of the normal display; so we have a white background with blue letters (foreground).

When still more video effects are needed, STORM uses Highlighted II display attributes. The only place these are currently used is at the bottom of Editor screens. There are two lines of special keys listed there. We use Highlighted I for the first set and Highlighted II for the second. The default selections are again a white background, but this time a cyan (light blue) foreground.

```
                    SELECTION OF DISPLAY ATTRIBUTES

                        Background           Foreground

Normal Display             1                    7

Highlighted  I             7                    1

Highlighted II             3                    1

Enter an attribute between 0 and 7 for each item


1-7 correspond to colors/shades as below (0 is black)
Blue    Green     Cyan     Red    Magenta   Brown    White
 1        2         3        4        5        6        7
```

Figure 8: Selecting Display Attributes

You may experiment with other values as you see fit. When you tell STORM you have finished making your selections, you will obtain a screen which shows you each of the three selections and asks if you are satisfied with them. If so, accept the default answer of *y* for *yes* to the question; otherwise, enter *n* for *no* to return to the display shown in Figure 8 and make additional changes.

6. Specifying a Disk File

Again a STORM form is used to facilitate this operation. Figure 9 presents the version used to name output report files, with all entries at their default values. The same File Specification form is used to specify data files, which you will want to do both to read in a previously prepared data set and to store the data of the current problem. The forms for those cases will differ only in the heading and the default extension.

6.1 Specifying the Drive

On the assumption that you will want your input and output files on floppy disks, the drive was initialized to A, unless you are running STORM from drive A. In that case, drive B will be assumed. As with any other default entry, you can change this to C if you want to use your fixed disk, or to anything else. You can also delete the entry and leave it blank. If so, STORM will assume that you wish to use the *current drive:* the drive you were (and still are) connected to when you entered STORM, identified by the DOS prompt (such as A>). If you have specified other disk default values for your data and reports and saved the results to the *Storm.cfg* file as indicated earlier in this chapter, then your saved defaults will appear each time you start the STORM program and enter a file specification form.

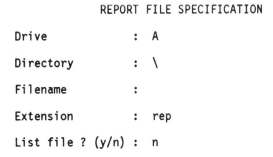

```
              REPORT FILE SPECIFICATION

    Drive              :  A

    Directory          :  \

    Filename           :

    Extension          :  rep

    List file ? (y/n) :  n
```

Figure 9: File Specification Form

6.2 Specifying the Directory

The directory selection is initialized to the root directory (\), unless you have changed this default and saved a *Storm.cfg* file. A blank entry is interpreted to mean the *connected directory* on the chosen drive. This will be the root directory, unless you have taken action to establish another. For example, if you specify the current drive, the connected directory is the one you are in.

6.3 Specifying the Filename

When you are reading in problem data files, STORM will default the filename to the name of the sample data file for the module which comes with the original diskettes. If you begin to type in some other filename, this default one will instantly disappear. The filename can include any letter or number or other special character permitted by DOS. If you leave it blank and attempt to leave the File Specification form by pressing the F7 key, you will be asked if you want to quit. If you do, you will be transferred to the appropriate menu.

If you are writing output files, no default values will appear for the filename. You will have to enter the desired value.

6.3.1 Getting a Directory Listing

Suppose you are in the File Specification form and find that you cannot remember the name of the file you want. Or perhaps you want to concoct a new name, and are concerned that you might be choosing one that you have used before. STORM makes it easy to obtain a listing of all the files that match the specified drive, directory, filename and extension. Obviously, if your specifications are unique and precisely defined in each category, then just one such file can exist, so when you press F7, STORM will understand that you want that file. However, note that the filename and extension entries can include the *wildcard* characters * and ? as described in the DOS manual. The rule is simple: *you will obtain a directory listing by pressing F7 if and only if at least one * or ? appears in either the filename or the extension*. For example, if filename *LP** and Extension *d?* are used, a directory listing will be presented that includes all files whose filename begins with *LP* (the asterisk represents any number of additional characters) and whose extension has two characters, with the first one a *d* (the question mark denotes precisely one character). As another example, an asterisk in both filename and extension will result in a complete listing of all files in the given directory, and in this most general case you will also receive subdirectory names that appear in the directory.

If you leave either filename or extension blank, it will be interpreted as an asterisk for directory purposes, but there must be an * or ? in the other entry or no listing will appear. Instead, a blank filename will be treated as described in Section 6.3, while a blank extension will be accepted as a perfectly legitimate option.

The files will be listed, one to a line, about as they are when you type DIR in DOS. The filename and extension are listed, followed by the size of the file in bytes and the date and time the file was last written. They will appear one page at a time (if the directory is too long to fit on one screen), advancing only when you press a key. In case you want to return to an earlier page, you cannot scroll back, but it is easy enough to complete the scan and start over. After the last page of the list you will return to the Filename line of the File Specification form, where you need only press the F7 key to repeat the directory listing. Otherwise, if the printer has been selected as an output device, you will have hard copy to study at your leisure.

6.4 Specifying the Extension

The default extension for data files is *dat,* and for output report files it is *rep.* These can, of course, be changed to almost any three characters or less, or eliminated.

6.5 Alteration of the Default Entries

The first time you visit a File Specification form, the default entries may be all wrong for your purposes. If so, you will have to fill them in only once. The most recent entries become the defaults for that type of file (that is, data files are treated separately from report files) until you change them again. Thus, each time you wish to read from or write to a data file, you will find the file name components set as you left them the last time you specified a data file, and the same is true for report files.

6.6 Typing the Entries

When typing in the entries of the File Specification form, the following points are worth noting. As usual, the Backspace key removes the character to the left of the cursor, and the Delete key removes the character the cursor is on. Because you will often want to replace a default entry with a totally different one, the present entry is cleared as soon as you start to type in a new one. Sometimes, this may cause you to regret a hasty move resulting in the loss of a string of characters you cannot quite remember and would like to restore. On such occasions, the Escape key re-enters what was there previously.

6.7 Listing the Specified File

There may be times when, having specified a file, you will want to have a look at its contents, perhaps to verify that it really is the file you think it is. If you enter *y* on the *List file?* line and press F7, the contents of the specified file will be listed on the screen. Since STORM creates and reads plain ASCII files, they can be readily viewed or printed out for reference or documentation.

After listing the file contents, STORM returns you to the File Specification form with the *List file?* row restored to its default entry *n*.

7. Transferring to the Process Menu: F7 (Edit/Save)

The F7 Function key takes you to the Process menu. This menu has four listings. The fourth, *Execute the module with the current data set*, is an unlikely choice at this point, since you were already at a menu within the module. The first, *Edit the current data set*, will return you to the Editor screen for data modification, in case you want to try again with new numbers. The second option, *Save the current data set*, may be your choice if you are through for the day and wish to store the data set on disk for future retrieval. The third, *Print the current data set*, produces a printout of the input data for further study. Only the last two options require discussion.

Incidentally, F7 is one of the three function keys which are used both in the Editor and in the menus. Although the other two serve quite different purposes, F7 always does the same thing: it signals the completion of your entries for the particular display.

7.1 Saving the Current Data on Disk

By selecting the option *Save the current data set*, you are asking STORM to store your problem data on disk. Remember, we are talking about the input data now, not the output that results from solving the problem, which was discussed in Section 5. The immediate result will be the presentation of a File Specification form just like the one shown in Figure 9, except that it will be headed *DATA FILE SPECIFICATION : SAVE* and the extension will be initially set to *dat*. Section 6 gives a full description of how to use such a form. When you have identified the file to be used, STORM will carry out the data transfer and return you to the Process menu. The data will be stored as ASCII characters, in a compressed format.

Once a data file has been defined, its specifications become the default entries as long as you remain in that module. Even if you switch to another module, the drive, directory, and extension will be left as you have set them; only the filename will be blanked. However, keep in mind that each time you wish to save data, if you use the same file, you will *overwrite* and hence lose the previous data set. STORM will warn you of this before carrying out such a command, which may be just what you intend. If it is not, be sure to specify a new file in which to store the second data set separately.

You will be given the opportunity to save the input data at various times as computing proceeds. Even if you do not remember to do so, the issue will arise. STORM keeps track of whether the current problem is freshly generated or was read in from a disk file. In the latter case, it also remembers whether you have edited it in this session. If the data set is new or modified and you are about to take any action that would result in its loss, STORM will interrupt to ask you if you wish to save it.

If you run out of disk space, or if there is any fatal disk error such as might be caused by a bad diskette, you will be informed of this and given a chance to start over.

7.2 Printing Out Current Data

If you want to obtain *hard copy* of your input data, you can choose the third option, *Print the current data set*. This choice will result in a printout of the problem data in essentially the same format as it appears on the Editor screen. After the Problem Description area has been printed, the detailed data will be given, five complete columns at a time, starting with the leftmost columns and proceeding left to right.

8. Transferring to the Input Menu: F8 (Input)

The F8 Function key brings you to the Input menu. Make this choice if you want to terminate work on the current problem and start afresh, but still remain in the same module. This is one of the many places where, if you have been using new or modified data and have not saved it, you will be given an opportunity to do so before leaving the module.

The second of your two choices, *Create a new data set,* will bring you to a fresh Editor screen. Option one, *Read an existing data file,* is our third occasion to visit a File Specification form (see Figure 9). The Title line will read *DATA FILE SPECIFICATION: INPUT;* otherwise nothing has changed. Section 6 tells you how to specify the file you want, whereupon the problem data will be read into core and will become the current data set. For large data sets, this transfer of data will take some time due to error checking of each item as it is read in.

After the data has been transferred, you will be brought to the Process menu, where you may choose the first option so as to look over and edit the new information, or proceed directly to analyze it (option 4: Execute).

9. Transferring to the Main Menu: F9 (Modules)

When you have finished using one module and wish to make use of a different module within STORM, the F9 Function key will bring you to the Main Menu. You can now start as though you had just signed on, except that default drives, directories, and so on for file reads and writes will remain as you last reset them. This is another occasion where you will be given the chance to save the data file that you may have forgotten to store.

10. Transferring Out of STORM: F10 (Exit STORM)

This function key terminates your use of STORM and returns you to DOS. Again, you will be asked if you want to save the input data in case you are about to lose it. Little else need be said, except so long and come back soon!

Chapter 4

THE STORM DATA EDITOR

The STORM Editor is a flexible, convenient facility which you will use to enter the data for a new problem and to modify existing data. It provides you with a tabular layout like a spreadsheet into which facts and figures can be entered systematically, and lets you move quickly over large arrays of data. Though the Editor is shared by all the computational modules, the organization of the display is individually tailored to the needs of each module. Within a module, it is further modified to fit your particular problem. If you change your mind, individual entries can be easily altered, and whole rows or columns of data can be added or removed. The Editor, in short, makes the preparation and modification of your input data file as painless as possible. It will signal you with beeps and error messages if you attempt the infeasible, and will display the options available to you if you ask for help by pressing the F8 function key.

1. Data Entry: Problem Description

We start at the point where you have chosen a module from the Main Menu. Next, the Input menu basically asks whether the problem data is to be entered at the keyboard or read from an existing data file. Let us suppose you choose to create a new data set. You are now presented with a tabular layout, largely blank, into which you will enter the problem data. An example is given in Figure 1. The top part, where entry headings appear, is called the *Problem Description area* (or simply the Description area), and must be completed first. Here you will specify the general characteristics of your problem, plus certain parameter values needed to tell the Editor the dimensions of the problem so it can prepare for the quantity of data to be input.

At the bottom of the screen, a reverse video line currently reads *Enter the title*. As you progress, this space, called the *Prompt line,* will give you instructions and advice about the current entry. At all times, the cursor, which is presently blinking at you at the top of the screen, indicates where the next character will appear. Type in an identifying name for the problem you are about to consider and then press the Enter key. Note how the *Pointer* (the reverse video box showing you your current location) moves from the title line to the next item to be entered. The Prompt line now has new instructions.

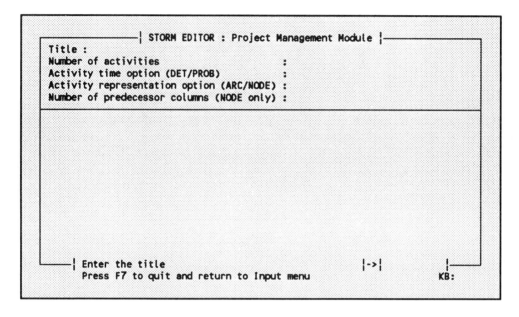

Figure 1: The Editor Screen for Data Entry

To its right, the smaller reverse video cell called the *Entry box* receives the datum as you type it in. Once an entry is to your liking (we will discuss how to correct slip-ups in Section 10), the Enter key will transfer it to its proper position above and advance you to the next entry. Try it. You will find it easy and convenient to use. Of course, the prompts are brief, and you will need to study the module in question to interpret some of them.

When you come to the end of the Problem Description entries, the Prompt line will ask you, *Ready to go on to detailed data? (y/n)*. This is your chance to look over what you have entered, spot any typos, and go back if necessary to make corrections. It is important to have this data correct before proceeding. If you type *n*, you will be taken back to the beginning and can use the Arrows to move to wherever a change is needed. A final Down Arrow will advance you to the next phase of data entry, as will the answer *yes* to the *Ready?* question.

2. Data Entry: Detailed Problem Data

At this point, the large blank rectangle in the center, called the *Problem Data area* (the Data area, for short), comes to life, as shown in Figure 2. A matrix is laid out, formatted as required by the chosen module and scaled in accordance with the problem description already entered. Each cell contains a dot (.) or other default entry which you can leave or alter. At the very bottom, a row of brief mnemonic codes remind you of the purposes of the eight function keys (F1 - F8) used within the Editor; they will be discussed in later sections.

A highlighted cell, the *Pointer,* will be found in the upper left corner. The row and column headers corresponding to its present position are also highlighted. You can move it from cell to cell using the four Arrow keys and in many other ways, as we shall see. The Pointer indicates where the next datum will be entered, and the Prompt line contains instructions on how to do it. Given an adequate understanding of the computational module you are using, the individual entries should be easy to make.

Having positioned the Pointer and typed a number into the Entry box, you can transfer it to its proper position in the Data area in several ways. All of these methods allow you not only to enter the datum but also to move the Pointer to a new location. One way is to use the Arrow keys, which now will simultaneously transfer the entry and shift one position in the indicated direction. Using them, you can work down one column and up the next, back and forth across successive rows, or move among the cells in any convenient order.

```
┌───────────────────────────────────────────────────────────────────────┐
│           ─────────────┤ STORM EDITOR : Project Management Module ├──────── │
│    Title : SAMPLE PROBLEM                                               │
│    Number of activities                        :        12             │
│    Activity time option (DET/PROB)             :       DET             │
│    Activity representation option (ARC/NODE) :       NODE              │
│    Number of predecessor columns (NODE only) :        6                │
│                                                                         │
│    R1  : C1        SYMBOL   ACT TIME   PRED  1   PRED  2   PRED  3   PRED  4 │
│    ACT   1           1        0.         .        .        .        .    │
│    ACT   2           2        0.         .        .        .        .    │
│    ACT   3           3        0.         .        .        .        .    │
│    ACT   4           4        0.         .        .        .        .    │
│    ACT   5           5        0.         .        .        .        .    │
│    ACT   6           6        0.         .        .        .        .    │
│    ACT   7           7        0.         .        .        .        .    │
│    ACT   8           8        0.         .        .        .        .    │
│    ACT   9           9        0.         .        .        .        .    │
│    ACT  10          10        0.         .        .        .        .    │
│    ACT  11          11        0.         .        .        .        .    │
│    ACT  12          12        0.         .        .        .        .    │
│           ──┤ Enter a symbol for ACT   1   (4 characters max) ├─->┤      ├── │
│    F1 Block  F2 GoTo  F3 InsR  F4 DelR  F5 InsC  F6 DelC  F7 Done  F8 Help  KB:C │
└───────────────────────────────────────────────────────────────────────┘
```

Figure 2: The Editor Screen Following Problem Description

Another way, of course, is to use the Enter key. This will automatically advance the Pointer to the next cell *down*. Thus, starting at the top left, you can work down each column (which experience has shown to be more convenient than traversing rows). When you reach the last entry in a column, the Enter key will jump you to the top of the next column to the right. Obviously, this is more limiting than using the Arrow keys. However, if you have large quantities of numeric data to enter, you may find it convenient to use the Numeric Keypad in its numeric mode, thus disabling the Arrow keys.

While these are the basic ways to transfer items from the Entry box to the designated cell, other means will be noted in Section 4, in conjunction with some additional modes of moving the Pointer.

3. Labeling Rows and Columns

In each module, the rows and columns will initially have general purpose headers or labels, often nothing more imaginative than ROW 1, ... and COLUMN 1, ... In most cases, these may be changed to whatever is appropriate to your particular problem. Each label can be up to ten characters long, and any characters can be used. When editing column labels, the Enter key will move the Pointer right, the only exception to the usual motion down.

Many labels, of course, are not subject to change. In the example of Figure 2, you can change the row labels to any activity names you like, but the column headers describe the kind of data that column contains and may not be altered.

4. Moving the Current Location Pointer

As explained above, once a legitimate set of characters has been typed into the Entry box, the Arrow keys perform the dual function of entering the data and moving the Pointer. However, if nothing has been typed, the Arrows will simply move the Pointer one cell in the designated direction. Thus, repeated use of an Arrow will carry you rapidly across the page; holding an Arrow key depressed generates even greater speed. If you start to type something and then decide you wish to move away without making (or altering) the entry in that cell, you may wipe the slate clean by striking the Escape (Esc) key.

When solving a large problem, not all the data will fit on the screen simultaneously. The amount that can be displayed in one screen is called a *page*. The extra columns and rows can be imagined as being in their proper positions offscreen, and can be reached by continuing to move in the appropriate direction using the Arrows. For example, if the problem requires 50 rows and 50 columns, the Editor will initially present the first (upper left) page: the first 15 rows of the first 6 columns. The Right Arrow, used repeatedly, will carry you to the edge of the screen. Press the Right Arrow key again, and the screen will scroll sideways, so that your view shifts one column to the right. All columns move one place left, with the leftmost column disappearing from view. If you continue to use the Right Arrow, you will scroll across the Data area, a column at a time. The Left Arrow will, of course, move the Pointer back across the screen and then scroll left. Thus, you can move back and forth over many pages. Vertical movement is similarly possible using the Up and Down Arrows.

With large data arrays, it may be desirable at times to move the Pointer more rapidly than one cell at a time. There are several ways to do this. The Page Up and Page Down (PgUp and PgDn) keys will cause the display to scroll one complete page up or down, leaving the Pointer in the same position on the screen. Likewise, the Tab key will move the screen a full page to the right. To scroll a page left, use the Tab key with the Shift key held down.

To move even greater distances across the Data area, you can use the Home key. After pressing it, an Arrow key will carry you to the farthest page of data in the indicated direction, skipping over all intervening pages. The End key will move the Pointer to the cell at the top of the next column to the right: a kind of vertical carriage return.

In all cases, if some item of data has been typed into the Entry box, it will be transferred to the location of the Pointer before it moves. If two key strokes, such as Home and Arrow, are required, the first will enter the datum.

In case you need to be reminded of these or other features of the Editor while in the process of entering or modifying data, you need only press the F8 Function key (the *Help* key at the bottom of the Editor screen) to have a summary appear on the screen, as reproduced in Figure 3.

4.1 Moving to a Specified Cell: F2

Rather than indicating how *far* you want the Pointer to move (one cell to the right, all the way to the bottom of the data, etc.), you may sometimes want it to go to a particular cell. Thus, in a large data base, with the Pointer at cell (1,1) (that is, row 1 and column 1), you may want to move it to cell (78,145). The *GoTo* feature, invoked by the F2 Function key, allows you to identify the next cell to be visited. Using two Candidate Selection screens, you choose the column and row of the target cell from the lists of labels provided. You are then returned to the Editor screen with the Pointer at the desired location. The chosen cell will be in the center of the screen, unless this would require scrolling beyond the data so that

```
                    STORM DATA EDITOR FEATURES

          KEY                      RESULTING ACTION
    --------------      -------------------------------------------
    Any Arrow           Pointer moves a cell in the indicated direction.

    Enter               • For column labels, Pointer moves a cell right.
                        • Otherwise, Pointer moves a cell down; and from
                          the bottom of a column to the top of the next.

    Tab/Shift-Tab       The display scrolls right/left one page.

    PgUp/PgDn           The display scrolls up/down one page.

    Home and Arrow      The display scrolls to the extremity of the data
                        in the indicated direction.

    End                 Pointer moves to the top of the next column.

    Esc                 The current entry is aborted.
    -------------------------------------------------------------------
    When any of the above keys (except Esc) is used with a valid item
    in the Entry box,  the item is transferred to the initial Pointer
    location before the Pointer moves to its new position.
```

Figure 3: Data Editor Features

empty rows or columns would appear. A brief reminder of the F2 key's use appears on the second screen of *Help* messages provided by F8, as shown in Figure 4.

5. Returning to the Problem Description Area

Having once left the Description area, you will not be permitted to change certain characteristics of your problem. Some of them are permanently locked in; to alter them, you will simply have to start over again. Others, specifically the problem dimensions, can be altered only by adding or deleting rows or columns in the Data area, as described in Section 8. This will cause the corresponding parameter values in the Description area to change automatically. Finally, in certain modules, some parameters in this area can be directly changed.

You may re-enter the Problem Description area by using the Up Arrow, which will jump you from the top row of the Data area (the row of column labels) to the Title line. You can now move among the entry cells using the Arrows as usual, making changes if desired and permitted. Where a change is not allowed, the Prompt line will inform you. The Down Arrow can be used to move the Pointer back into the Data area. Note that in doing so it skips the first line, which contains the column headers, and positions itself in the next row down. To edit the headers, you must approach them from below.

6. The Range and Precision of Data

Depending on the module in question, certain numeric data must be entered as integers, while with other kinds of data the Editor permits real numbers (with decimal parts).

6.1 Real Numbers

As a general rule, only six significant digits of a real number can be reliably entered using the STORM Editor. Even if an entry with a greater number of significant digits is made by the user, the least significant digits will be lost. The Editor uses a single precision storage scheme for all the real numbers in the problem data, which limits the maximal number of significant digits to six. Once the number has been typed in by the user, the Editor will choose to display it in either the decimal notation or the scientific (exponential) notation, depending on the magnitude of the number, independent of the format you used for entry. Keep in mind that the Entry box will accept a maximum of ten characters.

Whenever the number is displayed in the decimal notation, exactly six digits of precision are guaranteed, and this format is selected for numbers with magnitudes between 0.01 and 999,999. For numbers with magnitudes outside that range, the Editor will select the scientific notation. For example, if you type in 1234567.89, it will appear on the screen as 1.2346E+06 (which means 1.2346 times ten to the sixth power, or 1,234,600) with only five digits displayed. Since the Editor uses ten-character cells for displaying all the data, whenever a number is negative, only four significant digits can be shown in scientific format. For example, 0.00123456 will be displayed as 1.2346E-03, but -0.00123456 will be displayed as -1.235E-03. It should be emphasized that, **irrespective of the number of significant digits appearing on the Editor screen, the internal storage scheme will always have at least six digits of precision.**

In many modules, you will find dots (.) as default data entries. In some cases, if left unaltered, these entries will be interpreted as infinity. Some examples are the upper bound on variables in linear programming (a dot means an unbounded variable), the unit cost of a transportation route (a dot indicates a prohibited route), or the waiting room capacity in a queue. If you enter a finite value in such a cell and then change your mind, you will be allowed to enter a period to reset it to infinity.

Aside from these special cases, the largest number that you can enter is $1.0E+37$, and the smallest number is $-1.0E+37$. Any number between these two extremes may be entered, using either the decimal or the scientific format. For very large and very small numbers, you will have to use the scientific notation due to the ten-character width of the Entry box. When using the scientific notation for entry, choose the scheme that permits the maximal number of significant digits to be entered. For example, -0.0000000000000123456 can be entered as $-1.235E-13$ or as $-12346e-17$ (either "e" or "E" is accepted). They will appear the same on the screen, but the extra precision will be preserved internally. If you really want to enter six significant digits with full precision in a case like this, there is a trick you can use. Just enter the significant digits, say 123456. Then use the F1 key, described in Section 7 below, to multiply by $-1E-18$. This will show on the screen as $-1.235E-13$, but the internal representation will have six-digit accuracy.

6.2 Integers

The largest integer that is accepted by the Editor is 999,999,999. The use of scientific notation is not permitted when entering this kind of data, so no larger numbers are possible. On the other hand, greater precision is available since all digits typed in will be entered accurately. If the datum can be negative or positive, integers between -999,999,999 and 999,999,999 can be entered.

6.3 Alphanumeric Characters

In certain modules, there are entries other than the row and column labels that are symbols rather than numbers. For these, almost any character on the keyboard may be used. However, all such entries are restricted in STORM to a maximum of four characters. All letters will be converted to capitals, so do not try to differentiate on this basis: "bc1" and "BC1" are indistinguishable to STORM.

6.4 Use of the Dot Default (.)

The most common default entry you will find is the period or *dot*. It has a variety of interpretations, but most of the time it can be taken to mean that the datum is a *missing value*. Here are some of the ways it is used:

- When more cells are supplied than are needed, the extra ones are left at their dot default and ignored by STORM. This occurs in project scheduling when giving each activity's predecessors, in forecasting when listing the observations in a time series, and so on.

- Sometimes a parameter is made inoperative by leaving its value at the dot default, which can usually be interpreted as infinity. Examples include the upper bound of a variable in linear programming, and the capacity of a route in transportation. A dot means that there is no upper bound or capacity limitation.

- A dot may fill a cell that has been rendered inoperative by other choices the user has made. Thus, in queueing, the *lost customer cost* is not relevant if the chosen system never turns away a customer.

- When many entries are to be made which are frequently all the same value, STORM may provide a cell in which to enter a common value for all of them. Only those that differ need be entered; all others will be assigned the common value if left at the dot default.

There are other interpretations of a dot. Some appear in symbolic cells simply because no logical default exists. They have no significance and must be replaced before the module can be run. As you encounter dots in each module, their meanings will soon become clear.

7. Editing Existing Data using Block Operations: F1

You will have noticed that the Input menu gives you the option of reading an existing data file from disk storage. Thus, after working on a problem or entering part of the data, you may store it with the intention of coming back to it later, to complete work on it or to try variations. Having chosen option 1 of the Input menu, the old data set will be brought back for you to work on (see Chapter 3 for further discussion of file transfers). Whether or not the data set was previously stored, you may wish to make changes in a Data area to perform "what if" analysis. Of course, individual cells can be modified one by one as usual. In addition, special features of the Editor have been designed to facilitate altering a large array of data in certain ways.

Sometimes it may be desirable to make a whole series of similar changes, such as when you want to subtract 7 from every number in a certain column, or increase the first twenty entries in a given row by 15%. The F1 Function key, identified as *Block* at the bottom of the Editor screen, can be used to perform these operations. It will simultaneously modify the entries in every cell of any block (rectangular array) you specify.

Pressing F1 takes us to a Candidate Selection form where we choose one of the following types of block operations.

String constant : Enter in each cell a specified sequence of (up to four) characters, overwriting any previous entry, either letters or numbers.

Cell = A : Set each cell to a specified numerical value, A, regardless of its previous value.

Cell + A : Add the number A to each cell.

Cell - A : Subtract A from each cell.

*Cell * A* : Multiply each cell by A.

Cell / A : Divide each cell by A.

*A + B * Cell* : Each cell is multiplied by a constant, B, and another number, A, is then added to the product.

A + Cell / B : Each cell is divided by B, and A is added to the quotient.

*A * (Cell ** B)* : Each cell is raised to the power B, and the result is multiplied by A.

Import/Export : Retrieve (write) data from (to) a disk file. See Appendix D for a more detailed discussion of the Import/Export operation.

When we speak of operating on a cell (adding a number to a cell, etc.) we mean, of course, operating on the contents of that cell. For example, if we wish to increase a row of numbers by 15%, we would choose *Cell * A*. We are then given a STORM form in which to enter the specific values to be used for the string of symbols or A and B. In this form we are also asked if we want a *complete report;* we will come back to that later. Suppose that we leave it defaulted to *no,* set the constant values (for our example, set A to 1.15), and press F7.

We now return to the Editor screen. Superimposed on the Description area is a box containing a statement of the block operation in progress. In our case, it will read *Block operation selected: Cell * A. Constant A = 1.15.* The Data area is as we left it. However, the Prompt line now reads *Position Pointer & press F1 to begin (Esc to quit).* You can now move the Pointer to one end of the row or column to be altered, or at one corner (any of the four corners will do) of the rectangular block. By pressing F1, you signal your choice. The prompt will now change to *Position Pointer & press F1 to end (Esc to quit).* Shift the Pointer to the other end of the row or column of cells, or to the diagonally opposite corner of the block, and again use F1. If there are no potential difficulties, and if you have not requested a report, the changes will be made.

The prompt now invites you to mark another block, in case you want to modify additional cells in the same way. When you are finished, use Escape to return to normal operation. Press F8 and you will get a brief description of the use of the F1 key as shown in Figure 4.

```
                        FUNCTION KEYS

THE F1 KEY performs one of the following arithmetic operations on a rectangular
block of cells:

        String constant : Set each cell to a character string
        Cell = A : Set each cell to a numeric constant, A
        Cell + A : Add constant, A, to the contents of each cell
        Cell - A : Subtract A from the contents of each cell
        Cell * A : Multiply the contents of each cell by A
        Cell / A : Divide the contents of each cell by A
        A + B * Cell : Multiply the contents of each cell by B, and then add A
        A + Cell / B : Divide the contents of each cell by B, and then add A
        A * (Cell ** B) : Raise the contents of each cell to the power B, and
                          then multiply by A
        Inport/Export :  Retrieve (write) data from (to) a disk file

After you define the function, you mark the block to be modified by positioning
the Pointer at opposite corners (or at the ends of the row or column), pressing
F1 each time. You will be warned if any included cells cannot be altered in the
specified way. You can then identify other blocks to get the same treatment.

THE F2 KEY lets you specify the row and column of a cell in the Data area. The
Pointer is then moved to that location.
```

Figure 4: Use of F1 and F2 Function Keys

7.1 Conventions and Safeguards

There are a number of complications that can arise when you mark extensive blocks of cells to be modified. STORM will warn you before taking action in case you might want to reconsider. Following are three situations where action is taken automatically, and no special notification is considered necessary:

- Missing values or other dot defaults generally remain unaltered. The exceptions are the operations that reset the cell contents without regard to its previous value. *String constant* will operate on every symbolic cell in the block, even those that had dot entries. Similarly, *Cell = A* will enter the value A into all numeric cells including those containing dots.

- The entries in any cell are either *numeric* or *symbolic,* and numeric cells either require integer entries or accept any real numbers. If you specify a block that includes both numeric and symbolic cells, STORM will understand that you want to transform only those cells for which the chosen operation makes sense. Thus, an arithmetic function will be performed on all numeric cells in the specified block (except those where difficulties arise). Any symbolic cells included in the block will be left unaltered.

- If a number in an integer cell is to be altered to a noninteger value, the result will be rounded to the nearest integer (multiples of a half being rounded up).

Other complications can arise that you may not have foreseen. In such cases, STORM will first present an *exceptions report* of all cells where the transformation will not be straightforward, and your approval must be given before the operation is carried out. Here are some examples:

- If the result of an arithmetic operation produces a number that is out of range, it will be set at the appropriate limit (upper or lower).

- Cells will not be altered if the problem definition requires that they remain fixed. For example, in linear programming, if you have specified that no initial solution will be given, the entries in the INIT SOLN row are fixed at zero.

- Symbolic cells will be left unchanged if the new value does not match the set of symbols for which that cell is defined. In linear programming, for example, cells in the CONST TYPE column can only contain the constraint types "< =", "> =", or "="; and similarly for the VARBL TYPE row. Any other *String constant* entry would not be applied to such cells.

You will get a report listing all such cells with their current values and the values they will have after the operation has been carried out. You now have the opportunity to abort if you discover any unpleasant surprises, or to give the go-ahead signal.

7.2 Complete Report

As mentioned above, the STORM form asks you whether you want a complete report. As we have seen, even if you say "no," you will get an exceptions report if necessary, before any action is taken. If you answer "yes," you will get a more extensive report listing all changes to be made, even routine ones. You may want this for your records, and will again be given the chance to change your mind.

8. Inserting and Deleting Additional Rows or Columns

As you gain familiarity with STORM, you will find it increasingly easy to move around within a module. You will often solve a problem and look over the results, considering what alternatives might be open to a manager and how they would translate into different formulations of the problem. Returning to the Editor screen, you will make changes and solve the problem again with new assumptions. As a student in an introductory course, you may be content to find an answer to the assigned homework, but as you gain confidence and facility, and discover how easy it is to play "what if" games, it is our hope that you will be tempted to join in the fun.

The Editor, as you already know, makes it easy to change the numerical values of the input data. However, certain broad structural properties of the problem, which are determined in the Problem Description area, fix the size and sometimes the type of layout to be used in the Problem Data area, and altering them disrupts large portions of the data display.

Most important of these are the problem dimensions, such as the number of variables and constraints in a linear program, the number of activities in a project to be scheduled, or the number of inventoried items. In every module, being able to vary these parameters has great practical utility. Very often we will want to consider the effect of adding a source (a new factory or depot) in a transportation network, or an additional investment alternative, and so on. STORM permits you to do this easily, by adding or removing a row or column in the Data area.

8.1 Inserting a Row: F3

Suppose the Editor screen is displayed, and you want to add another row to your data base. Simply increasing the parameter value by one in the Description area would not be satisfactory, because the Editor would not know where to locate the new row. Instead, the procedure is simply this: position the Pointer anywhere on the line *above* the intended addition, and press the F3 Function key. A new row will be inserted with all entries initialized to the default values. In case a new first row is desired, the Pointer should be on a column header. On the other hand, if you have placed the Pointer in the bottom line on the screen (which may or may not be the end of the data base), the display will scroll up to bring the new row into view.

It goes without saying that, in situations where it makes no sense, attempts to insert a row will be disallowed and an appropriate message will appear. For example, in the Investment Analysis module, the first few lines in the Data area are for specifying the economic life span of each investment alternative, whether discounting is to be discrete or continuous, and several other specific points. A line added among these would have no meaning.

Further down in the same display, there is a series of rows containing the revenue per period for each period in the economic life of the alternative. Inserting a new row in this range would correspond to adding an extra period to the (maximal) life spans of the investment alternatives. Such a modification is feasible and is permitted.

The Investment Analysis module also illustrates another feature of row insertion. Below the Revenue rows there are an equal number of Expense rows, where the anticipated cash outlays for each period are entered. If a Revenue row is inserted, thereby increasing economic life spans, a corresponding Expense row should also be created. STORM will automatically take care of this. There are some other modules where "companion" rows or columns exist, and either one is always associated with the other. In the Facility Layout module, each department requires one column and two rows in the data base, so adding any one of the three brings the two others with it.

8.2 Deleting a Row: F4

To remove a line from the Data area, you should position the Pointer anywhere *on* (not above) the targeted line, and then press the F4 function key. The principal difference here is that the action contemplated is more serious: a line once deleted is forever lost. You will therefore be asked by STORM to confirm your decision, thereby giving you a chance to reconsider. If you remain steadfast, the designated line will disappear and the lower part of the screen will move up to fill in. Simultaneously, companion rows and/or columns will be deleted. As you would expect, the required rows for a module cannot be deleted, and STORM will so inform you if you accidentally try.

8.3 Inserting or Deleting a Column: F5 or F6

Little needs to be said about the corresponding column operations, which are exactly analogous. To add a column, place the Pointer anywhere in the column immediately *left* of the desired location. Then F5 will cause all data to the right to move one cell further right, making way for the new column and scrolling if necessary to bring it on to the screen. On the other hand, F6 will, after a warning, eliminate the column on which the Pointer is located, with an appropriate closing of ranks. As before, no infeasible actions will be taken, and companion rows/columns will accompany the affected column into or out of existence.

8.4 Other Consequences

Having successfully added or removed a row or column, you will observe one immediate result: the affected parameters in the Problem Description area will automatically be adjusted to their new values. It is up to you to take care of all other needed adjustments. Of course, you must fill in the new row or column, including the header. This will often be all that is required, but not always. For example, in the Project Management module, suppose we add a new activity to a project, and it must be completed before certain other activities are begun. Then, in addition to filling out the new activity's row, we must remember to modify some of the other rows to reflect the new precedence relationships.

9. Keeping on Track and how STORM can Help

Many safeguards have been built into the Editor to stop you from doing something you might regret, to facilitate making changes, to guide you from one step to the next, and to respond to your requests for help. Here are some of them.

9.1 Using the Insert Key

Sometimes, when altering a previous entry, the cursor will not be in its usual position at the end of the string of characters. When there are characters to the right of the cursor, you will find the Insert key useful. With the Ins key "on," you can type *into* the existing text (characters to the right move aside), while if you toggle it "off," you will type *over* the previous entry. Note that the Insert key will only function as a switch if the Num Lock key is "off"; otherwise you will simply be typing a zero. To remind you which mode you are in, an "I" appears in the lower right corner of your screen (see Section 9.7) when Ins is "on."

9.2 Error Detection by STORM

As you type a number or other character string into the Entry box, you will not be permitted to enter meaningless characters. For example, if the current entry is required to be a positive integer, any character other than the ten digits will be rejected. If you try to type in a minus sign or a decimal point, or accidentally strike a letter or other symbol, it will not be accepted, and the Editor will draw your attention to the fact with a gentle beep.

Possibly your error will not be detected until you try to transfer entry to the cell above. If, for example, you have typed several E's or decimal points into a real number, you will hear a beep and an error message will appear at the bottom of the screen. The cursor is now back at the far left of the Entry box, with all the characters you typed still in place. You can now type into or over them (depending on the status of the Ins key), or use the Delete key to eliminate some of them, or use the Escape key to clear them all out. *Do not forget they are there.*

For example, if you type 3333 and press Enter, you may be told that you are out of range for that particular entry; the largest number permitted is 125. You now decide to use that maximal value, so you type 125 (without looking at the screen) and Enter. Since you did not delete anything, you overwrote the first three digits but left the fourth, so you will again get an error message: 1253 is still too big.

9.3 Catching Your Own Mistakes

If you press the wrong key while typing data into the Entry box and notice it right away, press the Backspace key to wipe out the last character. If the whole entry is beyond repair, the Escape key will clean out the Entry box and put you back at the beginning.

9.4 Editing the Title

The one place on the Editor screen where greater flexibility is available in making changes is in the Title line. Since this entry is potentially so much longer than any other, the Right and Left Arrows may be used to move the cursor into position for corrections without altering the rest of the title. As usual, the status of the Ins key determines whether you are inserting new characters into the previous text or overwriting it.

9.5 On-Screen Help with Function Keys

Below the Prompt line at the bottom of the Editor screen, one more line appears. When you are in the process of making an entry, this line provides specific guidance (see Section 9.6). At other times, as shown in Figure 2, the space is used to list the function keys available to you with a very brief reminder of their uses. We have already noted how the F1 and F2 keys have the tags *Block* and *GoTo* to denote block operations and Pointer movement, as detailed in Sections 4 and 7. Next, F3 is labeled *InsR* for *Insert Row,* and similarly *DelR, InsC* and *DelC* are used to remind you of the purpose of the F4, F5 and F6 keys, as we saw in Section 8. The F7 key terminates the editing session, as described in Section 10, and so is labeled *Done.*

Finally, for more extensive on-screen help with these keys, press the Help key, F8. We have already discussed the first two screens that will appear; they are reproduced in Figures 3 and 4. Figure 5 shows the last Help screen, summarizing the use of the Insert and Delete keys, plus the Done key.

9.6 The Help Line

When you start to type something into the Entry box, a new message generally appears in the Help line, reminding you of the various keys available to advance you through (or extricate you from) the current entry, and to take you on to the next. A typical example, *Press Enter/Arrows/End/Tab/Home; or Esc to restart,* tells you that the Enter key or several others will transfer the contents of the Entry box to the present Pointer position, simultaneously moving the Pointer to a new position, while the Escape key is available to clear away the entry and start over.

```
                      FUNCTION KEYS

    Key       Purpose                 How to use it
    ---   ------------------   ------------------------------------
    F3    Inserts a row.       Position the Pointer anywhere on the
                                  line ABOVE the new row.  Press F3.
    F4    Deletes a row.       Position the Pointer anywhere ON the
                                  row to be deleted.  Press F4.
    F5    Inserts a column.    Position the Pointer anywhere in the
                                  column immediately to the LEFT of
                                  the new column.  Press F5.
    F6    Deletes a column.    Position  the Pointer anywhere ON the
                                  column to be deleted.  Press F6.
    F7    Ends edit session.   Press F7.
    -----------------------------------------------------------------

    For the four Insert and Delete keys, any companion rows and/or
    columns will be treated automatically and the Problem Description
    entries will be appropriately adjusted.

    THE F7 KEY  takes you to the Input menu if you have never entered
    the Data area. Otherwise, it takes you to the Process menu.
```

Figure 5: Use of the Editor Function Keys

The other kind of message that may occasionally appear in the Help line is an explanation of why an entry or other action that you attempted could not be carried out. For example, you may see *Error: Out of range* if you attempt to enter a number that is too big or too small, such as a negative number where only positive values are meaningful. At such times, STORM will tell you what the permissible range of values is, so that you can easily adjust your entry.

9.7 The Keyboard Status Indicator, KB

Keys that switch you into and out of a certain mode of operation may be called *toggle keys*. There are three toggle keys on your keyboard: Caps Lock, Num Lock and Ins. To help you keep track of the mode each of them is in, you will find keyboard status indicators in the lower right corner of all affected screens following the characters "KB:". For each toggle key, an appropriate initial will be displayed to indicate that it is switched "on." The letter will disappear when it is turned "off." Thus, as long as you are in the all-capitals mode, the letter C appears. Similarly, the letter N indicates that the Numeric Keypad is in numeric mode, and the letter I shows that the Ins key is in insert mode.

10. Terminating the Editing Session: F7

When you are finished entering or editing data, indicate this by pressing the F7 Function key. If you are just beginning to enter new problem data and have not yet left the Description area, the Editor will assume you have changed your mind and wish to start over. Consequently, you will be transferred to the Input menu. If you have advanced to the Data area, even if you then return to the Description area, F7 will be taken as a sign that the data has been fully and accurately entered and you are ready to compute, and you will be transferred to the Process menu.

The Process menu, which is reproduced in Figure 11 of Chapter 2, offers you four alternatives. The first of these, *Edit the current data set,* returns you to the Editor screen where you can modify the problem data. The second option, *Save the current data set,* allows you to specify a file where this data is to be stored, while the third, *Print the current data set,* provides you with a printout of the problem data. The fourth option, *Execute the module with the current data set,* will lead to another menu listing the various outputs that are available. From then on, each module goes its own way, as discussed in separate chapters beginning with Chapter 5.

LINEAR PROGRAMMING MODULE CAPABILITIES

PROBLEM FORMULATION OPTIONS
- Positive, negative or unrestricted variables
- Lower and/or upper bounds on each variable
- Range constraints
- User-supplied initial solution
- Option to exclude variables or constraints from the formulation, but keep them in the data base
- Maximize or minimize objective function
- Automatic scaling
- User-selected entering variable

OUTPUT OPTIONS AND OTHER FEATURES
- Problem statement in equation style
- Presentation of each iteration or optimal solution only
- Solution including
    - Reduced cost for each variable
    - Shadow price for each constraint
    - Tableau report
- Sensitivity analysis of
    - Cost coefficients
    - Right-hand side values
- Parametric analysis of right-hand side values
- Automatic scaling of problem data
- Save optimal solution as initial solution for future runs

MAXIMAL PROBLEM SIZES (VARIABLES, CONSTRAINTS)
- Personal version: (100, 50)

- Professional version
  Representative sizes, with 500K of net memory for STORM:
      (1250, 10)
      (625, 50)
      (125, 125)
      (50, 140)
      (10, 150)

FILE NAME FOR THE SAMPLE PROBLEM DATA
- LP.DAT

Chapter 5

LINEAR PROGRAMMING

Linear programming is a mathematical technique for finding the combination of levels for a given number of potential *activities* which best utilizes a given set of limited *resources*. A *solution* is a specification of a level for each activity being considered. Before applying linear programming, we require a linear *objective function* to provide a measure of the quality of each solution. Further, it must be possible to express the restrictions in the form of linear equations or inequalities which impose *constraints* on the activity levels. Since the level of an activity is under our control, we often refer to it as a *variable,* and to the activity levels as variable values. A *feasible solution* is one that satisfies all constraints, and an *optimal solution* is a feasible solution that maximizes (or minimizes) the objective function. We will let $x_1, x_2, \ldots$ denote the levels of the first, second, . . . activity.

1. The Solution Algorithm

The Revised Simplex algorithm is used by the STORM module to solve linear programming problems. The following generalizations are provided.

- Each variable may be constrained to be nonnegative (the usual assumption; this is the default value), nonpositive, or unrestricted.

- Other bounds can also be placed on the individual variables. Thus, if we require x_1 to lie between 20 and 100, or between -5 and +5, then upper and/or lower bounds can be specified for each variable. If no such bounds are required, the default values should be left unchanged (the upper and lower bounds are 1.0E+37 and -1.0E+37, displayed as ".").

- Inequality constraints can also be given upper and lower bounds. For example, the usual constraint is of the type:

$$a_1 x_1 + a_2 x_2 + \ldots + a_n x_n \leq B,$$

or else

$$a_1 x_1 + a_2 x_2 + \ldots + a_n x_n \geq B.$$

STORM also permits range constraints of the form:

$$b \leq a_1 x_1 + a_2 x_2 + \ldots + a_n x_n \leq B.$$

2. A Sample Problem

The Hamlin Company produces two related products, for which four centers or departments are required for various stages of their manufacture. In the coming month, each department has available a given number of machine hours to devote to the two products, which have specified production time requirements per unit. The data for the problem are as shown in Table 1:

	Department			
	1	2	3	4
Time Available (hrs.)	670	620	720	165
Time required per Item (hrs.)				
Product 1	0.9	0.7	1.0	0.2
Product 2	1.3	0.6	0.4	0.3

Table 1: Data for Sample Problem

To keep the problem simple, we will assume that fixed costs allocated to these products are constant, regardless of the quantity produced. Imagine, for example, that the equipment and workers in the four departments have no other function but to manufacture these two products; excess capacity is wasted. Thus, wages, overhead, etc. are sunk costs that must be paid anyway, and will be omitted from the calculations. The various capacities (such as times available) are determined by the workforce and facilities provided in each department, the anticipated down time, and so on.

Our objective will therefore be based on the contribution margin, namely the selling price minus the variable costs of materials. Assuming that the contribution margin per item produced is $26 and $28, respectively, we wish to determine the number of items of each product to manufacture this month so as to maximize the total contribution.

Written in mathematical form, this problem becomes the following linear program:

maximize $26x_1 + 28x_2$

subject to $0.9x_1 + 1.3x_2 \le 670$
$0.7x_1 + 0.6x_2 \le 620$
$x_1 + 0.4x_2 \le 720$
$0.2x_1 + 0.3x_2 \le 165$
$x_1 \ge 0,\ x_2 \ge 0$

where x_1 and x_2 are the number of items of Product 1 and Product 2, respectively, to be produced.

Incidentally, once you have entered the problem data, each menu will have an option *List problem data in equation style*. By selecting it, you will obtain a statement of the problem in the above form.

3. Data Entry Using STORM

Data entry for the given problem should terminate with a display like Figure 1. Note that in the Problem Description area you are asked whether you want to provide your own starting solution. Regardless of your choice, the row INIT SOLN will appear at the bottom of the Data area. Fill in your values if you answered "yes" to *Will the initial solution be provided?;* if your answer is "no," this row will be ignored, and the module will find a starting solution for you. Although the Simplex method normally starts with an arbitrary feasible solution, the initial solution you enter need not be feasible; STORM can handle it.

Also optional is the introduction of slack and/or surplus variables. You will probably enter the problem with original variables only, as in Figure 1, leaving the module to define any necessary additional variables for you; or you can define slacks and surpluses for yourself, and type in the problem in *standard form.*

3.1 Information about the Variables

For each variable, you must enter the objective function coefficient in the OBJ COEFF row, and in the following rows enter the coefficients of that variable in each constraint. The next row, VARBL TYPE, lets you modify the variable type, which determines the permissible range of values that this variable can take on. The possibilities are summarized in Table 2. The default setting is POS for nonnegative values. You can enter NEG (type "N") for nonpositive, or "U" for unrestricted. One of these options should be chosen when the variable can be any real number, fractional or whole, in the specified range.

```
------------| STORM EDITOR : Linear & Integer Programming Module |------------
Title : PRODUCTION PLANNING AT THE HAMLIN COMPANY
Number of variables     :      2
Number of constraints   :      4
Starting solution given :     NO
Objective type (MAX/MIN) :    MAX

R6  : C4    PRODUCT 1  PRODUCT 2 CONST TYPE     R H S      RANGE
OBJ COEFF     26.       28.      XXXX          XXXX       XXXX
DEPT. 1       0.9       1.3       <=           670.        .
DEPT. 2       0.7       0.6       <=           620.        .
DEPT. 3       1.        0.4       <=           720.        .
DEPT. 4       0.2       0.3       <=           165.        .
VARBL TYPE    POS       POS      XXXX          XXXX       XXXX
LOWR BOUND     .         .       XXXX          XXXX       XXXX
UPPR BOUND     .         .       XXXX          XXXX       XXXX
INIT SOLN     0.        0.       XXXX          XXXX       XXXX



------| No entry                                      |->       |------
```

Figure 1: Editor Screen After Data Entry

Variable Type	Symbol
Nonnegative continuous	P
Nonnegative integer	IP
Nonpositive continuous	N
Nonpositive integer	IN
Unrestricted continuous	U
Unrestricted integer	IU
Zero-one integer	0-1
Omitted from problem	0

Table 2: Available Types of Variables

If the variable can assume only integer values, you can impose this additional requirement by typing "I". Thus, type "IP" for nonnegative integer values, "IN" for nonpositive integers, and "IU" for unrestricted integers. A special type of integer variable that can only be zero or one is also available by entering "0-1". We will discuss the special features of integer-- valued variables in the next chapter, entitled *Integer Programming*. For the present, we shall assume that fractional values are permissible for all variables. Finally, you can also type the letter "O" for OMIT in this row, which has the effect of eliminating this variable from the problem. ***Be careful to distinguish the letter "O" from the number "0".***

In the next two rows, LOWR BOUND and UPPR BOUND, you can place bounds on the variable. The default values of "." make them effectively negative and positive infinity. Any real numbers can be entered, as long as the lower bound is no larger than the upper bound. You may observe that the variable type (aside from the integer specification) is redundant; the same information can be conveyed using bounds. In case the two constraints are not in agreement, the strictest bounds will be imposed. For example, if you specify that a variable be nonnegative and then give it lower and upper bounds of -5 and +10, respectively, the net result will be a variable bounded between 0 and 10. You might use this facility, for example, to limit the size of the workforce to a certain range when scheduling production.

3.2 Information About the Constraints

For each constraint, the value on the right-hand side (RHS) must be entered, and the default constraint type (CONST TYPE) adjusted if necessary; type "<" for *less than or equal to,* ">" for *greater than or equal to,* or "=" for *equal to.* You will find all the constraints defaulted to "<=" if the objective type is MAX, and to ">=" otherwise. You can also enter the letter "O" in the CONST TYPE column, which has the effect of excluding that constraint from the problem.

The final column (RANGE) permits both upper and lower bounds on the constraint. Thus, if we want

$$b \leq a_1 x_1 + \ldots + a_n x_n \leq B,$$

we can specify CONST TYPE: <=, RHS: B, and then RANGE: B-b. Equivalently, we might enter CONST TYPE: >=, RHS: b, and RANGE: B-b. That is, we pin down either end of the interval (b, B) and then give its width.

3.3 Removing Variables or Constraints Temporarily

As we have already said, by entering the letter "O" in the VARBL TYPE row or the CONST TYPE column, you have the facility to exclude variables and/or constraints from the formulation. You can, of course, always return to the Editor screen and replace the "O" with some other permissible entry to reinstate the variable or constraint. This allows you to perform "what if" analyses with great ease, without having to do extensive editing. For example, you might first solve a production scheduling problem, including the option of overtime work, and then resolve it with overtime disallowed, to assess the effect of this option on the total cost.

4. Execution of the Module

In executing the linear programming module, you will first be asked if you want to go directly to the final result, or if you would prefer to observe each solution as the algorithm progresses through successive iterations. If you are not concerned with intermediate output, you may skip Section 4.1.

4.1 Special Features of Intermediate Solution Reports

At each iteration of the Simplex algorithm, you will be presented with the menu given in Figure 2. The first option lets you skip to the final solution at any time. Instead, you may wish to step from one Simplex iteration to the next using option 4, pausing at will to explore the current solution. STORM also provides you with an option to proceed to the next solution by entering the variable of your choice.

```
        LINEAR PROGRAMMING PHASE 2 : ITERATION 3

    1)   Go to the optimal solution
    2)   Summary Report for current solution
    3)   Detailed Report for current solution
    4)   Go to the next iteration
    5)   Select entering variable, go to next iteration
    6)   List problem data in equation style
    7)   Tableau Report for current solution
```

Figure 2: Intermediate Menu

Information about each iteration may be presented in any of three ways: listings of the relevant information either summarized or in detail (options 2 and 3), or the traditional Simplex tableau (option 7). For further discussion of these reports, see Section 4.2. At each iteration of the algorithm, any of these reports may be obtained and you can then advance to the next iteration or skip to the optimal solution.

When observing each iteration in a problem where artificial variables are needed, Phase 1 of the simplex algorithm will also be presented. Phase 1 denotes those initial iterations used to drive the artificials out of the basis. This is done by solving the minimization problem in which the artificials are assigned a cost of 1 and all other objective function coefficients are set to zero, keeping the constraints unchanged. Once all the artificial variables have been removed, the original coefficients are restored and the remaining iterations take place in Phase 2.

4.2 Output Reports for the Optimal Solution

When optimality is reached, you will be offered the menu shown in Figure 3. The results are available in a variety of formats. In the various outputs, you will find that new variables have been introduced by the module. These represent the slack or surplus variables (both slack and surplus are called "slack") used in the constraints. As appropriate, a slack has been added to, or a surplus subtracted from, the left-hand side of each inequality constraint to make it an equation. The name assigned to each of these variables is the row label of the corresponding constraint.

```
LINEAR PROGRAMMING OPTIMAL SOLUTION : ITERATION 7

   1)   Summary Report for current solution
   2)   Detailed Report for current solution
   3)   Sensitivity analysis for optimal solution
   4)   Parametric analysis of right-hand side
   5)   Select entering variable, go to next iteration
   6)   Save optimal solution as initial solution
   7)   List problem data in equation style
   8)   Tableau Report for current solution
```

Figure 3: Final Menu

Options 1 and 2 present the basic information about the optimal solution in summary or detailed form, respectively. As we see in Figure 4, the detailed report gives for each variable:

- Its value in the solution.
- Its cost coefficient in the objective function.
- Its reduced cost: the amount by which the objective function will increase if one more unit of this activity is forced into the solution, with compensating changes of other activity levels.
- Its status: basic if it is part of the solution, and if nonbasic, whether it is at its lower bound or upper bound. For example, the usual nonnegative variable (lower bound of zero) without other bounds is at its lower bound when not basic.

```
                OPTIMAL SOLUTION  -  DETAILED REPORT
          Variable      Value      Cost    Red cost   Status
    1   PRODUCT 1      710.6383   26.0000    0.0000    Basic
    2   PRODUCT 2       23.4043   28.0000    0.0000    Basic

Slack Variables
    3   DEPT. 1          0.0000    0.0000  -18.7234 Lower bound
    4   DEPT. 2        108.5106    0.0000    0.0000    Basic
    5   DEPT. 3          0.0000    0.0000   -9.1489 Lower bound
    6   DEPT. 4         15.8511    0.0000    0.0000    Basic

        Constraint Type     RHS        Slack   Shadow price
    1   DEPT. 1    <=    670.0000     0.0000      18.7234
    2   DEPT. 2    <=    620.0000   108.5106       0.0000
    3   DEPT. 3    <=    720.0000     0.0000       9.1489
    4   DEPT. 4    <=    165.0000    15.8511       0.0000

Objective Function Value = 19131.92
```

Figure 4: Detailed Report of the Optimal Solution

For each constraint, we also have:

- Its type ($\leq$, $\geq$, or =).
- Its right-hand side (RHS) value.

- The value of the slack or surplus variable: the amount by which a resource is underutilized, or the amount by which we exceed minimal requirements, or generally, how close to being binding the RHS value is.
- The shadow price or dual price: the amount by which the objective function will increase if the RHS is increased by one unit; that is, if one additional unit of a resource is made available, or if a minimal requirement is increased one unit. Shadow prices are always zero if there is positive slack.

The summary report gives only the values and costs of the variables that have nonzero values in the solution, and the resulting value of the objective function.

The other means of presenting a solution is in the standard tableau format. If you choose this last option on the menu, you will be given a Candidate Selection form on which to select the subset of variables to be included as columns (remember, if you want to choose all of a long list, the F1 key toggles all candidates simultaneously). Since only four variables can be displayed as side-by-side columns before it is necessary to start a new set of rows, this facility has been added to allow you to obtain a more compact printout containing just the information desired. For example, basic variables whose columns are predictably all 1's and 0's can be omitted.

The final tableau for the sample problem is presented in Figure 5, where we chose to omit the columns representing the basic slack variables, SLACK 2 and SLACK 4. The first part of the report, which is always the same regardless of the variables chosen, gives the basic variables and their values. The second part has a column for each selected variable, in which is given its cost, its *exchange rate* with each basic variable and its reduced cost.

5. Alternative Optimal Solutions

Option 5 on the Optimal Solution menu is *Select entering variable, go to next iteration,* and you may wonder why one would ever want to modify a solution when it is already the best. Here is one situation where this facility could come in handy. If one or more nonbasic variables has a reduced cost of zero at optimality, this indicates that the problem has more than one optimal solution. STORM presents you with one of them. You may be interested in investigating the others. If so, choose alternative 5 and then select one of the nonbasic variables with zero reduced cost to enter. This will move you to a different optimum. By using this procedure repeatedly, you can generate all the basic optimal solutions.

```
                        TABLEAU REPORT
                 --------- Basis Information --------
        Constraint      Variable        Cost        Value
        DEPT. 1       PRODUCT 2        28.0000      23.4043
        DEPT. 2       SLACK   2         0.0000     108.5106
        DEPT. 3       PRODUCT 1        26.0000     710.6383
        DEPT. 4       SLACK   4         0.0000      15.8511

                    PRODUCT 1    PRODUCT 2    SLACK   1    SLACK   3
        Cost          26.0000      28.0000      0.0000       0.0000
                 -------------------------------------------------
        PRODUCT 2      0.0000       1.0000      1.0638      -0.9574
        SLACK   2      0.0000       0.0000     -0.3404      -0.3936
        PRODUCT 1      1.0000       0.0000     -0.4255       1.3830
        SLACK   4      0.0000       0.0000     -0.2340       0.0106
                 -------------------------------------------------
        Red. cost      0.0000       0.0000    -18.7234      -9.1489
```

Figure 5: Tableau Display of the Optimal Solution

6. Saving the Optimal Solution

If you select Option 6, *Save optimal solution as initial solution,* STORM will save your solution in the INIT SOLN row of the detailed data, and change the problem descriptor *Starting solution given* to *yes.* This option is useful in an operational setting where you may periodically resolve the same linear program with slightly different data. In such a case, we expect the new optimum to be close to the old one. Thus, the algorithm may converge much faster if we start from the previous solution.

7. Sensitivity Analysis

When the optimal solution is reached, two additional types of output are available: sensitivity analysis and parametric analysis. The sensitivity analysis of the sample problem is presented in Figure 6. It tells us over what range of values a given parameter of the problem can vary, all else being held fixed, without altering the nature of the solution in some way. The first kind of sensitivity analysis reported is *cost ranging:* the amount an objective function coefficient can vary without altering the solution. For example, we see in Figure 6 that the contribution margin of the first product, which we assumed to be $26 per unit, could actually be anywhere from $19.38 to $70.00, and it would still be optimal to produce the same number of units of each product.

Similarly, the second display in sensitivity analysis shows the interval over which any RHS value can be varied without changing the set of variables that are part of the solution. Thus, the 670 hours available in Department 1 could be as little as 648.0 hours or as much as 737.7 hours and the same variables would remain basic, though their values would change, as would the profit that could be achieved.

```
             SENSITIVITY ANALYSIS OF COST COEFFICIENTS
                           Current    Allowable   Allowable
              Variable      Coeff.     Minimum     Maximum
       1     PRODUCT 1     26.0000     19.3846     70.0000
       2     PRODUCT 2     28.0000     10.4000     37.5556

             SENSITIVITY ANALYSIS OF RIGHT-HAND SIDE VALUES
                           Current    Allowable   Allowable
         Constraint  Type   Value      Minimum     Maximum
       1   DEPT. 1   <=    670.0000    648.0000    737.7272
       2   DEPT. 2   <=    620.0000    511.4893    Infinity
       3   DEPT. 3   <=    720.0000    206.1539    744.4445
       4   DEPT. 4   <=    165.0000    149.1489    Infinity
```

Figure 6: Sensitivity Analysis of the Sample Problem

Remember, *the information in Figure 6 reflects the variation of one parameter only, with all others remaining constant.* Thus, we could not necessarily vary the available time (RHS) in both Departments 1 and 2 within their allowable ranges and retain the same basic variables.

8. Parametric Analysis

Parametric analysis reveals the way in which the optimal solution (that is, the set of basic variables and the objective function value) varies as a function of one of the RHS values. You will be given a form in which to specify which right-hand side (that is, which constraint) you want to investigate. If you need help remembering the precise constraint name, type F8 and a list of all the candidate row labels will appear at the right of the screen, with a Pointer you can move using the Up and Down Arrows. Make your selection by positioning the Pointer and pressing the Enter key. Next, you will be asked to select a range of values over which the RHS is to vary (default range: minus infinity to plus infinity). Having specified lower and upper limits, you will be presented with an output like Figure 7, containing the following information:

- The successive intervals of right-hand side values, within the overall span of values, in which the basis remains unchanged. For each range, the following facts are given.
- The shadow price of the RHS. This tells you the rate at which the function is increasing per unit change of the RHS value.
- The range of objective function values corresponding to the interval of RHS values. These values are displayed just below the right-hand side interval.
- The variable that leaves and the variable that enters, as the end of the interval is reached and the basis changes.

```
          PARAMETRIC ANALYSIS OF RIGHT-HAND SIDE VALUE - DEPT. 1
          COEF = 670.000      LWR LIMIT = -Infinity      UPR LIMIT = Infinity
                  ------- Range -------        Shadow   ---- Variable ----
                      From          To         Price      Leave      Enter
          RHS      670.000     737.727        18.723   SLACK    4  SLACK    1
          Obj    19131.920   20400.000

          RHS      737.727     Infinity         0.000   ----  No change  ----
          Obj    20400.000   20400.000

          RHS      670.000     648.000        18.723   PRODUCT 2  SLACK    3
          Obj    19131.920   18720.000

          RHS      648.000       0.000        28.889   PRODUCT 1
          Obj    18720.000       0.000

          RHS        0.000    -Infinity   ----  Infeasible in this range ----
```

Figure 7: Parametric Analysis of the First Constraint

Figure 7 gives the analysis for the first constraint of the example. The first row of numbers confirms what we have already learned in earlier outputs: at the present RHS value of 670 hours available in Department 1, the shadow price is 18.723 dollars per hour (see Figure

3), and remains so up to the *allowable maximum* of 737.727 hours (see Figure 6). As the available hours are increased over this interval, the profit grows from $19,131.92 to $20,400.00. At this point, a basic change takes place and SLACK 1 enters the basis. This means that further increases in this RHS parameter introduce slack time into Department 1; additional hours have no further value. The next row in the parametric analysis confirms that, from 737.727 hours on up, time in Department 1 has a shadow price (value) of zero, and contribution grows no further. Similarly, the rest of the report shows the consequences of decreasing the RHS value from its initial value of 670.

As was the case with sensitivity analysis, parametric analysis assumes that all other given values are held constant. When you wish to experiment with two or more parameters simultaneously, you will have to change them in the initial formulation and resolve the entire problem.

As we have seen, the simplest type of constraint, namely a variable bound such as $x_3 \leq 120$, can be conveniently entered in the Editor screen by typing 120 in the UPPR BOUND row. Alternatively, you could use an extra row and enter it as a separate constraint. Keep in mind that if you are going to want to do parametric analysis on the value 120, you must treat it as a constraint rather than as an upper bound. A similar situation arises with the range constraints. Recall from Section 3 that we can effectively enter two constraints on the same line by using the RANGE column. If we do so, parametric analysis is not available for either of these constraints.

9. Altering Problem Data Dimensions

The cost coefficients, lower and upper bounds, variable type and initial solution are all required rows in a data set. The columns for constraint type, RHS, and range are also not to be altered. Any constraint (variable) can be deleted as long as there is at least one more constraint (variable) in the data set. A constraint (variable) can be inserted if the total number of constraints (variables) does not exceed the maximal problem size. The procedure for inserting or deleting rows or columns is discussed in detail in Chapter 4.

Note that variables or constraints deleted will be permanently removed from the data set being edited. To omit a variable (constraint) for a particular session, simply enter "O" (the letter, not the number) for the variable (constraint) type. Variables (constraints) marked with an "O" will be excluded from consideration, but will remain in the data set and can be reactivated later.

INTEGER PROGRAMMING CAPABILITIES

PROBLEM FORMULATION OPTIONS
- Pure or mixed integer programs
- Any combination of positive, negative, unrestricted, or zero-one integer variables, with any number of continuous variables
- All the formulation options of linear programming

OUTPUT OPTIONS AND OTHER FEATURES
- Presentation of each solution found, or final solution only
- Branch-and-bound algorithm with running time controllable by
    - Prioritizing variables
    - Limiting number of nodes searched
    - Acceptance of a suboptimal solution
- Automatic scaling of problem data
- Save final solution as initial solution for future runs

MAXIMAL PROBLEM SIZES (VARIABLES, CONSTRAINTS)
- Personal version: (100, 50)

- Professional version
  Representative sizes, with 500K of net memory for STORM:
    (1250, 10)
    (625, 50)
    (125, 125)
    (50, 140)
    (10, 150)

FILE NAME FOR THE SAMPLE PROBLEM DATA
- IP.DAT

Chapter 6

INTEGER PROGRAMMING

Frequently, in a linear programming formulation, we will find that some or all of the activities are required by their very nature to take on integer values only. Thus, if a variable denotes the number of workers hired or number of cars produced, its value can only be a nonnegative whole number.

A linear program in which all variables must be integers is called an integer linear program or simply an *integer program*. If some activities must be integer-valued while others are not so constrained, we refer to a *mixed integer program*. Finally, a special kind of integer variable is frequently useful, which can take on only the values zero and one. Such variables are used as indicators of the presence or absence of some activity.

In STORM, the Linear and Integer Programming module permits you to define each variable separately to be real-valued (that is, not necessarily integral), integer-valued, or zero-one. You may have any mixture of variable types. This chapter discusses the integer extensions of linear programming. It depends heavily on the previous chapter, with which you should be familiar.

1. The Solution Algorithm

When integer variables are present, the module uses depth-first search in a branch-and-bound scheme, as discussed in most introductory management science textbooks. The problem is first solved as an ordinary linear program, the *linear relaxation*, in which all integer restrictions are ignored. Then, at each successive level of the search tree, one (or more) integer variables are fixed at integral values and a new solution is found. You can partially specify the order in which variables are chosen to branch on by assigning priorities, as described in Section 1.2. Beyond that, the algorithm chooses the integer variable with the largest fractional part, breaking ties arbitrarily.

1.1 Choosing the Quality of the Solution

For problems with many integer-valued activities, computer run times may be long. STORM therefore gives you the opportunity to curtail this time, if you are willing to accept a solution that is guaranteed to be within a certain per cent of the optimum. You can select the margin of error acceptable to you. For example, suppose you specify a solution quality of 5% (any solution within 5% of optimal is acceptable) in a cost minimization problem. Then as each improved feasible solution is found, it is compared to a lower bound that the module computes. When a solution is no more than 5% larger than the bound, the algorithm terminates and reports that solution as satisfactory. Note that the given solution may in fact be optimal, or perhaps only 2% more than the true optimum. Often, a branch-and-bound algorithm will find the optimum quickly, but will spend a lot of time checking out other likely candidates before it can be sure of its choice.

1.2 Setting Variable Priorities

Another means provided by the module to diminish computing time is prioritized variables. At any node in the search tree, a branching variable must be selected from among the integer variables which have not yet assumed integral values. You can influence the order of selection by assigning each variable a priority from zero to nine. A variable with a higher priority will always be chosen for branching before one with lower priority. Among variables with the same priority, we arbitrarily take one with the highest fractional part.

Judicious setting of priorities can have a considerable effect on the time needed to solve a (mixed) integer program, by influencing the number of nodes that must be examined. Each integer variable should be assigned a priority commensurate with its "importance," as best you can assess it. Usually this means a higher priority to those variables that are most critical to the outcome of the process being modelled. Zero-one variables are almost always most important, as they symbolize whether or not to undertake an activity rather than merely setting its level. Also, variables with higher cost or value coefficients in the objective should usually have higher priorities.

1.3 Limiting the Number of Nodes Generated

As a final control on running time, STORM lets you choose the number of nodes to be evaluated between reports. Each time STORM has searched another batch of nodes of the specified size, it will report the best objective value found so far (or, if no feasible solution has yet been found, it will report that), remind you of the upper bound, and ask if you wish to examine another batch. If you wish, it will continue searching this way until it finds and confirms the optimal solution (or reaches a solution of satisfactory quality, if so directed). At any step, you can terminate and receive a full output report. The dot default denotes a batch size of infinity. In this case, STORM will continue searching until a solution of the desired quality is reached.

2. A Sample Problem

In the last chapter, we discussed the manufacture of two products that shared the productive resources of four departments at the Hamlin Company. Given the total time available in each department and the four processing times for each product, as reproduced in Table 1 below, we sought to maximize total contribution when the contribution margin per item was $26 and $28, respectively. We found that it was optimal to produce 710.6 units of the first product and 23.4 units of the second, with departments 1 and 3 being fully utilized while departments 2 and 4 had some slack time remaining.

	Department			
	1	2	3	4
Time Available	670	620	720	165
Time required per Item				
Product 1	0.9	0.7	1.0	0.2
Product 2	1.3	0.6	0.4	0.3

Table 1: Data for Sample Problem

Let us now add the following considerations. First, the items being manufactured are indivisible; producing fractional amounts of either is meaningless. Second, the production manager at Hamlin notes that the available time in departments 1 and 3 is limited by a shortage of skilled personnel, not a lack of machine capacity. She is now presented with the opportunity of hiring an extra operator, capable of working in either of the two departments and thereby increasing the productive hours available in either or both. Specifically, at a cost of $2000 per month she can increase the available productive time by 154 hours each month (7 hours a day for 22 days), which can be shared between departments 1 and 3 in any proportion. Should Hamlin hire the additional operator, and if so, how should his time be apportioned?

To formulate this as a mixed integer program, we let x_1 and x_2 be the number of units of each product to be manufactured, and further define:

y = the extra time (hours) in department 1

so that 154 - y denotes the extra time for department 3, with the constraint: $y \leq$ 154. However, these times must both be zero if we decide not to hire the worker.

For this decision, we introduce a zero-one variable:

z = 1, if we hire the worker; 0, if not.

Since the hours are only available if z = 1, we replace 154 by 154z wherever it appears. Now, without our new employee, the constraint $y \leq$ 154z becomes $y \leq$ 0, or (since all variables are nonnegative) y = 0. This in turn implies that 154z - y = 0, as required.

Putting this all together, we have the mixed integer program:

$$\text{maximize} \quad 26x_1 + 28x_2 - 2000z$$

$$\begin{aligned}
\text{subject to} \quad & 0.9x_1 + 1.3x_2 \leq 670 + y \\
& 0.7x_1 + 0.6x_2 \leq 620 \\
& x_1 + 0.4x_2 \leq 720 + 154z - y \\
& 0.2x_1 + 0.3x_2 \leq 165 \\
& y \leq 154z \\
& x_1 = 0,1,2,\dots \quad x_2 = 0,1,2,\dots \\
& y \geq 0, \quad z = 0,1
\end{aligned}$$

3. Data Entry using STORM

After entering the above program in STORM, the Editor screen should look like Figure 1. The variables have been given more meaningful names; you will have no trouble identifying them. The final column, where range constraints can be specified, is off screen to the right, but no entries have been made there. The only place on the screen where an integer program differs from a linear program is in the VARBL TYPE row, where IPOS indicates a variable that can only take nonnegative integer values, and "0-1" forces the variable to be zero or one only. Table 2 in Chapter 5 lists all allowable variable types.

```
 -----------| STORM EDITOR : Linear & Integer Programming Module |-----------
 Title : PRODUCTION PLANNING AT THE HAMLIN COMPANY, WITH NEW WORKER
 Number of variables       :       4
 Number of constraints     :       5
 Starting solution given   :      NO
 Objective type (MAX/MIN) :     MAX

 R7  : C6   PRODUCT 1  PRODUCT 2  NEW HIRE? TIME IN D1 CONST TYPE    R H S
 OBJ COEFF       26.       28.      -2000.        0.    XXXX      XXXX
 DEPT. 1         0.9       1.3          0.       -1.      <=      670.
 DEPT. 2         0.7       0.6          0.        0.      <=      620.
 DEPT. 3         1.        0.4       -154.        1.      <=      720.
 DEPT. 4         0.2       0.3          0.        0.      <=      165.
 TIME LIMIT      0.        0.        -154.        1.      <=        0.
 VARBL TYPE     IPOS      IPOS        0-1       POS     XXXX      XXXX
 LOWR BOUND       .         .           .         .     XXXX      XXXX
 UPPR BOUND       .         .           .         .     XXXX      XXXX
 INIT SOLN       0.        0.          0.        0.     XXXX      XXXX




 -----| No entry                            |->|         |------
```

Figure 1: Editor Screen After Data Entry

4. Execution of the Module

When you proceed to execution, you will first be shown the STORM form illustrated in Figure 2. Here you can specify certain features of the branch-and-bound search procedure. Most importantly, since it may take some time to converge on the best solution, you may be willing to settle for a slightly suboptimal solution produced much more rapidly. Several of the available parameter settings allow you to do this in various ways, as already discussed in Section 1.

At the bottom of the screen, the value of the objective function is given when the problem is solved as a simple linear program, with integrality requirements ignored. Since a *relaxation* of certain requirements can only allow a better solution, this value is an upper bound for maximization problems (as here) and a lower bound on minimizations. This bound may give you insight into the magnitude of the search ahead, and help you decide what per cent from optimum you are willing to accept.

```
          SELECTION OF BRANCH-AND-BOUND PROCESS PARAMETERS

Desired solution quality (acceptable % from optimum) : 0.00
Set priorities on variables for branching ? (y/n)    : n
Report each improved solution found ? (y/n)          : n
Batch size for nodes to be examined (. if no limit)  : .


     Lower bound on objective function =    -Infinity
     Upper bound on objective function =    19520.43
```

Figure 2: Setting Parameters to Control Search Procedures

Most of the settings you must make in the STORM form have already been explained in Section 1. The first entry allows you to choose the acceptable margin of error. The larger the percentage below the optimal value (in a maximization problem) that you are willing to tolerate, the quicker the algorithm will terminate with an acceptable solution, as discussed in Section 1.1. If you answer *yes* in the second row, then at the time of execution you will first be taken to a Candidate Selection form where all integer variables are listed with their default priority settings (0-1 variables will have the highest priority of 9, while all others are given priority 1), and you can move up and down the column changing priorities at will. Prioritized variables are explained in Section 1.2. Skipping to the fourth entry in the form, you have another way to truncate the possibly lengthy calculations by instructing the program to search the nodes of the decision tree in batches of a specified size, with a brief progress report after each batch. You can then search another batch, or terminate at any time you think the reported objective value is satisfactory, as further discussed in Section 1.3.

The third row in the STORM form gives you the opportunity to inspect each solution as the algorithm discovers successively better ones. Note the difference between this and the fourth row entry. The third row option produces the full output reports whenever an improvement is found. On the other hand, choosing a batch size of ten in the fourth row gives you the value of the objective function (but not the complete solution) regularly every ten nodes, even if no improvement has occurred.

If you wish to be presented only with the final solution, leave the third and fourth entries at their default settings. Since Section 4.1 deals with intermediate outputs, you may wish to skip directly to Section 4.2.

4.1 Intermediate Solution Reports

If you answer *yes* to the question *Report each improved solution found?* and press the F7 key, then (after resetting the variable priorities if you chose to do so) you will go to the menu shown in Figure 3. The first two options provide information about the current best solution. They present the same information as the final solution reports in Figures 5 and 6, which will be discussed in the next section. By keeping in mind the upper (lower) bound on the optimum, you can decide whether to stop the process at any time, depending on how close the current solution is to the bound. Option 3 repeats the same menu with the solution number incremented by one. By repeated use of option 3, or by choosing option 4, we eventually come to the final solution, as described in Section 4.2.

```
           INTEGER PROGRAMMING SOLUTION NUMBER : 1


    1)    Summary Report for current solution
    2)    Detailed Report for corresponding LP solution
    3)    Go to the next solution
    4)    Go to the optimal solution
```

Figure 3: Menu for Intermediate Solutions

4.2 Output Reports for the Optimal Solution

When you arrive at the final solution (which we refer to as the "optimal solution," though it may not be if you have chosen any of the ways to terminate computation short of optimality), the menu shown in Figure 4 will appear. If you choose the first option, you will get the summary report presented in Figure 5.

```
           INTEGER PROGRAMMING OPTIMAL SOLUTION


    1)    Summary Report for current solution
    2)    Detailed Report for corresponding LP solution
    3)    Save final solution as initial solution and return
```

Figure 4: Menu for Final Solution

OPTIMAL SOLUTION - SUMMARY REPORT

Variable	Value	Cost	Lower bound	Upper bound
PRODUCT 1	792	26.0000	0	Infinity
PRODUCT 2	22	28.0000	0	Infinity
NEW HIRE?	1	-2000.0000	0	1
TIME IN D1	71.4000	0.0000	0.0000	Infinity

Constraint	Type	RHS	Slack
DEPT. 1	<=	670.0000	0.0000
DEPT. 2	<=	620.0000	52.4000
DEPT. 3	<=	720.0000	1.8000
DEPT. 4	<=	165.0000	0.0000
TIME LIMIT	<=	0.0000	82.6000

Objective Function Value = 19208

Figure 5: Summary Report for the Optimal Solution

The first part of the report simply gives the values of the variables, as well as echoing the objective function coefficients and the feasible ranges. As usual, figures required to be integers are given without decimal points. We can observe that it is desirable to hire the additional worker (NEW HIRE? = 1), that he should spend about half his time in Department 1 (TIME IN D1 = 71.4), and that the additional productive capacity he provides should be used entirely to manufacture more units of product 1. Specifically, PRODUCT 1, which we saw to be 710.6 units in the last chapter, and which would have been 708 units if both variables had been constrained to be integers, is now 792 units. PRODUCT 2, on the other hand, stays about the same.

The other part of the report gives the amount of slack that now remains in each constraint, as well as repeating its type and right-hand side value. We see that the capacity of Department 4 is now fully utilized, Department 2 still has some slack, and Departments 1 and 3, which share the services of the new worker, now have slightly more capacity (1.8 hours) than they can use, which has been arbitrarily allocated to Department 3. Finally, our total contribution is now $19,208, only slightly bigger than before. Probably in reality we need to analyze the situation more carefully, considering other actions available to us, market trends, etc., before making this hiring decision.

The second item on the menu, *Detailed Report for corresponding LP solution*, produces the output shown in Figure 6. This is useful when you are solving a mixed integer program, where some variables are required to be integers and some are not. Having solved the problem, STORM then fixes the integer variables at their optimal values and solves for the remaining continuous variables as an ordinary linear program. Of course, their values come out the same, but the output reports available for linear programs give more information than can be provided for integer programs. Specifically, we now have the reduced cost of each variable and the shadow price for the right-hand side of each constraint. For our small example, with only one continuous variable, there is nothing new to learn, since that variable, TIME IN D1, is basic and so has zero reduced cost.

```
               DETAILED LP REPORT FOR
                  OPTIMAL SOLUTION
           The following variables are fixed
                   PRODUCT 1          792
                   PRODUCT 2           22
                   NEW HIRE?            1

              OPTIMAL SOLUTION  - DETAILED REPORT
        Variable        Value        Cost   Red. cost   Status
   1    PRODUCT 1     792.0000     26.0000    26.0000 Lower bound
   2    PRODUCT 2      22.0000     28.0000    28.0000 Upper bound
   3    NEW HIRE?       1.0000  -2000.0000 -2000.0000 Lower bound
   4    TIME IN D1     71.4000      0.0000     0.0000    Basic

Slack Variables
   5      DEPT. 1       0.0000      0.0000     0.0000 Lower bound
   6      DEPT. 2      52.4000      0.0000     0.0000    Basic
   7      DEPT. 3       1.8000      0.0000     0.0000    Basic
   8      DEPT. 4       0.0000      0.0000     0.0000    Basic
   9    TIME LIMIT     82.6000      0.0000     0.0000    Basic

        Constraint  Type     RHS        Slack   Shadow price
   1      DEPT. 1    <=    670.0000     0.0000       0.0000
   2      DEPT. 2    <=    620.0000    52.4000       0.0000
   3      DEPT. 3    <=    720.0000     1.8000       0.0000
   4      DEPT. 4    <=    165.0000     0.0000       0.0000
   5    TIME LIMIT   <=      0.0000    82.6000       0.0000

Objective Function Value = 19208
```

Figure 6: Solution as a Linear Program

Be careful with your interpretation of these outputs. Although the integer variables are listed as though they were ordinary continuous ones, they are fixed and so their reduced costs are meaningless.

5. Tips on Using the Integer Programming Module

Option 3 of the optimal solution menu, *Save final solution as initial solution,* is particularly useful for problems that require long and unpredictable computational times. You may not have time to solve such a problem at one sitting. Instead, you can specify a solution quality of, say 10% to get close to the optimum in a reasonable time, and save the result as an initial solution. Having saved the data set to disk, you can return the next day and pick up from there, with solution quality set to 5%. This enables you to measure out the work to be done in each run, though it may be difficult to estimate how long it will take to reach a certain solution quality. Alternatively, using this same option, you can limit a work session by the number of nodes searched. This should give you better control over the time spent in each session, because the time required to search a node tends to be fairly constant.

6. Altering Problem Data Dimensions

The rules governing insertions and deletions in linear programming remain in effect here. Constraint rows and variable columns can be added or deleted, as long as at least one of each remains and the maximal problem size is not exceeded.

- NOTES -

ASSIGNMENT CAPABILITIES

PROBLEM FORMULATION OPTIONS
- Maximize or minimize the objective function
- Automatic insertion of dummy rows/columns for problems with an unequal number of rows and columns

OUTPUT OPTIONS AND OTHER FEATURES
- Report of partial assignment at each iteration
- Tableau output at each iteration for small problems

MAXIMAL PROBLEM SIZES (ROWS, COLUMNS)
- Personal version: (100, 100)

- Professional version, with 500K of net memory for STORM: (250, 250)

FILE NAME FOR THE SAMPLE PROBLEM DATA
- ASN.DAT

Chapter 7

THE ASSIGNMENT PROBLEM

Consider the problem of assigning a given set of jobs to a given set of machines, one job per machine. The desirability of each possible matching of a job to a machine has been previously evaluated, and we seek the particular assignment that minimizes or maximizes some objective such as cost or profit. Though we use the words *jobs* and *machines,* the same problem frequently arises in other connections. For example, we may be assigning workers to jobs so as to maximize the cost of completing all the work. Or we may wish to allocate projects to outside bidders, or territories to members of our sales force. Any time we wish to pair off two sets of objects efficiently, this module is probably applicable.

Though there will usually be equal numbers of jobs and machines, this need not be the case. If there are more jobs than machines or vice versa, assignments will still be one-to-one, and will be made purely on the basis of cost. For example, if there are more jobs than machines, the excess jobs will not get done, and the jobs chosen for assignment will be those that can be done most cheaply (or quickly, or desirably, according to the objective chosen), regardless of any other consideration such as urgency or importance.

1. The Solution Algorithm

The Assignment module utilizes the traditional reduction algorithm known as the *Hungarian method,* as discussed in most basic management science texts. The only required input data are the values associated with each assignment, which we assume to be laid out in a table or *matrix,* each row representing a machine and each column a job (or vice versa; rows and columns are interchangeable). We will refer to the positions in the matrix as *cells* and the numbers in each cell as *values* or *elements.* The often-used term *row or column* will be abbreviated *row/col,* and when we speak of performing some operation on a row/col, we will mean performing that operation on every element in that row/col. Throughout the ensuing discussion, we will assume that the given values are costs or other measures to be minimized. Understand, this is not a limitation of the module, which can handle either a maximization or a minimization objective.

If there are unequal numbers of jobs and machines, the algorithm requires dummy rows or columns with all-zero values to be added to the original matrix to make it square. STORM will take care of this automatically; you need not bother.

2. Problem Size

The Assignment module can handle matrices with up to 250 rows and 250 columns in the Professional version, and 100 by 100 matrices in the Personal version. For problems with no more than a six-by-six array, where the entire matrix fits on the monitor screen, results at each iteration of the algorithm can be displayed in tableau format. This is in addition to the listing of (partial) assignments that is available at each step, for any sized problem.

3. A Sample Problem

Suppose four project leaders are available for four research projects. Each project has equal priority. The time required to complete each project depends on which leader is assigned, as shown in Table 1:

```
                          Project

                     1     2     3     4

               1     1     4     6     3

    Leader     2     9     7    10     9

               3     4     5    11     7

               4     8     7     8     5
```

Table 1: Matrix of Project Completion Times

The entries in the four-by-four matrix are the predicted times each leader would require to complete each project. Our objective is to assign one leader to each project so as to minimize the total time needed to complete all projects.

4. Data Entry and Execution Using STORM

Using the Editor, the data are entered to produce the display shown in Figure 1. The numbers entered must be integers. The row and column headers (for which the default entries are ROW 1, . . . and COLUMN 1, . . .) have been changed to reflect the particular problem description. This, of course, is optional.

```
|-------------------------| STORM EDITOR : Assignment Module |----------------|
| Title : SAMPLE ASSIGNMENT PROBLEM                                            |
| Number of rows              :        4                                       |
| Number of columns           :        4                                       |
| Objective type (MAX/MIN) :        MIN                                        |
|                                                                              |
|                                                                              |
| R1  : C4      PROJECT 1  PROJECT 2  PROJECT 3  PROJECT 4                      |
| LEADER 1          1          4          6          3                         |
| LEADER 2          9          7         10          9                         |
| LEADER 3          4          5         11          7                         |
| LEADER 4          8          7          8          5                         |
|                                                                              |
|                                                                              |
|                                                                              |
|                                                                              |
|                                                                              |
|                                                                              |
|-----| Enter cost if PROJECT 4 assigned to LEADER 1     |->|       |----------|
```

Figure 1: The Editor Screen After Data Entry

Press F7 to return to the Process menu, where you are ready for option 4: *Execute the module with the current data set.* The next menu gives you the choice of going directly to the final solution or stepping through successive iterations of the algorithm. By choosing *Go to the next iteration,* you have the opportunity to observe the partial assignments listed in a format similar to Figure 2. Thereafter, at each step you can jump directly to the optimum, or advance one more iteration. Ultimately, the final solution is reached and can be displayed as in Figure 2, which gives the optimal assignments for the sample problem.

```
                  OPTIMAL SOLUTION
   Row               Column         Cost
   LEADER 1          PROJECT 1        1
   LEADER 2          PROJECT 3       10
   LEADER 3          PROJECT 2        5
   LEADER 4          PROJECT 4        5

   Total Cost = 21
   Number of iterations = 2
```

Figure 2: Optimal Assignment

5. Intermediate Tableau Output for Small Problems

The discussion in this section assumes that the reader is familiar with the step-by-step operation of the Hungarian method. If you are not acquainted with this algorithm, or not interested in interpreting intermediate outputs for small problems, you should skip directly to the next section.

For small problems (no more than six rows/cols), tableau outputs are available in addition to the listings described in Section 4. To begin with, the initial cost matrix can be displayed again, for final verification and to print it out if desired. Then, at each step, the reduced cost matrix can be observed (columns have been reduced before rows). An attempt has been made to find an all-zero set of assignments, and the selected cells are marked ASSIGN-MENT. Assuming a complete solution has not been found, the set of rows and columns chosen to cover all the zeros (the *crossed* rows/cols) are shown in reverse video, and the smallest uncrossed element is marked with an asterisk. Ultimately, when the optimal solution is reached, the menu option *View results in tableau format on monitor* produces successively the final reduced cost matrix with the optimal assignments indicated, and the optimal solution matrix with the original cost values restored. Also, since the last display shows the chosen cells only by reverse video, which will disappear when you produce hard copy on your printer, a third tableau simply gives the selected assignments. Remember, all of these tableau outputs are available only for 6 by 6 or smaller cost matrices.

6. Altering Problem Data Dimensions

Rows and columns can be freely inserted anywhere in the cost matrix until the data set reaches the maximal problem size. Any row/col can be deleted as long as there is at least one row/col left in the data set after the deletion.

TRANSPORTATION CAPABILITIES

PROBLEM FORMULATION OPTIONS
- Uncapacitated or capacitated routes
- Prohibited routes for uncapacitated problems
- Lower Bounds on shipments to/from each location
- Maximize or minimize objective function

OUTPUT OPTIONS AND OTHER FEATURES
- Initial solution algorithms:
  - Northwest corner rule
  - Matrix minimum
  - Row minimum
  - Vogel's approximation method
- Report of solution at each iteration, or optimal solution only
- Detailed or Summary Report of solution
- Tableau presentation for small problems

MAXIMAL PROBLEM SIZES (ROWS, COLUMNS)
- Personal version: (50, 50)

- Professional version
  Representative sizes, with 500K of net memory for STORM:

Uncapacitated	Capacitated
(50, 1000)	(50, 600)
(250, 250)	(175, 175)
(1000, 50)	(500, 50)

FILE NAMES FOR THE SAMPLE PROBLEM DATA
- For the uncapacitated problem: TR.DAT
- For the capacitated problem: TRC.DAT

Chapter 8

THE TRANSPORTATION PROBLEM

Suppose we wish to ship a product to several destinations (they may be customers, warehouses, etc.) from several sources (such as factories, regional warehouses, etc.). Each source has a given productive capacity or stock of the particular product to be distributed. Each destination has a given requirement or demand for it. A given per-unit cost is associated with shipping from any source to any destination, depending on distance, transportation modes available, unit production costs, and so on. We wish to determine how much of the product to ship from each source to each destination to satisfy the requirements at least total cost. Let us use the term *location* when we wish to refer to either a source or a destination.

1. The Solution Algorithm

In STORM, the Transportation problem described above is solved in its basic form using the well-known Modified Distribution or MODI method. You will find further details of this method in any standard management science text. If you wish, each iteration will be presented starting from an initial solution generated by any of four standard methods. Of course, if you wish only to obtain the final answer and are not concerned with the method used, you may ignore these options.

The term *basic form* means that we make two further simplifying assumptions:

- There is no limit on the amount that can be shipped over any route (that is, from any source to any destination). In this case, we say the problem is *uncapacitated*. With capacitated routes, which are discussed in Section 6, you can separately specify the maximal amount that can be shipped between each pair of locations, so that it may not be possible to transport as much over a route as economic considerations would indicate.

- In case the total supply from all sources is not equal to the total demand (and we need not require that they be equal), we wish to ship as much of the product as possible for the smallest total cost, regardless of how little some locations may send or receive. For example, if two warehouses, each with 1000 units, are to supply four customers who each require 1000 units, the 2000 available units will be distributed at minimal cost, with no concern for which customers are undersupplied and by how much. It may turn out to be most economical to send approximately equal amounts to each customer, in which case each will get about half his order. However, the solution may be to fully satisfy two of the customers, with the other two receiving nothing. Whatever the pattern of shipments, it will be based solely on cost considerations without regard to fairness, the relative importance of customers, etc. This is an important and frequently overlooked limitation of the classical transportation model. We shall later explain how to place limits on the amount shipped to or from each location. For the present, we shall say that these quantities are *unbounded*.

2. Problem Size

The largest problem that can be solved using the Transportation module of Personal STORM is one having 50 rows and 50 columns. With full core utilization, Professional STORM can solve much larger problems, depending on the amount of memory available in your computer. With variable dimensioning, you can trade off fewer rows for more columns or vice versa, and thus make fullest use of your computer's capacity. Assuming you have 500 kilobytes available for STORM to use, some representative examples of the largest uncapacitated problems that can be solved are: 50 rows and 1000 columns, 250 rows and 250 columns, and 1000 rows and 50 columns.

With capacitated routes, since we need double the number of rows for a given problem, the corresponding maximal problem sizes become 25 rows and 1000 columns, 125 rows and 250 columns, and 500 rows and 50 columns. Other examples are 50 rows and 600 columns, 175 rows and 175 columns, and 500 rows and 50 columns. Note how, since rows and columns may be interchanged in any transportation problem, we can solve a somewhat larger problem by letting the columns represent whichever is more numerous, sources or destinations. This is because we thereby choose the smaller of the two dimensions to be doubled.

For small unbounded problems (having up to 6 sources and 6 destinations, including any rows or columns STORM needs to add to solve the problem), each iteration may be displayed in Tableau format, showing in detail how the algorithm works (see Figure 4). Each solution can also be obtained in Report format (see Figure 3). For larger problems, the Report format is used for all output.

3. A Sample Problem

An oil company has orders for 80 units/day (measured in thousands of barrels) of a certain grade of gasoline from three terminals, which require 25, 45, and 10 units/day. The company has two refineries, each with a capacity of 50 units/day of this product. How should shipments be made to fill these requirements most economically, given the costs shown in Figure 1? The tabulated numbers are in units of $100 per unit delivered.

Terminal

		1	2	3	Supply
	1	2.0	2.8	3.8	50
Refinery					
	2	3.0	4.0	4.2	50
Demand		25	45	10	

Figure 1: Data for Sample Problem

4. Data Entry Using STORM

After the data for this problem have been entered using the Editor, the display should resemble Figure 2. In the Problem Description area at the top, we have indicated that the routes are uncapacitated and the total shipments into or out of a location are not bounded. Once you make the choice between capacitated or uncapacitated routes and leave the Description area, you cannot change this decision. Thus, if you are considering limiting the capacities of some routes, you may wish to start with the capacitated version, thus saving yourself the effort of reentering the cost data. The down side of doing this unnecessarily is that a block of cells is set aside to accommodate the capacity information, which uses up core storage.

The other entries in the Description area can be modified in later runs. The objective type can be directly changed, while the number of rows or columns can be changed by inserting or deleting extra rows or columns in the Data area. Since the rows and columns correspond to the sources and destinations, we have specified two rows and three columns.

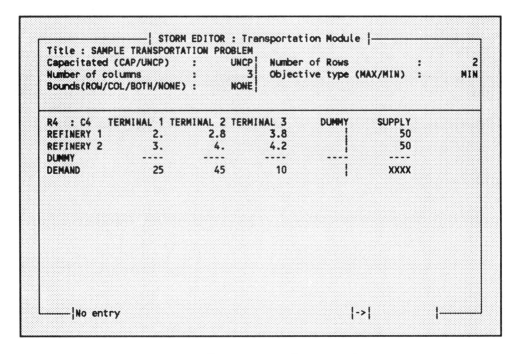

Figure 2: Editor Screen After Data Entry

Keep the following points in mind while making entries in the Data area:

- An extra row and column labeled DUMMY have been added, but the cells have been filled with dashes to indicate that you need not make any entries in those positions. They are there to partition the matrix and to indicate the possibility of a *dummy* source or destination as needed (again, in using this module simply to get the optimal solution, you need not be concerned with the concept of dummy locations). When you advance to such a cell, press the appropriate Arrow or other Pointer control key to move to the next required entry.

- As the module is set up, the rows represent sources and the columns represent destinations, but you are free to reverse these roles if you choose. For example, you will get a more compact display if you let the rows denote the more numerous category, because the Data area can accommodate 15 rows but only 6 columns on one screen. As usual, row and column labels can be changed at will.

- Costs can be any real numbers, positive or negative. However, the largest cost should not be more than 10^6 times the smallest nonzero cost, in magnitude.

- In case a route is prohibited, you should leave the cost entry at its default setting: a dot (.). This usually indicates a missing value. Here, it stands for a missing shipping option and hence for an effectively infinite cost of shipment. The algorithm handles this by assigning a capacity of zero to that route. Of course, if you have chosen the capacitated version of the model (to be discussed in Section 6), you may set the capacities of the unusable routes to zero.

- Supplies and demands can be any nonnegative integers. In case they are given as decimal numbers, they and the cost figures must be scaled accordingly. For example, if the commodity is measured in tons to one decimal place accuracy, you must redefine your units to be tenths-of-tons to make the quantities whole numbers, and also divide all cost figures (assuming they were originally dollars per ton) by ten. Generally, for each place you move the decimal point right in the supply and demand figures, you must move the point left in the cost figures.

- The objective may be to minimize (MIN) total costs, or, if cell entries denote the gain derived from each unit of shipment, to maximize (MAX) total profits.

5. Execution of the Module

Having instructed the program to proceed, you will be asked whether you wish to see only the final solution or would like to monitor every iteration. If you choose to skip straight to the optimum, you may request a summary and/or a detailed report, or for small problems, a tableau presentation of the answer. Figure 3 gives the solution to our sample problem in detailed report format. You will observe that some shipments go to or from a dummy location. These represent quantities of the product which are not in fact shipped at all. Thus, the twenty units shipped from REFINERY 2 to DUMMY denote unused capacity of that refinery.

```
                     SAMPLE TRANSPORTATION PROBLEM
            TRANSPORTATION - OPTIMAL SOLUTION - DETAILED REPORT
     ------- Cell  ------               Unit      Cell    Reduced
     Row          Column    Amount      Cost      Cost      Cost

     REFINERY 1 TERMINAL 1        5    2.0000    10.0000   0.0000*
     REFINERY 1 TERMINAL 2       45    2.8000   126.0000   0.0000*
     REFINERY 1 TERMINAL 3        0    3.8000     0.0000   0.6000
     REFINERY 1     Dummy         0    0.0000     0.0000   1.0000
     REFINERY 1 Subtotal = 136.0000

     REFINERY 2 TERMINAL 1       20    3.0000    60.0000   0.0000*
     REFINERY 2 TERMINAL 2        0    4.0000     0.0000   0.2000
     REFINERY 2 TERMINAL 3       10    4.2000    42.0000   0.0000*
     REFINERY 2     Dummy        20    0.0000     0.0000   0.0000*
     REFINERY 2 Subtotal = 102.0000

     Total Cost = 238.0000                       * Basic cells
     Number of iterations = 3
```

Figure 3: Detailed Report of the Optimal Solution

5.1 Output Reports of Intermediate Solutions

In this section, we discuss the intermediate output that is available to observe the algorithm as it advances through a sequence of improving solutions towards the optimum. We also describe the tableau reports that are available for small problems, where the numbers of sources and destinations are each six or less. If you are not interested in these features, which are provided largely for academic use, you may skip to Section 6.

If you wish to trace each iteration, you will be given a choice of procedures for finding an initial solution: the row minimum rule, the matrix minimum rule, Vogel's approximation method, or the northwest corner rule. You are then asked to choose the mode of presentation: summary report, detailed report, or, if the matrix is 6 by 6 or less, tableau presentation.

Figure 4 shows you what the initial solution will look like in the case of the sample problem, if you choose the northwest corner method with tableau display. In the upper left corner of the *Route cells* (the cells representing routes from a source to a destination) are the unit costs. Note that a dummy column has been added, with zero costs. In the occupied Route cells, shipment quantities appear in the lower right-hand corner in reverse video. We may call these the *basic cells,* with the amounts shipped being the values of the basic variables. In the lower portion of the unoccupied (nonbasic) Route cells, which represent unused routes in the current solution, appears the *reduced cost.* This is the increase in overall cost if one unit of the product is shipped over this route, with appropriate changes in other shipments to compensate.

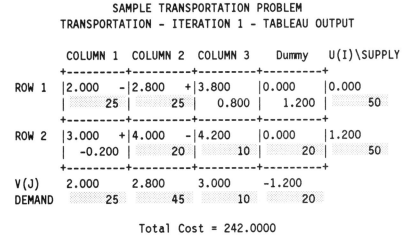

```
              SAMPLE TRANSPORTATION PROBLEM
          TRANSPORTATION - ITERATION 1 - TABLEAU OUTPUT

          COLUMN 1   COLUMN 2   COLUMN 3    Dummy    U(I)\SUPPLY
         +---------+---------+---------+---------+
  ROW 1  |2.000   -|2.800   +|3.800    |0.000    |0.000
         |     25  |     25  |  0.800  |  1.200  |      50
         +---------+---------+---------+---------+
  ROW 2  |3.000   +|4.000   -|4.200    |0.000    |1.200
         |  -0.200 |     20  |     10  |     20  |      50
         +---------+---------+---------+---------+
  V(J)     2.000     2.800     3.000    -1.200
  DEMAND        25        45        10        20

              Total Cost = 242.0000
```

Figure 4: Tableau Presentation of a Transportation Solution

Finally, blinking plus and minus signs mark the cells that will enter and leave the solution at the next iteration, while other plus and minus signs mark the cells in which shipments will be increased or decreased. In the *Marginal cells* (the ones in the far right column and bottom row), the numbers in the upper left corner are the row and column indices (called $U(I)$ and $V(J)$ respectively) used by the MODI method to compute reduced costs. Below them, the quantities of supply and demand are given in reverse video.

After each iteration, you are given the choice of advancing to the next iteration or skipping directly to the final solution. Enter the appropriate number and proceed. At last you will come to the optimal solution, which will be presented to you in any or all of the formats you choose.

6. The Capacitated Transportation Problem

It sometimes happens that transportation requirements include upper bounds on the amount that can be shipped over a particular route; that is, from a certain source to a certain destination. These limited capacities may exist over several routes, and each capacity may be different. Using the Transportation module in STORM, you can solve such a problem by selecting the capacitated option (CAP) in the Description area. To illustrate this, suppose that in our example the gasoline is conveyed over some routes through pipelines with limited pumping capacity. Specifically, a maximum of 30 units can be shipped from refinery 1 to terminal 2, and at most 5 units can be sent from refinery 2 to terminal 3. All other routes remain uncapacitated. Figure 5 shows how the Editor screen should look. Note that when a capacitated problem is called for in the Description area, the Data area is provided with a new set of rows at the bottom in which the route capacities are entered. Capacities must be specified as positive integers, with default values of (effectively) infinity. If you have changed a default value to a number and wish to change it back to infinity, simply enter a period. Figure 6 gives the optimal solution to the sample problem in summary report format.

```
-----------------------| STORM EDITOR : Transportation Module |----------------
Title : SAMPLE TRANSPORTATION PROBLEM: CAPACITATED ROUTES
Capacitated (CAP/UNCP)     :        CAP|  Number of Rows          :         2
Number of columns          :          3|  Objective type (MAX/MIN) :       MIN
Bounds(ROW/COL/BOTH/NONE) :       NONE|


R3 : C5      TERMINAL 1 TERMINAL 2 TERMINAL 3     DUMMY      SUPPLY
REFINERY 1        2.         2.8        3.8          |          50
REFINERY 2        3.         4.         4.2          |          50
DUMMY            ....       ....       ....        ....        ....
DEMAND            25         45         10           |         XXXX
CAP   1            .         30          .           |         XXXX
CAP   2            .          .          5           |         XXXX



-------| No entry                                         |->|        |------
```

Figure 5: Editor Screen for Capacitated Problem

```
          SAMPLE TRANSPORTATION PROBLEM: CAPACITATED ROUTES
          TRANSPORTATION - OPTIMAL SOLUTION - SUMMARY REPORT
          ------- Cell  ------                 Unit       Cell
          Row           Column    Amount       Cost       Cost
          REFINERY 1 TERMINAL 1       15      2.0000    30.0000
          REFINERY 1 TERMINAL 2       30      2.8000    84.0000
          REFINERY 1 TERMINAL 3        5      3.8000    19.0000
          REFINERY 1 Subtotal = 133.0000

          REFINERY 2 TERMINAL 1       10      3.0000    30.0000
          REFINERY 2 TERMINAL 2       15      4.0000    60.0000
          REFINERY 2 TERMINAL 3        5      4.2000    21.0000
          REFINERY 2     Dummy        20      0.0000     0.0000
          REFINERY 2 Subtotal = 111.0000

          Total Cost = 244.0000
          Number of iterations = 4
```

Figure 6: Summary Report for Capacitated Problem

Note in Figure 6 how the shipments are redistributed, and how the total cost has gone up since we are forced to ship less over certain routes than we would like. Note also that, in spite of the less economical pattern of shipment, we are still shipping the same amounts in total. The objective always remains to ship as much as possible, namely the smaller of the total supply and the total demand. In case the capacity constraints are so stringent that this is no longer possible, the module will report that the problem has no feasible solution as formulated.

The rest of Section 6 discusses technical issues that arise at early stages of the solution procedure or in small-problem tableau solutions. Those who are not concerned with such considerations should skip to Section 7.

6.1 Artificial Variables

If you observe each iteration of the solution algorithm, you will note that, with capacitated routes, it will sometimes be necessary to introduce artificial variables in order to find an initial feasible solution. For example, consider a two-by-two matrix with supplies of 50 and 100 and demands of 75 and 75. Then the northwest corner rule leads to an initial solution of 50 in cell (1,1), 25 in cell (2,1), and 75 in cell (2,2). But suppose cell (2,2) has a capacity of only 40. To accommodate the other 35 units, we introduce an artificial source and an artificial destination, with 35 units of supply and demand respectively, and with uncapacitated cells in the new row and column. The extra 35 units can now be shipped over artificial routes. If the problem has a feasible solution (this one does), a Phase 1 procedure similar to the one used in linear programming will drive all artificials out (actually, the artificial source will supply the artificial destination) and the row and column can be eliminated.

Figure 7 shows the initial solution for the sample problem using the northwest corner rule. The initial assignment is limited by the capacity of a cell, namely the cell in row 2 and column 3 as further discussed in Section 6.2. It follows that artificial locations are created, labeled ART-ROW and ART-COL. Since a Phase 1 procedure is now needed to get rid of them, the given costs have all been set to zero. The new artificial variables have unit costs assigned so that cost minimization will drive them out.

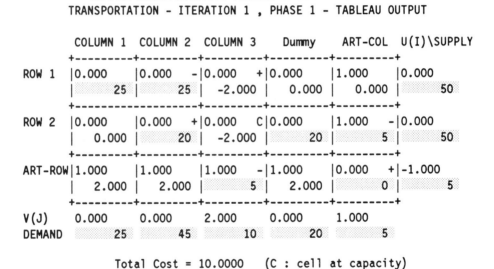

```
        SAMPLE TRANSPORTATION PROBLEM:CAPACITATED ROUTES
        TRANSPORTATION - ITERATION 1 , PHASE 1 - TABLEAU OUTPUT


         COLUMN 1  COLUMN 2  COLUMN 3    Dummy    ART-COL  U(I)\SUPPLY
        +---------+---------+---------+---------+---------+
 ROW 1  |0.000    |0.000   -|0.000   +|0.000    |1.000    |0.000
        |      25 |      25 |  -2.000 |   0.000 |   0.000 |      50
        +---------+---------+---------+---------+---------+
 ROW 2  |0.000    |0.000   +|0.000   C|0.000    |1.000   -|0.000
        |   0.000 |      20 |  -2.000 |      20 |       5 |      50
        +---------+---------+---------+---------+---------+
ART-ROW |1.000    |1.000    |1.000   -|1.000    |0.000   +|-1.000
        |   2.000 |   2.000 |       5 |   2.000 |       0 |       5
        +---------+---------+---------+---------+---------+
 V(J)     0.000     0.000     2.000     0.000     1.000
 DEMAND      25        45        10        20         5
```

              Total Cost = 10.0000   (C : cell at capacity)

Figure 7: Tableau Presentation of Initial Capacitated Solution

6.2 Cells at Capacity

In Figure 7, observe the letter "C" in cell (2,3). This cell could not accommodate all the flow that the northwest corner rule specified for it (a shipment of 10 units was indicated, but its capacity is only 5), so it has been assigned as much as it can carry. The letter "C" indicates those cells which are loaded to capacity. Such cells may occur, of course, at any stage, including optimal solutions.

Note that, when the shipment over a route is at its upper bound, that variable is not basic even though it is positive. We therefore report the reduced cost in the lower part of the cell. Although we cannot display the quantity shipped for lack of space, keep in mind that the route is being utilized to its full capacity.

7. The Transportation Problem with Bounds on Supply or Demand

This option is intended for the situation where total supply is not equal to total demand. In such a case, as discussed in Section 1, the minimal cost solution may not be desirable. Possibly a destination receives less than is acceptable, or perhaps a source is severely underutilized. To guard against this, you may want to add constraints on the minimal amount shipped to or from a location. In the STORM Transportation module, this can be done by entering the appropriate character in the Bounds field of the Description area. As the prompt will tell you, you should enter R for row or C for column if the lower bounds are on the supplies or demands, respectively, and B for both if there are bounds on some of each. Locations which are unconstrained can, of course, be left at their default settings (.). When the bound option is used, an additional column and/or row will be provided in the Data area by the Editor, where you can enter minimal permissible quantities to be transported to or from each location. Since the problem with bounds is solved by converting it to one with route capacities, an artificial row and column may appear in the early iterations of the solution procedure. The module will report infeasibility if the lower bound for any location exceeds its supply or demand, or if the sum of the lower bounds for all supplies (demands) exceeds the total demand (supply). Finally, it should be remarked that both location bounds and route capacities can be included in the same problem.

For example, suppose refinery 2, which is currently shipping only 30 of its 50 units of daily capacity (see Figure 6 where it ships 20 units to the dummy terminal), is required to utilize at least 40 units. Assuming we still have limited capacities on two routes, the problem now should be input as in Figure 8. The solution, given in Figure 9, shows that we must pay an extra 10 cost units ($1,000) to apportion the excess capacity equally to the two refineries.

```
┌─────────────────┤ STORM EDITOR : Transportation Module ├─────────────────┐
│ Title : SAMPLE TRANSPORTATION PROBLEM: CAPACITATED  AND BOUNDED           │
│ Capacitated (CAP/UNCP)      :      CAP│ Number of Rows            :      2 │
│ Number of columns           :        3│ Objective type (MAX/MIN)  :    MIN │
│ Bounds(ROW/COL/BOTH/NONE) :      ROW│                                      │
│                                                                            │
│  R3 : C6    TERMINAL 1 TERMINAL 2 TERMINAL 3    DUMMY LOWERBOUND    SUPPLY  │
│  REFINERY 1      2.        2.8        3.8          │        0          50   │
│  REFINERY 2      3.        4.         4.2          │       40          50   │
│  DUMMY         ----       ----       ----        ----     ----       ----   │
│  DEMAND          25         45         10          │      XXXX        XXXX   │
│  CAP    1        .          30         .           │      XXXX        XXXX   │
│  CAP    2        .          .          5           │      XXXX        XXXX   │
│                                                                            │
│                                                                            │
│                                                                            │
│                                                                            │
│                                                                            │
│                                                                            │
│                                                                            │
└───────┤ No entry                              │->│         │───────────────┘
```

Figure 8: Editor Screen For Capacitated and Bounded Problem

8. Altering Problem Data Dimensions

The Demand row, the Supply column and the Dummy row and column are all required in a Transportation data set. Any other row or column can be deleted. There must be at least one source and one destination in the data set after any deletions. Insertions are possible for new sources and for new destinations, as well as for the row and column bounds. To introduce row (column) bounds into a data set, the Pointer should be positioned on the Dummy row (column) before pressing the F3 (F5) key. There is no provision for converting an uncapacitated problem into a capacitated one. However, a capacitated problem may be rendered uncapacitated by setting all the route capacities to infinity (simply enter a period).

In the case of a capacitated transportation problem, each row operation will involve a companion row. For example, if you wish to add an additional source location and therefore insert a row to contain its route costs, another row will be automatically inserted at the appropriate place to contain its route capacities.

```
SAMPLE TRANSPORTATION PROBLEM: CAPACITATED AND BOUNDED
  TRANSPORTATION - OPTIMAL SOLUTION - SUMMARY REPORT
------- Cell  ------               Unit       Cell
Row            Column    Amount     Cost       Cost
REFINERY 1 TERMINAL 1        5     2.0000    10.0000
REFINERY 1 TERMINAL 2       30     2.8000    84.0000
REFINERY 1 TERMINAL 3        5     3.8000    19.0000
REFINERY 1      Dummy       10     0.0000     0.0000
REFINERY 1 Subtotal = 113.0000

REFINERY 2 TERMINAL 1       20     3.0000    60.0000
REFINERY 2 TERMINAL 2       15     4.0000    60.0000
REFINERY 2 TERMINAL 3        5     4.2000    21.0000
REFINERY 2      Dummy       10     0.0000     0.0000
REFINERY 2 Subtotal = 141.0000

Total Cost = 254.0000
Number of iterations = 4
```

Figure 9: Summary Report for Capacitated and Bounded Problem

DISTANCE NETWORKS (PATHS, TOURS, & TREES) CAPABILITIES

PROBLEM FORMULATION OPTIONS
- Shortest or longest paths from a node
- Traveling salesperson's tour
- Minimal or maximal spanning tree
- Symmetric or asymmetric distances
- Positive or negative distances
- Cyclic or acyclic networks

OUTPUT OPTIONS AND OTHER FEATURES
- Detection of negative (positive) cycles in shortest (longest) paths

MAXIMAL PROBLEM SIZES (NODES)
- Personal version: 50

- Professional version, with 500K of net memory for STORM: 250

FILE NAME FOR THE SAMPLE PROBLEM DATA
- DNET.DAT

Chapter 9

DISTANCE NETWORKS
Paths, Tours, and Trees

A *network* or *graph* consists of a finite set of points called *nodes* or *vertices,* with lines called *arcs* or *edges* joining some pairs of nodes. We are concerned only with *connected* graphs, in which every node can be reached from every other by traversing some sequence of arcs. Many systems, physical and abstract, can be represented by networks. An obvious example of a network is a map, where the nodes are locations (buildings or towns, perhaps) and the arcs are roads. Printed circuits, communications, and power grids are other examples of physical networks. Any system in which some pairwise relationship exists between elements can be so symbolized. In project management, nodes may represent tasks and an arc shows that one task must be processed before the other, as discussed in Chapter 11. Many other applications of the concept could be cited.

Usually, we assign a number to each arc. It may represent the distance between two cities, the capacity of an oil pipeline, the cost of constructing a link in a communications net, or the time required to process a task. For generality, we will refer to this number as the *weight* of the arc, although most commonly it represents a distance, as is reflected in the chapter title and elsewhere. The arcs may also be *directed* or *oriented,* meaning that the motion, communication, or other influence operates in one direction only. In this case, the arc is shown as an arrow pointing from its *start-node* to its *end-node.* Highways in a geographic network, for example, may be undirected (the distance is the same both ways), while city streets may be one-way. STORM treats all arcs as directed, recognizing that an undirected arc can always be represented by two directed arcs in opposite directions.

A *path* or *route* in a network is a sequence of nodes, all different, with an arc between each adjacent pair. A *closed* path (where the first and last nodes are the same) is called a *circuit* or *cycle.* A cycle that visits every node in the network is called a *tour.* A *tree* is any connected subgraph without cycles. That is, imagine picking an arbitrary node and choosing one or more arcs emanating from it. From each node connected to in this way, we may again reach out to other nodes. As long as we never extend to a node that is already connected and hence form a cycle, any such set of arcs with their associated nodes form a tree. A *spanning tree* reaches and hence interconnects all the nodes of the network. Though there are generally many spanning trees, all have the same number of arcs: one less than the number of nodes. This is the smallest number of arcs that can tie all the nodes together.

If the arcs are directed, we define directed paths and cycles in the obvious way: all arcs oriented consistently. In a directed network, paths and cycles will be understood to be directed without mention. However, we shall not be concerned with directed trees.

1. The Problems and Their Solution Algorithms

In this Distance Networks module, three principal problems are addressed. We now give a brief introduction to each, present some examples of their application, and identify the solution procedures used by STORM.

1.1 The Shortest and Longest Path Problems

Suppose that the weight assigned to each arc of a directed graph is its *length*. We may wish to trace the shortest or longest route through the network from a given origin node to one or more destination nodes. Applications of such an algorithm are numerous, some more obvious than others. For example:

- Imagine an independent trucker planning his trip home from an arbitrary location, with optional detours to pick up and deliver various loads he knows of. His truck is too small to handle more than one load at a time. The nodes are all the pickup and delivery points, and the "distance" between two nodes is the negative cost of making that run plus the revenue if the arc connects a pickup node to its delivery node. He now wants to find the longest route home. Of course, if we make costs positive and revenues negative, we have a shortest path problem.

- In project scheduling (see Chapter 11), a *precedence network* represents the tasks and their sequencing. Each task is a directed arc, the nodes being time instants at which all incoming tasks must be finished and all outgoing tasks may begin. The length of each arc is the processing time for that task, and the longest or *critical path* through the network turns out to be the time required to complete the project.

Depending on the characteristics of your network, either Dijkstra's, Bellman and Ford's, or Yen's algorithm is used, as described in *Combinatorial Optimization* by E. L. Lawler (Holt, Rinehart and Winston, 1976). Don't worry, you will not be involved in (or aware of) this choice. STORM will find the shortest or longest path from any specified node to any other one or more nodes. The network may contain cycles, and the arc lengths may include both positive and negative values. However, there must not be any cycles with negative total length in a minimization problem, nor positive cycles when maximizing. Such cycles would lead to unbounded solutions, as one could travel round and round a negative loop.

1.2 The Traveling Salesperson Problem

This problem is closely related to the Shortest Path problem. Again, the arc weights should be thought of as lengths, and we now seek the shortest cycle that traverses each node exactly once; that is, the shortest tour. The example of a businessman wishing to visit each of the branch offices or customers in his region is obvious from the problem's name, as are truck or bus routing applications. Less obvious is the problem of scheduling a set of jobs on one machine when the changeover or setup times between two successive jobs depends on the particular jobs and their order. If our goal is to minimize the total time required to complete the jobs, we can ignore the actual processing times as being independent of sequence and focus on minimizing total setup times. Viewing the changeover time from job A to job B as the travel time from city A to city B, we convert the production problem to a traveling salesperson problem.

STORM uses a composite algorithm for this problem. In the first stage, an initial tour is found by randomly generating one or by using either the Cheapest Insertion or the Greatest Angle Insertion algorithm. Both insertion algorithms start with a two-city cycle and add others one by one. Cheapest Insertion picks the one that contributes the least additional length to the existing cycle, while Greatest Angle Insertion chooses the node that makes the widest angle with its two new neighbors. In the second stage, we try to successively improve the given tour using the Two-Arc Interchange (or Two-Opt) algorithm. This procedure tests alternatives by removing two nonadjacent arcs and replacing them with two others. All possible pairs of arcs are tried, moving through a sequence of ever-shortening tours until a local optimum is found. The whole procedure is repeated several times from different starting points, and the best solution found is reported. Although we will often end up with the shortest possible tour, *we cannot guarantee the optimality of the solution.*

Arcs may have positive or negative weight, and be directed or not. In case the arcs are directed, STORM will only use arcs in a tour that are consistently oriented.

1.3 Minimal and Maximal Spanning Tree Problems

To find the minimal spanning tree is to find the set of arcs with smallest total weight that interconnect all nodes without including any cycles. Applications include laying out oil pipelines, communications nets, and temporary roads interconnecting work sites, as well as designing printed electronic circuitry. Wherever a set of points must be tied together using the shortest total length, a minimal spanning tree is called for.

Maximal spanning tree problems, where the largest total weight is sought, are less common. We might, for example, seek the most reliable military communications network, given that we can afford to build only the minimal number of links to join together all the installations. If the reliability of each link is the probability of its functioning, then the system reliability could be measured as the product of the reliabilities of the included links. By replacing the product of probabilities by the sum of their logarithms, we get an equivalent objective. Thus, if each link weight is its log reliability, we have a maximal spanning tree problem. We could, of course, replace the weights by their negatives and solve the minimization problem. This could be done for any maximal spanning tree problem, but we add this feature at no cost, for your convenience.

The following simple procedure, known as Prim's algorithm, is guaranteed to find the minimal spanning tree.

1. Pick any node and find its nearest neighbor. Those two nodes are now *connected.*
2. At any stage, find an unconnected node whose distance to any connected node is minimal. Make that connection.
3. Repeat step 2, each time adding one more node to the connected set, until all nodes are connected.

STORM uses this algorithm, starting always from the first node entered in the data set. The maximal spanning tree is found similarly, choosing largest distances instead of smallest. Arcs may be positive or negative, but are not viewed as directed by STORM. *If you enter different weights for the two directions of an arc, STORM will use the smaller for minimal trees and the larger for maximization.*

2. A Sample Problem

The Linton Oil Company owns a refinery and five terminals or depots which each supply the local market. Headquarters offices are located at the refinery. The geographical layout of the company's branches is shown in Figure 1. Mr. Linton, the founder's son, has several problems on his mind.

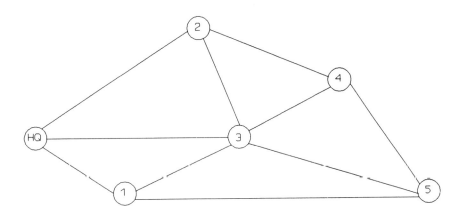

Figure 1: Map of Linton Oil Facilities

Travel Planning

Frequently, first thing in the morning, trucks must be sent from headquarters to one or other of the depots to transport workers and equipment. The system of roads and highways is such that only the routes indicated in Figure 1 are feasible. Since terminal 3 is located in the bustling city of Midland, rush hour congestion makes traffic entering node 3 much slower than outgoing traffic. For example, the trip in from headquarters takes an hour, while the return journey would only take 42 minutes. Routes that do not pass through Midland take about the same time either way. The times (in minutes) to travel each of the available routes in both directions are presented in Figure 2. The first question, then, is to find the quickest ways to get from headquarters to each of the depots.

A second question arises from the senior Mr. Linton's habit of occasionally spending a week on an inspection tour of each of the branch locations. He stays a day at each, and travels on the next morning. Given the travel times in Figure 2, in what order should he visit the depots, so as to waste the least amount of time on the road?

		T 0				
	Hq	D1	D2	D3	D4	D5
Headquarters	-	18	40	60	-	-
Depot 1	18	-	-	38	-	90
Depot 2	40	-	-	25	21	-
Depot 3	42	28	19	-	16	30
Depot 4	-	-	21	20	-	24
Depot 5	-	90	-	35	24	-

(Left margin label: F R O M)

Figure 2: Travel Times Between Locations

Pipeline Planning

A pipeline network is under consideration at Linton Oil, to tie the refinery to the five depots. Assuming it must follow the same highway routes as are shown in Figure 1, and taking the shorter travel times as proportional to the distances, young Mr. Linton wonders what layout will have the least total length.

3. Data Entry Using STORM

For all the problems solved in this module, the Editor uses the same simple layout, a square array into which you can enter the arc weights. In the Description area, the *Number of nodes* entry gives the dimensions of this matrix, each node being assigned a row and a column in the Data area. You will then enter the weight of the arc from node i to node j in the cell where row i intersects column j (cell (i,j)).

The other entry in the Description area, *Distance matrix type,* allows you to specify whether the arcs are directed, with different weights in either direction, or whether the weight is simply assigned to the arc without regard to orientation. By typing "A" for asymmetric, you signal that at least some arcs have two different weights, so that the entry in cell (i,j) will be different from that in cell (j,i). If you choose asymmetry, you will have to fill in every cell in the array where a (directed) arc exists, leaving all others at the default missing value setting. Even if you think of the arc as undirected with the same weight in both directions, STORM treats it as two directed arcs and you will have to enter the value in both cells.

If you choose the symmetric option, however, STORM will understand that all arcs are undirected, or equivalently that to every arc (i,j) there corresponds an arc (j,i) with equal weight. Since the matrix is symmetric, you need only fill in half of it. Indeed, you will only be able to make entries above the main diagonal (that is, in the upper right triangular portion of the Data area).

Data entry for our problem should conclude with an Editor screen looking like Figure 3. We have edited the column headers to reflect the sample problem, but the row labels at left cannot be changed.

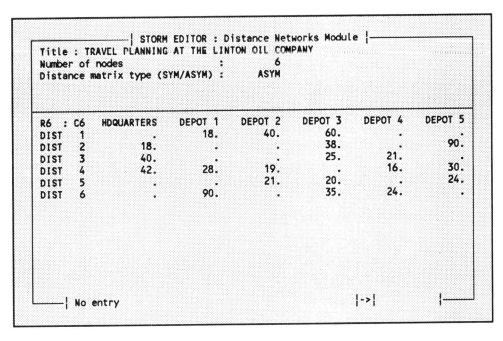

R6 : C6	HDQUARTERS	DEPOT 1	DEPOT 2	DEPOT 3	DEPOT 4	DEPOT 5
DIST 1	.	18.	40.	60.	.	.
DIST 2	18.	.	.	38.	.	90.
DIST 3	40.	.	.	25.	21.	.
DIST 4	42.	28.	19.	.	16.	30.
DIST 5	.	.	21.	20.	.	24.
DIST 6	.	90.	.	35.	24.	.

STORM EDITOR : Distance Networks Module

Title : TRAVEL PLANNING AT THE LINTON OIL COMPANY
Number of nodes : 6
Distance matrix type (SYM/ASYM) : ASYM

No entry

Figure 3: The Editor Screen After Data Entry

4. Execution of the Module

The first and only menu you will encounter is shown in Figure 4. We now discuss each of the three types of procedures available.

```
                    NETWORK ALGORITHMS

         1)    Shortest paths
         2)    Longest paths
         3)    Traveling salesperson's tour
         4)    Minimal spanning tree
         5)    Maximal spanning tree
```

Figure 4: Available Algorithms for Distance Networks

4.1 Shortest and Longest Paths

Choice of *Shortest paths* takes you to a Candidate Selection form to choose first a starting node and then the set of destinations to which shortest routes are wanted. Mark the chosen terminals with an asterisk in the usual way, toggling each one separately with the Space bar or using the F1 key to toggle the entire list simultaneously. If we ask for the shortest paths from headquarters to all other nodes, we get the output displayed in Figure 5. Sure enough, the congested direct highway into the big city (depot 3) should be avoided. We should enter instead via the less traveled road from depot 1. The city should be detoured entirely to get to depot 5.

```
               SHORTEST PATHS FROM HDQUARTERS

    Destination    Distance    Path
    DEPOT 1         18.0000    DEPOT 1
    DEPOT 2         40.0000    DEPOT 2
    DEPOT 3         56.0000    DEPOT 1--DEPOT 3
    DEPOT 4         61.0000    DEPOT 2--DEPOT 4
    DEPOT 5         85.0000    DEPOT 2--DEPOT 4--DEPOT 5
```

Figure 5: Shortest Paths from Headquarters to All Other Sites

In general, after each output, you will return to the Selection form where you can choose other destinations from the same origin. When you are finished, the Escape key takes you back a step to choose another source node and repeat the process if desired. If not, touch Esc again to return to the Algorithms menu. The only times that STORM will not provide you with the shortest path between two chosen nodes is when negative cycles exist in the network (just as positive cycles block the longest path algorithm; see below), or when no (directed) path exists, in which case the message *Not reachable* will appear.

If we choose *Longest paths* using the same data, we will get an error message, because positive cycles exist. Even a single positive arc is unacceptable if undirected, as we could travel back and forth on it forever. If we remove all entries below the main diagonal so that arcs are all one way "left to right" and no cycles remain, the report given in Figure 6 results. It has no significance in the present context, and is shown merely to demonstrate the module's capabilities.

```
             LONGEST PATHS FROM HDQUARTERS

     Destination    Distance    Path
     DEPOT 1         18.0000    DEPOT 1
     DEPOT 2         40.0000    DEPOT 2
     DEPOT 3         65.0000    DEPOT 2--DEPOT 3
     DEPOT 4         81.0000    DEPOT 2--DEPOT 3--DEPOT 4
     DEPOT 5        108.0000    DEPOT 1--DEPOT 5
```

Figure 6: The Longest Paths from Headquarters to All Depots

4.2 The Traveling Salesperson Problem

Choice of option 3 takes you directly to the output report, which looks like Figure 7 for our sample problem. The report gives the sequence of arcs that make up the best tour found by STORM, with the associated distances. The sequence of nodes is conveniently shown in the first column. Any tour presented will involve only arcs with consistent orientation. If no tour exists, the message *Cannot construct tour visiting all nodes* results. The procedure we use has been shown to produce excellent and often optimal solutions to real world problems, though it cannot guarantee optimality.

4.3 Minimal and Maximal Spanning Trees

If you choose the *Minimal spanning tree* option, the given data set produces the report shown in Figure 8. Since some arcs have different weights in either direction (we now think of the weights as representing miles instead of minutes), the shorter one is automatically used. Although the orientation is preserved in the report, STORM ignores it: a connection is a connection.

```
         BEST TRAVELING SALESPERSON'S TOUR FOUND

        -------  Arc  -------
        From Node      To Node    Arc Length
        HDQUARTERS     DEPOT 2      40.0000
        DEPOT 2        DEPOT 4      21.0000
        DEPOT 4        DEPOT 5      24.0000
        DEPOT 5        DEPOT 3      35.0000
        DEPOT 3        DEPOT 1      28.0000
        DEPOT 1        HDQUARTERS   18.0000

           Length of tour = 166.0000
```

Figure 7: The Shortest Way to Tour the Depots

The maximal spanning tree report is exactly analogous. The larger of the two oriented weights is chosen for each arc, and thereafter the algorithm picks largest connecting arcs to include instead of smallest. We show the output for the sample problem in Figure 9 for completeness, although it has no real significance.

```
              MINIMAL SPANNING TREE

        -------  Arc  -------
        From Node      To Node    Arc Length
        HDQUARTERS     DEPOT 1      18.0000
        DEPOT 3        DEPOT 1      28.0000
        DEPOT 3        DEPOT 4      16.0000
        DEPOT 3        DEPOT 2      19.0000
        DEPOT 4        DEPOT 5      24.0000

      Length of Minimal Spanning Tree = 105.0000
             Distance matrix is asymmetric
          Shorter arc used for each pair of nodes
```

Figure 8: The Shortest Possible Pipeline Network

MAXIMAL SPANNING TREE

------- Arc -------		
From Node	To Node	Arc Length
HDQUARTERS	DEPOT 3	60.0000
HDQUARTERS	DEPOT 2	40.0000
DEPOT 1	DEPOT 3	38.0000
DEPOT 1	DEPOT 5	90.0000
DEPOT 5	DEPOT 4	24.0000

Length of Maximal Spanning Tree = 252.0000
Distance matrix is asymmetric
Longer arc used for each pair of nodes

Figure 9: The Longest Spanning Tree

5. Altering Problem Data Dimensions

Rows and columns can be deleted down to a minimum of two nodes, or added up to the limit set for your version of STORM, but only in pairs. If you insert or delete a row, STORM will automatically insert or delete the corresponding column, and vice versa.

FLOW NETWORKS CAPABILITIES

PROBLEM FORMULATION OPTIONS
- Maximal flow problem
- Transshipment (minimal cost flow) problem
- Multiple sources and destinations
- Lower and upper limits on flows for arcs, sources, and destinations.

MAXIMAL PROBLEM SIZES (NODES, ARCS)
- Personal version: (50, 250)

- Professional version
  Representative sizes, with 500K of net memory for STORM:
  (100, 3000)
  (500, 2500)
  (1000, 2000)

FILE NAMES FOR THE SAMPLE PROBLEM DATA
- For the maximal flow problem: FNET.DAT
- For the transshipment problem: SHIP.DAT

Chapter 10

FLOW NETWORKS
Maximal Flow and Transshipment

Many managerial problems can be conceptually represented as a *network* consisting of *nodes* and *arcs* and solved using appropriate network analysis techniques. In Chapter 9, we introduced this idea and discussed one such class of problems, namely distance-oriented network problems. The Flow Networks module in STORM allows you to analyze two additional situations very common to the design of distribution, information, or traffic systems. Suppose the nodes of a network represent communication centers, highway interchanges, or plants, warehouses, or customers in a distribution network. The connecting arcs represent potential shipping routes, communication links, or highway segments. In addition, we now suppose that some commodity, be it product, information, or traffic, flows through the network.

As in the Distance Networks module, STORM treats all arcs as directed from one node to another, indicating that flow through this arc can occur only in this direction. However, an undirected arc (two-way information link or two-way highway) can always be represented by two directed arcs in opposite directions. Each directed arc is a possible shipment link from one node to another.

For each arc (i,j) from node i to node j, we can define three characteristics:

Symbol	Description
L_{ij}	Minimal amount of flow to be maintained in arc (i,j). Though in most situations we expect this value to be zero, in certain cases it may be a positive number. For example, a company's shipment of goods over some route may be contracted out to a carrier with a minimal shipment clause.
U_{ij}	Maximal amount of flow possible through arc (i,j). For example, monthly shipment quantities over a route may be limited by the number of trucks available.

C_{ij} Unit cost of shipment from node i to node j. Since no other costs are considered, we implicitly assume that the cost per unit is the same, irrespective of the amount shipped. Situations which require fixed (setup) costs or allow bulk discount are not considered by this module.

In addition, each node may be a source, a destination, or a transshipment point. Each *source* node may ship up to a specified *supply* quantity, each *destination* node must receive its specified *demand* quantity, and at all transshipment nodes, flow must be conserved: flow in must equal flow out.

1. The Problems and Their Solution Algorithms

Given all the (L_{ij}, U_{ij}, C_{ij}) values, the Flow Networks module allows you to answer the following strategic and operational questions.

1.1 The Maximal Flow Problem

In many situations, you may want to determine the largest total flow a network can support from its sources to its destinations. This is useful to know in the strategic planning of new facilities, or before launching a sales effort. For example, before building a new stadium, you may want to know if the highway network which will bring the fans from the city and suburbs to the potential stadium location has sufficient capacity to handle the expected traffic. In other circumstances, you may wonder if your current distribution network can handle the expected increase in customer orders if a proposed sales promotion is undertaken. Traditional management science texts discuss the maximal flow problem with a single source having an infinite supply and a single destination. However, STORM allows multiple sources and destinations with given finite supply and demands respectively.

STORM uses Dinic's algorithm based on the concept of layered networks (see "Graph Algorithms" by S. Even, published by Computer Science Press, 1979) to find the maximal flow in a network. This algorithm is a computationally efficient variation of the flow augmenting path algorithm discussed in most introductory management science books.

1.2 The Transshipment (or Minimal Cost) Problem

For many businesses, an ongoing operational problem is to periodically decide the most economical way to ship products from plants to customers. More generally, given the supply at each source node, the demand at each destination, and the characteristics of each arc of the given network, we seek the least costly shipping plan that satisfies all demands.

As a strategic planning tool, such a least cost shipping analysis may also be used to decide if the capital outlay to open a new warehouse (or plant), or expand an existing warehouse (or plant), is warranted by the consequent savings in the distribution costs.

To solve this transshipment problem, STORM uses the Network Simplex algorithm. The implementation of this algorithm in STORM is similar to one described by G. H. Bradley, G. G. Brown, and G. W. Graves in "Design and Implementation of Large Scale Primal Transshipment Algorithms", *Management Science,* Volume 24 (1977), Number 1, pages 1 - 34.

2. A Sample Problem

American Steel, an Ohio-based steel manufacturing company, produces steel at its two steel mills located at Youngstown and Pittsburgh. The company distributes finished steel to its retail customers through a distribution network of regional and field warehouses as shown in Figure 1. The network represents shipment of finished steel from American Steel's two steel mills located at Youngstown (node 1) and Pittsburgh (node 2) to their field warehouses at Albany, Houston, Tempe, and Gary (nodes 6,7,8, and 9) through three regional warehouses located at Cincinnati, Kansas City, and Chicago (nodes 3,4, and 5). Also, some field warehouses can be directly supplied from the steel mills. Table 1 presents the flow limits, L_{ij} and U_{ij}, and the unit costs C_{ij}, for each arc (i,j). For example, the shipment from Youngstown (node 1) to Kansas City (node 4) is contracted out to a railroad company with a minimal shipping clause of 1000 tons/month, hence $L_{14} = 1000$. However, the railroad cannot ship more than 5000 tons/month due a the shortage of rail cars, so $U_{14} = 5000$.

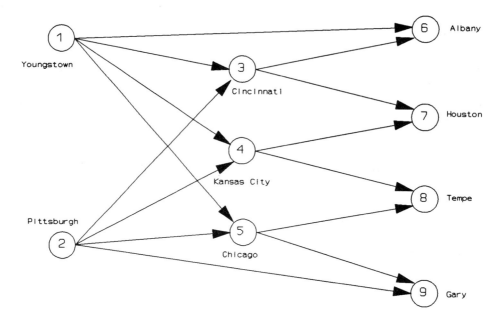

Figure 1: Distribution Network for American Steel

From node	To node	C_{ij}	L_{ij}	U_{ij}
Youngstown	Albany	500	0	1000
Youngstown	Cincinnati	350	0	3000
Youngstown	Kansas City	450	1000	5000
Youngstown	Chicago	375	0	5000
Pittsburgh	Cincinnati	350	0	2000
Pittsburgh	Kansas City	450	2000	3000
Pittsburgh	Chicago	400	0	4000
Pittsburgh	Gary	450	0	2000
Cincinnati	Albany	350	1000	5000
Cincinnati	Houston	550	0	6000
Kansas City	Houston	375	0	4000
Kansas City	Tempe	650	0	4000
Chicago	Tempe	600	0	2000
Chicago	Gary	120	0	4000

Table 1: Arc Data for the American Steel Example

2.1 Maximal Flow Problem

The monthly capacities of American Steel's Youngstown and Pittsburgh mills are 10,000 tons and 15,000 tons respectively. The management wants to know the maximal tonnage that can be shipped to the field warehouses over their existing distribution network. The demands at the field warehouses are not believed to be restrictive, as they can be controlled by reassigning retail customers to the field warehouse as appropriate. However, to be cost effective, each field warehouse should receive at least 2,000 tons/month. Also, the size of the warehouses restricts the maximal amount each field warehouse can receive to 8,000 tons/month.

2.2 Transshipment Problem

The table below gives the current monthly demand at American Steel's four field warehouses.

Field Warehouse	Monthly Demand
Albany, N.Y.	3000
Houston	7000
Tempe	4000
Gary	6000

Given that American Steel's Youngstown and Pittsburgh mills can produce up to 10,000 tons and 15,000 tons of steel per month, respectively, the management wants to know the least cost monthly shipment plan.

3. Data Entry Using STORM

Both maximal flow and transshipment problems share a common layout for the Editor screen. These are displayed in Figure 2 and Figure 3, respectively, for American Steel's problems. However, for a particular problem, certain entries may not be required and hence can be ignored as we explain below.

```
┌──────────────┤ STORM EDITOR : Flow Networks Module ├──────────────┐
│Title : American Steel Distribution Planning: Maximal Flow          │
│Number of nodes :        9                                          │
│Number of rows  :       20                                          │
│                                                                    │
├────────────────────────────────────────────────────────────────── │
│R1  : C1     FROM NODE    TO NODE   UNIT COST  LOWR BOUND  UPPR BOUND│
│ARC    1          .         YNTN        0          0         10000   │
│ARC    2          .         PITT        0          0         15000   │
│ARC    3        YNTN        ALBY        0          0          1000   │
│ARC    4        YNTN        CINC        0          0          3000   │
│ARC    5        YNTN          KC        0        1000         5000   │
│ARC    6        YNTN         CHI        0          0          5000   │
│ARC    7        PITT        CINC        0          0          2000   │
│ARC    8        PITT          KC        0        2000         3000   │
│ARC    9        PITT         CHI        0          0          4000   │
│ARC   10        PITT        GARY        0          0          2000   │
│ARC   11        CINC        ALBY        0        1000         5000   │
│ARC   12        CINC        HOUS        0          0          6000   │
│ARC   13          KC        HOUS        0          0          4000   │
│ARC   14          KC        TMPE        0          0          4000   │
│ARC   15         CHI        TMPE        0          0          2000   │
│ARC   16         CHI        GARY        0          0          4000   │
│ARC   17        ALBY          .         0        2000         8000   │
│ARC   18        HOUS          .         0        2000         8000   │
│ARC   19        TMPE          .         0        2000         8000   │
│ARC   20        GARY          .         0        2000         8000   │
└────────┤ No entry                              ├->│          ├─────│
```

Figure 2: American Steel's Maximal Flow Problem

3.1 The Problem Description Area

Besides the title, the problem description requires two other values as shown in Figures 2 and 3.

- *Number of nodes*
  This is the total number of nodes you have in your network. For our example, as shown in the network of Figure 1, this value is 9.

- *Number of rows*
  The detail data requires a row for each arc, each source (or supply) node, and each destination (or demand) node in the network. The value of this entry should therefore be (number of arcs) + (number of sources) +

(number of destinations). In American Steel's network, there are 14 arcs, 2 source nodes (nodes 1 and 2), and 4 destination nodes (nodes 6 through 9), hence a value of 20 is entered in this location.

```
|——————————————| STORM EDITOR : Flow Networks Module |——————————————|
Title : American Steel Distribution Planning: Monthly Shipping Plan
Number of nodes :        9
Number of rows  :       20


R1  : C1    FROM NODE   TO NODE  UNIT COST  LOWR BOUND  UPPR BOUND
ARC   1         .         YNTN       0          0         10000
ARC   2         .         PITT       0          0         15000
ARC   3        YNTN       ALBY      500          0          1000
ARC   4        YNTN       CINC      350          0          3000
ARC   5        YNTN        KC       450       1000          5000
ARC   6        YNTN       CHI       375          0          5000
ARC   7        PITT       CINC      350          0          2000
ARC   8        PITT        KC       450       2000          3000
ARC   9        PITT       CHI       400          0          4000
ARC  10        PITT       GARY      450          0          2000
ARC  11        CINC       ALBY      350       1000          5000
ARC  12        CINC       HOUS      550          0          6000
ARC  13         KC        HOUS      375          0          4000
ARC  14         KC        TMPE      650          0          4000
ARC  15        CHI        TMPE      600          0          2000
ARC  16        CHI        GARY      120          0          4000
ARC  17        ALBY        .         0        3000           .
ARC  18        HOUS        .         0        7000           .
ARC  19        TMPE        .         0        4000           .
ARC  20        GARY        .         0        6000           .
|——————| No entry                                   |->|       |——————
```

Figure 3: American Steel's Transshipment Problem

3.2 The Detailed Data Area

The detailed data contains a row each for all arcs, source nodes, and destination nodes. The row labels, of course, can be changed to give the corresponding arc, source, or destination a descriptive name. Each row requires five column entries labelled FROM NODE, TO NODE, UNIT COST, LOWR BOUND, and UPPR BOUND. These column labels cannot be changed. Also, the last three column entries are restricted to integers. If values for your problem have fractional parts, you should use appropriate transformations (for example, enter unit cost as cents rather than dollars, or limits as tenths of tons instead of tons) to convert them to integers. However, units for lower and upper limits should be consistent with the units used for the unit cost. That is, if the unit for limits is a tenth of a ton, the cost should be dollars or cents per tenth of a ton. The interpretation of these five column values is somewhat different depending on whether the row corresponds to an arc, a source, or a destination. We explain them for each row type. Note that all codes used to identify the nodes must be four characters or less.

Row Entries for Supply Nodes

FROM NODE   Should always be a dot.

TO NODE   A code name for the source.

UNIT COST   This value is not needed for the maximal flow problem, and can be ignored. For the transshipment problem, it is generally zero (the default value) for a source, as is the case in the American Steel example. However, see Section 6.3 for a generalization of the basic transshipment problem, where this value can be non-zero.

LOWR BOUND   Minimal amount that has to be shipped out of this supply node. If none, you can leave this at its default value of 0.

UPPR BOUND   The capacity of this source. For the maximal flow problem, this value should not exceed 999,999,999. The dot default denotes an unlimited supply. For the transshipment problem, the total capacity of all the supply nodes should not exceed 999,999,999.

The first two rows in the data sets displayed in Figures 2 and 3 corresponds to the steel mills at Youngstown and Pittsburgh for the maximal flow and transshipment problems, respectively.

Row Entries for Destination Nodes

FROM NODE   A code for the destination.

TO NODE   Should always be a dot.

UNIT COST	This value is not needed for the maximal flow problem, and can be ignored. For the transshipment problem, the default value (zero) is generally appropriate.
LOWR BOUND	For the maximal flow problem, this value should be the least amount of flow that should reach this node. For the example of American Steel, this value is 2,000 tons for each destination node as shown in Figure 2.
	For the transshipment problem, this value should be equal to the demand at this destination.
UPPR BOUND	For the maximal flow problem, this value is the largest amount this destination node can receive. This value should not exceed 999,999,999. A dot indicates infinity (or no limit). Note that for American Steel, this value is 8,000 tons for each field warehouse as shown in Figure 2.
	For the transshipment problem, this value is the maximum shipment allowed at this destination.

The last four rows in the two data sets correspond to the field warehouses located at Albany, Houston, Tempe, and Gary.

Row Entries for Arcs

FROM NODE	A code for the starting node of this arc.
TO NODE	A code for the ending node of this arc.
UNIT COST	This value is not needed for the maximal flow problem, and can be ignored. For the transshipment problem, this value is the unit cost of shipping over this arc. The unit cost for any arc should not exceed 10,000,000.
LOWR BOUND	Minimal amount of flow that must be maintained in this arc. The default value is 0.
UPPR BOUND	The maximal amount of flow this arc can support. The value should not exceed 999,999,999. Enter dot if unlimited.

Rows 3 through 16 in the data sets displayed in Figures 2 and 3 correspond to the arc data for the network of Figure 1, for the maximal flow and transshipment problems, respectively.

4. Executing the Module

The Flow Networks Options menu displayed in Figure 4 allows you to select the type of problem (maximal flow or transshipment problem) you want to solve. Once the problem type is selected, STORM will check your data set for consistency and give you the appropriate report if any inconsistencies exist in your data set. For example, STORM does not allow a dot entry in both the FROM NODE and TO NODE columns, which can occur if you have specified more rows than you need, or have just mistyped the entry. In the former case, all such rows should be deleted by using F4 key in the Editor. Also, for both the problems, at least one source and one destination node are expected, and for the transshipment problem, the total supply of all the sources should be equal to or exceed the combined demand of all the destinations. If these or other inconsistencies are found, STORM will report them and give you a chance to correct your data.

```
             FLOW NETWORKS OPTIONS

          1)      Maximal flow
          2)      Transshipment
```

Figure 4: The Flow Networks Options Menu

5. Output Reports

5.1 Maximal Flow Problem

The STORM Output Options menu gives you an option to obtain either a summary or detailed output. Figure 5 displays the detailed output report for American Steel, which lists the amount of flow through each arc, and also lists the amount of flow from each source and to each destination. The report shows that the current distribution network of American Steel can support a maximum of 21,000 tons of steel per month. The summary report lists the nonzero flows only and does not include the bounds in the output.

```
              MAXIMAL FLOW - DETAILED REPORT

                                          Lower      Upper
         Arc          From  To     Flow   Bound      Bound

         ARC   1       .    YNTN   10000     0       10000
         ARC   2       .    PITT   11000     0       15000
         ARC   3      YNTN  ALBY    1000     0        1000
         ARC   4      YNTN  CINC    3000     0        3000
         ARC   5      YNTN  KC      5000   1000       5000
         ARC   6      YNTN  CHI     1000     0        5000
         ARC   7      PITT  CINC    2000     0        2000
         ARC   8      PITT  KC      3000   2000       3000
         ARC   9      PITT  CHI     4000     0        4000
         ARC  10      PITT  GARY    2000     0        2000
         ARC  11      CINC  ALBY    5000   1000       5000
         ARC  12      CINC  HOUS       0     0        6000
         ARC  13      KC    HOUS    4000     0        4000
         ARC  14      KC    TMPE    4000     0        4000
         ARC  16      CHI   GARY    3000     0        4000
         ARC  15      CHI   TMPE    2000     0        2000
         ARC  17      ALBY   .      6000   2000       8000
         ARC  20      GARY   .      5000   2000       8000
         ARC  18      HOUS   .      4000   2000       8000
         ARC  19      TMPE   .      6000   2000       8000

         Maximal Flow = 21000
```

Figure 5: Detailed Report (Maximal Flow Problem)

5.2 The Transshipment Problem

Figure 6 displays the detailed output for the American Steel problem. For each arc, source, and destination, it reports the flow, the corresponding unit cost, shipping cost, and the reduced cost. As in the Linear Programming and the Transportation modules, the reduced cost indicates the increase in the total shipping cost if the flow in this arc (or source, or destination) is increased by 1. Finally, the last line of the report gives the total shipping cost.

TRANSSHIPMENT - DETAILED REPORT

Arc		From	To	Flow	Unit Cost	Shipping Cost	Reduced Cost
ARC	1	.	YNTN	10000	0	0	-25
ARC	2	.	PITT	10000	0	0	0
ARC	3	YNTN	ALBY	1000	500	500000	-600
ARC	4	YNTN	CINC	3000	350	1050000	-400
ARC	5	YNTN	KC	3000	450	1350000	0
ARC	6	YNTN	CHI	3000	375	1125000	0
ARC	7	PITT	CINC	2000	350	700000	-425
ARC	8	PITT	KC	3000	450	1350000	-25
ARC	9	PITT	CHI	3000	400	1200000	0
ARC	10	PITT	GARY	2000	450	900000	-675
ARC	11	CINC	ALBY	2000	350	700000	0
ARC	12	CINC	HOUS	3000	550	1650000	0
ARC	13	KC	HOUS	4000	375	1500000	-475
ARC	14	KC	TMPE	2000	650	1300000	0
ARC	16	CHI	GARY	4000	120	480000	-605
ARC	15	CHI	TMPE	2000	600	1200000	-125
ARC	17	ALBY	.	3000	0	0	1125
ARC	20	GARY	.	6000	0	0	1125
ARC	18	HOUS	.	7000	0	0	1325
ARC	19	TMPE	.	4000	0	0	1125

Total cost = 15005000

Figure 6: Detailed Report (Transshipment Problem)

The summary report is the same as the detailed report, except that only arcs, sources, and destinations with nonzero flow are included, and the reduced cost values are not reported.

6. Incorporating Some Generalizations into the Basic Transshipment Problem

Besides solving the basic transshipment problem described in the beginning of this chapter, STORM allows you flexibility to indirectly incorporate some generalizations which commonly occur in real world situations. We discuss some of them in subsequent subsections. By ingeniously creating appropriate network and corresponding flow and cost values, you should be able to incorporate many other variations.

6.1 Incorporating a Throughput Constraint at a Node

In many situations, a node may have a restriction which requires that the total flow through it (referred to as *throughput*) should satisfy some lower and/or upper limits. For example, in the American Steel problem, the size of the warehouse and the handling staff at Kansas City limits the monthly flow through the warehouse to 8,000 tons. In general, to incorporate such restriction for any node (say i), replace it in the network by two nodes, say j and k (where j and k are node names not used elsewhere), with an arc directed from j to k having lower and upper bounds equal to the respective limits on the throughput for node i, and unit cost of zero. Also, all the arcs coming into node i in the original network will now be ending at node j, and all arcs starting from node i will now start from node k. This is illustrated in Figure 7 for Kansas City in the American Steel example, where the arc (j,k) is given a lower bound of zero and an upper bound of 8,000.

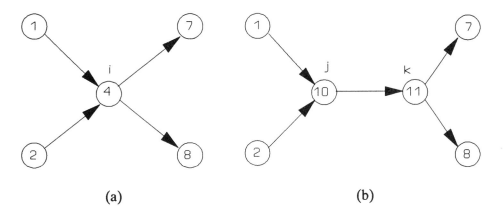

(a)   (b)

Figure 7: Incorporating a Throughput Constraint

6.2 Incorporating Excess Demand

In the transshipment problem, STORM does not allow the total supply or capacity of all sources to be less than the combined demand of all the destinations or customers. However, in such a case you may still want to ship the product to satisfy as much demand as possible at the least distribution cost. To do so, you should augment the original network by adding a "dummy" source or supply node with capacity equal to the total shortage (total demand minus total capacity). From this dummy node, you should then add arcs to each destination node. Since the flow in these arcs corresponds to shortage at the corresponding destination (or customer), these arcs should be given:

LOWR BOUND = 0
UPPR BOUND = Maximal allowable shortage at this destination.
UNIT COST   = Unit cost of shortage at this destination. This cost in many
                        situations may be zero, but in some cases a shortage may incur
                        some cost in the form of rebate to the customer on subsequent
                        orders, etc.

If you now create a data set corresponding to this augmented network, STORM will give you the distribution plan that minimizes total shipping and shortage cost.

6.3 Incorporating Unequal Production Costs

If the variable production costs at each source (or supply) node are unequal, it is possible that the distribution plan which minimizes total shipping cost may require producing more at the sources with higher variable production cost. In this situation, the logical objective is to find a plan which minimizes total shipping and production cost. To accomplish this, just enter the variable production cost for each source in its UNIT COST column.

6.4 Incorporating Unequal Selling Price

If the selling price of your product is different at each destination node, then in the excess demand situation (as described in Section 6.2), the solution which minimizes shipping cost may leave excessive shortage at destinations with high selling price, resulting in loss of potential profit. A more logical objective in this case is to minimize total shipping cost minus total sales. To achieve this objective using STORM, subtract the selling price at each destination from the unit cost of all the arcs directed into that destination node except for the arc from the "dummy" source node.

7. Altering Problem Data Dimensions

The columns in the data set cannot be deleted nor can new ones be inserted. The rows corresponding to arcs, sources, or destinations can be added at will by using F3 key in the editor. However, the number of rows and the nodes used should not exceed the allowable maximal limits for your version of the software. Also, STORM will automatically update the *Number of rows* entry in the problem description area. However, if you add new nodes in your network, you should move to the Problem Description area and change the *Number of Nodes* entry accordingly.

PROJECT MANAGEMENT (PERT/CPM) CAPABILITIES

PROBLEM FORMULATION OPTIONS
- Activity-on-arc or activity-on-node
- Deterministic or probabilistic activity times

OUTPUT OPTIONS AND OTHER FEATURES
- Activities listed in several orders
- Bar (Gantt) charts
- Deterministic solution including:
  - Early and late start times
  - Early and late finish times
  - Slack times and critical path
  - Project completion time
- Probabilistic solution including:
  - Deterministic outputs using mean times
  - Means and variances of activity times
  - Probability of meeting user-input deadline

MAXIMAL PROBLEM SIZES (ACTIVITIES, IMMEDIATE PREDECESSORS)
- Personal version: (100, 99)

- Professional version
  Representative sizes, with 500K of net memory for STORM:

Activity-on-node	Activity-on-arc
(3500, 5)	(3500, any)
(3000, 10)	
(2000, 20)	
(1000, 50)	
(500, 125)	

FILE NAMES FOR THE SAMPLE PROBLEM DATA
- The deterministic case: PM.DAT
- The probabilistic case: PERT.DAT

Chapter 11

PROJECT MANAGEMENT (PERT/CPM)

A *project* may be defined as a major undertaking made up of many tasks or *activities*. The activities are interrelated through *precedence* relationships: certain activities cannot be started until others are completed. If activity A must precede activity B, we say that A is a *predecessor* of B and B is a *successor* of A. If no other activity intervenes, so that B can start immediately upon completion of A, we use the terms *immediate predecessor* and *immediate successor*. Project management techniques, which developed independently under the acronyms of CPM (Critical Path Method) and PERT (Program Evaluation and Review Technique), are useful for planning, scheduling, controlling and evaluating the time aspect of large complex projects. Illustrative of these are the construction of buildings or bridges, and the development of new products or systems.

Assuming that only one resource, namely time, is in limited supply, with sufficient other production resources (materials, equipment and personnel) available at any time to proceed with any activities whose predecessors have all been completed, we may ask: (a) What is the expected project completion time? (b) What is the scheduled start time and completion time of each activity? (c) Which activities are *critical*, in the sense that if they are not completed on time the entire project will be delayed? (d) For each noncritical activity, how much *slack* or *float* is there; that is, how long can the activity be held up without delaying the project?

The time of each activity may be assumed to be either precisely known (the deterministic case), or of uncertain duration (the probabilistic case). In the latter case, each activity time is specified in terms of three estimates: a most likely or modal time, an optimistic or shortest feasible time, and a pessimistic or longest possible time. Traditionally, the deterministic case is associated with the name CPM, while probabilistic analysis is referred to as PERT.

The precedence relationships may be specified using either an *activity-on-arc* representation (an arrow network) or an *activity-on-node* representation (a node network). With the activity-on-arc approach, the project is portrayed as a network in which the arrows represent activities and the nodes are the *events* or time points at which the last of the incoming activities ends and the outgoing activities can begin. For example, if final assembly (activity FA) and tear-down of manufacturing equipment (activity TD) can both begin only after all three subassemblies (activities S1, S2, and S3) are complete, the arrow network is as presented in Figure 1a. Node 4 represents the event that all of the subassemblies have been completed, and FA and TD can start.

The activity-on-node model, on the other hand, represents activities by nodes, with an arrow directed from each activity to each of its immediate successors. Figure 1b gives the node network equivalent to the arrow network in Figure 1a. Node networks are generally easier to construct, particularly because arrow networks sometimes require that dummy, zero-duration activities be introduced to enforce certain precedence orderings.

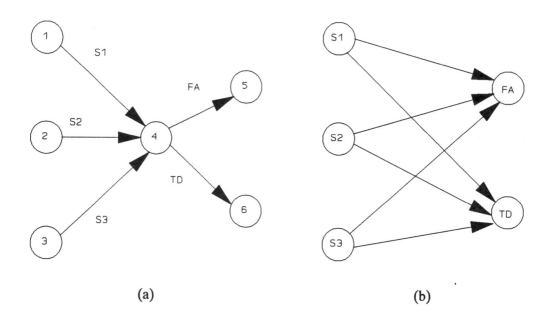

(a)   (b)

Figure 1: Arrow Network Versus Node Network

For instance, if in our example the tear-down activity could begin as soon as both S1 and S2 were finished, without having to wait for S3, while final assembly still must await completion of all three subassemblies, then the two network representations are given in Figure 2. The arrow network in Figure 2a now has a dummy activity d; the node network has only become simpler.

Actually, if the activity-on-node representation is to be used, there is no need for you to draw a network representation of the project before using STORM. You must simply be prepared to list all the immediate predecessors of each activity. With the activity-on-arc approach, you must draw the appropriate network and number all the nodes as a preliminary step, because you will be conveying the precedence information to the module by entering the starting and ending nodes for each activity.

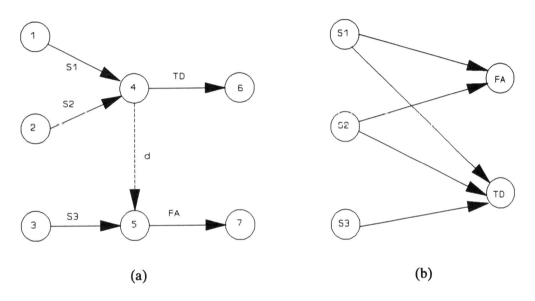

(a)   (b)

Figure 2: Modified Precedence Network

1. The Solution Algorithm

The basic problem of finding the critical activities, slack times, and minimal duration of a project with deterministic activity times is solved using the well-known Critical Path algorithm. The earliest start and finish times possible for each activity, and the latest such times that would not delay the project, are also generated.

With probabilistic activity times, the mean and variance for each activity are obtained as follows: If a_i, m_i and b_i are the estimates for the optimistic, most likely, and pessimistic duration of activity i, respectively, then the mean, t_i, and the standard deviation, d_i, are computed as

$t_i = (a_i + 4m_i + b_i) / 6$

$d_i = (b_i - a_i) / k$, where $k = 3.2$ or 6

The traditional formula for d_i involves division by 6 rather than 3.2. More recently, researchers have recommended the value 3.2. This is a technical issue involving the precise probabilistic meaning of a "pessimistic" or "optimistic" estimate. It is also an attempt to compensate for a tendency of the algorithm to underestimate the variance of the project duration. STORM defaults to 6, but you will be given the option to choose either value for the divisor.

The probabilistic critical path calculation is now performed using the mean time for each activity, and project mean and variance are estimated as the sums of means and variances of critical activities. Project duration is assumed to be normally distributed with these parameters.

2. Problem Size

If you are using Personal STORM, you can solve problems with up to 100 activities. Each activity can have any number of immediate predecessors, up to the obvious limit of 99. Professional STORM, with the capability for full core utilization, can solve much larger problems, depending on the amount of memory available in your computer. The precise limits will depend, for one thing, on the way you specify precedence.

With activity-on-node, you will be asked in the Problem Description area to indicate the largest number of immediate predecessors any activity in your network has. The Data area will then be set up to accommodate this many predecessor columns for any activity, and adequate space will be set aside in core storage. With variable dimensioning, STORM trades off fewer rows for more columns or vice versa, thus making fullest use of your computer's capacity. Consequently, overspecifying this parameter will waste storage space and limit the number of activities that can be accommodated. If you underspecify it, you can always increase it later by inserting columns. With this in mind, and assuming you have 500 kilobytes of core storage available for STORM to use, here are a few examples of the largest problems that Professional STORM can solve, where the first number is the number of activities and the second is the largest number of immediate predecessors any activity can have: (3500, 5), (3000, 10), (2000, 20), (1000, 50), and (500, 125).

If you use the activity-on-arc formulation, where immediate predecessors do not need to be explicitly listed, the item *Number of predecessor columns* in the Description area will be ignored. Without the need for predecessor columns, Professional STORM can accommodate 4000 activities, each with any number of immediate predecessors.

3. A Sample Problem: Deterministic Times with Activity-on-Node

The management of Aunt Hill's discount chain has decided to open its first branch outlet in Cleveland. It is about to launch a demographic study of the community to assess its socioeconomic make-up, the market potential for goods of various types and qualities, the relative desirability of several potential locations for the store, etc. In the coming weeks, it must select a manager to put in charge, hire and train a workforce, select and refurbish a building, choose the merchandise to be carried and contract with suppliers for it, and design and arrange for advertising in the local media. It could be argued that each of these activities is itself a more or less complex project, but as a first pass top management wishes to evaluate the undertaking without further refinement.

Obviously, some things must be done before others. After some consideration, it has been agreed that the required precedence is as listed in Table 1 and portrayed in the activity-on-node network of Figure 3. Also given in Table 1 are the estimated times (in weeks) that each activity will take.

Activity	Symbol	Time	Predecessors
Conduct market study	STDY	6	–
Appoint manager	MGR	3	–
Hire personnel	PER1	5	MGR
Train personnel	PER2	3	PER1, STDY
Acquire building	BLDG	3	STDY
Prepare building	FURN	5	BLDG
Select merchandise	PICK	3	STDY, MGR
Line up suppliers	DLRS	4	PICK
Acquire merchandise	STOK	3	PER2, FURN, DLRS
Advertise	ADV	2	PICK

Table 1: Given Data for Sample Problem

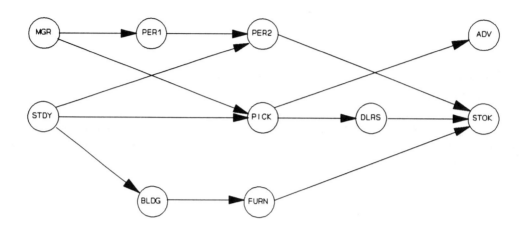

Figure 3: Node Network for Sample Problem

Management now wishes to know how long it will take before the store can open, and how much, if at all, each activity could be allowed to slip behind schedule before opening day would have to be postponed.

4. Data Entry Using STORM: Deterministic Times

Since we are provided with single-value estimates of activity times, we choose the deterministic (DET) option. We are given precedence information in the form of lists of predecessors, and this is precisely what is needed for the activity-on-node representation (NODE). Note that when using this approach, it is not necessary to draw a node network like Figure 3. In Figure 4, the data entry display for the sample problem is presented.

Following are some of the significant features of the input scheme.

- Activities can be entered in any convenient order.
- The activity name (default values ACT 1, ACT 2, . . .) can be any 10 characters or less.
- The activity symbol can be any 4 characters or less. Keep it as brief as possible, as you will have to type it each time you specify that activity as a predecessor.

```
┌────────────────────────────────────────────────────────────────────────┐
│              ─────────┤ STORM EDITOR : Project Management Module ├─────  │
│    Title : AUNT HILL'S STORE GRAND OPENING                               │
│    Number of activities                     :        10                  │
│    Activity time option (DET/PROB)          :       DET                  │
│    Activity representation option (ARC/NODE) :      NODE                  │
│    Number of predecessor columns (NODE only) :       3                   │
│                                                                          │
│    R10 : C5        SYMBOL   ACT TIME   PRED   1    PRED   2   PRED   3     │
│    ACT   1          STDY      6.         .          .          .         │
│    ACT   2           MGR      3.         .          .          .         │
│    ACT   3          PER1      5.        MGR         .          .         │
│    ACT   4          PER2      3.        PER1      STDY         .         │
│    ACT   5          BLDG      3.        STDY        .          .         │
│    ACT   6          FURN      5.        BLDG        .          .         │
│    ACT   7          PICK      3.        STDY       MGR         .         │
│    ACT   8          DLRS      4.        PICK        .          .         │
│    ACT   9          STOK      3.        PER2       FURN       DLRS       │
│    ACT  10           ADV      2.        PICK        .          .         │
│                                                                          │
│                                                                          │
│    ──────┤ Enter symbol of an immed predecessor of ACT  10  ├->┤   ├──── │
└────────────────────────────────────────────────────────────────────────┘
```

Figure 4: Editor Screen with the Sample Problem Entered

- The activity time (ACT TIME) can be any positive real number.
- The project may have any number of initial activities (activities with no predecessors) and any number of terminal activities (those with no successors).
- In the columns PRED 1, PRED 2, . . . , the immediate predecessors of the row activities are listed.

5. Errors Detected by STORM

If you make any of the following types of errors while entering data, STORM will detect them and inform you.

- Impossible precedence requirements, as evidenced by a loop in the node network. For example, you specify that activity A precedes B, B precedes C, and C precedes A.

- The same activity symbol used for more than one activity.
- A predecessor activity symbol which does not correspond to any code in the SYMBOL column.

These errors will not be caught as you enter the data, but will be detected and reported when you try to execute the module.

6. Execution of the Module: Deterministic Times

When you instruct the Project Management module to execute, you will be presented with a STORM form listing the output options, as shown in Figure 5. The first three available outputs are lists of the activities in various orders. As can be seen in Figure 6, the earliest start, earliest finish, latest start and latest finish times for each activity are given, as well as the amount of slack time available. Those activities which are on the critical path are indicated by a "c" in the final column.

```
                      SELECTION OF REPORTS

     List activities sorted by slack and earliest start ?        y
     List activities sorted by earliest start and slack ?        n
     List activities in the order entered ?                      n
     Bar chart: Noncritical activities sorted by slack ?         y
     Bar chart: Noncritical activities sorted by earliest start ? n
```

Figure 5: Available Output Reports

In the first of the three lists (the one illustrated in Figure 6), the activities are presented in increasing order of slack, so that, for example, the critical activities are first. This is the primary sort. Activities having equal slack are further ordered in increasing order of earliest start time (the secondary sort). The second list reverses priorities, sorting first by earliest start time and second by slack. This list produces *topological* or precedence ordering: each activity appears before any of its successors. The third list retains the order you used in entering the data.

AUNT HILL'S STORE GRAND OPENING
ACTIVITIES SORTED BY SLACK AND EARLIEST START

Activity Name		Symb	Activity Time	Earliest Start/Fin	Latest Start/Fin	Slack	
ACT	1	STDY	6.0000	0.0000	0.0000	0.0000	c
				6.0000	6.0000		
ACT	5	BLDG	3.0000	6.0000	6.0000	0.0000	c
				9.0000	9.0000		
ACT	6	FURN	5.0000	9.0000	9.0000	0.0000	c
				14.0000	14.0000		
ACT	9	STOK	3.0000	14.0000	14.0000	0.0000	c
				17.0000	17.0000		
ACT	7	PICK	3.0000	6.0000	7.0000	1.0000	
				9.0000	10.0000		
ACT	8	DLRS	4.0000	9.0000	10.0000	1.0000	
				13.0000	14.0000		
ACT	2	MGR	3.0000	0.0000	3.0000	3.0000	
				3.0000	6.0000		
ACT	3	PER1	5.0000	3.0000	6.0000	3.0000	
				8.0000	11.0000		
ACT	4	PER2	3.0000	8.0000	11.0000	3.0000	
				11.0000	14.0000		
ACT	10	ADV	2.0000	9.0000	15.0000	6.0000	
				11.0000	17.0000		

The computations were based on 10 activities
Earliest project completion time = 17.0000

Figure 6: Output with Activities Ordered by Slack

Two other outputs are available, and present much of the same information more graphical-ly. Here, each activity is represented by a bar of length equal to its duration laid out along a time scale and positioned at its earliest start time. Each critical activity is denoted by a string of c's, whereas the letter x is used for noncritical activities. The slack time of the noncritical activities is symbolized by a string of periods. The critical activities are listed first in time sequence. The rest of the activities are then displayed, sorted in either of the two ways described above. Specifically, the first bar chart, as shown in Figure 7, sorts primarily by slack and secondarily by earliest start time; the second option reverses the sorts.

```
                    AUNT HILL'S STORE GRAND OPENING
              BAR CHART: NONCRITICAL ACTIVITIES SORTED BY SLACK

         0                                                      17
         -----+-----+-----+-----+-----+-----+-----+-----+-----+-----+
    STDY |ccccccccccccccccccccc                                      |
    BLDG |                 ccccccccccc                               |
    FURN |                        ccccccccccccccccccc                |
    STOK |                                        ccccccccccc
    PICK |                 xxxxxxxxxxx...                            |
    DLRS |                        xxxxxxxxxxxxxxx...                 |
    MGR  |xxxxxxxxxxx..........                                      |
    PER1 |          xxxxxxxxxxxxxxxxx..........                      |
    PER2 |                   xxxxxxxxxxx..........                   |
    ADV  |                   xxxxxx.....................
         -----+-----+-----+-----+-----+-----+-----+-----+-----+-----+
```

Figure 7: Bar Chart with Activities Sorted by Slack

7. Sample Problem Continued: Probabilistic Times with Activity-on-Arc

The management of Aunt Hill's has studied carefully the outputs of the first computer run. It is reasonably satisfied with the projected opening date 17 weeks hence, but is concerned that unforeseen delays might cause a significant postponement. The market study, the single longest activity, is fairly well fixed; it cannot be shortened significantly, and its duration can be confidently forecast. The three other critical activities are locating and buying or leasing appropriate premises (BLDG), generally fixing them up (FURN), and then stocking the shelves (STOK). Almost as critical are deciding precisely what merchandise to stock (PICK), and selecting and contracting with wholesalers to supply the goods (DLRS). If these two activities between them are delayed over a week, they will become critical and force the grand opening to be postponed. The other four activities have ample slack and are in any case unlikely to encounter unexpected delays, but these five activities are cause for concern. Management has therefore decided to assess more carefully their possible durations, allowing for uncertainty. The results of many consultations and discussions are the time estimates given in Table 2. For example, the market study is unlikely to deviate by more than two days from its planned duration of six weeks, or 30 working days. Since it is as likely to be slightly shorter as slightly longer, the optimistic estimate is 28 days, most likely is 30 days and pessimistic is 32 days; that is, 5.6, 6 and 6.4 weeks. Other estimates have been similarly made, with the three numbers being chosen for each activity to provide an average activity time, t_i (as computed by the formula given earlier), consistent with the initial estimates. Those activities for which no significant variation is anticipated are given three identical times.

Activity	Activity Times			Node Numbers	
Symbol	Optim.	Likely	Pessim.	Start	End
MGR	3	3	3	1	3
STDY	5.6	6	6.4	2	4
PER1	5	5	5	3	6
d1	0	0	0	3	5
d2	0	0	0	4	6
d3	0	0	0	4	5
BLDG	2.4	2.6	5.2	4	7
PICK	2	3.2	3.2	5	8
PER2	3	3	3	6	9
FURN	4	4.6	7.6	7	9
DLRS	2.6	4.2	4.6	8	9
STOK	2	3	4	9	10
ADV	2	2	2	8	11

Table 2: Probabilistic Data for Sample Problem

Precedence information for Phase 2 of the study could be conveyed exactly as before: list all immediate predecessors after each activity. Instead, the activity-on-arc approach will be used for purposes of illustration. This requires that an Arrow network be prepared as a first step. In Figure 8, the Arrow network corresponding to the Node network of Figure 3 is displayed. You can see that it was necessary to add three dummy activities, which have been given symbols d1, d2 and d3. Having numbered the nodes, we need only give the start and end nodes of each activity to specify precedence. This information also appears in Table 2.

8. Data Entry Using STORM: Probabilistic Times

When the data have been entered, the display should look like Figure 9. Besides the features already mentioned, we note the following additional features when using the activity-on-arc representation:

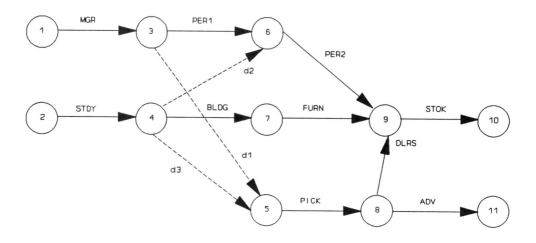

Figure 8: Arrow Network for the Sample Problem

```
|————————————| STORM EDITOR : Project Management Module |————————————
Title : AUNT HILL'S PROBLEM WITH PROBABILISTIC ACTIVITY TIMES
Number of activities                        :       13
Activity time option (DET/PROB)             :      PROB
Activity representation option (ARC/NODE) :      ARC
Number of predecessor columns (NODE only) :       3

R13 : C6        SYMBOL OPTIMISTIC      LIKELY PESIMISTIC START NODE    END NODE
ACT   1           MGR     3.             3.        3.           1            3
ACT   2           STDY    5.6            6.        6.4          2            4
ACT   3           PER1    5.             5.        5.           3            6
ACT   4           D1      0.             0.        0.           3            5
ACT   5           D2      0.             0.        0.           4            6
ACT   6           D3      0.             0.        0.           4            5
ACT   7           BLDG    2.4            2.6       5.2          4            7
ACT   8           PICK    2.             3.2       3.2          5            8
ACT   9           PER2    3.             3.        3.           6            9
ACT  10           FURN    4.             4.6       7.6          7            9
ACT  11           DLRS    2.6            4.2       4.6          8            9
ACT  12           STOK    2.             3.        4.           9           10
ACT  13           ADV     2.             2.        2.           8           11

|————| Enter the number of the end node for ACT  13      |->|        |————
```

Figure 9: Input Data Display with Probabilistic Times

- All activities must be entered, including dummy activities, which should be assigned zero duration. Thus, the number of activities has been increased accordingly.

- Events do not need to be numbered "left-to-right," with each activity's end node having a larger number than its start node. The STORM module checks for cycles and reports them with error messages. However, left-to-right numbering is considered good practice. You may even want to number in increments of five or ten to allow new activities to be inserted later without renumbering.

9. Execution of the Module: Probabilistic Times

Execution of the Project Management module with uncertain activity durations results in a set of output options similar to the selection with deterministic times. At the top of the list you are given the chance to specify which divisor you prefer when calculating the standard deviation of each activity time (3.2 or 6.0), as discussed in Section 1. The only other change is the added option of a probability plot, described below. The three lists of activities, sorted in various ways, are still available. Assuming we choose 3.2 as the denominator for computing standard deviations, the first list is shown in Figure 10, and may be compared with the corresponding deterministic list in Figure 6. Two new columns have been added, giving the mean and variance of each activity, and the project time variance has been added at the bottom. The two bar charts are essentially unchanged; compare Figure 11 to Figure 7.

The new menu item available when activity times are not precisely known is *Normal probability chart*. Remember, the assumption is that the project duration has an approximately normal distribution, so that we can compute the probabilities of achieving various project durations. In Figure 12 we plot the probability that all work will be completed by a certain time. The points marked along the time axis correspond to the probabilities listed vertically. For example, there is a 5% chance of opening the store within 14.41 weeks, a 10% chance of making 14.98 weeks, a 15% probability of being ready in 15.36 weeks, and so on.

AUNT HILL'S PROBLEM WITH PROBABILISTIC ACTIVITY TIMES
ACTIVITIES SORTED BY SLACK AND EARLIEST START

Activity Name	Symb	Mean Time /Std Dev	Earliest Start/Fin	Latest Start/Fin	Slack
ACT 2	STDY	6.0000	0.0000	0.0000	0.0000 c
		0.2500	6.0000	6.0000	
ACT 7	BLDG	3.0000	6.0000	6.0000	0.0000 c
		0.8750	9.0000	9.0000	
ACT 10	FURN	5.0000	9.0000	9.0000	0.0000 c
		1.1250	14.0000	14.0000	
ACT 12	STOK	3.0000	14.0000	14.0000	0.0000 c
		0.6250	17.0000	17.0000	
ACT 8	PICK	3.0000	6.0000	7.0000	1.0000
		0.3750	9.0000	10.0000	
ACT 6	D3	0.0000	6.0000	7.0000	1.0000
		0.0000	6.0000	7.0000	
ACT 11	DLRS	4.0000	9.0000	10.0000	1.0000
		0.6250	13.0000	14.0000	
ACT 1	MGR	3.0000	0.0000	3.0000	3.0000
		0.0000	3.0000	6.0000	
ACT 3	PER1	5.0000	3.0000	6.0000	3.0000
		0.0000	8.0000	11.0000	
ACT 9	PER2	3.0000	8.0000	11.0000	3.0000
		0.0000	11.0000	14.0000	
ACT 4	D1	0.0000	3.0000	7.0000	4.0000
		0.0000	3.0000	7.0000	
ACT 5	D2	0.0000	6.0000	11.0000	5.0000
		0.0000	6.0000	11.0000	
ACT 13	ADV	2.0000	9.0000	15.0000	6.0000
		0.0000	11.0000	17.0000	

The computations were based on 13 activities
Expected project completion time   = 17.0000
Activity std dev = (pessimistic - optimistic) / 3.2
Std dev of project completion time = 1.5762

Figure 10: Probabilistic Output with Activities Ordered by Slack

```
        AUNT HILL'S PROBLEM WITH PROBABILISTIC ACTIVITY TIMES
          BAR CHART: NONCRITICAL ACTIVITIES SORTED BY SLACK

      0                                                        17
     -----+-----+-----+-----+-----+-----+-----+-----+-----+-----+      |
 STDY |cccccccccccccccccccccc                                          |
 BLDG |                 cccccccccc                                     |
 FURN |                        cccccccccccccccccc                      |
 STOK |                                          cccccccccc
 PICK |                xxxxxxxxxxx...                                   |
 D3   |                x...                                            |
 DLRS |                        xxxxxxxxxxxxxx...                        |
 MGR  |xxxxxxxxxxx..........                                           |
 PER1 |       xxxxxxxxxxxxxxxxx...........                             |
 PER2 |                  xxxxxxxxxxx...........                        |
 D1   |        x.............                                          |
 D2   |              x................                                 |
 ADV  |                    xxxxxx....................                 .
     -----+-----+-----+-----+-----+-----+-----+-----+-----+-----+
```

Figure 11: Probabilistic Bar Chart

If you want the precise probability of achieving a target date not listed, you can enter a time in the Pointer at the bottom of the screen and your probability of making that deadline will be provided. In Figure 12, you can see that the management of Aunt Hill's has asked about their chances of opening within 18 weeks, and that the answer is 73.7%. You can query the module repeatedly about various target completion times; each time the probability will be given. In case you are in printer or disk output mode to save your results, column headers will automatically be produced when you first type in a target time, and you can thus generate a report giving the probability of project completions at a sequence of given dates.

10. Altering Problem Data Dimensions

New activities can be inserted in any position (any row), and old ones deleted. As always, STORM will simply add or remove the row in the Editor screen; it is your responsibility to fill it in with the appropriate entries. However, note that additional changes to the data will usually be required. In a node network, for example, the lists of predecessors for other activities may need to be changed. Thus, if activity A is an immediate predecessor of activity

C and you now wish to insert a new activity B between them, not only must you list A as a predecessor of B, but you must also change the predecessor of C from A to B. Similar considerations arise when removing an activity. Obviously, all references to a deleted activity should be eliminated. If they are not, the module will warn you. Other kinds of oversights will usually produce meaningful (though wrong) formulations which STORM will not be able to detect, so be careful.

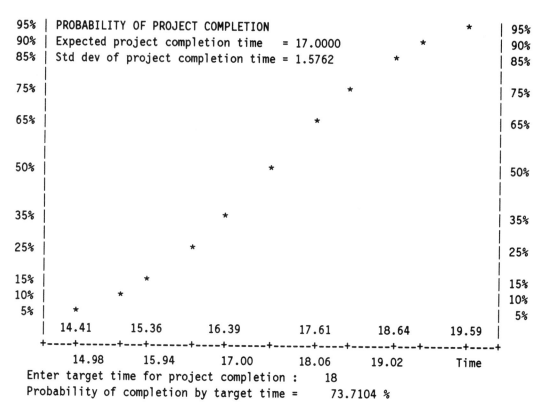

Figure 12: Distribution of Project Completion Time

With activity-on-arc representation, all the columns in the layout are required; column insertions and deletions are not permitted. With activities on nodes, additional predecessor columns can be added. STORM has no provision to convert activity-on-arc data sets to activity-on-node representations or vice versa, nor to switch between deterministic and probabilistic activity times. However, the probabilistic mode can be used for either fixed or uncertain times, or for a mixture of both. Simply enter the same value for all three times, when the activity time is deterministic.

QUEUEING ANALYSIS CAPABILITIES

PROBLEM FORMULATION OPTIONS
- Steady state analysis of:
  - M/M/c
  - M/G/c
  - M/D/c
  - M/M/c/K
  - M/M/c/K/K

OUTPUT OPTIONS AND OTHER FEATURES
- Steady state distribution and histogram
- Mean numbers in queues and in system
- Mean lengths of time in queues and in system
- Server utilizations
- Blocking probability
- Cost analysis

MAXIMAL PROBLEM SIZES (WORK STATIONS, SERVERS PER STATION)
- Personal version: (10, 50)
- Professional version: (2000, 100)

FILE NAME FOR THE SAMPLE PROBLEM DATA
- QUE.DAT

Chapter 12

QUEUEING ANALYSIS

Queues, or waiting lines, form in many situations in modern life. Customers in banks or supermarkets, cars at toll booths, and work awaiting processing at a job shop all encounter delays and must wait their turn when the system becomes congested. We will refer to entities seeking service as *customers* or *users* hereafter, whether they are in fact people, jobs, vehicles or whatever. Similarly, a *server* is anyone or anything providing service.

Questions concerning the amount of capacity that should be provided arise often in both manufacturing and service industries. Providing too many servers, or more rapid service than necessary, leads to idle workers and underutilized equipment. Too little capacity, on the other hand, produces long queues and consequently impatient customers and congested shop floors. While striking the correct balance must ultimately involve sound managerial judgment, such decisions are facilitated if their various consequences can be accurately assessed.

A location where a single line forms in front of one or several servers is called a *station*. In more complex situations, a customer completing service at one station may move on to join the queue at another station. A job shop is an example of a *network of queues* having several stations with customers (in this case jobs) following various routes from station to station. The current version of the Queueing Analysis module focuses on single station situations.

1. The Structure of a Queueing System

The mathematical study of queues has been extensive, and many formulas have been developed that help us estimate the characteristics of waiting lines. Such analysis must be based on a clear statement of the system's structure and how its parts interact. The general single-station waiting line model is made up of the following components.

1.1 The Input Population

The *input source* or *population* is the collection of all potential users that might arrive seeking service. The size of this population is often assumed to be effectively infinite (for example, people arriving at a movie theater), and this is the easier situation to analyze.

However, it may be unrealistic to assume an infinite source if the number of users is not very large, as in a repair shop dedicated to a limited number of machines. In such a case, we will have to enter the precise size of the population.

1.2 The Process of Arrivals

The way in which arrivals occur over time must be somehow described mathematically. This is usually given as a probability distribution of the time between successive arrivals, or an *interarrival time distribution*. A very common assumption is that arrivals from an infinite population are completely random, which leads to an exponential distribution for interarrival times. This is referred to as a *Poisson arrival process*.

If the input population is finite, the analogous assumption is that each user, when not in the system (that is, when not either awaiting or receiving service), makes demands on the system at completely random times, independently of the other users and at the same given rate.

1.3 The Waiting Line

The queue that is formed by waiting customers may also be assumed to have effectively infinite capacity, or be limited to a finite waiting room. In the latter case, any arrival finding the waiting room full is assumed to be turned away and denied service.

Incidentally, do not take the terms *arrival, waiting line,* and *waiting room* too literally. The customers may be massive pieces of machinery bolted to the floor, while the servers may be repairmen. In this case, it is the servers who arrive at the customers, and no queue actually forms. Nevertheless, the same concepts and formulas apply.

1.4 The Service Discipline

The sequence in which the waiting customers are chosen for service can be controlled in some situations. We shall assume that the order of service is always *first come, first served.*

1.5 The Number of Servers

Any number of servers can be specified. When the station has more than a single server, the multiple servers will be assumed to be identical and *in parallel,* which means that a customer seeks service from just one of them; any one will do.

1.6 The Distribution of Service Times

The times required to give service usually vary widely and unpredictably from one customer to the next. This uncertainty is captured by specifying a probability distribution for the service times. Again a common assumption is the exponential distribution. At the opposite extreme from this most unpredictable type of service time is the constant service time. Both of these lead to models which can be thoroughly analyzed. Limited results can also be obtained if no distribution is given, but instead the mean and standard deviation of the service times are specified.

2. Notational Conventions

The various components of a queueing system can be put together in many ways. The following widely accepted shorthand notation will be useful in specifying which combination we are concerned with. We write a series of letters separated by fraction bars, thus: a/b/c/d/e. The five symbols have the following significance.

a. The first position is used to indicate the type of arrival process. The only notation which STORM allows is:

> M - A "Markovian" input process, which simply means inputs which are generated by completely random arrivals. These may be from an infinite source, in which case the average arrival rate (number of arrivals per unit time) must be specified; or from a finite population, which will require you to give the average rate at which each customer arrives.

b. The second symbol denotes the distribution of service times. STORM offers three options:

> M - An exponentially distributed service time (again, M stands for Markovian). This is commonly assumed in theory, quite often encountered in practice, and gives in a sense the most *random* or unpredictable times.

D - Deterministic or constant processing times: the opposite extreme from the exponential. This may occur in manufacturing environments where machines have fixed cycle times.

G - General or unspecified probability distribution. Certain results can be obtained without making any assumption about the shape of the distribution, but using only the mean and standard deviation of the service time.

No matter which choice you make, you will then have to give the average service time. This is enough to fully determine the service process in the case of either exponential or deterministic times. For the general case, you must also input the standard deviation of the service times.

c. In the third slot, the letter stands for the number of parallel identical servers that make up the station.

d. The last two symbols are often omitted. In the fourth position we indicate the largest number of customers that can be in the system (that is, either being served or queueing). It is left off when there is no limit to the number of customers who can wait in line; that is, when the waiting room has infinite capacity.

e. The fifth indicator specifies the size of the input population. When it is omitted, a value of infinity is assumed. If the source is limited to K customers, we write a/b/c/K/K, implying that the capacity is also limited to K. This we can do even if the waiting room is unlimited, since we never need room for more than K.

3. Steady State Operation

When a complex random process like a waiting line starts up, as when a retail store first opens in the morning, there is a period of time during which the system conditions are influenced by the initial state. This *transient* phase is gradually replaced by a *steady state* in which a stable pattern emerges, even though random fluctuations are still observed.

The output reports of the Queueing Analysis module are based on the assumption that the system is operating in steady state. Among other things, this implies that the average arrival rate, the average service time, and all the other inputs that you will be asked to specify are constant over time.

Unless you are concerned with a *self-limiting* model in which either the waiting room or the input population is finite, you must be careful to enter an arrival rate that is smaller than the largest departure rate (which is the number of servers multiplied by one over the average service time). If customers arrive faster on the average than they can be handled, the queue will keep growing longer and longer and will never reach steady state. This is, of course, a theoretical result. In practice something will happen: perhaps the arrival rate will decrease as prospective customers turn away, or the departure rate may increase due either to more hurried service or to extra counters being opened. Whatever happens, the assumptions of the model will no longer be valid. Thus, all the formulas we use are based on steady state behavior, and you will not be permitted to use parameter values which violate this assumption.

4. The Performance Measures Reported

For each waiting line system that you solve, some or all of the following performance measures will be reported. In all cases, it is assumed that the system is in steady state.

- *The Server Utilization:* the fraction or per cent (as we report it) of time that each server is busy, on the average.

- *The Mean Queue Length:* the expected number of customers in the queue.

- *The Mean Number in System:* the expected number of customers either queueing or being served.

- *The Blocking Probability:* the probability that an arriving customer will find all servers busy and will be forced to wait for service. Equivalently, the fraction of customers who must wait to be served.

- *The Mean Queueing Time:* the expected time a customer spends in the waiting line before service begins.

- *The Mean Time in System:* the expected time a customer spends both waiting for service and receiving it.

- *The State Probabilities:* the probability distribution of the number in the system. That is, the probability that there are exactly n users either queueing or receiving service at any time, for $n = 0,1, \ldots$.

- *The Probability of Service Denial:* the probability that an arriving customer, finding the waiting room full, will be turned away; or, equivalently, the fraction of customers denied service. If the waiting room has infinite capacity, this probability is obviously zero and is not reported.

All of these results are obtained by direct evaluation of standard formulas. We will not present any of them here; many are quite complex. Most of them can be found in any standard text. Any expressions not so readily available will be referenced as they arise in the following sections, where we discuss each model in turn.

5. Cost Analysis

STORM provides the capability to perform a simple cost analysis aimed at determining the number of servers needed at the work station: the number of elevators to design into the new hotel, perhaps, or the number of toll booths to staff. The decision will be based on a trade-off between two basic costs: the cost of providing additional servers versus the cost attributed to delayed or denied service. We assume that the cost of delayed service is a given amount per customer per unit time spent in the system. While it is usually fairly easy to determine the cost of a server, the cost of making a customer wait is largely intangible and often hard to pin down. Suffice it to say that delay costs clearly exist and in extreme cases can become quite significant. They must be estimated somehow if a queueing system is to be intelligently designed and controlled.

We put both costs on the same basis by converting to cost per unit time. If the cost of a server is not already in this form (as the salary of an additional bank teller would be), any one-time outlays (like the down payment on an extra turret lathe) should be annualized (see the Investment Analysis chapter for details) and converted to the same time units you are using for the waiting cost rate.

If we define:

C_d = Delay cost per customer per unit time,
C_s = Cost per unit time of providing each additional server,
L = Average number in the system,
c = Number of servers

then the total cost per unit time for a station is:

$$LC_d + cC_s$$

As c increases, the additional capacity will speed service and L will decrease. STORM will explore this trade-off and, for the cost figures that you provide, will report the number of servers that minimizes total cost.

An extended analysis is performed for the queueing model that involves a finite amount of waiting room. Here, we trade off the cost of extra servers against the cost of lost business due to turning away customers, plus the delay cost for those customers who are admitted. Defining:

C_r = Cost of refusing service to a customer,
A = Arrival rate,
p = Probability that a customer is refused service,

the total cost rate now becomes

$$LC_d + cC_s + pAC_r$$

Cost analysis is an optional feature that may be omitted. If you wish to conduct a descriptive study of a queueing system without consideration of costs, simply do not enter any cost data.

6. The Queueing Models Analyzed

The components of a queueing model can be combined in various ways to reflect a great many situations that might be encountered. STORM provides you with the following selection of models to choose from. All of them permit you to specify any number, c, of identical parallel servers up to the limit of 200 servers for Professional STORM or 50 for the Personal version.

6.1 Poisson Input and Exponential Service Times (M/M/c)

This is probably the simplest queueing system to analyze. It assumes random arrivals from an infinite population (a Poisson input process), no limit on the waiting room, and exponentially distributed service times. STORM provides all of the measures of system performance listed above, using exact formulas.

6.2 Poisson Input and Constant Service Times (M/D/c)

Still with completely random arrivals, this model assumes fixed service times, the same for all jobs. In the multiserver case ($c > 1$), exact formulas are not available for the measures of interest, and we use Molina's approximation (see, for example, *Mathematical Methods of Operations Research,* by Thomas Saaty [McGraw-Hill, 1959]). For the single server station, exact formulas are used.

6.3 Poisson Input and Arbitrary Service Times (M/G/c)

Again assuming random arrivals and unlimited queue length, we now suppose that we know nothing of the distribution of service times beyond their mean value and standard deviation. As before, only in the case of a single server are exact expressions available. For $c > 1$, Lee and Longton's approximate formulas are used; see *Stochastic Models in Operations Research, Volume I,* by Daniel Heyman and Matthew Sobel (McGraw-Hill, 1982), for a discussion. These expressions are exact for the special cases of M/M/c and M/G/1, and are especially good in "heavy traffic" situations (that is, when the arrival rate is almost as large as the maximal departure rate). Only *mean value* performance measures are available with this model; the state probabilities cannot be determined with so little information.

6.4 Poisson Input, Exponential Service Times, and Finite Queue Length (M/M/c/K)

We now assume that the largest number of customers who can be in the system is limited to a finite number $K \geq c$, so that the waiting room capacity is $K - c$. Since we assume an infinite input population, there will continue to be arrivals when the system is full, so some customers will be denied service and turned away. This leads to some special features in the output reports of this model.

The average times spent queueing and in the system, which are reported for all other models, are omitted here because they are not clearly defined. What time shall we ascribe to a customer who never enters the system? On the other hand, an additional statistic is reported for this model only: the probability of service denial. Of course, this probability is zero when waiting capacity is unlimited.

The cost analysis is different for this model, also. As discussed in Section 5, we must add in the important cost of customers who are not merely delayed but actually lost.

6.5 Finite Input Source and Exponential Service Times (M/M/c/K/K)

Instead of a Poisson input stream, we now assume that a fixed finite number of customers use the service station. Thus the rate at which customers may be expected to arrive is a function of the number already in the system: the more of them present, the fewer who might decide to seek service. Assuming each customer independently and randomly places demands on the system, and that the service times are exponentially distributed, all of the performance measures listed in Section 4 are reported by STORM. It is understood that the input population has size $K \geq c$; otherwise one would certainly get rid of the excess servers.

7. Sample Problems

In order to illustrate the various models available, we will describe a situation in which the possible alternatives give rise to several scenarios. The columns in Figure 1 show the Editor screen after data entry for these scenarios. You may want to glance at the appropriate entry as you read the description.

7.1 Scenario 1 (M/M/c)

Your precision engineering firm uses two large drill presses for very accurate machining. It is considering adding a third because of long delays that have developed in this department. You charge a high price for this kind of work, and your customers are beginning to show some impatience. The jobs vary greatly in processing time (could this be part of your problem?), and an exponential distribution fits well, with mean value 2 hours.

You receive orders for this type of job at an average rate of 38 orders per week. Your people work an eight-hour day, five days a week. A new drill press will cost $1,500,000 and will have an estimated salvage value of $200,000 after 20 years. At a 15% annual interest rate, this gives it an equivalent worth of approximately -$238,000, or a cost of $4,600 per week. Finally, the hard question to answer: How much is it costing you to delay orders? Direct costs of handling complaints, expediting, etc. are, you suspect, much less significant than the possibility of losing business to your competition. Several valued customers have already mentioned this possibility, and a few have even carried through. Since the demand for your specialized services is not widespread, each such loss is very costly. At last, after estimating as best you can the cost of a lost customer and the chance of this happening as a function of waiting time, you come up with an overall delay cost per week per customer of $1,000.

```
┌─────────────────────────────────────────────────────────────────┐
│                                                                   │
│     ┌──────────────┤ STORM EDITOR : Queueing Analysis Module ├────────────┐
│     │ Title : DRILL PRESS PROBLEM                                          │
│     │ Number of independent queueing problems :          4                │
│     │                                                                      │
│     │                                                                      │
│     ├──────────────────────────────────────────────────────────────────  │
│     │ R11 : C4   SCENARIO 1 SCENARIO 2 SCENARIO 3 SCENARIO 4               │
│     │ # SERVERS      2          2          2          2                    │
│     │ SOURCE POP    INF        INF        INF        FIN                   │
│     │ ARR RATE      38.        38.        38.        0.2                   │
│     │ SERV DIST     EXP        GEN        EXP        EXP                   │
│     │ SERV TIME     0.05       0.05       0.05       0.05                  │
│     │ SERV STD       .         0.025       .          .                    │
│     │ WAIT CAP       .          .         10          .                    │
│     │ # CUSTMERS     .          .          .         200                   │
│     │ WAIT COST    1000.      1000.      1000.      1000.                  │
│     │ COST/SERV    4600.      4600.      4600.      4600.                  │
│     │ LOSTCUST C     .          .        5000.        .                    │
│     │                                                                      │
│     │                                                                      │
│     └─────────┤ Entry not required. No customer is denied service ├─>│  ├──│
│                                                                   │
└─────────────────────────────────────────────────────────────────┘
```

Figure 1: The Editor Screen After Data Entry

7.2 Scenario 2 (M/G/c)

You ask yourself again: How much of the difficulty you are experiencing in making timely deliveries is due to the highly unpredictable service times? You decide to see what would happen if you could reduce the standard deviation of these times. If great efficiencies result, it could be worthwhile seeking ways to work in this direction. Better maintenance or more operator training might help reduce the variation in processing times. To begin with, you will try halving the current standard deviation, which equals the mean value (two hours) for the exponential distribution.

7.3 Scenario 3 (M/M/c/K)

If you were to limit the number of jobs you would accept at any time, you might gain a better reputation for promptness and responsibility without having to turn away too many orders. You decide to try several values for this upper bound on the system state and see what effect it has. You will start with a maximal number in the system of twelve jobs. Since the average job produces a profit of $5,000, this is the cost of rejecting an order.

7.4 Scenario 4 (M/M/c/K/K)

You notice that all your business actually comes from just 200 customers, and none of them ever places another order until you complete whatever work you have for them. Shortening the turnaround time might stimulate more frequent orders. Your first analysis, by considering the calling population effectively infinite, has not allowed for this. Will a more careful analysis change your conclusions? On the average, each customer places an order every five weeks, or 0.2 orders per week.

8. Data Entry Using STORM

Figure 1 shows how the Editor screen should look after the four problems have been entered. We will briefly discuss each row.

8.1 Number of Servers (# SERVERS)

In all cases, simply enter the value of c, the number of servers at the station. In our scenario, $c = 2$.

8.2 Source Population (SOURCE POP)

Type the letter I or F, depending on whether the size of the input population is Infinite (the default entry, INF) or Finite.

8.3 Arrival Rate (ARR RATE)

For an infinite population, you should enter the average number of customers per unit time that you expect to arrive. For a finite input source, enter instead the average number of demands on the system that *each customer* is expected to make per unit time. Be sure to use a consistent time unit throughout.

8.4 Service Time Distribution (SERV DIST)

Type in here your choice among the three options available to you: E for Exponentially distributed or Markovian service times, D for Deterministic or constant service times, or G for General or arbitrary service times. The default entry is EXP.

8.5 Average Service Time (SERV TIME)

Enter the mean service time here. In the sample problems, since the 40-hour week is our time unit, the mean service time of 2 hours converts to 0.05 weeks.

8.6 Standard Deviation of Service Time (SERV STD)

This entry should only be made if the general service time distribution was chosen. For exponential or constant service times, the appropriate value (equal to the mean service time or zero, respectively) will automatically be used. Indeed, you will not be permitted to make an entry if you have chosen EXP or DET in the SERV DIST row. You could sneak one in by typing G above, entering a value here, and then going back and changing GEN to EXP or DET; but it would be ignored. Note that in Scenario 2 the standard deviation entered is half the mean value, as planned.

8.7 Waiting Room Capacity (WAIT CAP)

Enter here the amount of waiting room provided, or the maximal queue length, if this is limited. Otherwise, the default entry "." will denote an infinite waiting room capacity. Note that, if you enter a number here, it should not include the customers being served. In terms of the notation introduced earlier, you should enter $K - c$.

8.8 Number of Customers (# CUSTMERS)

This is the row in which to indicate the size of a finite input population. Use the dot default setting for an infinite number of customers.

8.9 Waiting Cost Rate Per Customer (WAIT COST)

Here you should enter the cost per unit time that you wish to charge yourself for making a customer wait, where waiting time is measured from the instant the order is placed until the job is finished. If this cost is left at its dot default and a cost per server is entered, a cost analysis will be performed assuming a waiting cost of zero.

8.10 Cost Per Server (COST/SERV)

The quantity to enter here is the cost *per unit time* that you ascribe to adding one more server. If you make no entry here, cost analysis will not be performed on that scenario.

8.11 Cost of Denying Service (LOSTCUST C)

If the waiting room capacity is finite, you should enter in this row the cost incurred when a customer finds no room to wait and is turned away: the *lost customer cost.* In scenarios where the queue length is unlimited, there will never be a lost customer so this cost is irrelevant; any entry you make will be ignored.

9. Execution of the Module

When you proceed to execute the module, the list of all the service facilities (or scenarios) you have entered will appear. You may wish to look at one or a few selected scenarios, in which case you should indicate your choices by marking them with asterisks. If you want to have the output reports for all the alternatives displayed in a continuous sequence, you can toggle them all simultaneously with the F1 key, as explained in Chapter 4.

Having selected the scenarios to be analyzed, you will be asked whether you wish to see a histogram of the state probabilities *(Show probability distribution of number in system?).* Since this may take a little time to compute for large problems, and may be more detailed information than you need, you are given the option to bypass it.

After this, the solutions to each selected queueing problem will be presented as follows. We illustrate with Scenario 1, the M/M/2 queue.

9.1 Summary Statistics

The first output report for any queueing problem will resemble Figure 2. After summarizing the input parameters on which the analysis is based, several statistics are given which describe how the queue is functioning. Thus, for Scenario 1, you can immediately confirm that the drill presses are heavily loaded: they are in use 95% of the time. The queue length does not seem all that excessive: an arriving job may expect to see about 17.5 jobs waiting ahead of it, or 19.5 including those being served. Of course, almost all jobs (92.56%) will experience some delay before being served, but it only takes about half a week (0.5128 weeks) on the average from arrival to departure.

```
            SCENARIO 1 : M / M / c
          QUEUE   STATISTICS

      Number of identical servers . . . . . . . . .         2
      Mean arrival rate . . . . . . . . . . . . .     38.0000
      Mean service rate per server  . . . . . . . .   20.0000

      Mean server utilization (%) . . . . . . . . .   95.0000
      Expected number of customers in queue . . . .   17.5872
      Expected number of customers in system  . . .   19.4872
      Probability that a customer must wait . . . .    0.9256
      Expected time in the queue  . . . . . . . . .    0.4628
      Expected time in the system . . . . . . . . .    0.5128
```

Figure 2: Summary Statistics for a Queueing Problem

9.2 Cost Analysis

The next report, shown in Figure 3, presents a cost analysis of the service system. The total cost per unit time is calculated (using the formulas of Section 5) and summarized for the given number of servers, and also for the number of servers that minimizes cost. You may be somewhat surprised to see that, although the average delays your customers are experiencing do not seem great, an additional drill press is indicated.

```
                  SCENARIO 1 : M / M / c
                  COST ANALYSIS PER UNIT TIME

                           Current System     Optimal System *
   Number of servers    |        2         |        3         |
   Cost per server      | 4600.0000        | 4600.0000        |
   Cost of service      |         9200.0000|         13800.0000|
   Mean number in system|    19.4972       |    2.5884         |
   Waiting cost/customer| 1000.0000        | 1000.0000        |
   Cost of waiting      |        19487.1900|          2588.4000|
                                 ----------           ----------
   TOTAL COST                    28687.1900           16388.4000

              * Optimization is over number of servers
```

Figure 3: Cost Analysis for a Queueing Problem

9.3 Probability Distribution of the Number in the System

The final output will be presented if you requested it by answering "yes" to the question *Show probability distribution of number in system?* which appeared on the screen earlier. Figure 4 shows what the first part of this output looks like for Scenario 1 (the entire display extends over three screens).

The plot is designed as follows. Each row represents a certain number of customers who may be in the system at an arbitrary time. This is often called the state of the system. There is one row for every state that has a *significant chance* of occurring, by which we mean a probability of 0.005 or more. For each such number, the probability of occurrence (or, if you like, the fraction of the time the system is in this state) given, followed by a graphical representation of the same probability. A bar chart or histogram is formed using asterisks for each 0.02 units of probability. The last fraction beyond a multiple of 0.02 is given by an asterisk if it is between 0.01 and 0.02, and by a plus sign if it is between 0 and 0.01. Table 1 illustrates this.

```
                     SCENARIO 1 : M / M / c
             PROBABILITY DISTRIBUTION OF NUMBER IN SYSTEM
     Number  Prob  0   0.1  0.2  0.3  0.4  0.5  0.6  0.7  0.8  0.9   1
                   +----+----+----+----+----+----+----+----+----+----+
         0  0.0256|*+                                                 |
         1  0.0487|**+-                                               |
         2  0.0463|**+---                                             |
         3  0.0440|**+-----                                           |
         4  0.0418|**+-------                                         |
         5  0.0397|**----------                                       |
         6  0.0377|**------------                                     |
         7  0.0358|**--------------                                   |
         8  0.0340|**----------------                                 |
         9  0.0323|**-----------------                                |
        10  0.0307|**-------------------                              |
        11  0.0292|*+--------------------                             |
        12  0.0277|*+----------------------                           |
        13  0.0263|*+-----------------------                          |
        14  0.0250|*+------------------------                         |
        15  0.0238|*+-------------------------                        |
        16  0.0226|*+---------------------------                      |
        17  0.0214|*+----------------------------                     |
        18  0.0204|*+-----------------------------                    |
```

Figure 4: Probability Distribution of the System State with Two Servers

When the probability for each separate state drops below 0.005, the plot terminates with a final row labeled OVER giving the total probability beyond this point. Sometimes the plot does not start at state 0, in which case a row labeled UNDER will come first.

Probability	Representation
0 - 0.01	+
0.01 - 0.02	*
0.02 - 0.03	*+
0.03 - 0.04	**
0.04 - 0.05	**+
. . .	. . .

Table 1: The Code Used in the Probability Histograms

To the right of each row of asterisks, a row of hyphens extends. This shows the *cumulative* distribution: the probability that the waiting line will be found in any state less than or equal to this one. Each hyphen denotes 0.02 probability.

For Scenario 1, much is now explained. The complete histogram (not shown) extends to 45 customers, and the OVER row shows that there is almost a 10% probability of having states even larger than that. Thus, while the average number in the system is fairly low, the variation over time is extreme, and delays of several weeks are not uncommon (40 jobs ahead of you means an average two-week delay, often longer).

You can confirm this diagnosis by looking at the probability distribution if you add the third drill press. As Figure 5 shows, long waiting lines have been eliminated. Incidentally, to modify and rerun a problem using STORM requires only that you press Esc and Enter to return to the Editor screen, make the appropriate changes, and then press F7 and Enter to return to the list of candidates.

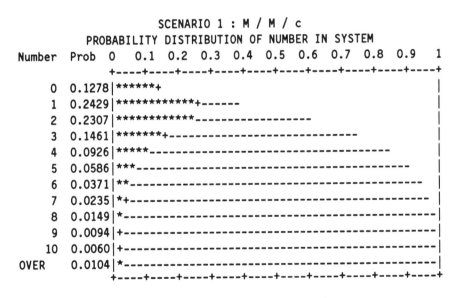

Figure 5: Probability Distribution with Three Servers

10. Special Features of Certain Models

For the most part, the output reports for each type of queueing model are the same. We will therefore not give a detailed discussion of each of the scenarios. Instead, in this section we will indicate the general differences between models, and in the following section we will comment briefly on how the reports can be interpreted to shed light on our sample problem.

10.1 The M/D/c and M/G/c Queues

For these models, the summary statistics reported are the same as those in Figure 2, and the cost analysis is just like the one in Figure 3. However, you are not given the opportunity to receive the third type of output, since formulas are not available for the complete probability distribution. If we know no more about the service times than their average and standard deviation, there is just not enough information to establish more than average performance measures.

10.2 The M/M/c/K Queue

There are several special features of this model, due to the possibility of denying service to a customer and thus losing an order. First, in the summary statistics, expected times do not appear because the *time in the system* for a lost customer is not well defined. Instead, the probability of service denial is reported. This is the fraction of arriving customers who are lost.

The cost analysis, shown in Figure 6 for Scenario 3, shows the additional cost that is included for this model, as discussed in Section 5.

11. Discussion of the Sample Problems

For those who may be interested in "how it all comes out," and to demonstrate how to use the STORM module efficiently, we close with some remarks about the sample scenarios.

```
                SCENARIO 3 : M / M / c / K
                COST ANALYSIS PER UNIT TIME

                        Current System      Optimal System *
Number of servers       |       2        |        3         |
Cost per server         | 4600.0000      | 4600.0000        |
Cost of service         |          9200.0000|         13800.0000|
Mean number in system   |    5.5735      |    2.5539         |
Waiting cost/customer   | 1000.0000      | 1000.0000         |
Cost of waiting         |          5573.5100|          2553.8800|
Prob of service denial  |    0.0585      |1.5213E-03         |
Arrival rate            |   38.0000      |   38.0000         |
Cost per lost customer  | 5000.0000      | 5000.0000         |
Cost of lost customers  |         11119.5300|           289.0500|
                                  ----------           ----------
TOTAL COST                        25893.0400           16642.9300

          * Optimization is over number of servers
```

Figure 6: Cost Analysis with Limited Waiting Room

11.1 Scenario 1

We saw how the initial analysis indicated that an additional machine should be acquired, and why it was desirable. There may be some lingering doubts in your mind concerning the sensitivity of this conclusion to the particular numbers you used. First, the cost of waiting was assumed to be $1,000 per customer per week. What if this figure is way off, as it may well be? You have only to return to the Editor screen, enter a different value, and solve the problem again. This is quickly done. You find that, even if this cost is reduced to $500, the recommendation is the same: get another drill press.

Suppose the arrival rate declines, as it is in imminent danger of doing? Changing it from 38 to 36 orders per week makes some dramatic changes. While the utilization remains quite high, the average queue length drops from 17.6 to 7.7 jobs, and the average time in the system is halved. Still, it remains desirable to add the third machine! Only if weekly arrivals fall to 34 do two machines become cost effective. Thus, there is considerably more sensitivity to arrival rate than to waiting cost, but the recommendation to add a machine holds up under a wide range of conditions.

11.2 Scenario 2

Here you are concerned with the effect of changing the variability of job times. By reducing the standard deviation from 0.05 to 0.025, the average queue length drops from 17.6 to 11.0. Even if we reduce the variance to zero (an unrealizable goal, presumably), the queue length only drops to 8.8. Throughout, the conclusion remains the same: three drill presses are better than two. Thus, variability of processing time is not a significant factor.

11.3 Scenario 3

You want to investigate the strategy of limiting the number of orders you will accept at any one time. If the present policy of never turning down a job (Scenario 1) is replaced by a maximal queue length of 10 orders, the average number in the system goes from 19.5 to 5.6, though the percentage of customers who are turned away (probability of service denial) is only about 6%. These numbers can be found in Figure 6. Figure 7 shows the probability distribution, where you can see how the truncation of the queue causes the graph to cut off rather abruptly at the maximal state, namely 12.

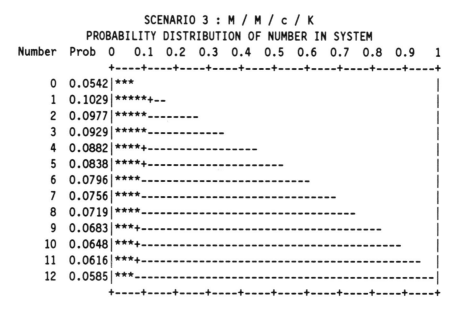

```
                  SCENARIO 3 : M / M / c / K
               PROBABILITY DISTRIBUTION OF NUMBER IN SYSTEM
        Number  Prob  0   0.1  0.2  0.3  0.4  0.5  0.6  0.7  0.8  0.9   1
                      +----+----+----+----+----+----+----+----+----+----+
            0  0.0542|***                                                |
            1  0.1029|*****+--                                           |
            2  0.0977|*****--------                                      |
            3  0.0929|*****------------                                  |
            4  0.0882|****+-----------------                             |
            5  0.0838|****+---------------------                         |
            6  0.0796|****-----------------------------                  |
            7  0.0756|****---------------------------------              |
            8  0.0719|****------------------------------------           |
            9  0.0683|***+-------------------------------------------    |
           10  0.0648|***+-------------------------------------------    |
           11  0.0616|***+-------------------------------------------    |
           12  0.0585|***------------------------------------------------|
                      +----+----+----+----+----+----+----+----+----+----+
```

Figure 7: Probability Distribution of System State
with Limited Queue Length

Allowing up to 20 jobs waiting, we only lose 2% of the orders, and the average system state is still only 9.1 jobs. Thus, it does seem possible to significantly curtail congestion in this way without losing too many orders.

Through it all, economic considerations continue to favor a third machine. One last concern of yours remains: how sensitive is the analysis to the estimate of $5,000 for the cost of losing an order? Another quick series of runs shows that, with waiting room for 10 jobs, this cost figure can range from $1,000 to $7,000 without changing the optimal number of servers from 3. If it rises to $8,000, you should add still another server.

12. Altering Problem Data Dimensions

In the Queueing Analysis module, columns (that is, service stations or scenarios) can be added or removed using the usual procedure for inserting or deleting columns. The rows, of course, have fixed functions and may not be altered.

INVENTORY MANAGEMENT CAPABILITIES

PROBLEM FORMULATION OPTIONS
- Economic order quantity model, production order quantity model or mixture of the two for item control
- Stochastic or deterministic demand
- Individual item and aggregate inventory analysis
- Allows for packaging quantity considerations

OUTPUT OPTIONS AND OTHER FEATURES
- Aggregate inventory values
  - Average working stock investment
  - Average safety stock investment
  - Cost of orders/setups
  - Average working stock carrying cost
  - Average safety stock carrying cost
  - Total number of orders/setups
  - Total expected stockouts
- Exchange tables
  - Working stock versus cost of orders
  - Safety stock investment versus stockouts
- ABC analysis report
- Ordering information for all items
- Cost information for all items
- Projected inventory status for all items
- Detailed reports for selected items

MAXIMAL PROBLEM SIZES (PRODUCTS)
- Personal version: 100
- Professional version, with 500K of net memory for STORM: 3200

FILE NAME FOR THE SAMPLE PROBLEM DATA
- INV.DAT

Chapter 13

INVENTORY MANAGEMENT

The inventory management module is devoted to the analysis and design of inventory control systems for independent demand inventory. This means that customers decide how much they are going to order and when, and that the supplier has little influence over customer actions. This is in contrast to dependent demand situations in which requirements for an item depend on the production schedule for products of which it is a part. Warehouse and retail inventories are examples of independent demand environments, whereas work-in-progress manufacturing inventories are examples of dependent demand. Dependent demand settings use the methods of material requirements planning, which are available in STORM and described in Chapter 19.

The inventory management module is designed to allow you to perform aggregate inventory analyses for all the items in an inventory grouping. For a small firm this could mean all items stocked as finished goods, whereas it may mean a product group for a larger organization. Strategic parameters such as total inventory investment and customer service level may be juggled until your inventory management objectives are achieved. Then the detailed tactical procedures necessary to implement the strategic plan may be determined. These may be transferred from STORM to an operating inventory control system. The strategic analyses that STORM supports include:

- Average working stock investment
- Average safety stock investment
- Annual ordering/setup costs
- Annual working stock carrying cost
- Annual safety stock carrying cost
- Number of orders/setups per year
- Expected stockouts per year

The more tactical/operational analyses supported by STORM are:

- ABC Analysis of inventoried items
- Determination of order quantities, reorder points
- Determination of item inventory costs
- Determination of projected item stock status

1. The Solution Procedures

The goal of this module is to allow the inventory manager to achieve the inventory goals of the organization. Customer service may be more important in one company, whereas minimizing inventory investment may be more significant in another. These are conflicting objectives which we allow you to evaluate and balance to your satisfaction.

All our analyses except the ABC analysis are based on an assumption that an economic order quantity system is the underlying inventory control system being used. We support either of two models of such order quantities which we term Economic Order Quantity (EOQ) or Production Order Quantity (POQ). The critical difference between them is that the EOQ system assumes lump sum delivery of all units ordered in a single batch, whereas the POQ system assumes that the batch will be manufactured internally. Figures 1 and 2 illustrate the assumed inventory behavior under each of these two systems. Figure 1 shows the EOQ system, where the arrival of an order causes the inventory level to jump immediately to the order quantity (EOQ). Then it is reduced gradually until a zero level is reached, at which time a new order is received. Real inventories do not behave so well, so we will relax certain assumptions of this system later in our discussion.

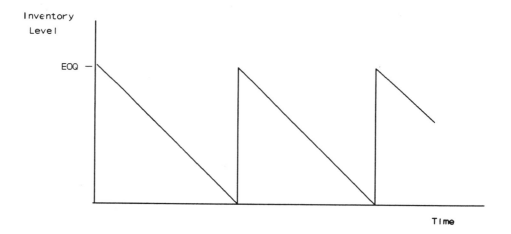

Figure 1: EOQ Inventory Behavior

Figure 2 shows the theoretical inventory behavior for the POQ system. In this case, we start the production of a replenishment quantity at the moment we run out of inventory. Some of the items being produced are immediately used up to meet demand, whereas the items in excess of that demand go into inventory. Thus, there is a gradual buildup of inventory until the batch quantity (POQ) has been produced. Because of the constant depletion, the peak inventory level shown in Figure 2 is somewhat less than the POQ. When production stops, inventory is withdrawn at the same constant rate as shown in Figure 1. It is assumed in this case that the production rate is significantly larger than the demand rate in order to allow the inventory buildup.

Several other assumptions on which both the EOQ and POQ systems rest are:

- All parameters are deterministic with their values known
- Lead times between placing and receiving an order are constant
- Inventory carrying charges are linear
- Inventory carrying charges are based on average inventory
- Inventory positions are monitored continuously
- Changes to inventory are reported instantaneously

The formulas are fairly robust in the face of violations of a number of these assumptions, but you should certainly keep them in mind when applying the module to your inventory situation.

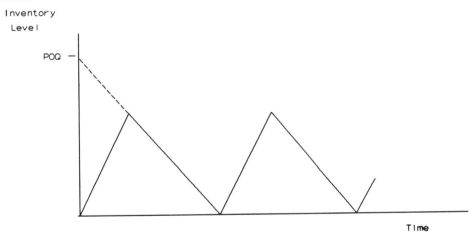

Figure 2: POQ Inventory Behavior

The EOQ system is appropriate in strictly warehouse or retail environments where no production takes place. The POQ system is appropriate in factories where an item is both produced and stocked (a factory-warehouse). There are also companies where some products are produced internally while others are ordered from suppliers, resulting in a hybrid of the two systems. STORM allows for such situations as well.

With this general introduction, we proceed to consider the strategic and operational outputs listed above. Throughout much of Section 1, the discussion will apply equally to the two systems. We will use terms that cover both when appropriate. For example, *inventory replenishment* refers to restocking, whether by external order or internal production. Otherwise, we will generally use the language of the EOQ system for simplicity, talking of orders where we mean orders/setups, etc.

1.1 Average Working Stock Investment

For each inventoried item, Figure 1 or 2 illustrates the expected inventory behavior. In each case, the average inventory of the item in units is expected to be one-half the maximal point of the respective graph. If we find this value for each item and multiply it by the unit value (in dollars) of the item, we will have the average amount invested in each item. We can then sum these for all the items in our inventory to yield the *average working stock investment*. We call this *working* stock since it is expected to be used up (withdrawn or sold) in each inventory cycle, in contrast to *safety* stock, which will be discussed later. Figures 1 and 2 clearly show that the larger the order quantities, the larger the required working stock and working stock investment. At the same time, the number of orders placed and the corresponding ordering/setup costs will be lower. Also, given the same level of customer service, there will be fewer opportunities to stockout and thus fewer expected stockout occurrences.

1.2 Average Safety Stock Investment

A safety stock of inventory represents units above the expected demand for an item which we use to absorb *excess* demand when it occurs. We will provide more explanation of this concept later in the chapter. For every item in inventory, the *safety stock investment* is computed by multiplying the units of safety stock by the unit value of the item. These investment values are then summed for all items to compute the total safety stock investment. It is not unusual in environments where a high variation in demand exists and/or a high service level is desired that this investment will be two or more times as great as the working stock investment.

1.3 Annual Ordering/Setup Costs

If we are simply ordering batch quantities of product from suppliers for lump sum deliveries, we must pay a certain variable cost to place such an order, independent of the amount ordered. This is typically a fairly small amount, especially if we have a computerized ordering system. In a manufacturing setting, however, we may have to set up equipment solely to produce a POQ, and this may be quite expensive. For each item, the number of orders/setups required annually is multiplied by the cost per order/setup. The sum of these figures over all items gives the total cost of all orders/setups per year. This is an expense item, as opposed to investment for working stock and safety stock listed above.

1.4 Annual Working Stock Carrying Cost

This is simply the average investment in working stock multiplied by the carrying charge rate. The carrying charge rate, expressed as a fraction of the unit value of the item, reflects expenses such as insurance, taxes, space charges, etc., along with the opportunity cost of having your money tied up in inventory. Typical values fall in the 25 to 35 per cent range.

1.5 Annual Safety Stock Carrying Cost

This is analogous to the working stock carrying cost. It is computed by multiplying the inventory carrying charge rate times the average investment in safety stock.

1.6 Number of Orders/Setups per Year

The total number of orders/setups per year is computed so that the workload on either the purchasing department or the setup personnel can be determined. Referring again to Figures 1 and 2, this value is obtained by first dividing the total annual demand for each item by its order quantity (EOQ or POQ) to determine the number of orders per year. Then we sum these numbers for all items.

1.7 Expected Number of Stockouts per Year

Let us now consider the consequences of relaxing the classical assumption of the EOQ and POQ models that demand is deterministic and known. Instead, we will assume that the *average* demand per unit time is known for each item, but that from month to month it may vary randomly about its mean value. Thus, at times of unusually high demand, we may find the stock on hand inadequate to satisfy all customers.

We define a *stockout* to be an inventory order cycle in which not all the demand can be met. We do not consider in our cost analysis the number of units short, nor the length of time for which we are in a shortage situation. Hence, the service level that you input refers to *the percentage of inventory order cycles in which we expect to meet all demand.*

The expected number of stockouts for each inventoried item is the proportion of inventory cycles in which we expect to stockout (100 - service level), times the number of orders per year (inventory cycles).

1.8 ABC Analysis of Inventoried Items

ABC analysis is simply a way of categorizing items according to their dollar importance. Various rules of thumb have been suggested for the categorization, but the fundamental concepts are always the same. Class A items represent the small proportion of inventoried items that account for the large proportion of the dollars. Class C includes the large proportion of inventoried items that account for a small proportion of the dollars. Class B items are in between. Class A items are subjected to the most rigorous monitoring and control actions followed by class B and finally class C. The rules of thumb that STORM uses are:

Class A	*10% of the Items*
Class B	*40% of the Items*
Class C	*50% of the Items*

Practically speaking, the user can always override this categorization when implementing these procedures.

The ABC analysis starts with the computation of the total dollar flow associated with each item. This is simply the product of the unit value times the annual demand. Then the list of items is sorted in descending order of this quantity in order to put the high dollar flow items at the top of the list. The first 10% of the items are classified as A, the next 40% as B, and the last 50% as class C items. A detailed report of this list is available during the output phase of the program, which will be described later.

1.9 Determination of Order Quantities/Reorder Points

The computation begins by applying the popular square root formula for either the EOQ or the POQ, depending on the value of the production rate. For lump sum deliveries, the production rate for an item is left at the default missing value.

In this case, the EOQ formula will be applied:

$$EOQ = \sqrt{\frac{2dk}{h}}$$

where d = demand rate
        k = cost to place an order
        h = inventory carrying charge $= iv$
        i = inventory carrying charge rate
        v = unit value

If a positive production rate, p, exceeds the demand rate that is entered, the POQ formula will be used:

$$POQ = \sqrt{\frac{2dkp}{h(p-d)}}$$

A production rate smaller than the demand rate is clearly an infeasible situation, and will be detected and reported as such.

The computed figure for the EOQ or the POQ may have a fractional part, so the next step is to convert it to an integer value. We do so by considering the next larger and next smaller value about the computed value, and choose the one with the smaller total cost. If there are no packaging quantity considerations, this concludes the computation of order quantities. Otherwise, there is one additional step.

Many products come in packaged quantities of a certain number of units. For example, soft drinks may come in cases of 24 bottles or cans per case. It is unlikely that a computed order quantity would be an integer multiple of the packaging quantity, yet it is clear that you may have to order such multiples. In the input data area, there is a column headed PACKAGING which has a default value of one. If a particular product must be ordered in multiples of a packaging quantity, you enter the packaging quantity in this column (24 in the soft drink example). If the computed order quantity (EOQ or POQ) is not an integral number of packages, the module will round up and round down to find the nearest integral values. It will compute the total cost for each, and select the one with the lower total.

Once the order quantity is determined, we need to know when to place the order, which will be determined by the reorder point. Up to now we have assumed in our discussion that reorders can be obtained, or production initiated, instantaneously. In practice there is usually a delay between initiating a request for replenishment and having it ready for use. This *lead time (LT)* is one of the parameters you will be asked to specify. Although in reality it is often of uncertain length, the module assumes that you can make a reasonably accurate estimate and treats lead time as a constant.

The *reorder point (ROP)* is the inventory position (defined as the inventory on hand plus on order) that triggers a replenishment order. The simplest example of this concept can be observed in Figure 3, which is a slightly altered version of Figure 1. Here the lead time is assumed to be small compared to the length of the *inventory order cycle:* the time between orders. Thus, the reorder point is simply the inventory level that is just enough to meet demand during the lead time. This will be modified later, when we discuss the effects of uncertain demand. It will be necessary then to increase the ROP by adding safety stock.

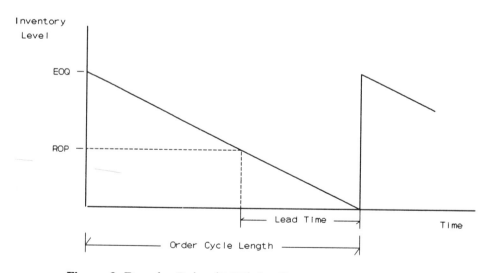

Figure 3: Reorder Point (ROP) for EOQ Inventory System

It may occur that the lead time to place and receive an order is longer than the inventory order cycle. In this case, more than one order may be outstanding for the same item at the same time. You might imagine that you have some inventory on hand, that a truck is on the way with an additional order quantity, and that you have just placed still another order with a factory that will take some time to produce and ship. For this reason, we also output the maximal number of orders expected to be outstanding at one time.

1.10 Determination of Item Inventory Costs

For each item, we know the ordering costs, the number of orders/setups required per year, the working stock carrying cost and the safety stock carrying cost. These were used to compute the aggregate values described earlier. A report is available which lists these values for each individual item in your inventory, along with the total cost for each. You may use it to determine which particular items contribute the most and the least to your total inventory associated costs.

1.11 Determination of Projected Item Stock Status

This analysis determines the minimal stock level you would expect to see for each individual item, the maximal level (just after receiving or completing an order) and the average level of stock on hand. The minimal quantity is simply the computed safety stock level. We introduce safety stocks for each item sufficient to reduce the chance of stockouts to acceptable levels. The determination of safety stock quantities can only be done if the user inputs the standard deviation (sigma in statistics texts) of demand per period for each item. Otherwise STORM will bypass this part of the computation as well as the safety stock investment described earlier. The maximal level is computed by adding the order quantity to the safety stock level for the EOQ situation, and the maximal height of the POQ curve (see Figure 2) to the safety stock level for the POQ situation.

Consider the graph in Figure 4 which represents the probability distribution of demand during the lead time. The area under the curve to the left of the mean is the probability that lead-time demand will not be greater than average. Thus, the number of units that equal mean lead-time demand represent the amount of inventory that is used up in an average cycle. These units are considered part of working stock (WS) and consequently part of the EOQ.

The area to the extreme right is the probability of a stockout (SO). These are extremely high demand values that could occur by chance, but only rarely. We do not keep enough safety stock to satisfy such demands since it is not cost effective to do so. The difference between demand large enough to cause a stockout and mean demand is the safety stock (SS). As long as demand exceeds its expected value by no more than this much, we will meet it.

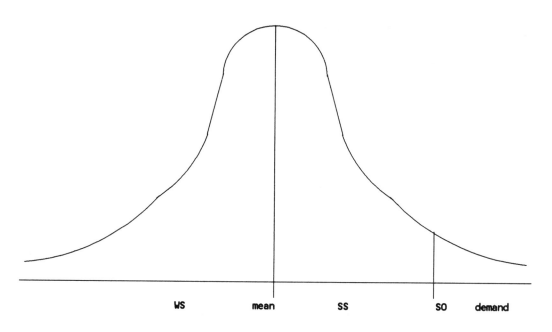

Figure 4: Probability Distribution of Lead Time Demand

Safety stock units behave differently from working stock units. Recall that the average working stock for an item is one-half the maximal height of the inventory level in Figures 1 and 2. Relaxing the assumption of constant demand, Figure 5 illustrates the inventory behavior we might observe in an EOQ system. The lower dashed line shows the safety stock level. In one half the cycles we expect to use none of it. Most safety stock simply waits in inventory for unusually high lead time demand to occur. Clearly, it is very expensive to carry safety stock in inventory. This is why forecast accuracy is important in independent demand inventory situations; it helps reduce safety stock required to guarantee the same service level.

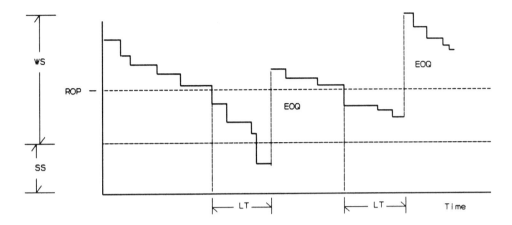

Figure 5: EOQ Inventory Behavior with Stochastic Demand

We assume in this analysis that the distribution of demand during the lead time approximates the familiar normal (bell-shaped) curve, as shown in Figure 4. When we input a service level, this means that we can determine how much more than the mean demand to stock to keep the chance of stockout at the desired value. Specifically, we can find the number of standard deviations to the right of the mean that corresponds to an area of [(100 - service level)/100] in the right tail of the normal distribution. This number of standard deviations we term k, the safety factor, and it may be obtained from standard normal tables. For each item, it is multiplied by the standard deviation of lead time demand to compute the safety stock in units.

You may be wondering how to obtain the standard deviation of demand per period to use in this analysis. If your company does not currently keep records to allow this to be computed, such a record-keeping system could be implemented internally. Modern, computer-based inventory control systems are now available to track such values automatically.

In the meantime, if you have a value for the standard deviation of demand on some time basis other than the standard time period (for example, you have an estimate of the quarterly sigma), it may be converted to an estimate of the standard deviation per time period as follows:

$$sigma(PD) \quad = \quad sqrt(PD/OT) \bullet sigma(OT)$$

where *sigma(PD)*   =   estimate of the standard deviation of per period (*PD*) demand

   sigma(OT)   =   the standard deviation of demand over some other time (*OT*)

   sqrt(PD/OT)   =   square root of the number obtained by dividing the time period by the other time (both times measured in the same units)

For example, assume that the standard deviation of quarterly demand *(sigma(OT))* for an item is 10 units, and the standard time (*PD*) is 2 months. Then, since two months is two thirds of a quarter,

   sigma(2)   = $[sqrt(2/3)](10) = (.816)(10) = 8.2$ units

2. A Sample Problem

Table 1 shows the problem description entries for a 10-item inventory problem, whereas Table 2 has the problem detailed data. The data are from a maintenance department so the items listed are maintenance spare parts.

```
Number of Items . . . . . . . . .      10
Cost to Place and Order . . . . .  $5.00
Default Carrying Charge Rate. . .     25%
Periods per year. . . . . . . . .      52
Default Service Level . . . . . .     95%
```

Table 1: Problem Description for the Sample Inventory Problem

3. Data Entry Using STORM

The problem appears as in Figure 6 after data entry has been completed. In the Problem Description area the entries include the title line, the number of items, the default order/setup cost, the default inventory carrying charge rate as a *percentage (%)*, the number of periods in the work year for your organization (used in computation of reorder points and to change your standard deviation values if you change your lead times) and your default service level. The default order/setup cost requires some explanation. Since you are allowed to mix EOQ and POQ situations, the order/setup cost may not be common to all items, yet many of them may have the same value. The value that you enter in the Problem Description will be assigned to every item in the Data area which you leave as a missing value (.) entry. Thus, you will only have to change the value for the items which have different order/setup costs.

Item Name	Item ID	Demand Per Period	Unit Value	Standard Deviation of Demand Per Period	Lead Time
Blades	1	4	$0.80	14	2
Switches	2	19	1.50	29	3
Plates	3	8	0.70	40	1
U-Joints	4	10	1.00	25	1
Elbows	5	8	0.60	35	1
Bolts	6	192	0.50	181	2
Valves	7	2	2.00	8	6
Elec Cords	8	2	12.00	5	7
Nuts	9	12	0.20	60	1
Screws	10	192	0.08	563	3

Table 2: Problem Data for the Sample Inventory Problem

The default service level works in the same fashion. You may have a general service level which you wish most items to observe. You may override it by making an entry in the detailed data area for a particular item.

The Problem Data area has a number of columns as shown in Figure 6 that must be explained. To begin, we see the row labels at the extreme left of the matrix that have been edited from the default values of ITEM 1, ITEM 2, etc. The next column is an item ID which must be a number of no more than ten digits. This is followed by the estimated demand rate *per period* (to keep all units consistent) for each item. Next, we input the unit value for each item. The item unit value may be the purchase price for commodities bought for resale. For manufactured items, it will include the price of purchased materials and components plus value added.

The next column is the ordering or setup cost for each item, depending on whether it is purchased or manufactured. Initially, a dot signifies the use of the default value from the Problem Description area. This may be overridden as needed. This is followed by the item carrying charge rate, which works the same way.

```
┌──────────────────────────────────────────────────────────────────────────┐
│         ┌───────────────┤ STORM EDITOR : Inventory Management Module├──────────┐
│ Title : TOOL CRIB PARTS ANALYSIS                                            │
│ Number of items        :       10 │ Default Order/Setup cost  :       5.    │
│ Default carrying rate, % :     25. │ Time periods per year     :      52.    │
│ Default service level, % :     95.                                          │
│                                                                             │
│ R1  : C1     ITEM  ID DEMAND/PD  UNIT VALUE ORDR/SETUP CARRY RATE  SIGMA(PD) │
│ BLADES           1      4.         0.8          .         .           14.    │
│ SWITCHES         2     19.         1.5          .         .           29.    │
│ PLATES           3      8.         0.7          .         .           40.    │
│ U-JOINTS         4     10.         1.           .         .           25.    │
│ ELBOWS           5      8.         0.6          .         .           35.    │
│ BOLTS            6    192.         0.5          .         .          181.    │
│ VALVES           7      2.         2.           .         .            8.    │
│ ELEC CORDS       8      2.        12.           .         .            5.    │
│ NUTS             9     12.         0.2          .         .           60.    │
│ SCREWS          10    192.         0.08         .         .          563.    │
│         └───┤ Enter item identification number for BLADES    ├->├      ├─────┘
└──────────────────────────────────────────────────────────────────────────┘
```

Figure 6: Sample Inventory Problem After Data Entry

```
┌──────────────────────────────────────────────────────────────────────────┐
│         ┌───────────────┤ STORM EDITOR : Inventory Management Module├──────────┐
│ Title : TOOL CRIB PARTS ANALYSIS                                            │
│ Number of items        :       10 │ Default Order/Setup cost  :       5.    │
│ Default carrying rate, % :     25. │ Time periods per year     :      52.    │
│ Default service level, % :     95.                                          │
│                                                                             │
│ R1  : C5    CARRY RATE  SIGMA(PD)  LEAD TIME SERV LEVEL  PACKAGING  PRODN/PD │
│ BLADES           .        14.         2.         .          1          .     │
│ SWITCHES         .        29.         3.         .          1          .     │
│ PLATES           .        40.         1.         .          1          .     │
│ U-JOINTS         .        25.         1.         .          1          .     │
│ ELBOWS           .        35.         1.         .          1          .     │
│ BOLTS            .       181.         2.         .          1          .     │
│ VALVES           .         8.         6.         .          1          .     │
│ ELEC CORDS       .         5.         7.         .          1          .     │
│ NUTS             .        60.         1.         .          1          .     │
│ SCREWS           .       563.         3.         .          1          .     │
│         └───┤ Carrying charge rate as % (. for default value)  ├->├   ├─────┘
└──────────────────────────────────────────────────────────────────────────┘
```

Figure 6 (continued): Sample Inventory Problem after Data Entry

Next, we come to the standard deviation of demand per period (SIGMA (PD)). It may be left as a missing value if it is not available and cannot be estimated, but the stockout and safety stock analyses cannot be done. These are important parts of an aggregate inventory analysis which should be done if at all possible. The lead time *in periods* between placing and receiving an order should be entered in the next column. If the lead time is any number other than 1.0, the standard deviation of demand per period will be modified by the formula listed earlier in the chapter to account for this. In general, anytime you lower the lead time, you will lower the safety stock required to provide the same customer service level, and vice versa. Fractional values may be input for the lead time if needed to reflect your suppliers' delivery schedules.

The next column is the item service level. This works exactly like the order/setup cost and carrying charge rate discussed above. The packaging quantity is the next entry, and it was discussed in detail in Section 1.4. The default value of 1 means that an item can be ordered in any integer quantity, so the user must override this value for any item that comes in a packaged quantity greater than one. We have kept the default values for our sample problem. The final column is the production rate, which applies only to the POQ items (if any) in the inventory analysis. Since we have none in our problem, we leave each entry in this column at the default missing value. This column will appear even if you have no POQ items. Note that you are allowed to mix EOQ and POQ items in the same inventory analysis.

4. Execution of the Module

For this module, considerable computation time may be required to complete the analyses for large inventory problems.

The first item on the output menu is aggregate inventory values. You may have certain inventory objectives for these values, such as a certain level of investment, customer service, etc. You may experiment with the aggregate analysis until you are satisfied, and then request the detailed reports listed later on the menu. The module provides a series of aggregate information outputs. The first of these is shown in Figure 7 for our sample problem. You may receive more or less information on this report, depending on the entries in your data set.

Most of the entries in Figure 7 are self-explanatory or are explained in Section 1. The first three items in Figure 7 (carrying charge rate, service level, and total number of items) are just an echo of input information to help you document this run. Note that EOQ and POQ statistics will be reported separately and then totaled for hybrid situations; otherwise only the appropriate one will have statistics reported. Also, the stockout and safety stock investment will only be reported if the standard deviation of demand per period was provided.

```
                    AGGREGATE INVENTORY VALUES
                 Inventory carrying charge = 25.00%
                       Service level = 95.00%


     Total number of items . . . . . . . . . . . . . . . .         10
     Average working stock investment ($) . . . . . . . . . .   846.46
     Average safety stock investment ($) . . . . . . . . . .    963.02
     Total inventory investment ($)  . . . . . . . . . . . .   1809.48

     Cost to order EOQ items ($/yr)  . . . . . . . . . . . .    210.42
     Average working stock carrying cost ($/yr) . . . . . . .   211.63
     Average safety stock carrying cost ($/yr)  . . . . . . .   240.76
     Total inventory cost ($/yr) . . . . . . . . . . . . . .    452.39
     Total cost ($/yr) . . . . . . . . . . . . . . . . . . .    662.81

     Number of orders for EOQ items  . . . . . . . . . . . .        42

     Expected stockouts  . . . . . . . . . . . . . . . . . .         2
```

Figure 7: Aggregate Inventory Values

The next two outputs available from this module are exchange tables. These allow you to answer managerial *what if* questions about inventory-related issues. For example, what if a cash flow problem exists and there is a need to reduce inventory investment? Both working stock and safety stock investment analyses need to be performed to answer this question. A useful way to proceed is to compute exchange tables that show the trade-offs to be made in such a case. The first one provided in the module shows working stock investment versus the cost of orders/setups as a function of the inventory carrying charge rate (Figure 8). The second shows safety stock investment versus stockouts as a function of the desired service level (Figure 9).

```
             WORKING STOCK EXCHANGE TABLE
     Carrying              Working         Cost  of
     Charge,%              Stock,$         Orders,$

      15.00                1089.91          163.39
      20.00                 944.02          188.64
      25.00                 846.46          210.42
      30.00                 770.95          231.00
      35.00                 715.12          249.03
```

Figure 8: Working Stock Exchange Table

If funds are becoming more scarce, it makes sense to *charge* yourself more for their use to invest in inventories. This would involve raising the carrying charge rate. This makes carrying inventory more expensive so the order quantity formulas will force a reduction in order quantities, which will reduce average inventory. The problem is that the smaller order quantities mean more frequent orders must be placed and we are therefore trading investment for expense. These effects are illustrated in Figure 8 for our example.

You can make a managerial choice as to what level of investment to support knowing the consequences in terms of ordering/setup expense. You should be advised, however, that there is an interaction effect between orders placed (which is influenced by the carrying charge rate) and stockouts. The more orders placed, given the same desired service level, the greater the number of stockout occurrences due to the larger number of inventory order cycles. To keep stockout occurrences constant, you would have to raise the desired service level which would force you to raise safety stock investment, thereby counteracting the earlier reduction in working stock investment!

The exchange table is set up to list only five different values of the carrying charge rate. These computations may be time consuming since they require five times as much work as the original aggregate value results. Default values for these five rates will be displayed. You may accept or change them via the use of a STORM form.

The other exchange table (see Figure 9) is for safety stock investment versus stockouts. In this case, the desired service level influences the trade-off. The higher the service level, the higher the safety stock investment, but the lower the resulting stockouts. Due to the interaction effect described above between the inventory carrying charge rate and this table, the carrying charge rate is also displayed here. Both the inventory carrying charge rate and the service levels desired may be changed via the STORM form.

```
              SAFETY STOCK EXCHANGE TABLE
               CARRYING RATE = 25.00 %
        Service          Safety          Annual
        Level,%          Stock, $        Stockouts

        90.00            750.60          4.21
        92.50            852.12          3.16
        95.00            963.02          2.10
        97.50           1142.96          1.05
        99.99           2172.56          4.21E-03
```

Figure 9: Safety Stock Exchange Table

The fourth item listed is a detailed ABC analysis report. This is a list of inventoried items sorted in descending order of total dollar flow, as described in Section 1.6. It is shown in Figure 10 for the sample problem listed earlier. The first column of this report is the item rank, which simply refers to the item's position in the sorted list. The *Item Name* and *Item ID* columns repeat the input data columns for your convenience in interpreting the output. The annual usage is the product of demand per period for each item times the number of periods per year times the unit value. The next two columns are *cumulative* in nature and are the basis for the ABC classification. The *% of Items* column gives the cumulative percentage of the items in inventory represented by all the items listed to this point. The *% of $* column gives the cumulative percentage of the total dollars spent on all inventoried items to this point. The final column lists the ABC class to which the item has been assigned. Until the *% of Items* column reaches 10%, all items are classified as A. The next 40% of the items are classified as B, so the cumulative per cent of items reaches 50% of the total (10% class A plus 40% class B). All other items are classified as C items.

The next item on the output menu is another detailed report (see Figure 11) that lists ordering information. The Item Name and Item ID are listed first for your convenience. Then the total number of orders (for EOQ items) or setups (POQ) for each item is listed. The next column lists the order quantity, followed by the reorder point. Finally, the maximal number of orders expected to be outstanding at any time is listed for each item. This information may be used to implement these results in an operating inventory control system. You may also get this same information for selected items rather than all of them. To do this simply select the last item on the output menu.

ABC ANALYSIS

Item Rank	Item Name	Item ID	Annual Usage, $	-- Cum. % of -- Items $ Usage		ABC Class
1	BOLTS	6	4992.00	10.00	49.52	A
2	SWITCHES	2	1482.00	20.00	64.22	B
3	ELEC CORDS	8	1248.00	30.00	76.60	B
4	SCREWS	10	798.72	40.00	84.52	B
5	U-JOINTS	4	520.00	50.00	89.68	B
6	PLATES	3	291.20	60.00	92.57	C
7	ELBOWS	5	249.60	70.00	95.05	C
8	VALVES	7	208.00	80.00	97.11	C
9	BLADES	1	166.40	90.00	98.76	C
10	NUTS	9	124.80	100.00	100.00	C

TOTAL ANNUAL USAGE = $10080.72

Figure 10: ABC Analysis Report

ORDERING INFORMATION

Item Name	Item ID	Orders / Setups	Order Size	Reorder Point	Max Orders Outstanding
BLADES	1	2.0	102	41	1
SWITCHES	2	6.1	162	140	1
PLATES	3	2.7	154	74	1
U-JOINTS	4	3.6	144	52	1
ELBOWS	5	2.5	167	66	1
BOLTS	6	11.2	894	806	1
VALVES	7	2.3	46	45	1
ELEC CORDS	8	5.5	19	36	1
NUTS	9	1.8	353	111	1
SCREWS	10	4.5	2234	2180	1

Figure 11: Ordering Information

The next report (see Figure 12) gives annual figures for the ordering/setup cost, the working stock carrying cost, the safety stock carrying cost and the total cost (sum of the previous three) *for each item*. This allows you to determine exactly how each item is contributing to the total inventory associated costs. Once again, if you want this information for only one or a few items, you may select the last menu item and choose the Item Names desired.

ANNUAL COST INFORMATION

Item Name	Item ID	Order Cost	Working Stock Cost	Safety Stock Cost	Total Cost
BLADES	1	10.20	10.20	6.60	27.00
SWITCHES	2	30.49	30.38	31.13	92.00
PLATES	3	13.51	13.47	11.55	38.53
U-JOINTS	4	18.06	18.00	10.50	46.56
ELBOWS	5	12.46	12.53	8.70	33.69
BOLTS	6	55.84	55.88	52.75	164.47
VALVES	7	11.30	11.50	16.50	39.30
ELEC CORDS	8	27.37	28.50	66.00	121.87
NUTS	9	8.84	8.83	4.95	22.62
SCREWS	10	22.35	22.34	32.08	76.77

Figure 12: Cost Report

The final report (see Figure 13) lists projected inventory levels for each item. The report begins with the Item Name and ID for each item. Then the minimal expected on hand quantity is listed, which is simply the safety stock. The maximal expected on hand inventory is the safety stock plus the peak of the working stock graph (see Figures 1 and 2). The expected average on hand quantity is midway between the minimum and the maximum.

You may wish to obtain a detailed report for only one or a few of the items in your complete data set. To do so, select the last item on the output menu. It will allow you to obtain outputs for any combination of items and any combination of the ordering information (Figure 11), the cost report (Figure 12) and the projected inventory status (Figure 13).

5. Tips on Using the Inventory Module

The inventory module was designed to allow you to investigate and experiment with aggregate inventory relationships. When using it, you should make a lot of changes in the data set and examine the results on aggregate inventory values. Two key variables to change in such experimentation are the default inventory carrying charge rate and the default service level. If all other values remain constant, raising the carrying charge rate has the effect of lowering the order quantities which in turn lowers the working stock investment, but raises the cost of orders/setups.

PROJECTED INVENTORY LEVELS

Item Name	Item ID	Minimal Quantity	Maximal Quantity	Average Quantity
BLADES	1	33	135	84
SWITCHES	2	83	245	164
PLATES	3	66	220	143
U-JOINTS	4	42	186	114
ELBOWS	5	58	225	141
BOLTS	6	422	1316	869
VALVES	7	33	79	56
ELEC CORDS	8	22	41	32
NUTS	9	99	452	276
SCREWS	10	1604	3838	2721

Figure 13: Projected Inventory Status

Similarly, raising the service level increases the required safety stock investment, but lowers the expected stockouts. There is an interaction between the carrying charge rate and the service received by customers as measured by stockouts. If the carrying charge rate is increased and the service level kept constant, the increased number of inventory order cycles will lead to an increased number of stockouts. Thus, if you desire to cap the number of stockouts at a certain level, you will have to raise the service level to do so.

When experimenting with data input values, we suggest trying *what if* scenarios involving different variables in isolation, and then examining their combined effects. In addition to the two mentioned above, you may experiment with the cost to place an order/setup to see what effect lowering these costs might have. If the impact is large, brainstorm with colleagues to try to determine ways to lower these costs. If the impact is small, you have found out without a lot of effort that it is not worth improvement attempts.

Another pair of variables frequently worth some experimentation are the standard deviation of demand and the lead time between placing and receiving orders. The standard deviation of demand per period may reflect the accuracy with which demand for a product can be forecasted. If so, improved forecasting may result in a need for less safety stock by reducing the standard deviation per period. You could try scenarios such as *what if we lowered these standard deviations by 10%; what would be the bottom line impact?* Similarly, shortening lead times will reduce the size of safety stocks needed in the square root fashion described earlier in the chapter. If you believe that you could work with your vendors to achieve lead time reductions, you could determine the estimated effect of different reductions via the inventory module.

As a final idea, many companies use different policies with respect to different classes (ABC) of inventory. For example, higher service levels may be set for class A items as compared to class C. You may wish to run the ABC analysis and obtain a listing, then go back to edit the data and change the default service level and/or carrying charge for different classes of items to see the resulting effects.

6. Altering Problem Data Dimensions

All columns are fixed in the Inventory Management module so that none can be added or deleted. Since each row represents an item, rows can be added or deleted as long as the minimum of 1 or the appropriate maximum is not violated.

- NOTES -

FACILITY LAYOUT CAPABILITIES

PROBLEM FORMULATION OPTIONS
- Equal department size problem
- Euclidean or rectilinear distance measure
- Symmetric or asymmetric matrix option for cost matrix, flow matrix or both for data input
- Fixed location assignments
- User-supplied initial solution (optional)

OUTPUT OPTIONS AND OTHER FEATURES
- Final layout diagram of relative department positions
- Sorted list of department interaction values
- List of departmental objective function values
- Generate random initial solution and resolve
- User-defined two department exchanges
- Save best solution found to data set
- Modified steepest descent pairwise interchange algorithm

MAXIMAL PROBLEM SIZES (DEPARTMENTS)
- Personal version: 50
- Professional version, with 500K of net memory for STORM: 150

FILE NAME FOR THE SAMPLE PROBLEM DATA
- LAY.DAT

Chapter 14

FACILITY LAYOUT

The facility layout problem consists of deciding where to place each department in the total floor space available. Such placements will influence material handling costs and whether the facility operates in a smooth and efficient manner. Facility layout in practice may involve a two-stage process. The first is deciding where the departments will be placed relative to each other, while the second involves exact architectural drawings that consider the placement of aisles, doors, windows, rest rooms, drinking fountains, etc. STORM supports only the first phase of layout analysis.

In many cases, the manufacture of the product (or service) dictates a serial flow layout arrangement termed a *product layout*. In that case Phase 1 of the layout analysis is essentially done and you bypass the need for the methods incorporated in STORM. The other type of layout is termed a *process layout* and is exemplified by a classic job shop. In the job shop, machines of the same type (lathes, milling machines, punch presses, etc.) are grouped together to form homogeneous work centers. Products are routed through the work centers (departments for layout purposes) depending on the processing needs for each product. The result appears to be random routing with jobs starting and ending at many different places. The objective in laying out such a facility is to place close together departments that have a high rate of product flow between them. This will minimize the distance over which material must be moved and thereby the material handling costs.

There are two generally recognized forms of the layout problem. The equal department size problem assumes all departments in the layout require the same amount of space and have the same rectangular shape (length and width dimensions). The unequal department size problem relaxes these assumptions and requires only that the sum of all departmental space requirements is less than or equal to the total space available.

Layout algorithms have been specifically designed to treat one or the other version of the problem, but both types can be used, with some ingenuity, to solve either type of problem. STORM uses an equal department size algorithm, but we discuss how to use it to analyze unequal department size problems in Section 5.4. First, there is another way to classify layout algorithms which we need to consider.

Layout algorithms may be said to be *construction* algorithms or *improvement* algorithms. Construction algorithms assume that no current layout exists and create one based on the problem data. Improvement algorithms assume a beginning layout (typically input by the user) and try to move departments around in the layout so as to decrease the materials handling costs. STORM allows you to input a beginning layout or, if you choose not to, it will generate a reasonable one for you. Then it uses an improvement algorithm to produce a heuristic solution (we cannot guarantee that the solution found is optimal).

1. The Solution Algorithm

The solution procedure is a modified steepest descent pairwise interchange method (SDPIM). The complete SDPIM considers the change in cost for exchanging the locations of every possible pair of departments. It then exchanges the pair that yields the greatest cost improvement, after which it restarts the whole move evaluation cycle. If there are N departments in the layout, there are [N(N-1)/2] possible exchanges which can be considered. The SDPIM considers all of them, makes the best one and then reconsiders all of them. It continues this process until no improvement results from any other two-department exchange.

To understand the modification of this procedure that has been incorporated into STORM, consider the way the complete SDPIM will probably work for most problems. Early in the solution process, there are usually many exchanges that will yield large improvements. Out of all such exchanges (we'll call them successes), we make only the best one, which may not be appreciably better than the next several. Still, we have used a lot of computation time to make this decision. On the other hand, later in the solution process we have a hard time finding *any* successes, so we must evaluate all possible moves.

The STORM strategy is to let you define the number of successes (successful exchange evaluations) you want the program to find before it goes ahead and makes the best exchange it has discovered so far. Of course, if it tries every exchange possible without reaching this number, it will select the best one available. If you set this triggering number to one, STORM immediately exchanges any two departments it finds that will reduce cost, and then continues to evaluate other exchanges from this point forward.

If you set the number of successes equal to [N(N-1)/2], you will get the full SDPIM. You may also select and experiment with intermediate strategies.

The logic of this approach is twofold. First, if in the early stages of computation many successes are being found, STORM will not continue exhaustive computations before exchanging two departments. Yet remember that unless you set the number of successes to one, we are still selecting the best exchange to make from all those that improve the solution. As the computations proceed, it will typically take more and more total *evaluations* to get the *same* number of successes. Thus, we focus computational effort where it is needed most.

Second, this procedure allows you to generate different heuristic solutions (called local optima) by simply changing the number-of-successes parameter. The complete SDPIM always yields the same answer with the same input data.

2. A Sample Problem

A local university is in the process of building a new business school and assigning faculty personnel to offices. The Operations Research Department has been called upon to assign faculty to offices so as to facilitate interaction among colleagues who routinely work together. In such cases, the office assignments will be as close together as possible. Each office will be 12' x 13' in size and there are a total of eight professors in the department. The department will occupy one floor of the new building and this floor has eight office spaces and a central 12' x 13' space reserved for the elevator and rest rooms. Figure 1 shows the schematic for this problem.

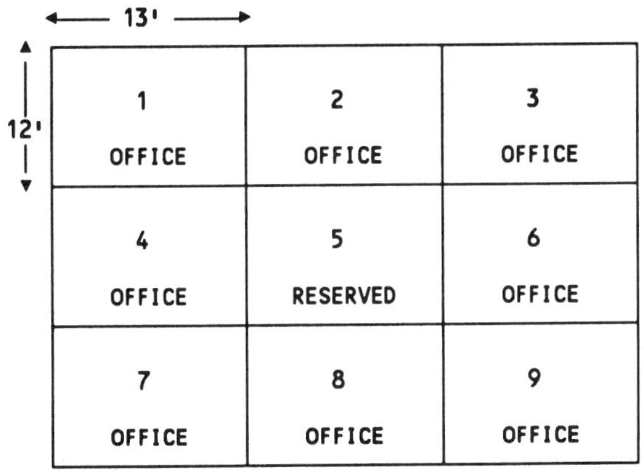

Figure 1: Operations Research Department Space

Table 1 shows a From-To Chart or flow matrix. It shows how many round trips per month each professor makes from his/her own office to the office of each colleague. The cost per unit distance per unit flow is assumed to be equal for all professors. Therefore, it can be assumed to be one in every case and we will simply be trying to minimize the total distance traveled by all the professors.

FROM \ TO	Prof 1	Prof 2	Prof 3	Prof 4	Prof 5	Prof 6	Prof 7	Prof 8
Prof 1	-	4	1	2	1	1	0	0
Prof 2	2	-	3	2	2	8	0	0
Prof 3	2	4	-	3	0	3	3	0
Prof 4	8	3	3	-	3	2	5	0
Prof 5	2	3	0	2	-	2	0	0
Prof 6	3	9	3	2	2	-	5	0
Prof 7	1	0	2	2	0	3	-	0
Prof 8	0	0	0	0	0	0	0	-

Table 1: From-To Chart Showing Frequency of Interoffice Visits

3. Data Entry Using STORM

The above problem appears as in Figure 2 once the data have been entered. Only that part of the data which fits in one screen is shown. There are several items in the Problem Description area in addition to the standard title line. Each is discussed below.

3.1 Number of Departments

This is the total number of real (non-empty) departments in the layout. There are nine in our problem including the reserved space.

3.2 Distance Measure

The distances between layout areas may be measured as either Euclidean or Rectilinear. Illustrations of each are shown in Figure 3. All distances are measured from department center to department center. Euclidean distances are appropriate when the layout area is very open and movement within it can follow a direct path. Rectilinear (sometimes called

```
┌─────────────── STORM EDITOR : Facility Layout Module ┤───────────────┐
│ Title : OPERATIONS RESEARCH FACULTY OFFICE ASSIGNMENT                 │
│ Number of departments  :      9 │ Distance (EUCL/RECT)  :    RECT     │
│ Number of depts down    :      3 │ Department width      :    13.      │
│ Department height        :     12. │ Symmetric matrices    :    NONE     │
│ Successful evaluations :      5 │                                      │
│                                                                       │
│ R15 : C6      PROF 1      PROF 2      PROF 3      PROF 4      PROF 5      PROF 6 │
│ FIXED LOC        .           .           .           .           .           . │
│ USER SOLN        .           .           .           .           .           . │
│ FLOW   1        .          4.          1.          2.          1.          1. │
│ FLOW   2       2.           .          3.          2.          2.          8. │
│ FLOW   3       2.          4.           .          3.          0.          3. │
│ FLOW   4       8.          3.          3.           .          3.          2. │
│ FLOW   5       2.          3.          0.          2.           .          2. │
│ FLOW   6       3.          9.          3.          2.          2.           . │
│ FLOW   7       1.          0.          2.          2.          0.          3. │
│ FLOW   8       0.          0.          0.          0.          0.          0. │
│ FLOW   9       0.          0.          0.          0.          0.          0. │
│ COST   1        .          1.          1.          1.          1.          1. │
│ COST   2       1.           .          1.          1.          1.          1. │
│ COST   3       1.          1.           .          1.          1.          1. │
│ COST   4       1.          1.          1.           .          1.          1. │
└──────┤ Enter the unit cost from PROF 4 to PROF 6      ┤->┤      ┤──────┘
```

Figure 2: Data Entry for Office Layout

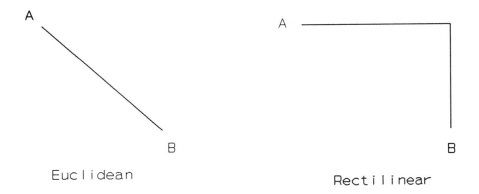

Euclidean   Rectilinear

Figure 3: Distance Measures

rectangular) distance is more appropriate for layouts with aisles or hallways where one generally reaches a destination after making one or more right turns. It tends to be much more useful in layout problems, whereas Euclidean distance is often preferred in Facility Location or Vehicle Routing problems.

3.3 Number of Departments Down

This is the number of departments required to stretch from the top to the bottom of our entire layout area. In Figure 1, office spaces 1, 4, and 7 reveal this number to be three offices down. We divide this number into the total number of departments to compute the number of departments across the layout area (again it is three in our example, as office spaces 1, 2, and 3 reveal). If the result of this division is not an integer, it will be rounded up to the next integer value. This means you can have more departmental spaces than you have departments, which is not unusual in new layouts where room has been left for expansion. Unless you specify otherwise in your starting solution (discussed later), STORM will assign all such unused locations around the edge of the layout and move them around if doing so improves the layout. You are not allowed to enter any flow or cost data for these unused locations: zero flow and zero cost will be assumed. If this assumption is invalid or if you wish to control the location of these areas, you will need to declare them as real departments, but you can still enter zero flow and cost for them. Then you can fix their position (discussed later) if you choose to control their location assignments.

You should also note that if you change this entry in subsequent analyses for your problem, you will need to reconsider any beginning solution or fixed location assignments you may have made, since the location numbers will now have different meanings. These assignments are discussed in Section 3.8.

3.4 Department Width

As shown in Figure 1, this is the distance across the top of any department (13' in our example). It, along with the height (to follow) are used by STORM to compute the distance from location to location. This saves you from putting in a distance matrix in addition to the flow and cost matrices required.

3.5 Department Height

This is the other dimension of the rectangular or square department area (12' in our example). It is important that this be consistent with the number of departments down (Section 3.3 above) to correspond to the total layout area.

3.6 Symmetric Matrices Declaration

A symmetric matrix is one in which the entries above the diagonal (that is, the *main diagonal* of a matrix, running from the upper left to the lower right corner) are mirror images of those below it. Thus, the entry in row 1, column 2 is equal to the value in row 2, column 1, and so on. In layout problems, it is frequently the case that the cost and distance matrices are symmetric, but the flow matrix is not. In STORM, the distance matrix is always symmetric, but the user must declare which of the others are symmetric. The options are:

    NONE = None
    FLOW = Flow matrix only
    COST = Cost matrix only
    BOTH = Both flow and cost matrices are symmetric

If you declare the flow matrix to be symmetric, then you enter data on only *one* side of the diagonal (your choice) and leave the remaining entries as dot defaults (.). However, if a cost matrix is declared symmetric, you will find that the upper right entries (above the diagonal) have been defaulted to 1, while the entries on and below the diagonal are dot defaults. As discussed in Section 3.8, a "cost" of 1 is the appropriate choice in the case that you simply wish to minimize the total "ton-miles" of material transported. If your costs vary depending on the two departments involved, you will have to change these default values. If you declare the cost matrix as asymmetric, all the default entries except the diagonal entries will be 1.

If you begin your analysis by choosing one of the options listed above, and then later change your mind, it will be your responsibility to change all the entries in the Problem Data area to match your choice. Otherwise, STORM will inform you that there are problems with your data and will not perform the layout analyses.

3.7 Number of Successful Evaluations Before Exchange

This is the number described in Section 1 in connection with the modified steepest descent pairwise interchange algorithm. It must be in the range 1 to [N(N-1)/2] where N is the total number of departments, including empty ones.

3.8 Data Entry in the Problem Data Area

Having completed the entries in the Description area, we proceed to the rows in the Data area. There are several different types of entries to make in this area.

Fixed location assignments (FIXED LOC)

The *fixed location* assignments allow you to declare any departments to be assigned to permanent locations. The locations are numbered in the layout from left to right and top to bottom as shown in Figure 1. Location numbers may be fixed, up to the total number of departments. Fixed location assignments are especially useful for departments like shipping and receiving, which must be on the perimeter of the layout. They must agree exactly with any initial solution you wish to submit. The default value of a dot (.) is used for departments that are not fixed. In the example, only the department called *Reserved* is fixed; it must remain in location 5. A 5 is placed in the FIXED LOC row (off-screen in Figure 2) for this department.

User supplied beginning solution (USER SOLN)

The USER SOLN row may be skipped (left as dots), in which case STORM will generate its own initial solution and then try to improve on it. If you choose to enter one, there is one strict requirement you must meet before STORM will solve your problem. These assignments must agree exactly with any fixed location assignments you have made. The solution you enter may be a complete solution (all departments are assigned to locations) or a partial solution (not all departments are assigned to locations). If you enter a partial solution, STORM will complete it to start the computational process.

The flow matrix (FLOW 1, FLOW 2, ...)

Next the flow matrix is entered according to whatever option you declared regarding its symmetry. If you declared this matrix to be asymmetric, you must make entries both above and below the diagonal. If you declared it as symmetric, you may enter the data *either* above or below, but not both. The flow data values are defaulted to dots (interpreted as zeroes), and should be in common units throughout (pallet loads, hand truck loads, pounds, pieces, or whatever), and apply to a common time period (week, month, year, etc.). They may be obtained from the combination of routings and sales volume statistics in manufacturing applications. If unavailable in any documented form, they may be physically observed and recorded over a representative time period.

The cost matrix (COST 1, COST 2, ...)

The last entries constitute the cost matrix. The values of these entries are defaulted to 1. These default values are chosen because in many layout problems the cost per unit distance per unit flow is assumed to be equal in every case. The objective is then simply to minimize the total flow-distance product. This can be accomplished by leaving the cost entries at their default values. Recall that if costs are symmetric, the ones will be found *above* the diagonal. The rest of the matrix is filled with dots.

If these costs differ, perhaps due to the use of different material handling devices, then it is important to understand how they are used in computing the objective function (cost) for the layout. For example, assume an entry of $0.01 in the cost matrix. This means it costs $0.01 to move one unit load over one unit distance. Thus, it would cost $0.05 to move five unit loads over one unit distance (1 foot, for example). Similarly, it would cost $0.10 to move one unit load over ten units of distance. Finally, it would cost (6 x 7 x 0.01) = $0.42 to move six unit loads over seven units of distance. The value to be input as cost is then *the cost per unit distance per unit load.* For any given layout, the program will compute the total cost of moving all loads over all distances by multiplying the corresponding entries in the three matrices, flow times cost times distance, and summing over all entries. The flow and cost matrices remain constant through all these computations, but the distance matrix is constantly changing as we move departments around in the layout.

4. Solving the Layout Problem

Once you complete the data entry and select *Execute the model with the current data set,* STORM will take your initial solution (if provided) or its own, and try to improve on it by moving departments around in the layout. It will go one iteration at a time if you want to see what is being moved where, or it will go all the way to a final local optimum solution if you so direct. A *local optimum* is a layout for which any pairwise exchange of departments would increase the cost. The solution cannot be claimed to be globally optimal, however, since we have not considered three-way exchanges (move A to B, B to C, and C to A), four-way exchanges, etc. To completely enumerate all these possibilities for even moderate-sized problems is beyond the scope of present day microcomputers. Therefore, you should plan to experiment with alternative solutions to your layout problem. STORM provides you with certain outputs and post-solution options to facilitate such experimentation. Figure 4 shows the menu from which you may review these outputs and exercise the options. You obtain this menu when STORM has found a local optimum for your problem.

```
      FACILITY LAYOUT : POST SOLUTION ANALYSIS

1)    Draw layout
2)    Department interaction values
3)    Objective function by department
4)    Generate a random initial solution and resolve
5)    Perform user defined exchanges
6)    Restart solution process from current solution
7)    Save best solution found as user solution
```

Figure 4: The Post Solution Menu

The Layout Matrix

The first output from the menu in Figure 4 is a layout matrix as shown in Figure 5. It shows the department assigned to each location in the current solution and the total cost of the solution.

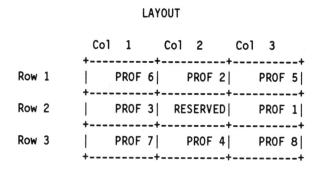

```
                    LAYOUT

            Col  1      Col  2      Col  3
            +----------+----------+----------+
    Row 1   |   PROF 6|    PROF 2|    PROF 5|
            +----------+----------+----------+
    Row 2   |   PROF 3| RESERVED|    PROF 1|
            +----------+----------+----------+
    Row 3   |   PROF 7|    PROF 4|    PROF 8|
            +----------+----------+----------+

   Total objective function value = 2287
```

Figure 5: Solution to the Layout Problem

Ranked Interaction Values

A second output, shown in Figure 6, is that of *Ranked Interaction Values*. This value is provided for every *pair* of departments and is presented in descending order. It is computed for a pair of departments by (1) multiplying the flow from the first to the second by its cost per unit distance per unit flow value, (2) making the analogous computation for the flow from the second department to the first, and (3) summing them. The result is the total cost of moving *all* flow between these two departments one unit distance. To minimize the costs of a layout, any two departments that have a high value of this interaction term (relative to other department pairs) should be located close together. Using this sorted list, you may examine the layout to see if highly ranked department pairs are *not* close together, and take action accordingly. The process to move departments around in the layout is described below. This output is independent of any particular layout. It depends only on the input data and will not change unless the input data changes. The other outputs will vary as a function of the layout being used at the time you request them.

Objective Function by Departments

A final output illustrated in Figure 7 lists the departments with the total interaction cost for each. This includes the cost of flows from the given department to all others, and from all others to that department, divided by two. The division is necessary to avoid double-counting and to have the departmental sums add up to the total cost. The objective of providing these values by department is to let you see if departments with a high total are generally more centrally located, and those with a low total more on the periphery. If not, a chance to change the layout will be presented later.

Generate a Random Initial Solution and Resolve

This is one of the options provided to help you search for better solutions to your layout problem. You may have STORM randomize the initial assignments (except for fixed location assignments), and rerun the analysis. This option recognizes that final solutions are sensitive to beginning solutions and allows you to have different beginning solutions generated for you automatically. This is a very convenient and powerful option which you may run repeatedly (10, 20 or more times) to generate a lot of solutions from which to choose the best.

```
DEPARTMENTAL INTERACTION VALUES  -  SORTED
   Department        Department     Interaction
   PROF 2             PROF 6          17.00
   PROF 1             PROF 4          10.00
   PROF 6             PROF 7           8.00
   PROF 4             PROF 7           7.00
   PROF 2             PROF 3           7.00
   PROF 1             PROF 2           6.00
   PROF 3             PROF 4           6.00
   PROF 3             PROF 6           6.00
   PROF 2             PROF 5           5.00
   PROF 3             PROF 7           5.00
   PROF 4             PROF 5           5.00
   PROF 2             PROF 4           5.00
   PROF 1             PROF 6           4.00
   PROF 5             PROF 6           4.00
   PROF 4             PROF 6           4.00
   PROF 1             PROF 3           3.00
   PROF 1             PROF 5           3.00
   PROF 1             PROF 7           1.00
   PROF 6             PROF 8           0.00
   PROF 5             PROF 8           0.00
   PROF 5           RESERVED           0.00
   PROF 2             PROF 7           0.00
   PROF 7             PROF 8           0.00
   PROF 6           RESERVED           0.00
   PROF 5             PROF 7           0.00
   PROF 7           RESERVED           0.00
   PROF 8           RESERVED           0.00
   PROF 2             PROF 8           0.00
   PROF 2           RESERVED           0.00
   PROF 3             PROF 8           0.00
   PROF 3           RESERVED           0.00
   PROF 1           RESERVED           0.00
   PROF 1             PROF 8           0.00
   PROF 3             PROF 5           0.00
   PROF 4             PROF 8           0.00
   PROF 4           RESERVED           0.00
```

Figure 6: Ranked Interaction Values

```
OBJECTIVE FUNCTION VALUES FOR DEPARTMENTS
                          Contribution
        Department         to objective

        PROF 1                352.00
        PROF 2                365.50
        PROF 3                267.50
        PROF 4                472.00
        PROF 5                195.00
        PROF 6                444.50
        PROF 7                190.50
        PROF 8                  0.00
        RESERVED                0.00

    Total objective function value = 2287
```

Figure 7: Cost Associated with Each Department

Perform User Defined Exchanges

We indicated above that the outputs from Figures 6 and 7 were to allow you to study the solution in Figure 5 and try to *second guess* it. This option allows you to experiment with the current solution by exchanging pairs of department locations and observing the cost effect. Figure 8 shows the Candidate Selection form you use to tell STORM which departments to switch. When you choose your first one, it will disappear from the list from which you will choose your second. Figure 9 shows the display you will receive informing you of the results of your switch. As you can see, our switch of departments 4 and 7 made the solution *worse*. This will always be true of the first such switch you make from a local optimum. Later switches may reverse this trend and eventually lead you to an improved solution. You may continue to exchange pairs as long as you like. After each exchange you may continue to make more exchanges or return to the output menu.

```
USER DEFINED EXCHANGES                          CANDIDATES

                                                PROF 1
                                                PROF 2
Select first department  :                      PROF 3
                                                PROF 4
                                                PROF 5
                                                PROF 6
                                                PROF 7
                                                PROF 8
                                                RESERVED
```

Figure 8: Candidate Selection Form for User Defined Exchanges

```
            USER DEFINED EXCHANGES


    Select first department  : PROF 4

    Select second department : PROF 7

    Objective value before change =        2287
    Objective value after change  =        2573
                                     ------------
                        Savings =            -286
```

Figure 9: The Results of a User Defined Exchange

Restart Solution Process from Current Solution

Anytime you make some user defined exchanges so as to create a different solution from the local optimum STORM had computed, you may want to let STORM restart the solution process with your new solution as the initial solution. If so, simply choose this option on the menu. This is still another way of experimenting with various solutions to your layout problem.

Save Best Solution Found as User Solution

When you experiment with the layout module to generate many solutions for your problem, you may forget exactly which solution provided the lowest total cost. Do not despair, for STORM remembers it and saves it in your computer's memory while you are experimenting. Anytime you obtain a new solution which is better than the previous best, STORM saves the new one. When you are ready to stop the session, you may want to save the best solution found to your data set for future reference. The selection of this option allows you to do so. You must save your data set to disk before exiting STORM to preserve the solution. When the solution is saved, it will be your initial solution the next time you use the layout module. This means you are starting off at a local optimum, so you will have to experiment with one of the approaches described above to learn anything new about your problem.

5. Tips on Using the Layout Module

We have already stressed the importance of computing many solutions to your layout problem and choosing the best one. In the previous section, a number of facilities which STORM provides for this purpose were explained. In particular, the relevant discussions were headed:

- Generate a random initial solution and resolve
- Perform user defined exchanges
- Restart solution process from current solution
- Save best solution found as user solution

There are a few additional tips which we list and explain below.

Following all these suggestions may seem too laborious. Remember, however, that layout problems are mathematically complex combinatorial problems for which good solutions may be hard to find. In addition, major investment decisions hinge on those solutions. Once implemented, they will be both costly and time consuming to reverse. Thus, it is imperative that we find the very best layout we can.

5.1 Solve Unconstrained Version of the Problem First

Regardless of the true situation, enter the most *unconstrained* version of your problem into STORM to begin and solve it. For example, if you have some departments which are considered fixed in their current locations, do not indicate this in your data set initially. Instead, solve the problem as though they could be placed anywhere in the layout and record the total cost of your best solution. Then systematically introduce your constraints one at a time and obtain additional solutions. You can observe *how much* it is costing you to impose these constraints, as opposed to relaxing them. If the costs of observing them is very great, you may have the justification you need to change the constraints.

5.2 Experiment with the Number of Successful Evaluations

In the Problem Description area (see Section 3.7) we described the parameter which controls the number of successful exchanges STORM tries to find before selecting the best one and making the exchange. This parameter provides still another means of experimenting with your problem to find different solutions. You could set this parameter to a value of 1 to begin, solve the problem, increase the parameter by 1 solve the problem, and so on. At some point, you will probably start to get the same final solution every time, which suggests terminating this mode of experimentation. You will have to go back to the STORM Editor to change this value, but it only takes a short time to do that.

5.3 Controlling the Location of Vacant Departments

In some problems, you may have more locations than you have real departments. For example, suppose you have 10 departments in a layout, and the facility could hold 12 (it is a 3 by 4 layout). Then there are two *vacant* departments which, if you do not declare as *real* departments, STORM will initially place in the last two positions in the layout. It will also assume it can move these departments to any location in the layout it desires. If you want to control the locations of such vacant spaces, you should declare, in this example, that you have 12 departments. Then you could name the two vacant ones VACANT 1 and VACANT 2, for example, and fix them in any two locations in the layout you desire. You would leave their flow matrix entries at the dot default value.

5.4 Solving Problems with Unequal Department Sizes

You can *trick* the STORM layout module into solving an unequal department size problem by a clever entry of the input data. There is a process which we recommend, which should work reasonably well for most problems.

To begin with, you should always first solve the problem as an equal department size problem with square departments (enter the department height and width as the same value in the Problem Description area). Allow each department to occupy only one space in the layout, regardless of its true size relative to the other departments. The purpose of this step is to determine a solution which tells you the *relative* positions in the layout which the departments should assume with respect to each other. Once you have a good solution to this problem, you would use it to guide a new data entry process (described below) which lets each department take up one or more spaces in the layout, depending on how much area the department truly needs.

For the entry of the new problem, you should compute a *common denominator* department size (we will call this a *block*) so that each department requires some rough integer multiple of this amount. The smallest department in the layout may provide a good value of the area needed for the common denominator. Convert this area to *square dimensions* so that the department height and width will be entered as the same in the Problem Description area (we can change this later). For each department, determine the number of these blocks required to provide all the space the department really needs. We will enter departments that need two or more blocks as two or more departments in the layout.

Now total the number of blocks needed for all departments, and decide how many blocks down and across you want in your layout. Next work out an initial solution for the revised problem which puts the departments in the same *relative locations* which resulted when you solved the problem as an equal department size problem with each department occupying only one space in the layout. Each department is now made up of several blocks. The department must be allowed to move, but the blocks which make it up must stay together. Two blocks can be forced to remain together by adding a large *dummy* flow between them. The dummy flow should be a large round number (such as 100,000), and the corresponding cost should be left at the default value of 1.0. This will make it easy to subtract these dummy costs out of the final solution STORM provides.

The blocks which make up a department should be bound together in a long chain, rather than in a box or rectangular shape. Thus, if department 1 is made up of five blocks, we might label these 1a, 1b, 1c, 1d and 1e. We should bind each of these blocks to its adjacent ones with a dummy flow, but not to the others (otherwise, the entire set will be locked in one position and unable to move). Thus, we would bind 1a to 1b, 1b to 1c, etc. This will allow the blocks to "*snake*" their way across the layout. Use one of the central blocks, such as 1c in our example, to enter the true flow between this department and all other departments. Leave the flows from all other blocks of this department to all other departments at the dot default. You are now ready to enter this solution and its corresponding data into STORM and solve the problem. Don't be surprised if your initial solution is a local optimum. Since we based it on a local optimum from the equal department-sized solution, it should be a very good solution to start. If it is a local optimum, proceed to use options such as *randomize the initial solution and resolve* as described in Section 4 to further experiment with your revised, unequal department size problem.

5.5 Moving Several Products Between a Pair of Departments

It may happen that the flow between two departments is comprised of several types of products, each with its own amount of flow and its own unit cost of transportation. Suppose there are two products, A and B, which have flows of fA_{12} and fB_{12} loads from department 1 to 2. The corresponding costs per unit load are cA_{12} and cB_{12}. If there is no flow from department 2 to 1, we could split these up and enter one of them as the latter flow. If there are other flows from 2 to 1, however, we must proceed in another manner.

Specifically, we will multiply the corresponding costs and flows together and enter the result in the flow matrix. Thus,

$$f_{12} = fA_{12} \cdot cA_{12} + fB_{12} \cdot cB_{12}$$

where f_{12} is the flow to be entered in the flow matrix. We will leave the cost matrix value at its default of 1.0. The extension to more than two products follows the same reasoning.

6. Altering Problem Data Dimensions

Adding or deleting a department from a layout problem can become tricky, so great care should be exercised when performing such an operation. Each such operation involves *two* rows (a flow matrix row and a cost matrix row) as well as a column headed by the department name. The first two rows of the Data area are fixed and cannot be deleted. Thus, row three is the first place a row may be inserted. When a row is inserted, STORM will automatically add its matching row and column in their appropriate locations. Similarly, when a column is inserted, the two rows will be added in their proper positions. Naturally, these inserted rows and column will be filled with default values, and it is your responsibility to enter the correct data. Row or column deletions behave similarly.

You may also need to make changes in other sections of the problem data, so that they will conform to the changes you make with insertions or deletions. These changes may be required for the following items (See Figure 2 and Section 3 of this chapter):

- Number of depts down (Problem Description area)
- FIXED LOC (Problem Data area)
- USER SOLN (Problem Data area)

STORM will keep track of the number of departments in the layout (a Problem Description area entry) for you automatically.

ASSEMBLY LINE BALANCING CAPABILITIES

PROBLEM FORMULATION OPTIONS
- Single-model, deterministic line balancing problems
- Automatic multiple operator stations for tasks with task times greater than the cycle time
- Tasks designated to be the only task at a station

OUTPUT OPTIONS AND OTHER FEATURES
- First pass fast heuristic, followed by second pass local optimization approach if the first solution is not optimal
- Automatic detection and reporting of *cycles* in input data (task A precedes B, B precedes C, and C precedes A)
- Work station information
    - Tasks assigned
    - Total productive time assigned
    - Total idle time remaining
    - Per cent idle time remaining
    - Number of operators assigned
- Summary information for line
    - Total operators assigned
    - Total number of work stations needed
    - Number of multiple operator stations
    - Balance delay (per cent idle time)
- Change cycle time and resolve

MAXIMAL PROBLEM SIZES (TASKS, IMMEDIATE PREDECESSORS)
- Personal version: (100, 99)
- Professional version
  Representative sizes, with 500K of net memory for STORM:
    - (235, 234)
    - (300, 150)
    - (400, 70)
    - (475, 25)

FILE NAME FOR THE SAMPLE PROBLEM DATA
- ALB.DAT

Chapter 15

ASSEMBLY LINE BALANCING

Assembly line balancing consists of assigning tasks to work stations so as to minimize balance delay (percentage of idle time) subject to certain constraints. These constraints include (1) cycle time, (2) precedence, (3) fixed location, and (4) fixed position or zoning restrictions. The *cycle time* is the amount of time initially allocated to each work station within which all tasks are to be performed. It is also the amount of time needed by an assembly line to produce one unit, and therefore may be dictated by the desired production rate. Precedence constraints restrict the order in which assembly tasks can be performed. For example, in the assembly of hand-held calculators, all internal components must have been assembled and the top and bottom case (housing) seated before the top and bottom can be fastened together with screws. Fixed location restrictions typically refer to heavy pieces of equipment used in the assembly process that are already in place and are not to be moved. Finally, positional restrictions refer to heavier product assemblies (major appliances, for example) where the assembler cannot pick up a unit and put it in any position. Thus, it may be positioned to allow front and back assembly on opposite sides of the line for a while, followed by top and bottom positioning. The changing of the position is generally accomplished by mechanical means.

STORM explicitly treats cycle time and precedence constraints. However, the user may treat the other two types by clever manipulation of our procedures. See the hints in section 6 of this chapter for more information on how to do this.

There are many other complications that may arise in assembly lines. Space must be allowed for the placement of components to be assembled. Time to obtain a tool or part may be needed at certain work stations. Time to return to a beginning work position may be needed if an operator moves along the line with the assembly. Pay rates may vary according to the most difficult task assigned to a work station. Assemblers may object if idle time is not evenly divided between work stations. Other considerations could be listed, but our point is that the person analyzing the assembly line will typically need to review computer-generated line balances, keeping in mind any practical considerations concerning the particular line. It will often be necessary to alter computer-generated balances to account for special conditions.

The STORM Assembly Line Balancing module focuses entirely on production efficiency by attempting to minimize the idle time at each work station along the line. It is a single-model line balancing procedure which assumes that only one product is assembled on a line at a time. This is in contrast to mixed model assembly lines such as those in the auto industry, where cars with different option packages, colors, etc., follow each other down the line.

Our procedures also assume deterministic or constant task times rather than stochastic or variable task times. Many companies treat the stochastic task time problem by first computing a balance using a deterministic procedure such as STORM's, and then simply adding a fixed amount of idle time to the cycle time. This practice has been demonstrated to be valid for a variety of situations.

The STORM package allows for two special features in balancing assembly lines which we wish to call to your attention. The first is the automatic handling of tasks with task times that exceed the cycle time. Suppose, for example, that a task requires 0.80 minutes to perform and the cycle time is 0.50 minutes. When this task comes up for assignment, the algorithm will automatically assign two operators to the work station since that is the minimum that will be required to complete the work. Each operator will take every other unit and each will effectively have two cycle times, or one minute, in which to complete the work. Since each will have one minute and the task requires only 0.80 minutes, the algorithm will try to assign one or more additional tasks to this station provided that the sum of all tasks assigned does not exceed 1.00. Each operator will then complete all assigned tasks on every other unit. Since multiple operator stations complicate the layout and physical realization of the line, STORM will only assign one such task to a work station even if the resulting balance at that work station exhibits a high percentage of idle time.

A second special feature allows you to isolate a task at a work station, so that no other tasks will be assigned to that station. In labor intensive assembly lines, there may be an occasional machine-based task. It would not be practical to have the operator at the station take a position to complete the machining task and then move to a new position to perform other manual tasks. It is this kind of situation for which this feature was added. To invoke this feature, the user simply leaves the dot default value for the task time of the task to be isolated. All such times will be changed to equal the cycle time when the balance is computed.

Two notes of caution are in order when using this isolation feature. First, you must take care that the cycle time you eventually adopt is never less than the true minimal task time for any isolated task in the line. Second, since we do not use such work stations in the resulting balance delay computations, you will need to check the solution carefully to insure that your criteria are being met. To illustrate, suppose you solve a line balancing problem assuming a single line which requires 17 operators, including one operator for the one isolated task in the line. Suppose you now triple the cycle time to see what will happen to balance delay if three identical lines are set up. This results in a six-operator-per-line solution (including one for the isolated task) which yields a lower balance delay. Even though the balance delay is lower, the number of operators required is 18 (3 lines times 6 operators per line) versus 17 for the single-line solution. Thus, the single-line solution is the more cost effective.

1. The Solution Algorithm

The solution procedure is a two phase heuristic algorithm which does not guarantee an optimal solution to the problem, although it may indeed find one. In the first phase, we use a fast heuristic procedure which has been shown to be a very good one. If we proceed to the second phase, we use a local optimization routine to try to improve on the first solution found. We describe each of these operations in the following sentences.

No matter which heuristic is being used, at each step the procedure must determine which tasks are available for assignment. This includes tasks for which all predecessors have been assigned to a work station or tasks which have no predecessors. Then, the set is further reduced by considering only those available tasks that fit into the time remaining to be assigned at a work station. The first phase heuristic selects a task from this set by the following rule:

> *Choose the task for which the sum of its task time and the task times of all the chains of tasks which it heads is a maximum.*

This is a slight modification of the classic Ranked Positional Weight technique. At each work station, tasks are assigned according to this rule until no other available tasks fit. Then, the next work station is completed and so on until all tasks are assigned. At this point, the program determines a lower bound on the number of operators required for the problem under consideration and compares it to the solution found. If they are equal, we can guarantee that an optimum has been found. If the solution requires more operators than the lower bound, we cannot say whether or not it is optimal. In the latter case, however, we proceed to a second stage procedure to try to improve the solution.

The second phase procedure tries all feasible combinations of tasks available at a particular station, and selects the combination which minimizes station balance delay. We call this algorithm the *Heuristic Branch and Bound Method*. This procedure may be more time consuming than our initial procedure, especially when there are many parallel tasks available for assignment at a work station. Thus our strategy is to try the first procedure and see if an optimum is found. If not, we go to the longer procedure, but use our first solution to stop computations in the second if it becomes clear that we will not improve.

2. A Sample Problem

The BAR-B-Q Grill Company is a manufacturer's outlet that sells barbecue grills to retail customers. The company is running a Saturday promotion for a rotisserie grill whereby all buyers will receive free assembly. Space does not allow all the grills to be preassembled before the sale. Therefore, the manager in charge of the promotion plans to hire students from the local high school to man an assembly line to assemble the grills as they are sold. The fastest selling rate for the grills has been estimated at one per minute, therefore the line should be able to produce at that rate. Figure 1 shows the precedence diagram for the grill and Figure 2 has a listing of the assembly tasks which are required. The task times in Figure 2 are in minutes. The manager would like to know how many students should be hired, and how to set up the line.

3. Data Entry Using STORM

The Problem Description area contains the title, number of tasks (which determines the length of the data set), maximal number of immediate predecessors (which determines the width of the data set), and cycle time. The Problem Data area includes the task number, the task time and the *immediate* predecessors for each task. Figure 3 shows the display after the data have been entered. We require that the user enter the task numbers since there is no requirement that the tasks be entered in any specific order. You may also edit the row labels on the left to assign any abbreviations that relate to the nature of the tasks, as has been done for the grill problem.

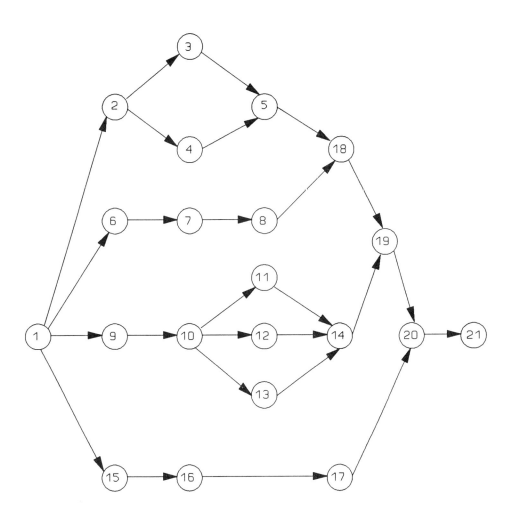

Figure 1: BBQ Grill Precedence Diagram

Task Number	Task Description	Task Time
1	Check to see that all parts are available	0.63

Hood Assembly

2	Fasten top to side	1.00
3	Attach rotisserie holder 1 to side	0.33
4	Attach rotisserie holder 2 to side	0.33
5	Inspect hood assembly	0.08

Bowl Assembly

6	Attach mounting bracket to bowl bottom	1.00
7	Insert rack into bowl	0.08
8	Inspect bowl assembly	0.05

Base Assembly

9	Connect three legs together at top	1.50
10	Connect each pair of legs with brace at bottom	2.00
11	Attach wheel to leg 1 with axle, secure hubcap	0.50
12	Attach wheel to leg 2 with axle, secure hubcap	0.50
13	Attach wheel to leg 3 with axle, secure hubcap	0.50
14	Inspect base assembly	0.17

Rotisserie Assembly

15	Slide prongs onto rod, secure	0.20
16	Attach motor to rod	0.05
17	Inspect rotisserie assembly	0.05

Final Assembly

18	Attach hood assembly to bowl assembly	1.00
19	Attach base assembly to bowl assembly	2.00
20	Insert rotisserie assembly in holder	0.05
21	Inspect completed grill	0.50

Figure 2: Assembly Tasks and Times for Grill

```
┌──────────────┤ STORM EDITOR : Assembly Line Balancing Module ├────────────┐
│ Title : BAR-B-Q Grill Company                                             │
│ Number of tasks                    :      21                              │
│ Maximal number of predecessors :          3                              │
│ Cycle time                         :      1.                              │
│                                                                           │
│ R1  : C1    TASK NUMBR   TASK TIME    PRED   1   PRED   2   PRED   3       │
│ CHECK PTS        1          0.63        .           .           .         │
│ TOP>SIDE         2          1.          1           .           .         │
│ HOLDER 1         3          0.33        2           .           .         │
│ HOLDER 2         4          0.33        2           .           .         │
│ INSP HOOD        5          0.08        3           4           .         │
│ MOUNT BRK        6          1.          1           .           .         │
│ RACK>BOWL        7          0.08        6           .           .         │
│ INSP BOWL        8          0.05        7           .           .         │
│ LEGS>TOP         9          1.5         1           .           .         │
│ BRACE LEGS      10          2.          9           .           .         │
│ WHEEL 1         11          0.5        10           .           .         │
│ WHEEL 2         12          0.5        10           .           .         │
│ WHEEL 3         13          0.5        10           .           .         │
│ INSP BASE       14          0.17       11          12          13         │
│ PRONGS          15          0.2         1           .           .         │
│ MOTOR           16          0.05       15           .           .         │
│ INSP ROTIS      17          0.05       16           .           .         │
│ HOOD>BOWL       18          1.          5           8           .         │
│ BASE>BOWL       19          2.         14          18           .         │
│ ROTIS>HOLD      20          0.05       19           .           .         │
│ FINAL INSP      21          0.5        20           .           .         │
└──────────┤ Enter the task number                    ├─>│        ├────────┘
```

Figure 3: Data Entry For Grill Problem

4. Execution of the Module

The solution output consists of two parts. The first lists the detailed solution by work station as illustrated in Figure 4. The work station information includes work station number, number of operators assigned, tasks assigned, task time for each task, idle time for the station, the idle time as a percentage and the total time for all tasks assigned to the station.

```
          FINAL SOLUTION - NOT GUARANTEED OPTIMAL
                  Cycle Time = 1.0000


   Work  Number of    Tasks                                   %
Station  Operators   Assigned    Task Time   Idle Time      Idle


    1        1     CHECK PTS      0.6300      0.0700        7.00
                  PRONGS         0.2000
                  MOTOR          0.0500
                  INSP ROTIS     0.0500
                  -----------------------
                  Total Time:    0.9300


    2        1     MOUNT BRK      1.0000      0.0000        0.00
                  -----------------------
                  Total Time:    1.0000


    3        1     TOP>SIDE       1.0000      0.0000        0.00
                  -----------------------
                  Total Time:    1.0000


    4        2     LEGS>TOP       1.5000      0.0400        2.00
                  HOLDER 2       0.3300
                  RACK>BOWL      0.0800
                  INSP BOWL      0.0500
                  -----------------------
                  Total Time:    1.9600


    5        2     BRACE LEGS     2.0000      0.0000        0.00
                  -----------------------
                  Total Time:    2.0000


    6        1     HOLDER 1       0.3300      0.0900        9.00
                  INSP HOOD      0.0800
                  WHEEL 3        0.5000
                  -----------------------
                  Total Time:    0.9100
```

Figure 4: Solution to the Grill Problem

```
            FINAL SOLUTION - NOT GUARANTEED OPTIMAL
                    Cycle Time = 1.0000
   Work  Number of    Tasks                              %
 Station Operators  Assigned    Task Time   Idle Time   Idle

    7        1      HOOD>BOWL     1.0000      0.0000     0.00
                    ----------------------
                    Total Time:   1.0000

    8        1      WHEEL 1       0.5000      0.0000     0.00
                    WHEEL 2       0.5000
                    ----------------------
                    Total Time:   1.0000

    9        1      INSP BASE     0.1700      0.8300    83.00
                    ----------------------
                    Total Time:   0.1700

   10        2      BASE>BOWL     2.0000      0.0000     0.00
                    ----------------------
                    Total Time:   2.0000

   11        1      ROTIS>HOLD    0.0500      0.4500    45.00
                    FINAL INSP    0.5000
                    ----------------------
                    Total Time:   0.5500
```

Figure 4(continued): Solution to the Grill Problem

Figure 5 illustrates the second part of the solution output, which is a summary of the solution for the entire line of work stations. It lists the cycle time, number of work stations, number of operators, number of multiple operator stations, and the balance delay for the line.

5. Post-Execution Option

After reviewing your initial run, you will be offered the opportunity to change the cycle time and resolve the problem. This could be useful in a variety of circumstances. If you are considering a one-shift versus two-shift, or a two-shift versus three-shift operation, you can simply change the cycle time accordingly. You may investigate alternative numbers of identical (or different) assembly lines. If you want to minimize the cycle time for a given number of work stations, this option may be used to experiment and try to find the answer.

```
          FINAL SOLUTION - NOT GUARANTEED OPTIMAL
                    Cycle Time = 1.0000
            Summary information for this balance

   Total number of work stations  . . . . . .      11

   Total number of operators  . . . . . . . .      14

   Number of multiple operator stations . . .       3

   Balance delay (%)  . . . . . . . . . . . .    10.57
```

Figure 5: Summary of the Solution to the Grill Problem

6. Tips on Using the Assembly Line Balancing Module

You should experiment a lot with this module to obtain alternative solutions to your line balancing problem. If you can consider going to more shifts, you should compute balances for the various options which are feasible. Then compare the solutions based on the most important criteria for your company. For many companies, this will be the total number of operators required to staff the line.

For light assembly operations requiring no expensive equipment in duplicate lines, you should experiment with adding lines until the number of assembly tasks per employee gets too large for them to be mastered. Then examine the various solutions to choose the one which best fits your needs.

It is possible to solve line balancing problems which exhibit fixed location or fixed restriction constraints by use of the STORM module. Specifically, the line may be broken down into two or more subproblems which are solved individually, and then reassembled into a complete solution. Such breakdowns are not simple and straightforward, but with some effort and experimentation, adequate results should be achieved.

7. Altering Problem Data Dimensions

The first and most important point to make about altering the problem data set for this module is that *the precedence data will not be automatically adjusted*. It is your responsibility to ensure that it is correct after all insertions/deletions have been completed. The task number and task time columns (first two in the data set) are fixed so that they cannot be deleted, nor can any new columns be inserted between them. The number of columns containing predecessors in the data layout may be altered by either insertions or deletions. Insertions are allowed only at the right extremity of the data set. You may insert columns as long as the number of columns is less than the maximum allowed by your version of STORM. Deletions are allowed until no predecessor columns remain.

Rows represent tasks and may be changed by insertions or deletions provided that certain conditions are met. First, you must always have a minimum of one task in the data set. Second, you must have one more task than the number of predecessor columns. Finally, you cannot have more rows (tasks) than the maximum allowed by your version of STORM.

INVESTMENT ANALYSIS CAPABILITIES

PROBLEM FORMULATION OPTIONS
- Multiple investment alternatives in one data base
- Different economic lives for different alternatives
- Discrete or continuous discounting
- Cash flow timing at beginning, middle or end of period
- Different cash flow timing allowed for revenues and expenses
- Different hurdle rates for different alternatives

OUTPUT OPTIONS AND OTHER FEATURES
- All or selected alternatives in each report
- Choose any combination of the following reports:
    - Present value report
    - Payback period report
    - Rate of return report
    - Plots of equivalent worth versus interest rate

MAXIMAL PROBLEM SIZES (ALTERNATIVES, PERIODS)
- Personal version: (5, 100)

- Professional version
  Representative sizes, with 500K of net memory for STORM:
    - (5, 1185)
    - (50, 675)
    - (300, 110)
    - (2350, 10)

FILE NAME FOR THE SAMPLE PROBLEM DATA
- FIN.DAT

Chapter 16

INVESTMENT ANALYSIS

Investment analysis, often applied to equipment investment and replacement decisions, is a special kind of capital budgeting. The objective is to make intelligent comparisons of alternative investment proposals. These proposals may involve different initial investment values, different operating revenues and/or costs over the lives of the investments and different salvage values at the end of their useful (economic) lives. The length of such lives may also differ from one alternative to another. To properly interpret such a diversity of cash flows so that sound investment decisions can be made requires the use of tools to convert the unequal, uneven flows into measures which can be compared.

Central to the achievement of this goal is the concept of the time value of money. If we invest $1 today at a 10 per cent simple annual interest rate, one year later we receive $1.10. This illustrates the *compounding* effect of the time value of money. Conversely, if someone offers us an investment proposal to pay us $1 one year from now, how much should we pay for such an investment? This value is called the *present value* of some future payment. Clearly, the present value is less than $1 in our example. How much less depends on what interest rate we require on our investments. The higher the rate, the *less* we're willing to pay for the same future sum. In our example, assuming a 10 per cent interest rate, we would be willing to pay $0.909 or 91 cents.

STORM treats investment proposals as being made up of some combination of (1) a purchase price, (2) a salvage value, (3) a revenue stream, and (4) an expense stream. It allows an investment proposal to be treated as a single alternative over one economic life, or as an infinite chain of alternatives. The infinite chain analysis effectively equates the economic lives of alternative investments. STORM assumes any tax effects are considered prior to data entry, so that the results are after tax results.

1. The Solution Procedures

STORM computes the values of seven different investment criteria and allows you to compare alternatives based on all of these. Five of the criteria use methods which consider and account for the time value of money in their computational procedures. The other two, simple payback period and simple rate of return, do not. These last two criteria are included in STORM because of their popularity.

1.1 Net Present Value: Single Investment

The net present value is equal to the sum of the present values of all cash inflows and outflows. The present values of the inflows (revenues and salvage value) have positive signs, while those of the outflows (purchase price and expenses) have negative signs. If the net present value is positive, it means the inflows exceed the outflows by this amount *at the given rate of interest,* and vice versa if negative.

1.2 Net Present Value: Infinite Chain

If you reinvest in another identical investment as soon as the economic life of an alternative is reached, and continue to do that ad infinitum, an infinite chain of investments of the same type would result. We can compute the net present value of such an infinite chain. As a practical matter we do not invest in the same investment over and over. However, this criterion may be used to compare investment alternatives which exhibit different economic lives. By imagining an infinite chain of investments of each type, we equate the economic lives.

1.3 Equivalent Worth

In this method, we compute the constant cash flow per period (positive or negative) which, at the given interest rate, yields the same net present value as the user-projected cash flows. This method effectively converts the net present value to a *per period* or annuity basis which may be useful in comparing alternatives of unequal lives.

1.4 Discounted Payback Period

This is the length of time required for an investment to pay back its principal plus interest at the given interest rate. Since all the cash flows resulting from the investment must be taken into account, it is possible to have several values of this measure. Thus, an investment could pay for itself by a certain time and then incur a negative cash flow which puts it back *in the red.* Conceivably, this could occur repeatedly. STORM will find all points in the economic life where *paybacks* occurred.

1.5 Simple Payback Period

This is analogous to the discounted payback period described above except that the cash flows are all considered at their user input values rather than their discounted present values. Multiple values of this measure may occur, analogously to the discounted payback period.

1.6 Discounted Rate of Return

This is the value of the interest rate which causes the present value of all outflows to equal the present value of all inflows (that is, the net present value equals zero).

1.7 Simple Rate of Return

This measure results from dividing the average cash flow per period by the average investment, and then converting it to a percentage. The average cash flow per period is defined as the average value of (Revenue - Expense) over the economic life of the investment alternative. The average investment is computed by first subtracting the salvage value from the purchase price, and then dividing this difference by 2. The division assumes a straight line decrease in asset value over the economic life.

2. A Sample Problem

A hospital lab director has been asked to add laboratory equipment for tests that have typically been done by outside contractors. The first approach available is to use four small testing machines, each of which requires an operator. Another alternative is to purchase a large automatic machine which requires only one operator to run. The large machine could accommodate a larger volume of tests, but costs more in initial investment. A summary of these alternatives appears in Table 1.

Alternative A: Small Machines

```
Purchase Price . . . . . . .    $12,500    per machine
Economic Life . . . . . . .           5    years
Capacity . . . . . . . . . .      1,000    tests/year
Operator Wages Per Year . .     $15,000    per operator
Salvage Value . . . . . . .      $2,000    per machine
Estimated Tests/Year . . . .      4,000    for years 1-5
Charge per Test . . . . . .         $20
```

Alternative B: Large Machine

```
Purchase Price . . . . . . .   $175,000    per machine
Economic Life . . . . . . .           8    years
Capacity . . . . . . . . . .     10,000    tests/year
Operator Wages Per Year . .     $20,000    per operator
Salvage Value . . . . . . .     $20,000    per machine
Estimated Tests/Year . . . .      4,000    for years 1-6
                                  5,000    for years 7-8 (new wing)
Charge per Test . . . . . .         $20
```

Table 1: Summary of Investment Alternatives

3. Data Entry Using STORM

After the data for this problem have been entered using the Editor, the display should resemble Figure 1, which has been enlarged to show all the data. There are various options available to you to analyze your problem. We will use Figure 1 to explain each of them.

In the Problem Description area, there are only three entries to make. The first is the number of investment alternatives to be considered. Since each alternative becomes a column in the Problem Data area, this entry specifies the *width* of the detailed data matrix. The second entry is the *maximal* economic life of all the alternatives. Since the cash flows are entered row by row, this determines the *length* of the data matrix. If there are unequal economic lives among the investment alternatives, all but the maximum will have excess rows which may be left at the default missing values. Finally, you choose whether to enter interest rates as fractions or percentages.

```
                ┌─────│STORM EDITOR :Investment Analysis Module │──────────┐
                │ Title : HOSPITAL LAB CASE                                 │
                │ Number of investment alternatives :        2              │
                │ Maximum economic life              :        8             │
                │ Interest rate (fraction / %)       :     PERC             │
                │                                                           │
                │                                                           │
                │ R23 : C2   SMALL MACH LARGE MACH                          │
                │ ECON LIFE          5          8                           │
                │ DISCOUNTNG      DISC       DISC                           │
                │ REV TIMING       END        END                           │
                │ EXP TIMING       END        END                           │
                │ INTEREST         15.        15.                           │
                │ PURC PRICE     50000.    175000.                          │
                │ SALV VALUE      8000.     20000.                          │
                │ REVENUE  1     80000.     80000.                          │
                │ REVENUE  2     80000.     80000.                          │
                │ REVENUE  3     80000.     80000.                          │
                │ REVENUE  4     80000.     80000.                          │
                │ REVENUE  5     80000.     80000.                          │
                │ REVENUE  6         .      80000.                          │
                │ REVENUE  7         .     100000.                          │
                │ REVENUE  8         .     100000.                          │
                │ EXPENSE  1     60000.     20000.                          │
                │ EXPENSE  2     60000.     20000.                          │
                │ EXPENSE  3     60000.     20000.                          │
                │ EXPENSE  4     60000.     20000.                          │
                │ EXPENSE  5     60000.     20000.                          │
                │ EXPENSE  6         .      20000.                          │
                │ EXPENSE  7         .      20000.                          │
                │ EXPENSE  8         .      20000.                          │
                └───────│ Enter the expense for LARGE MACH in period  8   │->│      │──┘
```

Figure 1: Data Entry for the Sample Problem

Moving now to the Problem Data area, we have the following entries to make for each alternative:

Row 1: The Economic Life (ECON LIFE)

Enter the economic life of the investment in this column. The units are whatever time units you have chosen for your analysis (years, months, weeks, etc.). Note, however, that all other data entries for each alternative, such as interest rate and cash flows, must be based on this same time unit.

Row 2: The Type of Discounting (DISCOUNTNG)

Discounting can be done on either a discrete or continuous basis corresponding to discrete or continuous compounding of interest. The default option is discrete discounting, but you may change it to continuous by simply entering a "c."

Row 3: The Timing for Receiving Revenues (REV TIMING)

The timing option on receipt of revenues allows you to enter either E = End of time period, M = Middle of time period, or B = Beginning of time period. STORM assumes this is the time at which the actual cash flow for an investment takes place. The default option is End of the time period. Choose the one that most closely approximates the timing of cash flows you expect. The choice being made in this row applies *only* to revenues. The purchase price is always assumed at time zero, and the salvage value is always assumed at the end of the economic life.

Row 4: The Timing for Paying Expenses (EXP TIMING)

This is analogous to the previous item with the same choices, except that it applies to expenses. STORM allows you to specify each separately since the timing could be different for revenues and costs for the same investment proposal.

Row 5: Interest Rate (INTEREST)

This is the desired interest rate or discount rate to be used in all present value computations. Your choice of whether to express this as a per cent (9, for 9%) or as a fraction (.09) must, of course, be consistent with your earlier selection in the Description area.

Row 6: Purchase Price (PURC PRICE)

This is the net installed price of the investment alternative (net of any salvage value of an asset which would be replaced by the proposed one). The timing of this outflow is assumed to be at time zero to start the economic life.

Row 7: Salvage Value (SALV VALUE)

This is the salvage value of the investment, if any. It is assumed to occur at the end of the last period in the economic life of the alternative. The timing of any other revenue in the last period of the economic life can thus be separated from this flow through the revenue timing option described earlier.

Row 8 and following: Revenues for Each Period (REVENUE)

This is the cash inflow, if any, for each period in the life of the investment. For example, rows 8, 9, and 10 are for the revenues from periods 1, 2, and 3, respectively, up to the economic life.

Rows following revenue rows: Expenses for Each Period (EXPENSE)

This is analogous to Revenue except that it applies to outflows. The revenues and expenses may be consolidated into a single revenue or expense by netting them before entry. The disadvantage of such netting is that if analyses are to be done for different estimates of one or the other or both, all computations will have to be done by the user before data entry. However, if each cash flow is left in its basic form, the module will perform the netting for you.

4. Execution of the Module

When you choose to execute the module from the Process menu, you will obtain the STORM form shown in Figure 2. It allows you to include all or only selected investment alternatives in your reports. If you do not want all alternatives, you will be presented with a Candidate Selection form from which you can choose the ones you want. The STORM form also allows you to select which reports you want. Figure 3 lists the investment criteria contained in the various reports.

For both the payback period and rate of return report, multiple values of an investment criterion may occur for the same investment proposal. If this occurs, STORM will find all such values and list them for you. If any measures cannot be computed, the letters *N/A* will appear in their position of the reports.

Figures 4 through 8 illustrate these reports for our sample problem. The present value report in Figure 4 favors the large machine investment alternative on all three criteria.

```
                    SELECT ALTERNATIVES

          Include all alternatives in report : y


                      SELECT REPORTS

          Present value report     : y

          Payback period report    : y

          Rate of return report    : y

          Plot of equivalent
            worth vs interest rate : y
```

Figure 2: STORM Form for Report Selection

This is due to the extra revenue we receive in years 6 through 8. The payback criteria in Figure 5 show a slight edge to the small machine due to its lower purchase price. Figure 6 shows a very close comparison for the discounted rate of return criterion, with the small machine better on the simple rate of return (this is again due to the lower purchase price for the small machine).


```
Report                 Investment Criteria

Present Value          Net Present Value (NPV)
                       NPV of an Infinite Chain
                       Equivalent Worth

Payback Period         Discounted Payback Period
                       Simple Payback Period

Rate of Return         Discounted (Internal) Rate of Return (IROR)
                       Simple Rate of Return

Plots                  Equivalent Worth versus
                       Discounted Rate of Return (Interest Rate)
```

Figure 3: The Contents of the Reports

```
                        PRESENT VALUE REPORT
                  Net Present   Net Present Value    Equivalent
   Alternative       Value      of Infinite Chain      Worth

   SMALL MACH      21020.5200         41804.9800      6270.7470
   LARGE MACH     114834.1000        170605.3000     25590.7900
```

Figure 4: Present Value Report

So far, we have mixed reviews about which investment to choose. This is very common in investment problems. We typically look at other factors to help us make these decisions. For example, do we think the technology of the equipment will change dramatically during the next five years? If so, we may prefer the small machine to minimize the purchase price, thus saving the money to invest in the new technology when it is available. If not, the large machine looks like the better choice.

```
              PAYBACK PERIOD REPORT
      Alternative  Discounted      Simple

      SMALL MACH      3.38          2.50
      LARGE MACH      4.12          2.92
```

Figure 5: Payback Period Report

```
            RATE OF RETURN (%) REPORT
      Alternative  Discounted      Simple

      SMALL MACH     30.86         95.24
      LARGE MACH     31.86         83.87
```

Figure 6: Rate of Return Report

Figures 7 and 8 show the plots for each alternative. The objective of the plots is to show how the attractiveness of the investment changes as a function of the interest rate. For our problem, the figures reveal that the alternatives are about equal at a 30 per cent interest rate. We also saw this in the rate of return report in Figure 6. We can further determine that the large machine shows greater movement as the interest rate changes. For example, if the interest rate was 10 per cent, the equivalent worths for the alternatives are roughly $10,000 (small machine) and $37,500 (large machine). Thus, if we think the interest rate might decrease from our current 15 per cent, the large machine becomes an even more attractive investment. Conversely, if interest rates were to skyrocket above 30 per cent, the large machine's equivalent worth decreases at a more rapid rate. The decision maker could take all of the above into account in considering the decision.

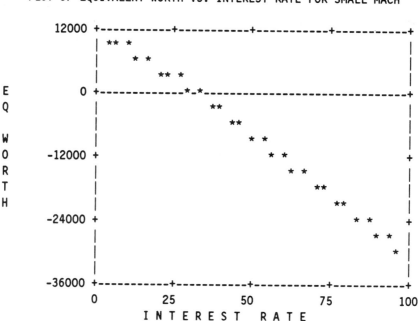

Figure 7: Plot for Small Machine

5. Tips on Using the Investment Module

The only hint we provide for this module has to do with investment proposals that have a revenue at time zero. An example of such a proposal occurred in a distribution problem where the option existed to sell some warehouses and increase transportation costs. The question was whether the sales revenue more than offset the increased operating costs. STORM requires that the purchase price be positive, and interprets it as an outflow. You can change *revenue timing to the beginning of the period, and put any such immediate inflow* in period one. If there are other inflows that would be received at the end of period one, they must be moved to period two, and so on. This will not work if other revenues have *middle of the period* timing.

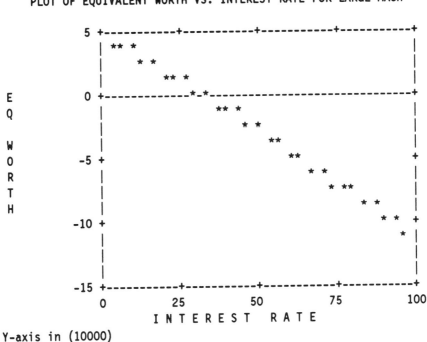

Figure 8: Plot for Large Machine

6. Altering Problem Data Dimensions

Investment proposals may be added or deleted by inserting or deleting columns in the Problem Data area. A minimum of one column (alternative) must be maintained at all times. The first seven rows of the Data area are required; therefore, no deletions nor insertions are permitted in those rows. Following row seven, you may add a period to the maximum economic life by inserting a row in either the revenue or expense section. The corresponding row will automatically be added by STORM to the other section. Deletions of periods follow an analogous procedure.

FORECASTING CAPABILITIES

PROBLEM FORMULATION OPTIONS
- Univariate time series analysis using exponential smoothing
- Automatic model selection from the following four:
    - Level model
    - Level and trend model
    - Level and seasonal model
    - Level, trend, and seasonal model
- Computer search for best smoothing constants
- User-controlled search parameters (if desired)
- Nonnegative, nonpositive or unrestricted observation values
- Integer or real valued observations
- Model fitting and model validation available
- User-controlled planning horizon for computing error statistics during model validation

OUTPUT OPTIONS AND OTHER FEATURES
- User preselects all outputs desired
- Batch mode processing for more than one series at a time, or
- Analyze mode for detailed analysis of a single series
- Summary and/or detailed reports available
- Five different error measures computed and output, including measures of bias and accuracy
- Reports available for initial conditions, model fitting, and model validation
- Future forecasts for periods beyond data base values
- Plots of actual values versus forecasts

MAXIMAL PROBLEM SIZES (TIME SERIES, MAXIMAL LENGTH OF A SERIES)
- Personal version: (5, 100)

- Professional version
  Representative sizes, with 500K of net memory for STORM:
    (10, 2850)
    (100, 600)
    (500, 120)
    (1000, 50)
    (1250, 36)

FILE NAME FOR THE SAMPLE PROBLEM DATA
- FC.DAT

Chapter 17

FORECASTING

Time series forecasting is a method for projecting past values of a regularly observed quantity into the future. There are several different ways of doing this, each with its own advantages and disadvantages. Since all assume the past is a good guide to the future, all must be used with caution. Projections should not be made so far into the future that the underlying forces creating the results are likely to have changed.

1. The Solution Algorithm

The method used by STORM belongs to the class of methods known as *exponential smoothing*. Exponential smoothing is actually a procedure for *revising* estimates of the forecast model components, so named because of the manner in which past observations are *weighted* to produce current component values. Starting with the latest observation and going backwards in time, weights applied to historical observations decrease exponentially (that is, each weight is a certain fixed fraction of the one following). Thus, the most recent observation receives the most weight, followed by the second most recent value, and so on.

The basic operation of exponential smoothing is:

New Estimate   =   Old Estimate + A Fraction of the Error

where:

New Estimate   =   The revised estimate of a forecasting model component after a new observation has been obtained and incorporated

Old Estimate   =   The most recent value of the component before the new observation became available

Error   =   The latest value of the component, as indicated by the most recent observation, minus the forecasted value for it made one period earlier (the old estimate)

Fraction   = A value between zero and one which is termed the exponential smoothing constant; it determines the responsiveness of the revision system to new observations

While this may seem a bit confusing, the effect it has is very simple. If a forecast for the current period turns out to be too low, it will be raised for the next period. If it is too high, it will be lowered. This intuitively appealing result has caused exponential smoothing systems to become the most widely used methods for operational forecasting.

When only short-term forecasting is being performed, the components of a time series requiring consideration are:

Level   = The long-run average or *level* component of a time series; it is the base component with reference to which the other components are defined

Trend   = The per period change in the level which may be linear (constant) or nonlinear; in keeping with popular practice, we consider only a linear trend

Seasonal   = This is a recurring pattern about the level component or level and trend components, which may occur in response to natural or artificial forces; the seasons of the year are illustrative of natural forces, while regular sales promotions may induce an artificial seasonality into a time series

Random   = The unexplained period-to-period fluctuations in demand not due to any of the above effects; also called noise

To illustrate the above concepts, consider a simple example. Assume that only a level component is evident in historical data for a particular product. The most recent estimate of demand is 50 units per month. This is the current value of the level component, which is also the forecast for any future period. At the end of the ensuing month, the actual demand turns out to be 60 units (the extra units being sold from safety stock). Assume that we are using an exponential smoothing constant value of 0.1. Then applying the above operation to these data we obtain:

New level $= 50 + 0.1(60 - 50) = 51$

Notice that since the forecast was too low, we raised our estimate of the level, which will increase the forecast for the next time period.

The choice of exponential smoothing constants is of great importance in these forecasting systems because of their impact of the forecast accuracy achieved. In general, the more volatile the time series, the lower the smoothing constants must be in order to avoid "chasing" the random fluctuations in the time series. The objective in forecasting such unstable series is to stay near the center rather than to chase the randomness up and down. Conversely, when the time series exhibits more stable characteristics, we are more confident that when an unusual observation occurs, it may signal a change in the demand pattern. In such a case, a larger smoothing constant is called for to incorporate the change into the forecast coefficients.

STORM allows you to select and/or modify the values of the exponential smoothing constants, or it will search for good values for you. Good values are those which minimize the error rate when we fit a model to historical data. Such values should allow the model to adjust promptly to true shifts in the behavior of the time series, but not make major adjustments in response to random fluctuations.

A second critical decision affecting forecast accuracy is the forecasting components included in the model. Of course, randomness is always present. Without it, we would have certainty, and there would be no need to forecast. A level component is always included, too, since it forms the basis of our model. The only question remaining is whether trend and/or seasonality exist. The possible answers are that neither exists, one or the other is present, or both occur. This results in four possible models:

- Level model
- Level and trend model
- Level and seasonal model
- Level, trend and seasonal model

STORM will either allow you to choose the model you wish to use for a time series, or it will select one for you. In the latter case, it selects the model which yields the greatest forecast accuracy when it fits the models to the historical data.

2. A Sample Problem

A large paint manufacturer sells pigmented acrylics for the automotive aftermarket under various labels in two basic forms: factory packs of ready-to-use colors and mixing colors. There are several thousand stock keeping units (s.k.u.'s), each with its own pattern of demand. This makes accurate forecasting of sales vitally important for inventory control.

The company wishes to include four representative products in a preliminary study. Table 1 displays the quarterly sales data over a five year period for the following products:

- An individual s.k.u. of the mixing colors sold under the Apex label.
- An individual s.k.u. of the factory packs marketed under the Bestrim label.
- The aggregate sales of all mixing colors sold as Colormatch paint.
- The aggregate sales of all products (factory packs and mixing colors) sold under the Dabiton label.

	Apex	Bestrim	Colormatch	Dabiton
	Indiv Mix	Indiv Pack	All Mix	All
1st Qrtr, 1979	1519	3071	55880	22560
2nd Qrtr, 1979	2307	3024	50832	25498
3rd Qrtr, 1979	2434	2765	72392	19956
4th Qrtr, 1979	1352	2775	89886	13142
1st Qrtr, 1980	2084	2614	77421	19940
2nd Qrtr, 1980	2329	2765	107846	20638
3rd Qrtr, 1980	3330	3348	90628	24534
4th Qrtr, 1980	2260	2931	96574	18392
1st Qrtr, 1981	3811	3136	134883	21996
2nd Qrtr, 1981	4926	2692	163524	23080
3rd Qrtr, 1981	4505	3062	160059	24660
4th Qrtr, 1981	1972	2794	116367	16049
1st Qrtr, 1982	3874	2836	133721	22526
2nd Qrtr, 1982	4775	3168	182356	24044
3rd Qrtr, 1982	4981	2539	169950	24470
4th Qrtr, 1982	3252	3092	187333	15598
1st Qrtr, 1983	3965	3220	160017	18550
2nd Qrtr, 1983	6166	3414	160910	24191
3rd Qrtr, 1983	5845	3561	170692	25076
4th Qrtr, 1983	4184	2733	200664	19225

Table 1: Sales Data for Four Paint Products

3. Data Entry Using STORM

There are just two data items required for Problem Description: the number of independent series you wish to investigate, and the largest number of observations to be entered for any one of them. Immediately after you enter these, the Editor screen will look like Figure 1. Of course, the rows at the bottom labeled PERIOD 1, PERIOD 2, etc. are for entry of the time series data (initialized to dots by STORM). There are as many such rows (most of them off screen in Figure 1) as you need for the longest series. Hereafter, we will let n denote the length of a series.

Before you reach the area where observed values are to be entered, there are several rows in which to list other characteristics of each time series, and to indicate how you want the forecasting model to be selected and designed. We will discuss each entry in the following sections. The combination of these entries allows you a great deal of control over the module, but also requires you to make many decisions. If you do not wish to consider all the options, just review the first two entries for now (sections 3.1 and 3.2), and then skip to section 4. STORM will use its default values for the other entries. These values were carefully selected to be fairly robust values. After you have gained some experience with the module, you may want to return and review the rest of the items listed below.

3.1 Type of Data Values (DATA TYPE)

Here you indicate whether the observations to be entered in this column are in the form of integers (type I) or real numbers with decimal parts (type R). If the data are integer-valued (which is the default assumption), forecasts will be rounded off to the nearest integer. Once you have entered any historical data in a column, this entry cannot be changed. Thus, be sure it is correct before entering your data.

3.2 Range of Data Values (DATA RANGE)

Specify whether the series is entirely made up of positive numbers (enter P for positive; the default option), or entirely negative numbers (enter N), or is a mixture of both (enter U for unrestricted). Actually *positive* means *nonnegative:* there can be some zero entries intermixed with the positive numbers. Similarly, *negative* means *nonpositive.*

```
|─────────────────────| STORM EDITOR : Forecasting Module |─────────────────
| Title : FORECASTING SALES: FOUR SAMPLE PAINT PRODUCTS
| Number of time series        :        4
| Maximal length of any series :       20
|
|
| R1  : C1   SERIES   1 SERIES   2 SERIES   3 SERIES   4
| DATA TYPE       INT        INT        INT        INT
| DATA RANGE      POS        POS        POS        POS
| SEASON LNG       12         12         12         12
| MODEL VAL         0          0          0          0
| PLAN HORIZ        1          1          1          1
| LEVL ALPHA      0.2        0.2        0.2        0.2
| TRND ALPHA      0.2        0.2        0.2        0.2
| SEAS ALPHA      0.2        0.2        0.2        0.2
| SEARCH ?        YES        YES        YES        YES
| STEP SIZE       0.1        0.1        0.1        0.1
| MODEL          BEST       BEST       BEST       BEST
| PERIOD   1        .          .          .          .
| PERIOD   2        .          .          .          .
| PERIOD   3        .          .          .          .
| PERIOD   4        .          .          .          .
|─────────| Enter the type of data (Integer / Real)        |→|      |─────
```

Figure 1: The Editor Screen In Initial Default State

There are several reasons why we ask for this information. The unrestricted alternative is useful when the series is actually made up of differences between two series or between successive elements of the same series. While it is convenient to be able to forecast such series (many other packages do not), it requires more computation. This can be avoided if all data is known to be of the same sign. Also, in the latter case, STORM can be helpful in detecting data entry errors such as a negative point in a positive series. It will also keep forecasts in the correct range. For example, if the series is given as positive but the forecast at some point is calculated to be negative, the module will round it up to zero.

3.3 Length of Seasonal Pattern (SEASON LNG)

This entry specifies the length of time to repeat any seasonal pattern. We will use m to represent this number of periods. It is defaulted to twelve to accommodate monthly data. An entry of four would be appropriate for quarterly data. Seasonality other than annual may occur. For example, you may have daily observations and enter seven (or five for work days) so as to reflect a weekly pattern.

3.4 Number of Periods to be Used for Model Validation (MODEL VAL)

To explain the use of this parameter, we must now go a little deeper into the functioning of the module. To begin with, STORM will divide the given series of observations into three groups, to be used for Initial Conditions, Model Fitting, and Model Validation. You are allowed to control the number of data points used for model validation, while STORM decides the others. General descriptions of the calculations performed with each of these data groups follow.

3.4.1 Initial Conditions

The earliest data are used to calculate initial values for the components of the forecasting models. Since we have not yet decided which exponential smoothing model is most appropriate, starting component values for each of the four models are found. The formulas used are quite complicated and will not be given here. For adopters of STORM who are interested in such details, they are available from Storm Software Inc. A minimum of $m+3$ periods are used to make these initial estimates, m being the length of the seasonal pattern.

After the formulas have been applied, a backsmoothing procedure is used to further improve the estimates. Backsmoothing essentially *backs* the model components to time zero, and then *walks* them through the data one period at a time, revising them by exponential smoothing.

3.4.2 Model Fitting

The data from the next set of periods are used to test the forecasting ability of each of the four models using various smoothing constant values, so that the choice of smoothing constants can be properly made. The most effective of the models is then be selected. The way in which the algorithm searches for a good set of smoothing constants is described in Section 3.7. At least one period must be used for model fitting.

Instead of allowing STORM to make these decisions for you, you may wish to specify the values of the smoothing constants to be used and/or the model desired. This can easily be done, as explained in Sections 3.7 and 3.9.

3.4.3 Model Validation

The observations used for initial conditions and model fitting may be called *estimation data.* All the remaining data, often referred to as *prediction data,* are used for validating the selected model. That is, the model is used to forecast the observations, period by period, just as it would be employed in practice. The smoothing constants are held fixed in this phase, and the estimates of the components are updated at regular intervals equal to the planning horizon to be described in Section 3.5. The results are then output, as we will see in Figure 6, to show you how accurate the forecast was in each of the validation periods. Also, summary statistics are given in other outputs (see Table 3) to help you get a sense of the accuracy you can anticipate when using the model.

Note that such an assessment can only come from a validation phase, after the model has been predetermined using other data. Sometimes a forecasting model will be touted on the basis of excellent model fitting error statistics, but this performance cannot be expected in practice, since the parameters were tailored to fit precisely those data (with benefit of hindsight).

3.4.4 Choosing the Value of MODEL VAL

Given the number of observations, n, and the length of the seasonal pattern, m, you must decide how much of the data is to be used for model validation (MV). We know from our earlier discussion that STORM requires $m+3$ observations for initial conditions, and at least one for model fitting. Thus, the value you choose for model validation must leave at least $m+4$ observations. If it does not, STORM will ignore it and use the total number of observations minus $m+4$ for MV.

How, then, should you set the value of MV? With small amounts of data, you will want to give priority to model fitting over validation. At least one seasonal pattern of periods should be available for fitting ($\geq m$) before any data is allocated to validation. Indeed, if you do not have at least this much data ($2m+3$ observations, permitting initial conditions $= m+3$ and model fitting $= m$), you would be well advised to make judgmental forecasts rather than use quantitative methods. When your file contains $3m+3$ observations, you can set $MV = m$ and perform your first model validation experiment. We suggest leaving $MV = m$ until your total observations reaches $5m$. This will allow $2m$ for inial conditions, $2m$ for model fitting and m for model validation. When you have more than $5m$ observations, you may allocate more to model validation, as you wish.

3.4.5 How STORM Allocates Data for Initial Conditions and Model Fitting

As stated previously, STORM requires a minimum of $m+3$ observations for initial conditions and one observation for model fitting. When more data than $m+4$ observations are available for these computations, STORM initially adds more to model fitting until it "catches up" with initial conditions. Then it roughly splits the data between the two until each has been allocated $2m$ observations. After that, no more data is allocated to initial conditions; the excess goes to model fitting. This is because the purpose of initial conditions is to provide crude estimates of the model coefficients which the exponential smoothing process can then revise.

3.5 Length of Planning Horizon (PLAN HORIZ)

This parameter applies *only* to the *model validation* process in STORM. In many applications, forecasts are used in operations planning to prepare rolling schedules for a number of periods into the future. This number is termed the planning horizon. You may want to see how accurate the forecasts will be over such a horizon. If so, the number of periods used by your organization should be entered here. Once STORM reaches the model validation phase, it will produce forecasts for each period in the horizon, using the values of the model components which just precede the horizon. Then the components will be updated to the end of this horizon, and the resulting values will be used to compute forecasts for the periods in the second planning horizon. This process will continue throughout the model validation phase. Of course, the default value of 1 may be accepted if you want new values computed every period. Conversely, if you want no updating, the planning horizon should be set equal to the number of periods used for model validation.

3.6 Initial Values of Smoothing Constants (LEVL ALPHA, TRND ALPHA, SEAS ALPHA)

If you wish to specify the values of the smoothing constants to use when updating the level, trend, and seasonal components, this is the place to do it. We call these *alphas* because this Greek letter is often used in texts to denote the smoothing constant. The three entries are defaulted to 0.2. In section 3.7 we describe a search option which will change these values. Thus, the entries here have a dual interpretation. If there is no search, they are the final values of the smoothing constants. Otherwise, they are the starting values for the search. The lower limit on all alphas is 0.01 and the upper limit is 1.0.

3.7 Search for Improved Smoothing Constants (SEARCH?)

In this cell, a *yes* response (the default entry) will prompt a search for good smoothing constant values, and a *no* will leave the values as specified in Section 3.6. If you decide to conduct the search, the step size specified in section 3.8 will be used in the search process. For each smoothing constant (level, trend and/or seasonal, whichever are appropriate for the particular model), STORM will determine a high, middle and low value. Initially, it uses the values from section 3.6 as the *middle* values. It first adds and then subtracts the step size (section 3.8) to determine the high and low. It tries each combination of high, medium and low values in a historical simulation, and chooses the combination which yields the lowest root mean squared error (see section 4.1.2 for a definition of this term) to be the next set of middle values. It continues this process until it reaches a point where the middle values give the best results twice in a row. This means all other combinations gave higher errors, so we have found a local optimum. We cannot say this is the global optimum because we have not tried every possible combination.

3.8 Grid Size for Smoothing Constant Search (STEP SIZE)

The step size that you specify here will determine how coarse or fine the search described in section 3.7 will be. You should be careful of very small values (0.01 for example), which may cause excessive computation times. We recommend you start with the 0.1 default value, and then use the option described in section 4.2.5 to save the results of the search to your data set. Then specify a smaller step size (for example, 0.05) and make another run. See if your errors decrease appreciably, especially your model validation errors (if you have specified a model validation period). Continue this process until the errors stop decreasing. Step sizes smaller than 0.01 are not accepted.

3.9 Choice of Model (MODEL)

This is your opportunity to pick the model to be used, rather than leaving it up to STORM to make this decision for you. You can choose any of the four models by typing *L* for the level model, *T* for the trend model, *S* for the seasonal model and *F* for the full or trend-seasonal model. The selected model will then have its smoothing constants adjusted to the *best* values, namely those that produce the smallest root mean squared error in the Model Fitting phase, as described in Section 3.8. Of course, if you have responded *no* to the SEARCH? prompt, the smoothing constants will simply be left at their initial values.

If you want STORM to make this decision for your, you should accept the default value of *B* for best. In this case, after the smoothing constants of each of the four models have been set, the model with the smallest error rate will be chosen.

3.10 Data Entry for the Sample Problem

After the data for the sample problem have been entered, the first screen will look like Figure 2. Many default options have been left unaltered. The exceptions to this, aside from the actual data at the bottom of the screen, are the seasonal length (SEASON LNG), which is four to reflect the quarterly data, and the number of periods of data to be used for model validation (MODEL VAL), which is six. As a consequence, seven periods (the minimal number) will be used to compute initial conditions, leaving seven periods for model fitting. All three are rather skimpy allocations, but with only 20 data points our options are limited.

```
-----------| STORM EDITOR : Forecasting Module |-----------
      Title : FORECASTING SALES: FOUR SAMPLE PAINT PRODUCTS
      Number of time series       :       4
      Maximal Length of any Series :      20


      R1  : C1   APEX:INDIV BEST:INDIV  COLOR:MIX DABITN:ALL
      DATA TYPE      INT        INT        INT       INT
      DATA RANGE     POS        POS        POS       POS
      SEASON LNG       4          4          4         4
      MODEL VAL        6          6          6         6
      PLAN HORIZ       1          1          1         1
      LEVL ALPHA     0.2        0.2        0.2       0.2
      TRND ALPHA     0.2        0.2        0.2       0.2
      SEAS ALPHA     0.2        0.2        0.2       0.2
      SEARCH ?       YES        YES        YES       YES
      STEP SIZE      0.1        0.1        0.1       0.1
      MODEL         BEST       BEST       BEST      BEST
      QTR 1,1979    1519       3071      55880     22560
      QTR 2,1979    2307       3024      50832     25498
      QTR 3,1979    2434       2765      72392     19956
      QTR 4,1979    1352       2775      89886     13142
      -----| This entry cannot be changed         |->|     |----
```

Figure 2: The Editor Screen After Data Entry

4. Execution of the Module

Having proceeded to the execute phase, the Forecasting Options menu shown in Figure 3 will appear. We will discuss each of the three alternatives on that menu.

```
                    FORECASTING OPTIONS

            1)   Summary report for selected time series
            2)   Detailed report for selected time series
            3)   Analyze a time series
```

Figure 3: The Forecasting Options Menu

4.1 Summary Report

If you pick the first option, you must first choose which of the time series you wish to consider at this time. To facilitate your selection, a list of all the names of the time series (the column headers) will appear in the format of Figure 4, with a Pointer that can be positioned using the Up and Down Arrow keys. Mark the selected series with an asterisk, which can be toggled on or off using the space bar. (See Chapter 3 for more information on using such Candidate Selection screens).

```
        SELECTION OF TIME SERIES                CANDIDATES

    Select time series for reports          *  APEX:INDIV
                                            *  BEST:INDIV
    Note : * marks selected series          *  COLOR:MIX
                                            *  DABITN:ALL
```

Figure 4: Form Used to Select Time Series

4.1.1 Model Selection

Having starred all four time series, we press the F7 key and the module performs the calculations we have requested. For each series, these may include the initial conditions, model fitting and model validation. While these rather computations are in progress, status reports will appear on the screen to reassure you that things are progressing.

The end result will be a report as shown in Table 2 which shows, for each series selected, the chosen model along with its smoothing constants. If a problem is encountered with some series, such as fewer data points than the minimum required, you will receive a message as to the difficulty and the action taken.

SUMMARY REPORT

	APEX:INDIV	BEST:INDIV	COLOR:MIX	DABITN:ALL
Number of Periods	20	20	20	20
Model Selected	Trend-Seas	Level	Trend	Seasonal
Level Smoothing Constant	0.200	0.100	0.100	0.200
Trend smoothing Constant	0.100	N/A	0.100	N/A
Seasonal Smoothing Constant	0.200	N/A	N/A	0.400

Table 2: Specifications of the Selected Models

4.1.2 Error Statistics

The next output provided in the summary report is a list of the statistics used to measure how well a model forecasts a time series. These statistics are computed separately for the Model Fitting and the Model Validation phases for each series, as shown in Table 3. They allow you to judge how well each selected model performs. STORM computes and reports five statistics.

```
                           SUMMARY REPORT

                  APEX:INDIV  BEST:INDIV   COLOR:MIX  DABITN:ALL
```

Model Fitting Error Statistics

```
Number of Periods         7           7          7           7
Mean Err             330.714      28.286   4330.714     868.714
Mean % Err             6.512       0.617      0.426       4.702
Mean Absolute Err    703.286     158.286  23675.290    1323.571
Mean Abs % Err        20.387       5.353     17.065       6.547
Root Mean Sq Err     836.797     178.925  24900.320    2108.906
```

Model Validation Error Statistics

```
Number of Periods         6           6          6           6
Mean Err              32.833     140.167 -14236.670      86.000
Mean % Err             1.021       3.139     -8.755       0.122
Mean Absolute Err    699.833     375.833  16863.330    1869.000
Mean Abs % Err        14.878      12.128     10.157       9.232
Root Mean Sq Err     720.939     394.710  21425.060    2275.321
```

Table 3: Performance Measures for the Selected Models

The *Mean Error* is the average of the forecast errors, or:

$$ME = [(D_1 - F_1) + (D_2 - F_2) + \ldots + (D_k - F_k)] / k,$$

where

k = Number of periods of data
D_i = Actual observation for period i
F_i = Forecast for period i

This statistic and the next one are common measures of bias. Since forecasts that are too high cancel those that are too low, *ME* will be close to zero if the model is unbiased (even if the separate errors are large).

The *Mean Per Cent Error* is just the *ME* converted to a percentage. Each error, D_i-F_i, is replaced by $100(D_i$-$F_i)/D_i$. This statistic performs the same function as *ME*, but it is a relative measure which may be compared across series. It will not be reported if any D_i

equals zero, since we cannot divide by zero.

The *Mean Absolute Error, MAE*, is computed by replacing $(D_i\text{-}F_i)$ with $|D_i\text{-}F_i|$ in the expression for *ME*. This and the two following statistics are measures of accuracy, since they penalize deviations in either direction equally.

The *Mean Absolute Per Cent Error* comes from the *MAE* by replacing $|D_i\text{-}F_i|$ by $100|D_i\text{-}F_i|/D_i$. Again a percentage error, being a relative value, is more meaningful, and again no report is provided if any D_i equals zero.

The *Root Mean Squared Error, RMSE*, is the measure of forecast accuracy used in the Model Fitting phase to choose the best model. To compute it, we average the squares of the separate errors, $(D_i\text{-}F_i)^2$, and then take the square root of the average. Squaring the errors has the same effect as taking their absolute values in that overestimates and underestimates are penalized equally. In addition, it penalizes large errors much more than small ones. The latter is especially important in practice since it is typically easier to adjust to several small errors than to one huge error.

4.1.3 Final Model Components

The last output of the summary report displays the final values of the components of the forecasting model, as of the end of the Model Validation phase. The results for the sample problem appear in Table 4. Note that components which are not part of the chosen model are marked *N/A* for *not applicable*.

4.2 Detailed Report

The second alternative on the Forecasting Options menu should be chosen if you want a more extensive report on some or all of the time series. As with the summary report, you will first be asked to indicate your selection by marking each chosen series with an asterisk, as shown in Figure 4. The ensuing reports will deal with one series at a time. We will now detail the reports we would get if we chose the first series: the single product in the Apex line. If additional series had also been requested, STORM would immediately follow these reports with the corresponding outputs for the next time series selected.

```
                          SUMMARY REPORT

                 APEX:INDIV  BEST:INDIV   COLOR:MIX  DABITN:ALL

   Final Model Components

   Level                5354.426    3016.047  202965.400   21853.360
   Trend                 194.496         N/A    7511.045         N/A
   Seasonal  1             0.969         N/A         N/A       0.987
   Seasonal  2             1.134         N/A         N/A       1.121
   Seasonal  3             1.268         N/A         N/A       1.191
   Seasonal  4             0.689         N/A         N/A       0.800
```

Table 4: Final Component Values of the Selected Models

4.2.1 Choice of Desired Outputs

Since several extensive reports are available, you will first be asked to select the ones you wish to receive. You do this using the Output Reports Selection form shown in Figure 5. You simply position the Pointer using Up and Down Arrow keys, and enter y or n to indicate inclusion or exclusion of the report (the space bar toggles the y/n choice). There is one entry on this form which asks you for how many periods ahead do you desire future forecasts. The default value is 12, which we have changed to 4 for our problem. If you want no future forecasts, enter a zero in this space.

The first three reports are on the three phases of model development: Initial Conditions, Model Fitting, and Model Validation. These reports are for the model selected by STORM or by you if you did not request the best model. A plot is also available, which presents graphically the same information contained in the Model Fitting and Model Validation tables. The Summary Error Report is typically the smallest and most important of the reports. It lists the model fitting and model validation (if appropriate) error statistics. It is here that you can easily observe whether the forecasts were as good for the model validation phase as for model fitting. There are reports for the models *not* selected if you so desire. If you choose these, you will receive quite lengthy reports which may take some time to review or print. Lastly, the input data base can be modified to reflect STORM's choice of model and smoothing constants. This is a useful feature if you want to run the module on a periodic basis to add new data as it becomes available. You may not want to go through the long set of computations to try every model every time.

In Figure 5, the default selections are shown (except for the number of periods for extended forecasts). Note that all the reports selected are for the single selected model. The omitted reports would give some of the same information for the three other models. Since the extra reports would be of the same type, we will not request them.

Keep in mind, however, that you will not get the extra reports even if you ask for them if your input data set specifies a particular model rather than indicating BEST. This is because, when the model has already been chosen, STORM performs no calculations on the others and so has no output to offer you.

```
                   OUTPUT REPORTS SELECTION

      Initial Conditions Report                              : y

      Model Fitting Report for Selected Model                : y

      Model Validation Report for Selected Model             : y

      Plots for Selected Model                               : y

      Number of Periods for Extended Forecasts (0 for none)  : 4

      Summary Error Report                                   : y

      Model Fitting Report for Other Models Tried            : n

      Model Validation Report for Other Models Tried         : n

      Plots for Other Models Tried                           : n

      Update Smoothing Constants & Model in Data Set         : n
```

Figure 5: The Output Reports Selection Form

4.2.2 Initial Conditions Report

The results of the Initial Conditions calculations for all four models are shown in Table 5. However, only the selected model will be included in the other reports, since that is all we requested. You may recall that we selected only the APEX:INDIV product so it is the only one listed in this and the following reports.

```
                    INITIAL CONDITIONS FOR APEX:INDIV
                      Level       Trend     Seasonal    Trend-Seas
       Component      Model       Model       Model        Model

       Level        2235.8000   2567.1530   2209.3590    2474.6280
       Trend             N/A     125.3712        N/A      124.3340
       Seasonal  1       N/A         N/A     0.8994        0.9366
       Seasonal  2       N/A         N/A     1.0294        1.0174
       Seasonal  3       N/A         N/A     1.4384        1.3418
       Seasonal  4       N/A         N/A     0.5974        0.6468

       Above values are based on the first 7 periods of data
```

Table 5: Initial Conditions for All Models for a Time Series

4.2.3 Model Fitting and Validation Reports

The next two reports, shown in Table 6, give step-by-step calculations of the Model Fitting and Validation phases. For each period, the forecast value is compared with the value actually observed and the difference (the error) is reported. In addition, the updated values of the components of the forecasting model are output. In the sample problem, we have a full trend-seasonal model so all these components are listed.

The next display, shown in Figure 6, repeats part of this information graphically. In this figure, data points are represented by asterisks, model fitting forecasts by the letter M, model validation forecasts by the letter V and future forecasts by the letter F. Of course, some of these may not be plotted, depending on your selections. For model fitting and model validation data points, the observations and the forecasts are plotted so that their distance apart conveys the error.

```
           TREND-SEAS MODEL FITTING STATISTICS FOR APEX:INDIV
      SMOOTHING CONSTANTS USED : 0.20(LEVEL), 0.10(TREND), 0.20(SEASONAL)
   Period         Actual    Forecast      Error      Level      Trend Seasonal

   QTR 4,1980       2260       1681         579    2777.9960   142.2373    0.680
   QTR 1,1981       3811       2735        1076    3149.9830   165.2123    0.991
   QTR 2,1981       4926       3373        1553    3620.4900   195.7418    1.086
   QTR 3,1981       4505       5121        -616    3724.4720   186.5658    1.315
   QTR 4,1981       1972       2660        -688    3708.7050   166.3325    0.650
   QTR 1,1982       3874       3841          33    3881.6710   166.9959    0.993
   QTR 2,1982       4775       4397         378    4118.2650   173.9557    1.101

           TREND-SEAS MODEL VALIDATION STATISTICS FOR APEX:INDIV
      SMOOTHING CONSTANTS USED : 0.20(LEVEL), 0.10(TREND), 0.20(SEASONAL)
   Period         Actual    Forecast      Error      Level      Trend Seasonal

   QTR 3,1982       4981       5646        -665    4191.1400   163.8476    1.290
   QTR 4,1982       3252       2833         419    4483.8950   176.7384    0.665
   QTR 1,1983       3965       4626        -661    4527.4160   163.4167    0.969
   QTR 2,1983       6166       5163        1003    4873.0090   181.6342    1.134
   QTR 3,1983       5845       6520        -675    4949.9330   171.1633    1.268
   QTR 4,1983       4184       3408         776    5354.4260   194.4962    0.689
```

Table 6: Details of Fitting and Validation of Selected Model

The next report provides all the error statistics for all four models, as can be seen in Table 7. The trend-seasonal model has been selected by STORM since it has the lowest model fitting RMSE. We report the model fitting and validation statistics for all models, so we can see that the chosen model also performed best in the validation phase. If it had not, STORM would have so informed us with a message at the bottom of Table 7. We may also note that the model validation errors for the selected model are *better* than the model fitting ones, which is unusual. It signifies that either the model has *homed in* on the time series during model fitting, or that the time series is simply better behaved in the validation phase.

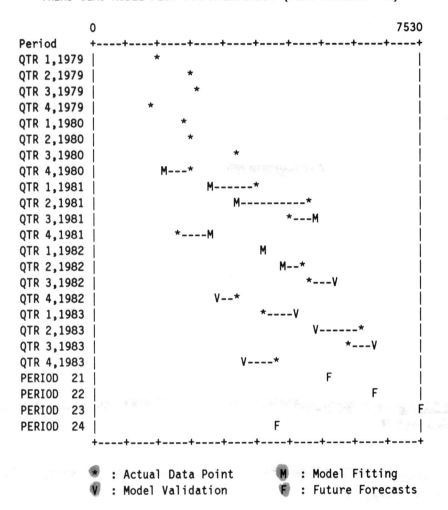

```
        TREND-SEAS MODEL PLOT FOR APEX:INDIV (PLAN HORIZON = 1)

             0                                              7530
Period       +----+----+----+----+----+----+----+----+----+----+
QTR 1,1979 |            *                                        |
QTR 2,1979 |                *                                    |
QTR 3,1979 |                *                                    |
QTR 4,1979 |           *                                         |
QTR 1,1980 |              *                                      |
QTR 2,1980 |              *                                      |
QTR 3,1980 |                  *                                  |
QTR 4,1980 |        M---*                                        |
QTR 1,1981 |             M------*                                |
QTR 2,1981 |                M----------*                         |
QTR 3,1981 |                        *---M                        |
QTR 4,1981 |        *----M                                       |
QTR 1,1982 |                     M                               |
QTR 2,1982 |                   M--*                              |
QTR 3,1982 |                       *---V                         |
QTR 4,1982 |           V--*                                      |
QTR 1,1983 |                  *----V                             |
QTR 2,1983 |                       V------*                      |
QTR 3,1983 |                         *---V                       |
QTR 4,1983 |             V----*                                  |
PERIOD  21 |                         F                           |
PERIOD  22 |                             F                       |
PERIOD  23 |                                               F     |
PERIOD  24 |                    F                                |
             +----+----+----+----+----+----+----+----+----+----+

            * : Actual Data Point      M : Model Fitting
            V : Model Validation       F : Future Forecasts
```

Figure 6: Plot of the Performance of the Selected Model

4.2.4 Forecasts Beyond the Given Data

The final output is the one for which all the rest are preparatory: actual forecasts of the time series beyond the given observations. One full year of quarterly forecasts is given, as shown in Table 8, using the selected model with the most recently updated component values. These are the values you would typically use in your planning processes. We could obtain forecasts for the second year and beyond by specifying more than four periods in Figure 5.

```
        MODEL FITTING / VALIDATION ERROR STATISTICS FOR APEX:INDIV
                              Level      Trend    Seasonal  Trend-Seas
        Statistic             Model      Model      Model      Model

        Model Fitting Error Statistics for 7 periods from QTR 4,1980

        Mean Err             627.1429   401.1429   475.0000   330.7143
        Mean % Err             6.1245     0.3082    12.0398     6.5123
        Mean Absolute Err   1211.7140  1032.2860   949.8571   703.2857
        Mean Abs % Err        35.7681    31.5139    26.4989    20.3872
        Root Mean Sq Err    1397.8160  1196.8160  1005.7510   836.7965

                    Model selected was Trend-Seas

        Model Validation Error Statistics for 6 periods from QTR 3,1982

        Mean Err             343.8333   -33.6667   376.5000    32.8333
        Mean % Err             2.3117    -5.6143     8.6245     1.0213
        Mean Absolute Err   1073.5000  1017.3330   717.8333   699.8333
        Mean Abs % Err        22.3427    22.7459    15.9186    14.8780
        Root Mean Sq Err    1246.9170  1063.7610   827.1357   720.9389
```

Table 7: Error Statistics for All Models of a Selected Series

```
            TREND-SEAS MODEL FORECASTS FOR APEX:INDIV
            Extended Forecasts for Periods beyond QTR 4,1983

                    Period              Forecast

                    PERIOD  21            5378
                    PERIOD  22            6511
                    PERIOD  23            7530
                    PERIOD  24            4223
```

Table 8: Extended Forecasts using the Selected Model

4.2.5 Revision of the Data Base

In the initial data entry we may have asked the module to search for smoothing constants within each model, and/or to select the best model. Now that STORM has made those decisions, you may wish to modify the input data to incorporate these choices for future use. This is what the final option in the Output Reports Selection form permits you to do. By making these changes now, you will not have to wait so long in future runs to obtain forecasts, provided you believe that the same model remains your best choice. If you suspect that the new data reflect altered conditions, you can change the MODEL entry back to BEST.

Of course, once a selected model has been written into the data base, it will be interpreted in all future runs as though you had specified it that way from the start; STORM will not know the difference. For example, if you start out leaving the choice of models open and ask for a detailed report with every option in the Output Reports Selection form (see Figure 5) set to *y*, all four models will be reported and the chosen model saved to your data set. Then, if you immediately request exactly the same output, you will receive reports on only the saved model.

4.3 Analysis of a Time Series

Up to now we have simply been viewing the results of our initial inputs supplemented by the automatic procedures of STORM. This final alternative on the Forecasting Options menu is designed to let you experiment with any one time series, easily and conveniently. You would typically use this capability to investigate very important series, such as total sales dollars for your organization.

If you pick this option, you will again be offered a list of the candidate series, but this time you may choose just one. Then the menu shown in Figure 7 will appear. The first two options on this menu (described below) allow you the ultimate control over experiments you wish STORM to conduct. The third choice allows you to obtain a plot similar to Figure 6, except that only your historical data will appear. The purpose of this is to let you study the plot to determine if seasonality or trend effects occur, and if so to select the models to be tried accordingly. The fourth choice takes you to the report selection screen of Figure 5 so you can see the results of your experiments. The last choice returns you to the menu in Figure 3, where you may choose any of the options to continue your analyses.

If you choose option 1) in Figure 7, the STORM form in Figure 8 will appear. You may use it to select *any* combination of the four forecasting models to be tried. Thus, if you believe your data are seasonal, but are not sure about a trend, you may select only the two models which include seasonality.

```
            FORECASTING CONTROL OPTIONS

        1)   Select models to be fitted
        2)   Set smoothing constant values
        3)   Plots of historical data
        4)   Review results for current parameters
        5)   Return to Forecasting Options Menu
```

Figure 7: Analyze a Time Series Options

```
        SELECTION OF MODELS TO BE FITTED

    Try Level Model ? (y/n)          : y

    Try Trend Model ? (y/n)          : y

    Try Seasonal Model ? (y/n)       : y

    Try Trend-Seas Model ? (y/n)     : y
```

Figure 8: Selecting Models for Analyze a Time Series

If you choose option 2) in Figure 7, the STORM form in Figure 9 will appear. You may use it to modify any or all of the search parameters to be used in the computations. Thus, you may change the starting values for any or all of the exponential smoothing constants, turn the search "on" or "off" and change the step-size to be used in the search using this screen.

You may continue to experiment using these options until you are satisfied with the results. After each experiment, you will be given the opportunity to save the results to your data set.

```
                    SMOOTHING CONSTANT SELECTION

    Level smoothing constant                        : 0.200

    Trend smoothing constant                        : 0.200

    Seasonal smoothing constant                     : 0.200

    Conduct search starting from above values ? (y/n)  : y

    Step-size to be used during search              : 0.100
```

Figure 9: Choosing the Search Parameters

5. Tips on Using the Forecasting Module

The STORM module for forecasting is designed for maximal flexibility and convenience. You can easily modify your assumptions and try different scenarios, either by using the analysis option described in Section 4.3 or by returning to the input data and editing it directly. Here are some points to keep in mind.

In discussing the number of periods to be used for Model Validation, we have assumed throughout that we were still in doubt about the best model to use. However, once you have chosen a model, there is no longer need to validate it. To establish the best set of smoothing constants and the best component values from which to make projections into the unknown, you should make a final run with MV set to zero, devoting all your available data to initializing and fitting the model.

In searching for the best set of smoothing constants, the default step size of 0.1 has been used throughout without much discussion. If accurate forecasts are vital, you may want to try the following strategy: (1) try several very different sets of starting values for the alphas to see if the search converges to different local optima; (2) having found a local optimum, use that as a starting point for a search over a finer grid, say with a step size of 0.05.

We end with the same warning with which we began: times change, economic forces are unpredictable, and the uncritical extrapolation of the past may not always provide you with an accurate picture of the future. Your knowledge of the market or other qualitative factors which might influence the future course of the time series should be used to guide your final selections of both model and smoothing constant values.

6. Altering Problem Data Dimensions

Columns, which correspond to time series in this module, can be added (up to the maximum allowed) or deleted in the usual way. Similarly, when you wish to add additional observations to any of your series, extra rows can be inserted; or you can delete rows of observations if you wish. Of course, the first eleven rows are always required and cannot be deleted, nor can other rows be inserted between them. If you insert or delete rows or columns, STORM will automatically update the proper Problem Description entries to have them accurately reflect your modified data base.

PRODUCTION SCHEDULING CAPABILITIES

PROBLEM FORMULATION OPTIONS
- Multiple products, equal or unequal capacity required per unit for each
- Multiple methods of production (regular time, overtime, etc.)
- Multiple periods in planning horizon
- Lower bounds on capacity utilization for each method of production in each period
- Backorders or lost sales allowed
- Lower bounds on ending inventory for each product in each period

OUTPUT OPTIONS AND OTHER FEATURES
- Production schedule by product by method for each period
- Cost report by product and summary
- Product report showing supply, demand, and inventory status by product for each period
- Capacity utilization report by method by period and summary
- Customer service report by product

MAXIMAL PROBLEM SIZES (PRODUCTS, PERIODS, METHODS)
- Personal version
  Representative sizes
  - (2, 16, 1)
  - (24, 2, 1)
  - (6, 6, 2)
  - (9, 4, 3)

- Professional version
  Representative sizes, assuming 500K of net memory for STORM:
  - (48, 4, 2)
  - (13, 13, 2)
  - (5, 26, 2)

FILE NAME FOR THE SAMPLE PROBLEM DATA
- PS.DAT

Chapter 18

PRODUCTION SCHEDULING

Scheduling the operations of any productive organization is a central activity of great importance. The schedule commits personnel, money, materials, and machines to certain activities for the immediate planning horizon. Thus, the success of the firm in matching supplies to the customer demands in an efficient manner will be critically affected by the scheduling activity. This efficient matching of resources to demands is the objective of the STORM Production Scheduling module.

There are many different kinds of scheduling which may be undertaken in either manufacturing or service organizations. Our focus in this module is the manufacturing environment. Even with this limitation, there are at least the following four levels of scheduling problems:

- Production Planning
- Master Scheduling
- Lot Sizing
- Sequencing

The STORM Scheduling module focuses on the first two of these levels. To put them in proper perspective, we offer a brief explanation of all four scheduling functions in the next few paragraphs, along with information about other relevant STORM modules.

Production planning is a top management responsibility that involves establishing resource levels and the general approach to be taken in meeting customer demand. A typical time horizon for the production planning activity would be one to five years. The general approach might be characterized along a continuum as follows:

Level Production   Varying Production

Fluctuating Inventories   Constant Inventories

At the extreme left, we try to achieve a constant work force size and production rate and allow inventories to absorb demand variations. Thus, the inventories may build during slow demand periods only to be drawn down during seasonal peaks of demand. At the extreme right, we vary production so as to satisfy demand exactly as it occurs, and maintain constant (presumably low) inventories. Obviously, there are tradeoffs, and the most economical policy usually lies somewhere between these two extremes. STORM is designed to help you evaluate these tradeoffs.

Master scheduling is usually more detailed and immediate than production planning. The results of the master scheduling activity should be a statement of which products are to be made in each period in the planning horizon (perhaps one month to one year in length) and in what quantities. The master schedule typically drives the MRP system (see Chapter 19) in manufacturing environments.

Lot sizing involves the batching of two or more production requirements into a single production run. The objective of such batching is to obtain production efficiency by spreading the setup cost over more units of production, but being careful that increased inventory carrying costs do not more than offset the savings. Once we know that we need a certain number of units of a part, component, assembly, or finished product in each of several periods, is it more economical to combine these requirements into one large batch run? Or is it better to incur the costs for more setups to reduce the inventory costs and produce several smaller batches? Various lot sizing procedures are available to support such decisions both in the MRP module (Chapter 19) and the Inventory module (Chapter 13).

A final, even more detailed level of scheduling is that of job shop scheduling or sequencing. Once we have specified which items are to be produced this period and their respective production quantities, we must decide which should be produced first, second, etc. Alternatively, if several batches of product are waiting for processing at a particular work station, we need a way to choose which batch should be processed when the station is next available. Many such selection criteria are discussed in the job shop scheduling and sequencing literature. STORM does not currently contain a module devoted to this problem.

As indicated earlier, the STORM Scheduling module may be used in a Production Planning or a Master Scheduling environment. The major difference between these two is frequently the unit of time used. Months or even quarters may be used in production planning, whereas weeks or months would be more typical of master scheduling. It may also occur that resources can be varied in the production planning setting, but are fixed in a master scheduling scenario. Both kinds of scheduling can be supported by STORM due to the ease with which input data can be varied to test different resource availabilities for production planning. Some of the assumptions we make about the production environment are:

- There are one or many *products* or product groups to be scheduled
- There are one or many *methods* of production such as regular time, overtime, subcontracting, backup equipment, etc.
- There are one or more *periods* in the planning horizon over which a schedule is to be computed
- *Demand* in any period can be met from production in that period or from inventory carried over from previous production
- If demand cannot be met, one of the following options must be chosen for all products:
  - Declare the problem to be infeasible since you *require* all demand to be met (in practice, more resources must be made available)
  - Incur lost sales, which means the unmet demand will *not* be made up later when additional supplies become available
  - Backorder the unmet demand and meet it as soon as supplies become available. This assumes the customer is willing to wait.
- Scheduling costs consist of production costs, inventory carrying costs, and lost sales or backorder costs if allowed
- Cost minimization is the primary goal of the scheduling activity
- The demand for each product and the productive capacity by each method are known, for each period in the planning horizon
- The capacity required per unit to produce each product in each period by each method is known
- The costs per unit of production, carrying inventory, and incurring lost sales or backorders (if allowed) are known for each product in each period
- Minimal ending inventory requirements to meet unexpected increases in demand may be specified for each product in each period
- Minimal capacity utilization for each method of production in each period may be specified

1. The Solution Algorithm

The solution algorithm consists of a linear programming optimization technique. Chapter 5 briefly describes these techniques and the Linear Programming module. The Production Scheduling module organizes your data into the linear programming format and then calls those routines to solve the problem. The advantages of using this module rather than the linear programming module (assuming either one fits your problem) are:

- The input format is much more concise in this case
- The outputs are designed to meet the scheduler's needs, rather than those of general linear programming

Our reliance on linear programming methods means that answers with fractional parts may occur. In some instances, this poses no real problem. For example, if we are to produce 10.6 units of a product on regular time and 4.4 units on overtime, it is easy to assume that a unit may be started on regular time and completed during overtime production. Conversely, if the methods of production are two different machines, we would typically confine production of the divided unit to one or the other. You should manually shift the unit to the more expensive method in such cases, since STORM will have utilized all the less expensive capacity first. Even so, you will need to verify that enough capacity exists for the more expensive alternative to accommodate the added production. If it does not, the unit must be shifted to a third, even more expensive alternative, etc. Such adjustments, which may sound tedious, typically have a small effect on total costs and are therefore frequently ignored in practice.

2. Problem Size

Since this module uses the Linear Programming module, you are limited to a certain number of constraints and variables. Professional STORM restricts you to 200 constraints and 1500 variables, while Personal STORM restricts you to 50 constraints and 200 variables. No single statement of problem size is possible, but simple formulas to allow you to determine if your problem fits are offered below. Let's consider how you can compute the total number of variables and constraints for your problem.

The total number of variables (TV) is equal to the number of production variables (PV) plus the number of inventory variables (IV) plus the number of lost sales (LS) or backorder (BO) variables, if either are allowed. Thus,

$$TV = PV + IV + (LS \text{ or } BO)$$

The number of production variables is the number of products (P) times the number of methods of production (M) times the number of periods in the planning horizon (T), or

$$PV = P \cdot M \cdot T$$

The number of inventory variables is:

$$IV = P \cdot T$$

The same formula also applies to the number of lost sale or backorder variables, so

$$LS = P \cdot T$$

or

$$BO = P \cdot T$$

The total number of constraints (TC) is equal to the number of capacity constraints (CC) plus the number of demand constraints (DC), or

$$TC = CC + DC$$

where

$$CC = M \cdot T$$

and

$$DC = P \cdot T$$

The example problem described in the next section has two products, four periods, two methods, and allows for lost sales. The sample computations to determine the problem size are:

$$PV = 2 \cdot 2 \cdot 4 = 16 \text{ production variables}$$

$$IV = 2 \cdot 4 \quad = 8 \text{ inventory variables}$$

$$LS = 2 \cdot 4 \quad = 8 \text{ lost sales variables}$$

$$TV = 16 + 8 + 8 = 32 \text{ total variables}$$

For constraints, we have:

$$CC = 2 \cdot 4 \quad = 8 \text{ capacity constraints}$$

$DC = 2 \cdot 4 \quad = \text{8 demand constraints}$

$TC = 8 + 8 \quad = \text{16 total constraints}$

We have computed a few other problem sizes for your convenience. Table 1 shows these for Personal STORM, while Table 2 contains the list for Professional STORM. All entries in these tables assume you have either *backorders* or *lost sales*. If you have neither, your problem sizes may be larger than those shown in the Tables. If you are unsure about your problem, simply try to create a new data set and enter your dimensions. STORM will inform you if the problem is too big.

Products	Periods	Methods	Total Variables	Total Constraints
2	16	1	96	48
24	2	1	144	50
6	6	2	144	48
2	12	2	96	48
20	2	3	200	46
9	4	3	180	48
5	6	3	150	48

Table 1: Personal STORM Problem Sizes

Products	Periods	Methods	Total Variables	Total Constraints
25	6	8	1500	1500
30	6	3	900	900
20	8	5	1120	1120
12	12	4	864	864

Table 2: Professional STORM Problem Sizes

3. A Sample Problem

The Charlesville Furniture Company (CFC) manufactures a variety of high quality wood furniture products for sale to distributors. As a member of the management team at the

Blue Ridge assembly plant of CFC, your responsibilities include scheduling the operations of the Bar Stool assembly line. The company produces two kinds of bar stools: the *standard* and the *deluxe* models. The deluxe model has the added attractions of a back rest and attractive leather upholstery on both the seat and the back. Otherwise the products are identical.

The workers in the assembly section produce complete units. The assemblers are paid $8.00 per unit to put together the standard model on regular time and $12.00 for overtime. The corresponding figures for the deluxe model are $12.00 and $18.00. While assemblers vary in their individual abilities, you can assume for planning purposes that they require 1 hour on the average to complete the assembly of one standard bar stool, and 1.2 hours to assemble the deluxe model. Generally, adequate stocks of all components and materials necessary to assemble the products are available. The assembly section currently has five employees available to work 40 hours per week each on regular time and up to ten hours per week on overtime. They have on hand 41 units of the standard model and 23 units of the deluxe model completed and ready to ship. These units cost $38 per standard model and $55 per deluxe model in direct material and labor expenses, and sell for $53 and $80 per unit, respectively. Due to the volatile nature of the furniture industry, high cost of capital to borrow money, and risk of damage and obsolescence of the products, CFC management assesses a 39% inventory carrying charge rate per unit per year.

The competitive nature of the industry is such that if the CFC cannot supply the distributors with bar stools as promised, the distributors will buy them from other companies, with the resulting loss of business to CFC.

As the manager, you want to determine the weekly production schedule for the four-week period, so that the total cost (production cost plus inventory cost plus lost sales cost) is a minimum.

At the end of each week, the company likes to have 50 units of the standard model and 25 units of the deluxe model on hand so that they may replace any returned units or perhaps pick up some extra business. The forecast demand for standard and deluxe units for the next four weeks (the planning horizon) is as follows:

Week	Standard Demand	Deluxe Demand
1	122	103
2	108	93
3	106	89
4	120	97

4. Data Entry Using STORM

Data entry for a given problem should terminate with a display like Figure 1 (parts a, b and c), which gives the complete data for the example of Section 3. We will discuss the various entries in these three screens, beginning with the Problem Description entries.

Title - We have entered the company name for the title.

Capacity/unit = 1? (Y/N) - If all products to be scheduled require one unit of capacity to produce one product unit, the correct response is *yes*. A *yes* response allows us to use a more efficient solution method as well as ask you for less input data. In our example, the two products require different amounts of capacity per unit.

Planning Horizon Length - This is the number of periods in the planning horizon for the scheduling problem. In our case, it is four.

Number of Products - This is the total number of products (or product groups) to be scheduled; two for our example.

Number of Methods - This is the number of methods of production available to us to meet demand. Typical methods include regular time, overtime, subcontracting, etc. We will use only regular time and overtime for our problem so our response for this entry is two.

Shortage Policy - We offer three shortage policies from which one must be selected. The *B* response signifies a backorder situation in which customers are willing to wait for a product until we can supply it; they will not buy it elsewhere. The *L* response signifies that customers will go elsewhere if we do not have the product available and we will incur a *lost sale* or sales. Finally, an entry of *N* means we allow neither backorders nor lost sales; all demand must be met from some supply source as the demand occurs. If there is inadequate capacity to meet all demand and you choose this last policy, you will get a message that your problem is infeasible; that is, there is no solution which meets all your requirements.

```
┌──────────────┤ STORM EDITOR : Production Scheduling Module ├──────────────┐
│ Title : THE CHARLESVILLE FURNITURE COMPANY CASE                           │
│ Capacity/Unit = 1? (Y/N) :        N │ Planning Horizon length :         4 │
│ Number of Products        :        2 │ Number of Methods        :        2 │
│ Shortage Policy (B/L/N)   :        L │                                     │
│                                                                            │
│                                                                            │
│ R1 : C1       STANDARD PR 1/MTH 1 PR 1/MTH 2  PR 1 REQS LOST SALES  INV COST│
│ PERIOD   0      XXXX       XXXX       XXXX       XXXX       15.     0.285   │
│ PERIOD   1      XXXX        8.        12.        122         .         .    │
│ PERIOD   2      XXXX        8.        12.        108         .         .    │
│ PERIOD   3      XXXX        8.        12.        106         .         .    │
│ PERIOD   4      XXXX        8.        12.        120         .         .    │
│ CAP / UNIT      XXXX        1.         1.        XXXX       XXXX      XXXX   │
│                                                                            │
│                                                                            │
│                                                                            │
│ └──────┤ This entry can not be changed               ├─>┤        ├──────  │
└────────────────────────────────────────────────────────────────────────────┘
```

(a)

```
┌──────────────┤ STORM EDITOR : Production Scheduling Module ├──────────────┐
│ Title : THE CHARLESVILLE FURNITURE COMPANY CASE                           │
│ Capacity/Unit = 1? (Y/N) :        N │ Planning Horizon Length :         4 │
│ Number of Products        :        2 │ Number of Methods        :        2 │
│ Shortage Policy (B/L/N)   :        L │                                     │
│                                                                            │
│                                                                            │
│ R1 : C7      INV LEVEL   DE LUXE PR 2/MTH 1 PR 2/MTH 2  PR 2 REQS LOST SALES│
│ PERIOD   0      41         XXXX       XXXX       XXXX       XXXX       25.  │
│ PERIOD   1      50         XXXX       12.        18.        103         .   │
│ PERIOD   2      50         XXXX       12.        18.         93         .   │
│ PERIOD   3      50         XXXX       12.        18.         89         .   │
│ PERIOD   4      50         XXXX       12.        18.         97         .   │
│ CAP / UNIT      XXXX       XXXX       1.2        1.2        XXXX      XXXX   │
│                                                                            │
│                                                                            │
│                                                                            │
│ └──────┤ Enter Beginning Inventory in Units for Standard  ├─>┤    ├──────  │
└────────────────────────────────────────────────────────────────────────────┘
```

(b)

Figure 1: Editor Screens After Data Entry

```
┌──────────────────────────────────────────────────────────────────────┐
│    ┌──────────────┤ STORM EDITOR : Production Scheduling Module ├──────┐│
│    Title : THE CHARLESVILLE FURNITURE COMPANY CASE                     │
│    Capacity/Unit = 1? (Y/N) :        N │ Planning Horizon Length  :   4 │
│    Number of Products       :        2 │ Number of Methods        :   2 │
│    Shortage Policy (B/L/N)  :        L │                                │
│    ─────────────────────────────────── ──────────────────────────────  │
│    R1 : C13      INV COST  INV LEVEL   REGULAR  MIN UTIL  OVERTIME  MIN UTIL │
│    PERIOD   0    0.4125       23         XXXX     XXXX     XXXX     XXXX  │
│    PERIOD   1      .          25         200        0       50        0   │
│    PERIOD   2      .          25         200        0       50        0   │
│    PERIOD   3      .          25         200        0       50        0   │
│    PERIOD   4      .          25         200        0       50        0   │
│    CAP / UNIT    XXXX        XXXX        XXXX     XXXX     XXXX     XXXX  │
│                                                                        │
│                                                                        │
│    └─────┤ Default inventory cost/unit/period for DE LUXE   ├─>│    ├──┘│
└──────────────────────────────────────────────────────────────────────┘
                                   (c)
```

Figure 1: Editor Screens After Data Entry

Once the preceding entries are completed, the detailed data must be entered to complete the data set. Figure 2 shows the general layout for the Problem Data area. It reveals that we generally group all the entries for a particular product as a set of columns. These sets go from left to right until the last product in our problem appears. Following the last product, we enter capacity data for each method of production. The rows in the data area generally signify *periods* in the planning horizon. With the general overview provided by Figure 2, we proceed to describe the specific entries illustrated in Figure 1 for the Data area, starting at the left.

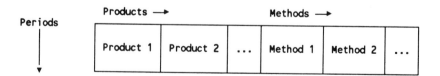

Figure 2: General View of the Data Area

Product Naming Column - The first column for each product is simply a blank column except for the column label. We enter the product name which we wish to appear on all reports as the column label. We have entered the word STANDARD for our first product.

Production Cost Columns - The next column or columns will be for entering the production cost for the particular product in question for each of the methods by which it can be produced, and in each period in the planning horizon. The entry in the last row for each of these columns is the capacity required to produce one unit of this product by the method the column represents. This row will not be included if the capacity per unit for all products is one (from the Problem Description entry). For our problem, the cost to produce on regular time was entered in the column headed PR 1/MTH 1 and was $8.00 per unit for all time periods. The capacity required per unit on regular time was 1.0 hour. The analogous numbers for overtime production were $12 per unit and 1.0 hour. If the methods of production involved different processes, the capacity per unit might very well be different for different methods for the same product.

Product Requirements - After the product cost columns have been completed for all methods, we reach a column in which we enter the production requirements (or demand) for the product in each period. For our problem, we have entered the sales forecasts for the standard product. Of course, there is no entry for this column in the last row, the capacity-per-unit row.

Lost Sales or Backorder Cost Column - If either of these were chosen while entering the Problem Description, then the associated cost per unit for the product in each period in the planning horizon must be entered here. Since you may want this value to be different from period to period, the capability is provided for you to enter a different value every period. However, if the value should not change, you need only enter the first value (which is the default value for all periods) in the row labeled PERIOD 0. We have used this latter option to declare a lost sales cost of $15 ($53 selling price minus $38 direct costs) per unit for the standard product in all periods.

Inventory Cost - In this column goes the inventory carrying cost per unit per period for this product. We enter the default value in the first row, which is labeled PERIOD 0. Then we enter the inventory carrying cost for any other period only if the cost is different from the default value. For our example, this cost is computed by first converting the 39% rate to a weekly rate by dividing 0.39 by 52 weeks per year. The result, 0.0075, is then multiplied by the $38 direct cost per unit to obtain the default carrying cost per week: 0.285.

Ending Inventory Units - In this column (labeled INV LEVEL) we enter the required ending inventory in units for each period in the planning horizon. The entry for the first row, PERIOD 0, is the actual inventory on hand to begin the planning horizon.

The above columns are duplicated in Figure 1 for the deluxe product, and would be repeated for each product to be scheduled.

In part (c) of Figure 1, the last four columns list capacity information for the two different methods of production allowed in our problem. In general, there will be two columns for each possible production method. The first of each pair is headed by a label which we have edited to read REGULAR and OVERTIME. These labels will be used on reports, so we recommend that you modify them appropriately. The entries to be made in these two columns are:

Capacity Available Column - In the left column of each pair where the label for the production method appears, we enter the amount of capacity available in each period of the planning horizon, using that method. Thus, using regular-time production, we have available five employees times 40 hours per week, giving 200 hours per week.

Minimal Utilization Column - It is frequently true that we wish to guarantee some minimal utilization of capacity. This may be due to a union contract or projected seasonal demand or any of a number of other reasons. STORM allows you to simply enter the number of capacity units which you require to be used. We placed no limits on these in our sample problem, but it would frequently be true that we would want to fully utilize regular time production. If so, in our example we would enter 200, since the entry is made in *capacity units,* not as a per cent. You can not enter a value larger than that in the Capacity Available Column in the same row.

Having completed the data entry for the Charlesville Company, we are ready to proceed to execution of the module.

5. Execution of the Module

Execution of the module results in a choice of five output reports designed to provide different kinds of information about the scheduling problem. The types of information include the schedule itself, cost information, product availability, capacity utilization, and customer service. Each of these is briefly discussed and illustrated below.

5.1 Production Schedule

The production schedule for Charlesville is shown in Figure 3. As is evident, it is time based. The listing shows, for each week, which products are to be produced, by what method or methods, and in what quantities. This is the kind of information needed for production planning and shop floor control activities, and to tell us if the schedule can be met and how.

```
              PRODUCTION SCHEDULE

                  PERIOD    1
   Product          Method        Units
   STANDARD         REGULAR       74.00
   STANDARD         OVERTIME      50.00
   Deluxe           REGULAR      105.00

                  PERIOD    2
   Product          Method        Units
   STANDARD         REGULAR       88.40
   STANDARD         OVERTIME      19.60
   Deluxe           REGULAR       93.00

                  PERIOD    3
   Product          Method        Units
   STANDARD         REGULAR       93.20
   STANDARD         OVERTIME      12.80
   Deluxe           REGULAR       89.00

                  PERIOD    4
   Product          Method        Units
   STANDARD         REGULAR       83.60
   STANDARD         OVERTIME      36.40
   Deluxe           REGULAR       97.00
```

Figure 3: The Production Schedule

5.2 Cost Report - By Product and Summary

The second report available is directed toward financial analysis of the schedule and would be a primary input to the cash flow analysis for a typical manufacturing firm. It is illustrated in Figure 4 for Charlesville. It is a two-part report with the first part being product oriented. Thus, for each of our two products, we see in Figure 4 the regular time cost for the units produced by that method, the overtime costs for same, the inventory carrying costs (if any), and the lost sales or backorder costs if either is allowed. The total cost for the planning period is shown after the last product listing. It is followed by a summary of total production costs by method, inventory costs, and lost sales or backorder costs if appropriate.

```
                   COST REPORT  -  BY PRODUCT

                      STANDARD
                        Cost                Units
        REGULAR        2713.60             339.20
        OVERTIME       1425.60             118.80
        Inventory        57.00             200.00
        Lost Sales      105.00               7.00

                       Deluxe
                        Cost                Units
        REGULAR        4608.00             384.00
        OVERTIME          0.00               0.00
        Inventory        41.25             100.00
        Lost Sales        0.00               0.00

    Total Cost = 8950.45


                   COST REPORT  -  SUMMARY
                            Production Cost

          REGULAR             7321.60
          OVERTIME            1425.60
          Inventory             98.25
          Lost Sales           105.00

        Total Cost = 8950.45
```

Figure 4: Cost Report

5.3 Product Report

This report, shown in Figure 5, provides a period-by-period summary of the activity associated with each product. It lists the sources of supply in the first few rows, including beginning inventory and production on all available methods. Then the demand is listed and netted from the available supply to produce the ending inventory balance. If lost sales or backorders are allowed, there will be a row for same at the bottom of this display. Notice that 7.00 units of lost sales occurred in period 1 for the standard product, while 50 units are projected in ending inventory. The ending inventory constraints are treated as binding by our module, but the sales manager will sell those units to any customer who wants them! What we should do in this case is return to the Editor, reduce the ending inventory requirement for period 1 to 43 units (50 - 7 lost sales), and recompute the solution. This kind of report can be very valuable to marketing by showing projected available balances for each product on a period-by-period basis.

PRODUCT REPORT

	STANDARD			
	PERIOD 1	PERIOD 2	PERIOD 3	PERIOD 4
Beg Inventory	41.00	50.00	50.00	50.00
Production				
REGULAR	74.00	88.40	93.20	83.60
OVERTIME	50.00	19.60	12.80	36.40
Demand	122.00	108.00	106.00	120.00
End Inventory	50.00	50.00	50.00	50.00
Lost Sales	7.00	0.00	0.00	0.00

	Deluxe			
	PERIOD 1	PERIOD 2	PERIOD 3	PERIOD 4
Beg Inventory	23.00	25.00	25.00	25.00
Production				
REGULAR	105.00	93.00	89.00	97.00
OVERTIME	0.00	0.00	0.00	0.00
Demand	103.00	93.00	89.00	97.00
End Inventory	25.00	25.00	25.00	25.00
Lost Sales	0.00	0.00	0.00	0.00

Figure 5: Product Report

5.4 Capacity Utilization

This report, which is illustrated in Figure 6 for our example, parallels the approach taken in the Cost Report. It starts with a detailed report for each method in each period, listing the capacity available, the minimal utilization required, the amount actually utilized, and the utilization as a percentage. This is followed by a summary of the total utilization of each method over the entire planning horizon. Notice in Figure 6 that full utilization is made of regular time production for Charlesville, with overtime utilization varying from 25.5% to 100.0%. If we wanted to use at least 50 per cent of the overtime capacity in every period, we could go back and edit the data set to require that 25 hours (50 per cent of 50 hours) be used each week, and solve the problem again. You may want to try this and see what happens.

```
                CAPACITY UTILIZATION REPORT : DETAILED


                               REGULAR
                    Capacity    Minimal        Amount    Per cent
        Period      Available  Utilization    Utilized   Utilized
        PERIOD  1    200.000      0.000       200.0000    100.00
        PERIOD  2    200.000      0.000       200.0000    100.00
        PERIOD  3    200.000      0.000       200.0000    100.00
        PERIOD  4    200.000      0.000       200.0000    100.00


                               OVERTIME
                    Capacity    Minimal        Amount    Per cent
        Period      Available  Utilization    Utilized   Utilized
        PERIOD  1     50.000      0.000        50.0000    100.00
        PERIOD  2     50.000      0.000        19.6000     39.20
        PERIOD  3     50.000      0.000        12.8000     25.60
        PERIOD  4     50.000      0.000        36.4000     72.80



                CAPACITY UTILIZATION REPORT : SUMMARY

                      Total        Total       Per cent
        Method       Available    Utilized     Utilized
        REGULAR       800.00       800.00       100.00
        OVERTIME      200.00       118.80        59.40
```

Figure 6: Capacity Utilization Report

5.5 Customer Service Report

The customer service report is shown in Figure 7 and reveals, for each product, how well the projected balances would meet customer demand. It shows units supplied versus units demanded, the difference between them, and the difference expressed as a per cent. This is a summarized figure over the entire planning horizon.

CUSTOMER SERVICE REPORT

Product	Units Supplied	Units Demanded	Difference	Per cent Difference
STANDARD	449.00	456.00	-7.00	-1.54
Deluxe	382.00	382.00	0.00	0.00

Figure 7: Customer Service Report

6. Altering Problem Data Dimensions

Due to the layout of the data in this module, altering the problem size is an intricate procedure. Much of it may take place *off* your screen, and unless you carefully examine the data you may leave some important entries blank.

Row one is required and cannot be deleted. If the answer to the *capacity per unit = 1?* question is *no,* there will be a row at the bottom of the display for the capacity per unit that is also required. Otherwise, rows represent periods in the planning horizon and we can add or delete them as we see fit. We must maintain a minimum of one period in the planning horizon which requires a minimum of two or three rows, the latter being the case if the capacity per unit row is required at the bottom of the matrix. STORM will keep track of the correct planning horizon for you in the Problem Description area.

Columns may be considered in either the product area (see Figure 1) or the capacity area. For the product area, we know each product will occupy $4 + M$ columns if neither backorders nor lost sales are allowed, and where M is the number of methods of production. A product will occupy $5 + M$ columns, otherwise. Thus, a request to insert or delete a column will result in a multi-column operation. Specifically, a request to delete any column for a product will result in *all* columns for that product being deleted. A request to enter a column when the Pointer is on any product column will cause a new set of columns to be inserted to the right of the product on which the Pointer is located. STORM will keep track of the number of products for you.

In the columns at the right of the Data area where productive capacity is recorded, column operations also result in multi-column impacts. Suppose you wish to remove one of the methods of production. A request to delete a column in this area will result in the deletion of two adjacent columns: the capacity and the minimal utilization column for the method on which the Pointer is located. Both will be deleted regardless of which column the Pointer is on. In addition, one column will be deleted from each product area, resulting in the deletion of P more columns if P is the number of products in the problem. Of course, in each case the deleted column will be the one related to the deleted method. The reverse action takes place if a request is made to insert a column in the capacity area. Two columns are inserted in that area to the right of the Pointer's current position, and P additional columns are inserted back in the product area. STORM automatically keeps track of the number of methods for you in the Problem Description area. Insertions in the capacity area should be done very carefully, as the product columns added are typically out of view of the user and may easily be forgotten.

- NOTES -

MATERIAL REQUIREMENTS PLANNING CAPABILITIES

PROBLEM FORMULATION OPTIONS
- Material requirements planning
- Capacity requirements planning
- Individual item lot sizing rules
- Seven lot sizing rules including user-supplied lot sizes (fixed quantity rule)
- Gross requirements backlog may be input
- Single level bill of material format
- Items at any level may be master scheduled
- User-supplied planning horizon
- User-defined time bucket
- User-specified safety stock for each item
- Firm planned orders

OUTPUT OPTIONS AND OTHER FEATURES
- Bill of material explosion
- Load reports for each capacity center
- Indented bill of material list(s), single- or multi-level
- Indented where-used list(s), single- or multi-level
- File utilities for sorting and copying item numbers and descriptions from file to file

MAXIMAL PROBLEM SIZES (ITEMS, DESCENDANTS, PLANNING HORIZON)
- Personal version: (100, 25, 15)

- Professional version
  Representative sizes, with 500K of net memory for STORM
  (240, 25, 104)
  (265, 50, 52)
  (485, 25, 26)
  (270, 50, 13)
  (See Section 2 for more details)

FILE NAMES FOR THE SAMPLE PROBLEM DATA
- For the Bill of Material file ...... BOM.DAT
- For the Master Schedule file ..... MAST.DAT
- For the Inventory Status file ..... MRPINV.DAT
- For the Item Master file .... ITEM.DAT
- For the Capacity file .... CAP.DAT

Chapter 19

MATERIAL REQUIREMENTS PLANNING

Material Requirements Planning, popularly called MRP, is a methodology used for managing dependent demand inventory situations. Dependent demand simply means that demand for one part, component or subassembly is dependent upon the demand for its parent component(s). For example, assume you are assembling chairs which have four legs each. If you are to assemble 100 such chairs, then you will need 400 legs to complete the assembly. The STORM MRP module allows you to analyze such inventory situations. Of course, there is a lot more to it than implied by the chair example, but dependent demand is the crux of MRP applications.

The MRP module is different from all other STORM modules in one very important respect: it utilizes either four or five input data files to completely define the problem, whereas all other modules use only one. If you have been using other modules, you will need to adapt your thinking to accommodate this difference. If this is your first or one of your first modules, you should be aware that this module is nonstandard in this respect.

1. The Solution Algorithm

There are a number of computational and file handling procedures available in this module. The most critical of these can be summarized under the headings:

- Bill of material explosion
- Indented bill of material listing
- Where-used report
- Shop load reporting (capacity requirements planning)

The *bill of material (BOM) explosion* is the most important part of any MRP system, since it provides the detailed guide for operations. The process of computing and presenting the BOM explosion involves:

- Determining gross requirements for each item tracked by the system
- Netting out available quantities of each item, offsetting for required lead times
- Determining the resulting net requirements
- Lot sizing these net requirements into production quantities

The STORM module includes all these processes, and further allows you to select from among several lot sizing rules for each inventoried item.

The module employs a *regenerative* scheme to perform the BOM explosion, which means that each time you execute the module, the entire set of computations is performed. This is true even if you've only made one small change to the data base. Large scale MRP systems frequently use a *net change* logic wherein only computations affected by changes are redone and displayed. Such logic is beyond the scope of our MRP module.

One critical problem in using MRP systems is that complete, accurate, and up-to-date BOM records must be maintained. STORM simplifies this process by allowing you to obtain the BOM printout directly from STORM after you have built the BOM file. As you will see in the example, building this file is relatively easy since we use a single-level BOM file structure. *The indented BOM listing* links together all the levels of a particular product's bill of material, which you may then list out for documentation purposes.

A third process provided is the production of a *where-used report*. A typical need for such a document occurs if a supplier notifies you that a shipment of a part is going to be late. One obvious question is, "What will this affect?" To answer it, we must first find out the parent assemblies in which this part is used, and secondly which of these parents are scheduled, when, and in what quantities. STORM does not have the capability to answer all these questions. It will answer the first one quickly, which is frequently the most difficult one to answer. By telling you where the part is used, you can then examine your most recent BOM explosion report to survey the damage (if any) the late shipment will cause. There are other uses for the where-used report that reflect more pleasant conditions. For example, a design engineer who is to redesign an existing part may profit from knowing all parent items which use this part, so that the new design will meet all the different needs.

In addition to material, other resources may be planned and scheduled via MRP techniques. Labor and machine hours may be necessary to complete manufacturing shop orders, and the amount of each needed per part is typically available. If so, STORM allows you to declare such capacity items in the BOM file, and it will compute and prepare time-phased capacity load reports for each resource. In this way you can compare capacity available to the projected need.

Further details of MRP are available in standard production planning and inventory control reference books. We will allude to some of these points in Section 3 when we solve a sample problem.

2. Problem Sizes for Professional STORM

There are several dimensions to consider in an MRP problem including:

- Number of items in the BOM file
- Number of descendants for any item
- Number of periods in the planning horizon

Unfortunately, there is no simple formula to allow an easy determination of whether an MRP problem will fit in STORM. Each file has its own requirements when you are editing it. In addition, there are times during execution when STORM needs more than one file at a time. STORM builds a complex tree structure during execution which also requires memory. As you can see, this gets very confusing!

To assist you in evaluating whether STORM can help you with your MRP problem, Table 1 has been prepared. This table is based on *worst case scenarios*. It assumes that the maximal lead time for any item and the maximal number of periods for firm planned orders in the Inventory Status file (see Section 4.6 for more information) are both equal to the planning horizon length in time buckets in the Master Schedule file (see Section 4.5 for more information). Both are likely to be less than the planning horizon length, and possibly by large amounts. The table also assumes a *dense* Bill of Material (BOM) file (see Section 4.1 for more information). That is, it assumes that a high proportion of the items listed in this file have a lot of descendants. To the extent that our worst case assumptions do not apply to your problem, you may be able to solve slightly larger problems than those listed in Table 1. Nonetheless, the table may be used as a rough guideline.

The first row of the table reveals the largest number of periods in a planning horizon, assuming a minimal number of two items in the BOM file and only one descendant. After that row, the table contains blocks of four rows which each illustrate a different planning horizon length (number of periods). Rows 2 through 5 use a planning horizon of 104 corresponding to weekly time buckets and a two-year planning horizon. The maximal number of descendants of any item in the BOM file is increased in these rows from a minimum of 0 to a maximum of 119. The minimum was chosen to reflect a reorder point system in a distribution requirements planning environment. The maximum was chosen so as to allow one item in the BOM file to have all others as its descendant. This same four row pattern is repeated in rows 6 through for a planning horizon of 52 (weeks in a year), in rows 10 through 13 for a horizon of 26 (weeks in a six month period), and finally in rows 14 through 17 for a horizon of 13 (weeks in a quarter). You may note that when the maximal descendants is 119, the maximal items in the BOM file is 120 *regardless of the planning horizon length.* This is because the planning horizon length is not the bottleneck constraint in this case.

Row Number	Number of BOM Items	Maximal Number of Descendants	Number of Periods
1	2	1	3600
2	315	0	104
3	240	25	104
4	190	50	104
5	120	119	104
6	570	0	52
7	360	25	52
8	265	50	52
9	120	119	52
10	950	0	26
11	485	25	26
12	270	50	26
13	120	119	26
14	1400	0	13
15	500	25	13
16	270	50	13
17	120	119	13

Table 1: MRP Problem Sizes for Professional STORM with 500K Memory

3. A Sample Problem

The sample problem we will use to illustrate this module is for an assembly department of a furniture manufacturing company. This company, the Blue Ridge Furniture Company, manufactures a wide variety of products including tall stools which are used in laboratory settings for research scientists. The marketing department of Blue Ridge has just received an order for 300 of the standard stools and 80 de luxe stools from a research lab embarked on a modernization program. The customer would like the standard stools to be available three weeks from now and the de luxe stools in four weeks. Given the current availability of both labor and material resources, can Blue Ridge meet this date?

To answer this question requires the use of all five files in the MRP module and considerable data. Rather than presenting all the data in this section, we will introduce most of it in Section 4 where we enter it into STORM. For now, we will focus our attention on Figures 1 and 2 which show the product structure tree for each of the standard and de luxe stools.

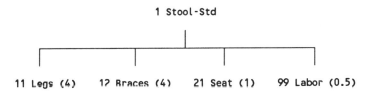

Figure 1: The Standard Stool Product Structure Tree

At the top of Figure 1 we see that the standard stool has been assigned the number 1 by our product numbering system. By convention in the MRP literature, we refer to the top of the product structure tree as level 0 (zero), and succeeding lower levels are numbered 1, 2, 3, etc. Level 0 items are frequently finished goods, as is the case in Figure 1. The interpretation of the entries at the bottom of Figure 1 is as follows. First we list the item number, then the item name and finally the quantity per assembly (in parentheses). The quantity per assembly is the number of units required to make *one* unit of the parent item at the next level up in the tree. Thus, we need 4 legs (item number 11) to make one standard stool, 4 braces to connect the legs, 1 seat and 0.5 hours of assembly labor. Figure 2 reveals a more complicated structure for the de luxe stool. It has a padded seat and a padded back to differentiate it from the standard model. Both the seat and back use the same pad and fabric, which are attached to the seat and back before the seat and back are joined to the legs and braces. Notice that in Figure 2 the seat and back assemblies (items 13 and 14) both have immediate descendants only to level 3, even though it appears that the back assembly (14) goes to a lower level. This was done simply to fit everything into the display.

With this brief introduction to the assembly department's problem in mind, let's proceed to enter the data.

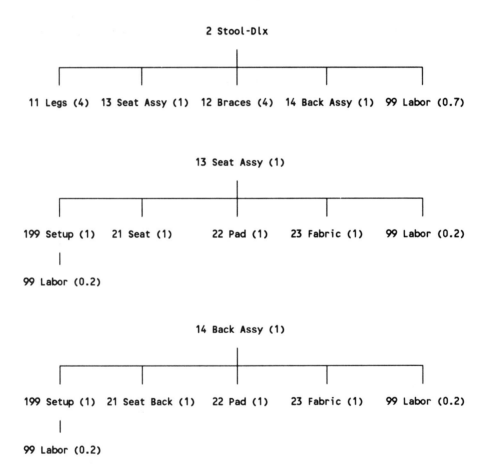

Figure 2: The De luxe Stool Product Structure Tree

4. Data Entry Using STORM

We begin by selecting Material Requirements Planning from the STORM Main Menu, and obtaining the menu shown in Figure 3. Due to the complexity of this module, it was necessary to add this preliminary menu which offers you two principal choices: proceed to execute the module if all the files are ready, or else create new files or editing existing ones.

```
MATERIAL REQUIREMENTS PLANNING : FILE SELECTION

1)    Execute the module (if all files ready)
2)    Bill of Material file
3)    Master Schedule file
4)    Inventory Status file
5)    Item Master file
6)    Resource Capacity file
7)    Create new data files from BOM file
```

Figure 3: The MRP File Selection Menu

If you simply want to rerun a previously prepared set of files, you can choose option 1 and proceed to execute the module as described in Section 5. In the present case, we cannot proceed with execution until we first create all new files, so we start with option 2, the Bill of Material (BOM) file. Incidentally, it is desirable to have all these files together on one diskette to avoid frequent exchanges of diskettes when running the module.

Having chosen option 2, the input menu in Figure 4 will appear.

```
MRP, BILL OF MATERIAL : INPUT

1)    Read an existing data file
2)    Create a new data file
```

Figure 4: The BOM Input Menu

4.1 The Bill of Material File

The entry of the BOM file requires us to convert the information in Figures 1 and 2 to a file format. After we have done so, the file will appear as shown in Figures 5A and 5B. The file was too large to fit in one screen, so we have simply reproduced in these figures the displays that you obtain if you tab to the right in the Editor. Let's examine each type of data entered in this file using the labels as they appear in these figures.

Title - This is self-explanatory.

Total number of items in the file - This is the total number of unique items that we need to enter into the BOM file. This entry determines the total length of this file. Notice that each item is entered only one time, no matter how many parent items it has. The LABOR entry, item number 99, appears several times in Figures 1 and 2, but is only entered once in the BOM file.

Maximal number of immediate descendants of any item - This entry determines the width of the BOM file. It is important to note that the number to be entered here is the number of *immediate* descendants, not the total number of all descendants of an item. Thus, although Figure 2 reveals that the de luxe stool has 17 total descendants, the correct entry here is 5. This is because at level one in the tree structure (where 11 Legs, 13 Seat Assy, ... appear) there are 5 immediate descendants of item 2, the Stool-Dlx.

ITEM ID - This is the item identification number that you wish to assign to this particular part or component, which must be an integer. We have numbered the material items in this example so that the first digit is the level number for the item and the second digit is an item identifier. However, this is not the recommended practice as product redesigns would create confusion due to product re-numbering requirements.

ITEM TYPE - Enter an M for Material, C for Capacity or S for Setup. An M means that a physical part or component is being described. For such items, an entry must also appear in the Inventory Status file and the Item Master file. A C means that it is used for planning capacity utilization for labor or machines or some other such resource. An S means that a setup must be performed before the parent item can be made.

```
┌──────────┤ STORM EDITOR : Bill Of Material File - MRP Module ├──────────┐
│ Title : BLUE RIDGE FURNITURE COMPANY                                    │
│ Total number of items in the file                    :        12        │
│ Maximal number of immediate descendants of any item :         5         │
│                                                                         │
│ R1  : C1      ITEM ID   ITEM TYPE   DESC  1 Q/ASSY  1   DESC  2 Q/ASSY  2│
│ STOOL-STD        1        MAT        11      4.         12      4.       │
│ STOOL-DLX        2        MAT        11      4.         12      4.       │
│ LEG             11        MAT         .       .          .       .       │
│ BRACE           12        MAT         .       .          .       .       │
│ SEAT ASSY       13        MAT        21      1.         22      1.       │
│ BACK ASSY       14        MAT        24      1.         22      1.       │
│ SEAT            21        MAT         .       .          .       .       │
│ PAD             22        MAT         .       .          .       .       │
│ FABRIC          23        MAT         .       .          .       .       │
│ BACK            24        MAT         .       .          .       .       │
│ LABOR           99        CAP         .       .          .       .       │
│ SETUP STPL     199        SET        99      0.2         .       .       │
└──────────┤ Enter the item ID number for STOOL-STD          ├─→│   │─────┘
```

Figure 5A: The First Screen of the BOM File

```
┌──────────┤ STORM EDITOR : Bill Of Material File - MRP Module ├──────────┐
│ Title : BLUE RIDGE FURNITURE COMPANY                                    │
│ Total number of items in the file                    :        12        │
│ Maximal number of immediate descendants of any item :         5         │
│                                                                         │
│ R1  : C7     DESC  3 Q/ASSY  3   DESC  4 Q/ASSY  4   DESC  5 Q/ASSY  5   │
│ STOOL-STD      21      1.          99      0.5         .       .         │
│ STOOL-DLX      13      1.          14      1.          99      0.7       │
│ LEG            .       .           .       .           .       .         │
│ BRACE          .       .           .       .           .       .         │
│ SEAT ASSY      23      1.          99      0.2        199      1.        │
│ BACK ASSY      23      1.          99      0.2        199      1.        │
│ SEAT           .       .           .       .           .       .         │
│ PAD            .       .           .       .           .       .         │
│ FABRIC         .       .           .       .           .       .         │
│ BACK           .       .           .       .           .       .         │
│ LABOR          .       .           .       .           .       .         │
│ SETUP STPL     .       .           .       .           .       .         │
└──────────┤ Enter ID number for descendant   3 of 1       ├─→│   │───────┘
```

Figure 5B: The Second Screen of the BOM File

A setup must use some capacity resource to complete, such as labor and machine time. The distinction between a capacity (C) item and a setup (S) item is that *the setup capacity will only be "charged" once, regardless of the number of units of the parent being made. The capacity item will be charged once **per unit** as is the common definition of a descendant.* We have one capacity item, LABOR, and one setup item, SETUP STPL, which appear as the last two entries in our file. The setup item refers to loading a stapler before making the seat and back assemblies.

DESC 1, 2, ... - These are the Item ID numbers of the immediate descendants for this item. This is what was meant in our earlier discussion of the single-level BOM file. For item 2, Stool-Dlx, the descendants are items 11, 12, 13, 14, and 99.

Q/ASSY 1, 2, ... - This is the *quantity per assembly,* that is, the number or amount of the descendant item required for completion of one unit of the parent item. This forms a paired entry with the Desc entry listed above which is repeated as many times as necessary to list all the immediate descendants for a parent. This value must be entered as 1.0 for all SETUP items, or STORM will not execute your data set.

Note that we have also edited the default row labels (which read ITEM 1, ITEM 2, ...) to enter a brief item description.

4.2 The MRP Process Menu

After we have completed data entry for the BOM file (or any other) and have pressed the F7 key to leave the Editor, we are transferred to the Process menu shown in Figure 6. There are the usual options to edit, save, or print the data file or to execute the module. However, since we have several files to be concerned with in this module, there is the additional option to return to the File Selection menu to prepare other files. If you have edited the file, the pointer will be on option 2, Save the current data file, when you leave the Editor. Otherwise, it will be on option 4, Return to File Selection menu. The Execute option should not be selected until all files are ready.

```
MRP, BILL OF MATERIAL : PROCESS

1)    Edit the current data file
2)    Save the current data file
3)    Print the current data file
4)    Return to File Selection menu
5)    Execute the module (if all files ready)
```

Figure 6: The MRP Process Menu

4.3 Default File Names for MRP Files

When we select the Save option on the Process menu, a STORM form will appear which already has the file name *bom.dat* entered as the default name. This feature was added to make it easier to use, given the large number of file names that must be entered. If the default names are not acceptable, simply enter other file names more to your liking. The default file names provided for the MRP files are shown in Figure 7.

```
File                                File Name

Bill of Material .  .  .  .  .    bom.dat
Master Schedule  .  .  .  .  .    mast.dat
Inventory Status .  .  .  .  .  mrpinv.dat
Item Master.  .  .  .  .  .  .    item.dat
Capacity.  .  .  .  .  .  .  .    cap.dat
```

Figure 7: Default File Names for MRP Module

4.4 Creating Other Files from the BOM File

If you were following along with the Blue Ridge example and had created the BOM file as described in Section 4.1, you could use it to save yourself some work in creating row labels and item ID numbers for other files. For example, when you select the Master Schedule from the File Selection menu and view its input menu, one of the options is to create the Master Schedule file from the BOM file. The BOM file occupies this special position since every item that appears in another file must also be entered in the BOM file. Thus, if you have created the BOM file with the desired row labels and item ID numbers, you may wish to copy those to the other files, instead of laboriously re-entering them each time. If so, first select the *Create from BOM file* option from the menu under consideration. STORM will copy the title of your problem from the BOM file into the title area of the Problem Description. You will be allowed to edit the title if you wish, and then the number of entries for the file in question will be automatically entered by the MRP module. You will not be allowed to change that number, since it matches the BOM file which is being used to create the new file. After you have completed any remaining entries in the Problem Description area and proceeded to the Problem Data area, the copied labels and IDs will already be there. You will only need to add the new data for each file.

There are certain rules that STORM follows in executing this copy procedure, which vary among the files. For the Master Schedule file, STORM will only copy the items which have a lowest level code of zero in the BOM file (STORM automatically determines the lowest level code for any item in the BOM file). These are the items that occupy the highest level in the product structure tree. Thus, for Blue Ridge, this includes items 1 and 2, the stools. For the Inventory Status file (see Section 4.6) and the Item Master file (see Section 4.7), all items which have the Item Type *MAT* (for material) will be copied over from the BOM file. For the Capacity file (see Section 4.8), all items which have the Item Type *CAP* will be copied. The *SET* (setup) entry is only used in the Bill of Material file, and so will not be copied to any other file.

4.5 The Master Schedule File

The Master Schedule file is the next file we will create for the Blue Ridge example. Typically, level 0 items are master scheduled in a company. However, you may enter any items in this file which you need to master schedule. In our example, we assume only the two finished products, Stool-Std and Stool-Dlx, are master scheduled. If customers occasionally experience tears in the fabric for the de luxe stools, we could master schedule additional fabric and/or seat and back assemblies. Figure 8 contains the display of the Master Schedule file after all data have been entered. The data items necessary and their brief descriptions are:

Title - Self-explanatory.

Number of items master scheduled - This is the total number of items you have to enter into this file, and determines its length.

Planning horizon length in time buckets - This is the number of periods or time buckets in your planning (scheduling) horizon, irrespective of the time unit (week, day, month, etc.) being used. For Blue Ridge it is four periods, which the next line will reveal to be four weeks.

Number of time buckets per year - STORM needs this information in order to properly assess inventory carrying charges in the lot sizing computations described later in this chapter. The 52 entry means that Blue Ridge has a weekly time bucket. A monthly time bucket would cause us to enter 12, a quarterly time bucket a 4, and so on.

ITEM ID - This is the same as described in Section 4.1 for the BOM file.

PERIOD 1, 2,... - We replaced the default word *PERIOD* with the word *WEEK* in Figure 8 for our sample problem. In these columns you enter the master scheduled quantities for every item listed in the ITEM ID column for each period in the planning horizon. These entries become the gross requirements for the BOM explosion described in Section 5.3.1. We have entered the Blue Ridge information in weeks 3 and 4.

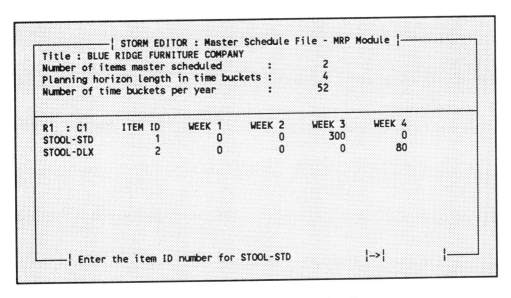

Figure 8: The Master Schedule File

4.6 The Inventory Status File

This file is the one in which current on-hand and on-order inventory balances are kept, along with any other conditions affecting current and expected inventory balances for each material item. The information for the Blue Ridge example is shown in Figures 9A and 9B. The required data items are:

Title - Self-explanatory.

Total number of material items - The number of material items to be recorded in this file, which determines the file length.

Maximal lead time in time buckets - Lead times may be purchasing lead times or manufacturing lead times for items produced in house. The one item among all material items that requires the longest lead time either to procure or produce should determine this entry. This entry partially determines the width of this file. This is also the number of periods into the future we should allow for projected receipts of this item due to either an open purchase or shop order. It must be less than or equal to the planning horizon value you entered in the Master Schedule file (see Section 4.5), or the module will not execute.

Maximal number of periods for firm planned orders - If you wish to enter any firm planned orders, this entry determines how far into the future planning horizon you may do so. It partially determines the width of this file. It may not be longer than the planning horizon entered in the Master Schedule file. Firm planned orders will be explained below.

Annual carrying charge rate, per cent - This is the inventory carrying charge rate appropriate for your inventory investment. It includes the opportunity cost for having capital funds tied up in inventory plus taxes, insurance, space charges and other costs incurred for carrying inventory. It is expressed as a per cent and must be an annual rate. Typical values range from 25 to 35 per cent, although yours may be higher or lower, and may fluctuate with changes in the interest rate. The only place it is used is in selected lot sizing computations.

ITEM ID - The same as in Section 4.1.

```
┌──────────┤ STORM EDITOR : Inventory Status File - MRP Module ├──────────┐
│ Title : BLUE RIDGE FURNITURE COMPANY                                    │
│ Total number of material items                    :        10           │
│ Maximal lead time in time buckets                 :         2           │
│ Maximal number of periods for firm planned orders :         2           │
│ Annual carrying charge rate, per cent             :        25.          │
│                                                                         │
│ R1  : C1      ITEM ID SAFE STOCK    ON HAND    PAST DUE RECEIPT 1 RECEIPT 2 │
│ STOOL-STD        1        50          53          0        0        0    │
│ STOOL-DLX        2        25          36          0        0        0    │
│ LEG             11         0         112          0        0        0    │
│ BRACE           12         0          36          0      500        0    │
│ SEAT ASSY       13         0           1          0        0        0    │
│ BACK ASSY       14         0           0          0        0        0    │
│ SEAT            21         0          45          0        0        0    │
│ PAD             22         0          22          0       50        0    │
│ FABRIC          23         0           9          0        0        0    │
│ BACK            24         0          14          0        0        0    │
│                                                                         │
└──────────┤ Enter the item ID number for STOOL-STD        ├─→├     ├──────┘
```

Figure 9A: The Inventory Status File

```
┌──────────┤ STORM EDITOR : Inventory Status File - MRP Module ├──────────┐
│ Title : BLUE RIDGE FURNITURE COMPANY                                    │
│ Total number of material items                    :        10           │
│ Maximal lead time in time buckets                 :         2           │
│ Maximal number of periods for firm planned orders :         2           │
│ Annual carrying charge rate, per cent             :        25.          │
│                                                                         │
│ R1  : C4    PAST DUE RECEIPT 1 RECEIPT 2    FPO ->   FPO 1    FPO 2     │
│ STOOL-STD       0          0        0       XXXX       0        0        │
│ STOOL-DLX       0          0        0       XXXX       0        0        │
│ LEG             0          0        0       XXXX       0        0        │
│ BRACE           0        500        0       XXXX       0      100        │
│ SEAT ASSY       0          0        0       XXXX       0      100        │
│ BACK ASSY       0          0        0       XXXX       0        0        │
│ SEAT            0          0        0       XXXX       0        0        │
│ PAD             0         50        0       XXXX       0        0        │
│ FABRIC          0          0        0       XXXX       0        0        │
│ BACK            0          0        0       XXXX       0        0        │
│                                                                         │
└──────────┤ Enter the number of units of 1 past due       ├─→├     ├──────┘
```

Figure 9B: The Inventory Status File

SAFE STOCK - This stands for *safety stock.* This is the minimal level of inventory you wish to maintain for this item. If your on-hand inventory drops below this amount at any time, STORM will add enough to planned orders to cover the gross requirements plus the safety stock replenishment.

ON HAND - This is the number of units of the item identified in the Item ID column which we have in inventory.

PAST DUE - This is the amount of this item, if any, which was supposed to be delivered (purchased item) or produced (manufactured item) prior to this time, but wasn't. It will be added to the Gross Requirements and used in the BOM explosion described in Section 5.3.1. It is listed separately to distinguish it from new gross requirements.

RECEIPT 1, 2, ... - These are planned receipts for this item for 1 period from now, 2 periods from now, etc. which result from open orders (purchasing or manufacturing). These quantities will affect projected inventory balances in the BOM explosion (see Section 5.3.1) by acting as *supplies* in their scheduled periods. We have purchase orders outstanding at Blue Ridge for braces and pads, as indicated in the figures.

FPO -> - This is a divider column which separates scheduled receipts columns (to the left) from firm planned order columns (to the right).

FPO 1, 2, ... - Firm planned orders are planned orders input by the user which *override* those normally computed by STORM. If a firm planned order is insufficient to meet the net requirements in the following period, it will be increased by STORM according to the designated lot sizing rule. Otherwise, STORM will never change an FPO value. In our example, we have two firm planned orders in period two for subassemblies, because an assembler who is particularly good at these is only available in week two of our planning horizon. *Please take special note of the fact that the first column of entries in this firm planned order section will be placed in the first period of the planning horizon, the second column in the second period, etc., regardless of the labels at the top of the FPO columns.*

4.7 The Item Master File

This file, in contrast to the Master Schedule and Inventory Status files, contains data that are expected to change only very gradually over time. For this reason, the item labels from this file will be used on reports for all material items. Figures 10A and 10B illustrate these data for the Blue Ridge example, since all would not fit in one screen. Starting with Figure 10A, the data items and their explanations are:

Title - Self-explanatory.

Total number of material items - This is the same as for the Inventory Status file, and is the number of material items in the BOM file. It determines the length of the Item Master file.

ITEM ID - The same as for the BOM file (see Section 4.1).

CLASS - This is an item for your use in characterizing products. It could be used to identify products as Class A, B, or C as in traditional inventory analysis (see the Inventory module), or to classify products as to their methods of manufacture (fabricated, assembled, etc.). STORM does not use this item; it is provided strictly for your convenience.

LOT SIZE - This is the rule to be used by STORM for lot sizing the net requirements of this item. There are seven different rules from which you may choose. The abbreviations used in the STORM prompt line and the definitions of the lot sizing rule they represent are listed in Section 4.7.1.

MULTIPLE - If you specify either FP (fixed period) or FQ (fixed quantity) for the lot sizing rule, then you must specify with this entry either the number of periods for FP or the number of units for FQ, to guide the lot sizing decisions.

LEAD TIME - This is the time from placing a purchasing or shop order for an item until the required quantity is available. Remember to express this and all other time quantities in consistent time units (time buckets).

SCRAP % - This is a percentage allowance for scrap for the item in question. If a nonzero entry is made, the lot sized planned orders column for this item in the BOM explosion report (see Figure 15 later in this chapter) will be inflated to account for this expected loss.

```
┌─────────────────────────────────────────────────────────────────────────┐
│    ┌──────────────┤ STORM EDITOR : Item Master File - MRP Module ├───     │
│    Title : BLUE RIDGE FURNITURE COMPANY                                   │
│    Total number of material items :           10                          │
│                                                                           │
│                                                                           │
│    R1  : C1      ITEM ID      CLASS   LOT SIZE   MULTIPLE  LEAD TIME  SCRAP % │
│    STOOL-STD        1                   LFL         0          1        0.   │
│    STOOL-DLX        2                   LFL         0          1        0.   │
│    LEG             11                   LFL         0          1        2.   │
│    BRACE           12                   LFL         0          1        2.   │
│    SEAT ASSY       13                   LFL         0          1        0.   │
│    BACK ASSY       14                   LFL         0          1        0.   │
│    SEAT            21                   LFL         0          1        0.   │
│    PAD             22                   LFL         0          1        1.   │
│    FABRIC          23                   LFL         0          2        1.   │
│    BACK            24                   LFL         0          1        0.5  │
│    └─────┤ Enter the item ID number for STOOL-STD        ├─>│      ├──────  │
└─────────────────────────────────────────────────────────────────────────┘
```

Figure 10A: The First Screen of the Item Master File

```
┌─────────────────────────────────────────────────────────────────────────┐
│    ┌──────────────┤ STORM EDITOR : Item Master File - MRP Module ├───     │
│    Title : BLUE RIDGE FURNITURE COMPANY                                   │
│    Total number of material items :           10                          │
│                                                                           │
│                                                                           │
│    R1  : C6      SCRAP % UNIT VALUE ORDER COST  DEMAND/YR DATA FIELD DATA FIELD │
│    STOOL-STD        0.        50.       23.       5000                     │
│    STOOL-DLX        0.        75.       28.       1500                     │
│    LEG              2.         3.        5.      30000                     │
│    BRACE            2.        1.5        5.      30000                     │
│    SEAT ASSY        0.        22.       12.       7000                     │
│    BACK ASSY        0.        22.       12.       1750                     │
│    SEAT             0.         8.        5.       7500                     │
│    PAD              1.         5.        5.       9000                     │
│    FABRIC           1.         6.        5.       9000                     │
│    BACK             0.5        8.        5.       2000                     │
│    └─────┤ Enter the per cent scrap allowance for 1      ├─>│      ├──────  │
└─────────────────────────────────────────────────────────────────────────┘
```

Figure 10B: The Last Screen of the Item Master File

UNIT VALUE - This is the dollar value of the item for inventory evaluation purposes. It is used to compute inventory carrying costs for the lot sizing analysis.

ORDER COST - This is the fixed cost per order to place either a purchasing or a manufacturing order. In the latter case, it is typically the setup cost for the manufacturing operation.

DEMAND/YR - This is the expected demand per year in units for this item. It is used to compute the lot size (or order quantity) if EOQ is picked as the lot sizing rule.

DATA FIELDS - Two additional user-defined data fields have been added for your convenience in augmenting this product information file. These items (along with several others in this file) will not be displayed anywhere on MRP module reports, but you may use these entries for your own internal use.

4.7.1 Explanation of Lot Sizing Rules

Lot-for-lot: LFL

This is a popular method which does not lump any two periods' net requirements together, but instead meets each one with a separate planned order.

Fixed Period: FP

This method lets you specify that the net requirements for a fixed number of periods be added together to provide a lot size. If you choose this, you must make a corresponding entry in the column labeled *multiple* which is described later in this section.

Fixed Quantity: FQ

This rule allows you to specify that the same number of units be ordered or produced every time; every lot has the same lot size. Selection of this option also requires you to enter the quantity desired in the column labeled *multiple,* described later in this section. If the fixed quantity is less than the net requirements for one period for some product, the lot size will be determined by taking the minimal integer multiple of your lot size which meets or exceeds the net requirements.

Economic Order Quantity: EOQ

This choice causes your lot sizes to be computed by the classical square root formula. This is not generally recommended for MRP systems, but is sometimes used in reorder point systems, so we provide it. If you select this rule, you must enter the setup/ordering cost and the expected annual demand in the Item Master file. Otherwise, STORM defaults to the LFL (lot-for-lot) rule. Furthermore, if the net requirement for a period is larger than the computed EOQ, the net requirement quantity will be used as the lot size.

Least Unit Cost: LUC

The lot size is computed by starting with the first nonzero net requirement quantity, and sequentially adding the inventory carrying charges to the setup cost, if the next nonzero requirement is added, then the next, and so on. The lot size which yields the lowest cost per unit is chosen, and the process is restarted.

Part Period Balancing: PPB

This procedure attempts to produce lot sizes with setup/ordering costs approximately equal to carrying costs. To apply this rule, the setup/ordering cost is first divided by the cost to carry one unit of inventory for one time period. This gives the number of so-called *economic part periods* in future lots before the carrying costs would equal the setup/ordering cost. Thus, suppose the first positive net requirement, R_1, occurs in period one. If the next positive requirement is for R_2 units in period three, then the number of part periods in the second lot is R_2 times two (periods). If this is less than the economic number of part periods computed above, we add it to the previous lot size; that is, we plan a lot size of $R_1 + R_2$ units for period one. We then subtract the number of part periods consumed by the second positive requirement (R_2 times two) from the original balance to obtain the net part periods available. We next consider the third period with positive requirements in an analogous way by multiplying its quantity by the number of periods since period one, and comparing it to the net part periods available, and so on. At some point the part periods consumed will exceed those available. We will choose the lot size that most closely equates the setup cost to the carrying cost, and restart the process from the first positive net requirement not included in this lot size. This process is continued until the end of the planning horizon is reached.

Wagner-Whitin Method: WW

This method is based on the technique of dynamic programming and will determine the optimal lot sizes for an individual item, to minimize the combined setup/ordering plus inventory carrying costs over the entire planning horizon. It is beyond the scope of this manual to provide the technical details of this procedure.

4.8 The Capacity File

For any item listed in the BOM file as a CAP (capacity) item, you must tell STORM how much of that resource is available for each period in the planning horizon via entries in the capacity file. The Blue Ridge Capacity file is shown in Figure 11. Note that if you have no CAP items in the BOM file, you do not need to change the default filename for the capacity file specified by STORM for it (see section 5.1 and Figure 12), nor does any file by that name need to exist. STORM will determine if this file is needed and will ignore the filename if it is not. The labels entered in this file will appear on the Capacity Load report (see Figure 15E).

The entries for this file when it is needed are:

Title - Self-explanatory.

Total number of capacity items - This must be the exact number of items listed in the BOM file as CAP items, and determines the length of this file.

Planning horizon length in time buckets - This is the number of periods for which you will enter resource availability data. It must be at least as long as the planning horizon entered in the Master Schedule file (see Section 4.4) in order to execute the module.

ITEM ID - The same as in Section 4.1.

DEFAULT - This is the default capacity per period for this particular resource. It will be used for all entries to its right which are left as "."

CAP 1, 2, ... - The capacity available in each period for this resource if other than the default value, in the same units as recorded in the BOM file. The projected resource usage will be compared to this amount in the Capacity Load Report, produced in conjunction with the BOM explosion.

```
┌──────────────────────────────────────────────────────────────────────────┐
│  ┌────────────────┤ STORM EDITOR : Resource Capacity File - MRP Module ├─────────┐  │
│  │ Title : BLUE RIDGE FURNITURE COMPANY                                         │  │
│  │ Total number of capacity items        :        1                             │  │
│  │ Number of periods in planning horizon :        4                             │  │
│  │                                                                              │  │
│  ├──────────────────────────────────────────────────────────────────────────────┤  │
│  │ R1  : C1        ITEM ID    Default    CAP  1     CAP  2     CAP  3     CAP  4   │  │
│  │ LABOR               99        50.        .          .          .          .    │  │
│  │                                                                              │  │
│  │                                                                              │  │
│  │                                                                              │  │
│  │                                                                              │  │
│  │                                                                              │  │
│  │                                                                              │  │
│  └──┤ Enter the item ID number for LABOR              │->            │──────────┘  │
└──────────────────────────────────────────────────────────────────────────┘
```

Figure 11: The Capacity File

5. Execution of the Module

When all files are ready, we select the Execute option from any Process menu or the File Selection menu to proceed. In this phase, too, there are a number of special features of this module to be considered.

5.1 The MRP File Specification Form

The first task we must perform is to enter the names of all the files we will be using. The STORM form used to do this is shown in Figure 12. It is a multiple-file modification of the standard File Specification form discussed in Chapter 3. For each of the five types of files, cells are provided into which we can enter the four components of a file specification: drive, directory, filename, and extension. Your directory specification can have a maximum of 36 characters. All cells are provided with default entries, including the filename cells. If you have just been entering or editing any of the files, the defaults will conform to your latest specifications, and you need only press F7 and proceed. Otherwise, default entries similar to Figure 12 will appear.

```
                    FILES NEEDED FOR RUNNING MRP


    File                Drive   Directory        Filename Ext List?

    Bill of Material      A    \                 bom      dat   n

    Master Schedule       A    \                 mast     dat   n

    Inventory Status      A    \                 mrpinv   dat   n

    Item Master           A    \                 item     dat   n

    Resource Capacity     A    \                 cap      dat   n
```

Figure 12: The File Specification Form for MRP

The capacity file is optional for the MRP module, but a default file name has been provided for it anyway. There is no need to *erase* these entries if you do not need this file; STORM will ignore them if the contents of the BOM file indicate that a capacity file is redundant.

In other ways, this STORM form is like the usual File Specification form. Using the Arrow keys, you may move about the form in any direction to make whatever modifications are necessary. You can indicate if you wish to have the contents of the file displayed on your monitor. You can also obtain directory listings by entering "*" or "?" in the filename or extension, as fully described in Chapter 3.

5.2 The Execution Process

When you have finished editing the names, press the F7 key to advance to the execution process outlined in Figure 13.

```
           STEPS IN THE MRP EXECUTION PROCESS

      • Check filenames
      • Check file syntax for each file
      • Check item number consistency between files
      • Build tree structure
```

Figure 13: The Execution Process

The process begins by checking to see if the files exist as specified. If not, the form in Figure 12 must be used to correct the entries. If the filenames were correct, the file syntax for each file will be checked by opening and reading the contents of each of the files specified. Any errors detected will be reported and an opportunity to correct them will be provided.

Once the checks on individual files have been completed, the third step is to check for item number consistency within and between the files. Thus, the BOM file is checked to insure that all descendants of a particular item exist in the file. In addition, each item scheduled in the Master Schedule file must exist as a material item in the BOM file. The BOM file material items must match perfectly those in the Inventory Status and Item Master files. The BOM capacity items must perfectly match those in the Resource Capacity file. There must not be any *cycles* in the BOM data (that is, item A is a parent to B, B to C, and C to A), nor can any resource capacity items have descendants. SETUP items must have a quantity per assembly of 1.0. Finally, proper relationships must be maintained between lead times in the Inventory Status file and the planning horizon in the Master Schedule file. As above, any errors detected will cause processing to stop to allow for correction.

Next, the tree structure necessary for the BOM explosion and associated output processing is created. Status messages informing you about all the steps listed in Figure 13 will appear as they are completed. Finally, the Output menu will appear on your monitor.

5.3 The Output Menu

The first four selections on the Output menu in Figure 14 are reports which you may obtain. The last selection is a special feature of the MRP module. It may not appear to belong on the Output menu, but this is the logical place to list the file utilities which it offers.

```
            MATERIAL REQUIREMENTS PLANNING : OUTPUT

   1)   Explosion Report (Exclude items with no activity)
   2)   Explosion Report (All items)
   3)   Indented Bill of Material Report
   4)   Where-Used Report
   5)   File Utilities
```

Figure 14: The Output Menu

The first two options appear in the same identical format, but simply contain a different selection of items. The first report excludes any items for which no quantity is expected to change during the planning horizon. You may prefer this in order to focus your attention on the active items. On the other hand, if you wish to see all items, selection 2 will allow you to do so. We will discuss the report for either of these two options in Section 5.3.1 and the other menu selections in the sections to follow.

5.3.1 The Explosion Report

The BOM Explosion Report is quite lengthy, even for our small example. Nonetheless, on the assumption that you may want to replicate our example to familiarize yourself with this module, we have reproduced in Figures 15A through 15G all the output you would receive if you made selection 1 or 2 from the Output menu (the outputs are the same for our particular example, although this is not generally true). These figures were produced using the F6 function key to select output devices and routing the report to the printer. Thus, we call the displays pages instead of screens.

We will only explain one sample section of the Explosion Report since all are in the same format. We refer you to the top of Figure 15A, to the section headed STOOLSTD. Here a set of information about the item is listed. Most of it is from the Item Master file. The *level* is the *lowest level code* for the item which was computed by STORM. That is, this is the lowest level at which this item appears in any product structure tree to which it belongs (refer to Figures 1 and 2). The *Total order/setup cost* in the right column of this information is the *Order/Setup Cost* per occurrence which was entered in the Item Master file, times the number of orders or setups suggested by the *planned order* (PO) column. The entry in Figure 15B for LEG (top of the figure) indicates that two orders for LEGS are suggested in WEEK 1 and WEEK 2. The purpose of this header information is to allow you to interpret the entries that follow.

After the next line in the figure, the explosion results begin. In the first column of entries are labels for Past Due and the periods in the planning horizon. The next column, headed GR, contains the Gross Requirements, period by period, for the item being considered. If there are any past due units for this item, they will be reported as the first entry in this column. Notice that at the very top of this figure, the column header Gross Reqts appears above the column subsequently headed GR as a reminder to you of what the GR stands for.

Following the GR column is the SR or scheduled receipts column which shows the expected arrival of any ordered units of this item during the planning horizon. These units will be used to meet gross requirements whenever they become available. The column headed OH contains the Projected On Hand balances, period by period, assuming everything goes exactly as planned.

The last two columns both relate to the lot sizing activity. The first column, headed LFL, shows the lot sizes that would result if the LFL rule was used. These reflect the latest possible time the quantities must be available to meet the schedule. The PO or Planned Order column reflects the final lot sizing suggestions of the MRP system after the LFL lot sizes have been replanned using the lot sizing rules selected in the Item Master file. In our example, it happens that LFL was the rule chosen so these are the same, but that is generally not the case. We show both the LFL and PO columns for your convenience.

If capacity problems arise with a lot sizing rule which produces relatively large lot sizes, manual adjustments can be made knowing the LFL lot sizes.

You may examine Figures 15B through 15E to see the remainder of the explosion results. Notice that all these figures contain *exception notices* in a footnote style following the explosion results for particular items. These footnotes inform us that scrap adjustments have been made to the planned orders, that firm planned orders caused certain results in the planned order column, and so on. Figure 15E reveals that we are in trouble with item FABRIC (the first in the figure). There is a projected on hand balance of -191 in period 2. This is an MRP convention for letting you know that some action needed to be taken *before* the planning horizon started in order to meet the schedule. There is a corresponding footnote at the bottom of that section of the figure which informs us that two planned orders for this item should have been placed prior to this time. This means the current schedule for Blue Ridge is infeasible. We cannot meet the expected demand unless we can expedite the receipt of the fabric. Perhaps we can air freight it in from our supplier, since it is not too heavy.

```
                          EXPLOSION REPORT
       Planning      Gross    Sched'd  Projected --- Planned Orders ---
       Period        Reqts    Receipts On hand  Lot for Lot   Lot sized
```

```
STOOL-STD            1        Level  0   LT =  1    Lot size LFL
Annual demand = 5000          Scrap % = 0.00
Order/Setup Cost = 23.00      Total order/setup cost = 23.00
Unit Value = 50.00            Total carrying cost   = 49.52
Safety stock = 50
```

	GR	SR	OH	LFL	PO
PAST DUE	0		53		
WEEK 1	0	0	53	0	0
WEEK 2	0	0	53	297	297
WEEK 3	300	0	50	0	0
WEEK 4	0	0	50	0	0

```
STOOL-DLX            2        Level  0   LT =  1    Lot size LFL
Annual demand = 1500          Scrap % = 0.00
Order/Setup Cost = 28.00      Total order/setup cost = 28.00
Unit Value = 75.00            Total carrying cost   = 47.96
Safety stock = 25
```

	GR	SR	OH	LFL	PO
PAST DUE	0		36		
WEEK 1	0	0	36	0	0
WEEK 2	0	0	36	0	0
WEEK 3	0	0	36	69	69
WEEK 4	80	0	25	0	0

Figure 15A: Page 1 of BOM Explosion

```
                      EXPLOSION REPORT
    Planning          Gross    Sched'd  Projected --- Planned Orders ---
    Period            Reqts    Receipts  On hand Lot for Lot  Lot sized
```

```
    LEG                 11     Level  1  LT =  1     Lot size LFL
    Annual demand = 30000      Scrap % = 2.00
    Order/Setup Cost = 5.00    Total order/setup cost = 10.00
    Unit Value = 3.00          Total carrying cost   = 1.62
    Safety stock = 0
```

	GR	SR	OH	LFL	PO+
PAST DUE	0		112		
WEEK 1	0	0	112	1098	1098
WEEK 2	1188	0	0	282	282
WEEK 3	276	0	0	0	0
WEEK 4	0	0	0	0	0

+ Values adjusted to account for scrap; total scrap = 28

```
    BRACE               12     Level  1   LT =  1    Lot size LFL
    Annual demand = 30000      Scrap % = 2.00
    Order/Setup Cost = 5.00    Total order/setup cost = 10.00
    Unit Value = 1.50          Total carrying cost   = 3.87
    Safety stock = 0
```

	GR	SR	OH	LFL	PO+
PAST DUE	0		36		
WEEK 1	0	500	536	666	666
WEEK 2	1188	0	0	282	282
WEEK 3	276	0	0	0	0
WEEK 4	0	0	0	0	0

+ Values adjusted to account for scrap; total scrap = 20

Figure 15B: Page 2 of BOM Explosion

```
                            EXPLOSION REPORT
       Planning       Gross    Sched'd  Projected --- Planned Orders ---
       Period         Reqts    Receipts  On hand Lot for Lot  Lot sized
```

```
SEAT ASSY           13      Level  1   LT = 1     Lot size LFL
Annual demand = 7000        Scrap % = 0.00
Order/Setup Cost = 12.00    Total order/setup cost = 12.00
Unit Value = 22.00          Total carrying cost   = 6.98
Safety stock = 0
```

	GR	SR	OH	LFL	PO
PAST DUE	0		1		
WEEK 1	0	0	1	0	0
WEEK 2	0	0	1	0	100#
WEEK 3	69	0	32	0	0
WEEK 4	0	0	32	0	0

100 is firm planned order

```
BACK ASSY           14      Level  1   LT = 1     Lot size LFL
Annual demand = 1750        Scrap % = 0.00
Order/Setup Cost = 12.00    Total order/setup cost = 12.00
Unit Value = 22.00          Total carrying cost   = 6.56
Safety stock = 0
```

	GR	SR	OH	LFL	PO
PAST DUE	0		0		
WEEK 1	0	0	0	0	0
WEEK 2	0	0	0	0	100#
WEEK 3	69	0	31	0	0
WEEK 4	0	0	31	0	0

100 is firm planned order

Figure 15C: Page 3 of BOM Explosion

```
                        EXPLOSION REPORT
   Planning       Gross    Sched'd  Projected --- Planned Orders ---
   Period         Reqts    Receipts  On hand  Lot for Lot  Lot sized
```

```
SEAT              21       Level  2   LT =  1     Lot size LFL
Annual demand = 7500      Scrap % = 0.00
Order/Setup Cost = 5.00   Total order/setup cost = 5.00
Unit Value = 8.00         Total carrying cost   = 1.73
Safety stock = 0
```

	GR	SR	OH	LFL	PO
PAST DUE	0		45		
WEEK 1	0	0	45	352	352
WEEK 2	397	0	0	0	0
WEEK 3	0	0	0	0	0
WEEK 4	0	0	0	0	0

```
PAD               22       Level  2   LT =  1     Lot size LFL
Annual demand = 9000      Scrap % = 1.00
Order/Setup Cost = 5.00   Total order/setup cost = 5.00
Unit Value = 5.00         Total carrying cost   = 1.73
Safety stock = 0
```

	GR	SR	OH	LFL	PO+
PAST DUE	0		22		
WEEK 1	0	50	72	130	130
WEEK 2	200	0	0	0	0
WEEK 3	0	0	0	0	0
WEEK 4	0	0	0	0	0

+ Values adjusted to account for scrap; total scrap = 2

Figure 15D: Page 4 of BOM Explosion

```
                               EXPLOSION REPORT
        Planning        Gross    Sched'd  Projected --- Planned Orders ---
        Period          Reqts    Receipts On hand Lot for Lot  Lot sized
```

FABRIC	23		Level 2 LT = 2 Lot size LFL		
Annual demand = 9000			Scrap % = 1.00		
Order/Setup Cost = 5.00			Total order/setup cost = 5.00		
Unit Value = 6.00			Total carrying cost = 6.03		
Safety stock = 100					

	GR	SR	OH	LFL	PO+
PAST DUE	0		9		
WEEK 1	0	0	9*	294	294
WEEK 2	200	0	-191*	0	0
WEEK 3	0	0	100	0	0
WEEK 4	0	0	100	0	0

* 91 units for WEEK 1 offset into past by 2 period(s)
* 200 units for WEEK 2 offset into past by 1 period(s)
+ Values adjusted to account for scrap; total scrap = 3

BACK	24		Level 2 LT = 1 Lot size LFL		
Annual demand = 2000			Scrap % = 0.50		
Order/Setup Cost = 5.00			Total order/setup cost = 5.00		
Unit Value = 8.00			Total carrying cost = 5.38E-01		
Safety stock = 0					

	GR	SR	OH	LFL	PO+
PAST DUE	0		14		
WEEK 1	0	0	14	87	87
WEEK 2	100	0	0	0	0
WEEK 3	0	0	0	0	0
WEEK 4	0	0	0	0	0

+ Values adjusted to account for scrap; total scrap = 1

Figure 15E: Page 5 of BOM Explosion

Figure 15F shows a short Cost Summary report for our run. It totals the ordering or setup cost plus the inventory carrying costs for *all* items in the run. It will allow you to evaluate the cost effectiveness of different schedules and lot sizing rules. It also lists the inventory carrying charge rate which was used for the computations.

```
              EXPLOSION REPORT : COST SUMMARY
              (Carrying Charge Rate = 25.00%)

    Total order/setup cost for all items =      115.00
    Total carrying cost for all items    =      126.52
    Total cost for all items             =      241.52
```

Figure 15F: The Cost Summary Report

Figure 15G contains the Capacity Load Report for our example. In general, if there is such a report, it will appear at the end of the BOM explosion. From a computational perspective, this is the optimal time to prepare and output this report. The header line lists the resource in question (LABOR in our example) and its Item ID (99 for Blue Ridge LABOR). Then for each period, the capacity available versus the capacity *loaded* (or used) and the per cent utilization are listed for this resource. In addition to the infeasibility noted above, this report reveals a very uneven use of the labor force for Blue Ridge. We could try to reschedule the finished products in the Master Schedule file, and/or use firm planned orders to try to *smooth* the capacity utilization.

```
                   CAPACITY LOAD REPORT

                   LABOR          99
    Planning       Available    Loaded       Per cent
    Period         Capacity     Capacity     Utilized
    CAP    1         50.00        0.00          0.00
    CAP    2         50.00      188.90        377.80
    CAP    3         50.00       48.30         96.60
    CAP    4         50.00        0.00          0.00
```

Figure 15G: Capacity Load Report

5.3.2 The Indented BOM Report

The primary purpose of this report is to help you document your BOM structure for each item. It allows you to do this in a variety of ways. If you select option 3 from the Output menu, you will obtain the Indented BOM menu as shown in Figure 16. The first two choices on this latter menu apply to all levels from the requested level to the bottom of the BOM structure. You may either request this multi-level output for all items at the requested level (menu option 1) or for a specific item ID (menu option 2). In either case you will use the STORM Candidate Selection process to make your choice of level or item.

```
MATERIAL REQUIREMENTS PLANNING : INDENTED BOM

          1)   By level, all levels
          2)   Single item, all levels
          3)   By level, single level
          4)   Single item, single level
```

Figure 16: The Indented BOM Menu

Options 3 and 4 on the Indented BOM menu are analogous to options 1 and 2 except that only the immediate descendants of any item are shown. This is essentially the single-level bill concept used in building the BOM file.

We selected option 1 from the Indented BOM menu, and subsequently chose level 0 to produce the display in Figure 17.

Notice that this display is not physically indented, as the name implies. However, the column headed LEVEL does reveal the indented or hierarchical structure. Any time you see the level increase from one row to another in this display, you know the lower of the two rows represents a descendant of the parent in the row above it. The item ID, name and quantity per assembly are also shown in this report. This report is exactly analogous to Figures 1 and 2 which show the product structure in tree format.

5.3.3 The Where-Used Report

If you choose option 4, the Where-Used Report, on the Output menu, you will elicit a parallel process to the Indented BOM Report. First a Where-Used Report menu will appear with exactly analogous options to those of the Indented BOM menu. After selecting from that list, a second selection process will follow wherein you specify the level or the

```
                    INDENTED BOM
                      LEVEL 0

             STOOL-STD              1
   Item ID    Level      Item Name      Qty/Assy
     11         1             LEG        4.000
     12         1           BRACE        4.000
     21         1            SEAT        1.000
     99         1           LABOR        0.500

             STOOL-DLX              2
   Item ID    Level      Item Name      Qty/Assy
     11         1             LEG        4.000
     12         1           BRACE        4.000
     13         1        SEAT ASSY       1.000
     21         2            SEAT        1.000
     22         2             PAD        1.000
     23         2          FABRIC        1.000
     99         2           LABOR        0.200
    199         2       SETUP STPL       1.000
     99         3           LABOR        0.200
     14         1        BACK ASSY       1.000
     24         2            BACK        1.000
     22         2             PAD        1.000
     23         2          FABRIC        1.000
     99         2           LABOR        0.200
    199         2       SETUP STPL       1.000
     99         3           LABOR        0.200
     99         1           LABOR        0.700
```

Figure 17: Indented BOM Listing

item ID for which you desire the Where-Used Report. For the Blue Ridge data, we selected all items at level 2 for all levels to produce the display in Figure 18.

If you select a single-level Where-Used Report, you also obtain the quantity per assembly. Note that, in this case, quantity per assembly means the quantity of the item listed in the heading required to make one unit of the parent item listed in the row. For multi-level listings, this column does not appear since the entries would be ambiguous.

```
                    WHERE-USED REPORT
                        LEVEL 2


              SEAT                  21
        Item ID        Level      Item Name
        13                 1      SEAT ASSY
        2                  0      STOOL-DLX
        1                  1      STOOL-STD


              PAD                   22
        Item ID        Level      Item Name
        14                 1      BACK ASSY
        2                  0      STOOL-DLX
        13                 1      SEAT ASSY
        2                  0      STOOL-DLX


              FABRIC                23
        Item ID        Level      Item Name
        14                 1      BACK ASSY
        2                  0      STOOL-DLX
        13                 1      SEAT ASSY
        2                  0      STOOL-DLX


              BACK                  24
        Item ID        Level      Item Name
        14                 1      BACK ASSY
        2                  0      STOOL-DLX


              SETUP STPL           199
        Item ID        Level      Item Name
        14                 1      BACK ASSY
        2                  0      STOOL-DLX
        13                 1      SEAT ASSY
        2                  0      STOOL-DLX
```

Figure 18: Where-Used Report

5.3.4 File Utilities for MRP

If you select the File Utilities option from the Output menu, you will see the display reproduced as Figure 19. You should not choose this option until you are finished with all other Output menu items, however, since you cannot return to the Output menu from this menu. The reason for this restriction is simple. If you alter the files via the file utilities, the results of other processes listed on the Output menu would no longer be correct.

The File Utilities menu allows you to conveniently perform two housekeeping functions. The first of these is simply to copy item labels from one file to another. If you have already created your MRP files and have edited the row labels in one file, but not in the others, option 1 on this menu allows you to copy your edited labels to other files. You will first have to declare a source file to copy from and a destination file to copy to, from among the five files used in MRP. Then each Item ID that STORM matches between the two files will result in the label from the source file being placed in the label area of the destination file. All other contents of the destination file will be left unchanged, including row labels for which no match between the two files occurred.

```
MATERIAL REQUIREMENTS PLANNING : FILE UTILITIES

1)   Copy item labels between existing files
2)   Sort items by level and ID and save on disk
```

Figure 19: File Utilities Menu

The second choice on this menu allows you to sort items in the MRP files first by level, then within level by item ID number to arrange them in ascending order. Thus, all level zero items would come out at the top of the file, then level one, etc. Within level zero, item 1 would precede 2, 2 would precede 3, etc. Many users prefer such a tidy listing within files, and this order will also speed processing within the MRP module for the BOM explosion, since this is the order in which it is done.

6. Tips for Using the MRP Module

The tips which we provide may be conveniently divided between the mechanics of using the module and the substance of solving your problem. In the first category, we will discuss data entry and *transaction processing* (defined later) in the next two sections. Following that, some ideas concerning the substantive issues of infeasible schedules and uneven capacity utilization will be presented.

6.1 Data Entry Tips

The major point we want to emphasize here is *create your Bill of Material file first,* and then use STORM to create the other files from it so that you do not repeat typing in row labels or Item ID numbers. Be sure that you have completed all entries in the BOM file before starting to create the others to further save time.

A second tip is that when you must add items to the files at a later time, you may edit the labels in the BOM file, and then copy these to the other files. Note, however, that you must first insert the item in the other file or files to which it belongs. For material items, this includes the Inventory Status file, the Item Master file, and the Master Schedule file if the new item is master scheduled. In all these cases, the Item ID number will have to be entered in the file. For capacity items, only the Resource Capacity file will be affected. A final note is that when you delete an item from the system, you must delete it from all applicable files. Otherwise, STORM will indicate a file error condition and no execution will take place.

6.2 Transaction Processing (Moving Through Time)

As you move through time, you will want to replan your operations using information about what actually happened in the most recent time period. STORM has no automatic facility to do this, since plans and reality often diverge in practice. However, it is fairly easy to use the STORM Editor to edit the files to achieve the updating desired. The Bill of Material file and the Item Master file are generally unchanged from period to period, and so will be left out of this discussion.

6.2.1 Transaction Processing: Master Schedule File

In the Master Schedule file, the columns indicate time as we move from left to right. If our actual results exactly matched our plan from one period earlier, we would simply delete the first column from this file and add a new last column. The last column's label may need to be changed to reflect our time period (such as week 5, 6, etc. in the example in this chapter). Then we would only need to delete old and/or add new products to this file, depending on what we needed to master schedule for the next planning horizon.

6.2.2 Transaction Processing: Inventory Status File

There are several items which require updating from period to period in this file. The first and most obvious is the ON HAND column for each material item. If your actual operations matched your BOM explosion report from the previous period *exactly,* then the projected on hand balances as of the end of the first period on that report would be the new actual balances. This is unlikely to occur for all material items, but at least gives you a place to start. You may either take the actual balances from a physical inventory count or an inventory record-keeping system and enter them into this column using the STORM Editor. If you must perform this operation frequently, you may want to develop or to have developed a computer program to take this information from your inventory control system and put it into the STORM Inventory Status file. A data base management system may be used to develop such a program. The file format information in Appendix C would be helpful to any effort to develop such a program.

The same comments as listed above for ON HAND balances also apply to PAST DUE quantities. We provide the PAST DUE column in STORM so you don't have to keep rolling past-due orders into new periods in the Master Schedule file. Instead, you may consolidate them all in this one place. You will generally have to either update these using the STORM Editor, or develop a program if your inventory control system tracks these balances to copy them into the STORM file.

Both the scheduled receipt columns (RECEIPT 1, RECEIPT 2, ...) and the firm planned order columns (FPO 1, FPO 2, ...) work the same way and will be discussed as one. If everything happened exactly as planned in the preceding BOM explosion report, we would only need to delete the first column from each of these areas, and add a new last column or columns (if we needed to extend the time frame for either). For each material item listed in this file, we would need to update the receipts and firm planned orders entries to reflect exactly what did happen, and what we expect or want to happen in the future. An inventory control system might provide this information for scheduled receipts, as indicated above for ON HAND, but we will likely have to enter firm planned order quantities via the STORM Editor.

6.2.3 Transaction Processing: Resource Capacity File

This operates similarly to the Master Schedule file described above, only more easily. The resource capacity items listed in this file are likely to be very constant. To the extent that their capacities per period do not change dramatically, the DEFAULT entry may suffice for most periods in the planning horizon. Thus, we may only need to delete the first period in the old file (CAP 1 in our sample problem in this chapter), add a new last period and edit the column label for the new last period. Of course, if we want the capacity for any of the items to differ from the default value for this new last period, we will have to edit that row.

6.3 Infeasible Material Schedules

An infeasible schedule occurs from a material standpoint if one or more purchasing or manufacturing orders should have been released prior to the current time in order to produce the master scheduled quantities of items. This infeasibility assumes that the lead times for each of these items are absolutely fixed. The fact that they generally are not is what allows us to try to work around such infeasibilities.

For a purchasing order, we may ask the supplier to expedite shipment of the order. If that is not possible, we may investigate alternative transportation modes (truck rather than rail, air rather than truck, for example) to see if the lead time can be shortened. Another strategy is to try an alternate supplier, if one exists who can meet your quality standards. Any of these strategies may cause additional costs which must be considered prior to any final decision.

For a manufacturing order, we may check with the department or departments in which the item requires processing to determine if we can get a high priority assigned to it to expedite it through our system. We must be careful not to fall into the trap where everything is expedited, but this strategy may be successful if used selectively. In some cases, working overtime or transferring personnel from a less busy department may help in this situation.

6.4 Uneven Capacity Utilization

When we see uneven capacity utilization in the capacity utilization section of the BOM explosion report (see Figure 15E), there are three strategies which we may use to try to smooth it. The first of these involves moving master scheduled quantities around in the Master Schedule file. To determine which ones to move, you may need to use the Where-Used report for the capacity item in question to trace it to master scheduled items. For this strategy to be truly effective, there must be some slack capacity in earlier periods in the planning horizon. In this way, we may move master scheduled quantities to periods *earlier* than when they are required so that schedule integrity is assured. We suggest you save your original Master Schedule file under a new name before you start this procedure. Then if this procedure is unsuccessful, you do not have to undo all the editing work you've done during your experiments.

A second strategy is to examine the BOM explosion report to see if the lot sizing procedures you are using are causing *lumpy* capacity utilization. If, as above, you have used the Where-Used report to identify the parent items for the resource, you may check the lot sizes determined for the parents on the explosion report. If there are some large lot sizes, the lot sizing rule may be changed so as to decrease them. This will typically smooth capacity utilization, but you must remember to change the lot sizing procedure back when the problem has passed.

Possibly the best way to treat uneven capacity utilization is with firm planned orders. Firm planned orders allow us to move capacity usage in the most micro way for finished goods, components, assemblies, etc. We again assume that there is some slack capacity earlier in the planning horizon so that we can place firm planned orders for parents which use this capacity in these periods with slack. Naturally, we must rerun the BOM explosion to make sure *material* items needed to support this plan are available. We continue this type of juggling until we reach a plan we decide to implement.

Even though the discussion above focused on situations where excess capacity existed early in the planning horizon, we can use similar logic when overutilization of capacity occurs. First, we try to see if the amount of capacity available can be increased through overtime, subcontracting, transfers from other departments, etc. If not, we must change the schedule and perhaps notify our customers that we cannot meet some due dates. One other item to check here is required safety stocks. We may be able to temporarily reduce them during the capacity crunch to free capacity for production, and then rebuild them at a later time. While not desirable, this may be the only way to meet our commitments.

7. Altering Problem Data Dimensions

Since the MRP module has five files, we will discuss how to alter each of their dimensions in separate sections. However, you should be very careful in making such changes since STORM cannot ensure that your resulting files will be consistent with each other.

7.1 Altering the BOM File Size

You may insert or delete rows at will. STORM will automatically keep track of the total number of items in the file for you. It will not keep track of parent/descendant relationships, however. Thus, if you delete the row containing a descendant of an item, and do not remove it from the list of descendants for that item, you will get an error message if you try to execute the module. You must keep at least one row at all times in the BOM file. Further, the number of rows must always be at least one greater than the number of descendant columns.

Columns one and two of this file are required and cannot be deleted, nor can any columns be inserted preceding these. Columns beyond column two exist in pairs of descendant ID and quantity per assembly for each descendant. The only time it should be necessary to add a pair is when the maximal number of descendants for any item increases above its current limit. In such a case it is desirable to *add columns at the right extreme of the data area,* so that is the only place STORM allows you to do so. It will automatically update the maximal number of descendants entry in the Problem Description area. You may not add any column if the number of columns is one less than the number of rows.

Beyond column two, you may delete any *pair* of descendant ID and quantity per assembly columns by placing the pointer on either of them and pressing the function key to delete a column. Again, you should exercise care to ensure that the correct parent/descendant structure is intact after such deletions.

7.2 Altering the Master Schedule File Size

You may insert or delete rows at will, but must always maintain a one row minimum for this file. STORM will automatically update the Problem Description area entry for the number of items in the file.

Column one in this file is required and cannot be deleted, nor can any column be inserted to precede it. Columns beyond it can be deleted or have new columns inserted to precede or follow them. A minimum of two columns must be maintained at all times, including column one. STORM will automatically keep track of the planning horizon in the Problem Description area as the number of columns changes.

7.3 Altering the Inventory Status File Size

Rows may be inserted or deleted at will, with the proviso that a minimum of one row must be maintained. STORM will automatically keep track of the number of items in the file for the Problem Description area.

Columns one to four are required, thus no columns can be inserted to precede one of these, nor can any of these be deleted. At least one scheduled receipt column is also required. Other scheduled receipts columns may be inserted anywhere to the right of the PAST DUE column, and to the left of the FPO -> divider column. STORM will automatically keep track of the maximal lead time for any item in the Problem Description area as the number of these columns changes. If you insert new receipt columns, the default labels INSERT n (where n is a number STORM assigns) will be used. *STORM assumes that scheduled receipts start with period one in the planning horizon, and increase by one as we move from left to right in the Inventory Status file.*

The FPO -> divider column is required, but no columns are required to its right if you do not wish to use any firm planned orders. Columns may be inserted to the right of the divider column and STORM will automatically keep track of the maximal number of periods for firm planned orders. If you insert new FPO columns, the default labels INSERT n (where n is a number STORM assigns) will be used. *STORM assumes that firm planned orders start with period one in the planning horizon, and increase by one as we move from left to right in the Inventory Status file.*

7.4 Altering the Item Master File Size

You may insert or delete rows at will, provided that a minimum of one row be maintained at all times. STORM will automatically keep track of the total number of items in the file for you. All columns are fixed and therefore neither insertions nor deletions are allowed.

7.5 Altering the Capacity File Size

Rows may be inserted or deleted at will, provided a one row minimum is maintained. STORM will automatically keep track of the number of capacity resources listed in the file.

Columns one and two for this file are required. They cannot be deleted, nor can a column be inserted to precede either of them. Columns beyond them may be deleted or have new columns inserted before or after them. A minimum of three columns must be maintained in the file at all times, corresponding to a planning horizon of at least one period. STORM automatically keeps track of the planning horizon value, and updates the entry in the Problem Description area as the number of columns changes.

- NOTES -

STATISTICAL PROCESS CONTROL CAPABILITIES

PROBLEM FORMULATION OPTIONS
- Variables control charts
    - Mean (x-bar chart)
    - Range (R chart)
    - Standard deviation (s chart)
    - Variance (s-squared chart)
- Attributes control charts
    - Fraction nonconforming (p chart)
    - Nonconformities per unit (c chart)
- Design based on history or standards
- Single or double limit charts
- Common or individualized plan parameters
- Raw or summarized variables data

OUTPUT OPTIONS AND OTHER FEATURES
- Control chart plots with plan design information
- Automated out-of-control criteria selected by user; includes statistical runs tests
- Automated chi-squared test for normality
- Assignable cause samples plotted, but ignored in computations
- Save plans to data base for later use
- Data set allows for user coded potential assignable causes

MAXIMAL PROBLEM SIZES (VARIABLES, SAMPLE SIZE, ATTRIBUTES, SAMPLES)
- Personal version: (5, 25, 5, 100)

- Professional version
  Representative sizes, with 500K of net memory for STORM:
    (5, 25, 5, 445)
    (100, 5, 100, 65)
    (See Section 2 for more details)

FILE NAME FOR THE SAMPLE PROBLEM DATA
- SPC.DAT

Chapter 20

STATISTICAL PROCESS CONTROL

In recent years, statistical process control (SPC) has gained much popularity in manufacturing companies. It is based on our knowledge of the theory of random behavior. A primary goal of SPC is to detect *nonrandom* behavior in a process as soon as possible after it starts. In this way, the process can be adjusted to correct the problem and bring it back into control before heavy material losses occur. Naturally, we would prefer that processes never go out of control, but they do.

The basic approach to such detection is to plot points on control charts which may have upper and/or lower *control limits*. A point falling outside a limit is unlikely to occur by chance, and is therefore subject to suspicion of nonrandom influences. When that occurs, a search is performed for an *assignable cause* which might explain the nonrandom behavior. Potential assignable causes include:

- Operators
- Machines
- Materials (vendors)
- Relationships of the above to each other, including over time
- Others

If an assignable cause is found for a particular sample result, it is excluded from the computations to establish revised control chart limits.

SPC is frequently used in a proactive way by companies. The control charts which are the heart of SPC are used to measure the impact of process changes. If these changes produce improved performance, they become the standard way of running the process.

Another use of SPC is to define a standard for a process based on its past or *historical* performance. After any historical data points are removed for which assignable causes are found, the remaining data may be used to compute control chart limits. These limits are the *natural tolerance limits* of the process. They are the limits the process is capable of maintaining.

Many control charts are based on the statistical assumption that the characteristic being measured follows a normal distribution. It is particularly important that this assumption be tested when small sample sizes are used. Therefore, STORM includes an automatic chi-squared goodness-of-fit test for normality. The results of the test are provided with the control chart plot.

The proper interpretation of control charts is critical to their use. Many different out-of-control criteria have been suggested for interpreting the charts. Some are rules of thumb which are particularly useful when only a small number of samples are available for analysis. When a larger data set is available, we recommend the use of statistical *runs tests* to properly interpret control charts. Both simple criteria and runs tests are available in STORM, and you can turn them on or off at will. This capability allows you to automate part of the process of interpreting control charts. Of course, a decision maker must still review the chart, conduct the assignable cause searches that are indicated, and take action accordingly. The exact charts and criteria and some suggestions for using them are the subject of this chapter.

1. The Solution Procedures

There are a variety of control charts as well as out-of-control criteria for interpreting them which are presented below. First, there are some generic concepts which we need to define which apply to all the charts.

Control charts may be designed based on *history* or *standards*. History simply means we have data available from the past which we use to compute control chart limits. The advantage of using history is that the limits which result are real. We know the process is capable of staying within these limits because it has in the past. We recommend a minimum of 30 acceptable samples to establish control charts based on history. The process for defining limits is an iterative one. When 30 or more samples are available, control chart limits can be computed and the samples plotted. If there is any nonrandom behavior in the samples, assignable cause searches must be performed to see if there are explanations for the nonrandom behavior. If so, the data points should be excluded from computations in the next iteration. This process should continue until no points exhibit nonrandom behavior, or no assignable causes can be found for those that do. If the number of points remaining in the data set is at least 30, control chart limits can be established and used. Otherwise, we need to collect more samples.

There are several situations in which standard values may be used in lieu of limits based on historical data. The most obvious is when there is no history, so we use estimates of the process capability. Such estimates may be based on manufacturer's specifications for the equipment being used in the production process.

A second situation arises when a customer has provided us with tolerance limits which we must meet in order to win his business. Our process may be incapable at present of meeting these specifications. We will use the standards provided to us by the customer to show exactly how much we must improve. As process changes are made, we can track the improvement as we come inside the specification limits.

One other situation which may occur is that the process is capable of producing products within tighter limits than those specified by our customers. It is possible to use the customer specifications to establish wider limits than the process would normally meet. Such situations are properly called *acceptance control charts*. The problem with using them is that the products may be within customer specifications, but the process is out-of-control. That is, the process is operating outside control limits based on its history, but inside control limits based on the customer standards. Many companies feel this is a bad practice for that reason, and use historically based standards even if they result in better quality products than required.

Finally, we introduce the concept of upper and lower control chart limits. In some situations, we may only be concerned about deviations on one side or the other of a measurement, but not both. In such cases, we may use a single limit plan on the appropriate end (upper or lower). An example of this is any control chart which measures variability in a process. We are concerned if the variability is too high, but not if it is low. Thus, we may use only an upper limit on our control chart. We point out that also using a lower control limit may be beneficial, even in this case. If unusually low variation occurs in a process, we may want to investigate for an assignable cause for *favorable* deviation. If we find a cause, it may lead to a process improvement such that smaller variability is always the result. If we want to monitor deviations in either direction, we specify a double limit control chart.

1.1 The Control Charts

The control charts may be broadly classified as variables and attributes control charts. *Variables* control charts are used to measure a continuous dimension such as length, width, temperature, etc. The variables control charts which STORM supports include:

- Mean (x-bar chart)
- Range (R chart)
- Standard deviation (s chart)
- Variance (s-squared chart)

Attributes control charts are appropriate when the measurement is a *categorical* or two level one. For example, we may only observe that a product is conforming or nonconforming, or it has a nonconformity or it doesn't. (Previously, nonconforming products were called defective and nonconformities were called defects. More recently the terminology we are using has been adopted.) The attributes charts which STORM supports include:

- Fraction nonconforming (p chart)
- Nonconformities per unit (c chart)

We will provide brief descriptions and explanations for each of these six control charts.

• Mean (x-bar chart)

The *mean* or *x-bar chart* is used to monitor and control the *level* of some variable of interest. It is based on the arithmetic mean computed from samples drawn from the process. For example, if we were bottling beverages in twelve ounce cans, we need to control the average contents of each can so that it corresponds to its labeling. The mean chart is probably the most commonly used variables control chart and certainly an important one. We use the normal probability distribution for computations for this chart.

• Range (R chart)

The range is used to measure the variability in the process. As compared to the level of the variable measured in a mean chart, the goal in this case is consistency in production. In the early days of statistical quality control, the *range chart (R chart)* was used heavily because inspectors had to manually compute and plot the variables. The range offered a far easier measure of variation to compute than, for example, the standard deviation. In addition, if the sample sizes are small (twelve or less), the power of the range approaches that of the standard deviation. If the sample size exceeds 25, the range is not appropriate and will not be plotted. We use the normal probability distribution for computations for this chart. Due to the widespread availability of computing resources, it is now possible to use the standard deviation or variance which employ *all* measurements in the sample to monitor and control variability.

• Standard deviation (s chart)

The *standard deviation (s chart)* is also a measure of variability in the process. It has the advantage, as compared to the range chart, of being based on every measurement in the sample rather than just the two extreme points. When the sample size is large, it is a more powerful statistic than the range. It is a biased statistic, whereas the variance listed next is not. However, the standard deviation is easier to interpret than the variance, thus many process engineers prefer it. Computations for this chart are based on the normal probability distribution.

• *Variance (s-squared chart)*

The *variance (s-squared chart)* is a third way to measure the variability of a process. It and the standard deviation give very similar results. The advantage of the variance, as mentioned above, is that it is statistically unbiased. The variance control chart is not symmetrical, however, and is therefore more difficult to read and interpret than the standard deviation chart. Computations for this chart are based on the chi-squared distribution.

• *Fraction nonconforming (p chart)*

When products are classified as either conforming or nonconforming to specifications, we may use this chart. It is called a *p chart* in statistical quality control references. An example of its use would be in functional testing of electronic devices. When we test a calculator, for example, it either functions properly and gives the right answer, or it doesn't. If it does, it's a conforming unit; otherwise, it's nonconforming. We desire to keep the fraction as low as possible and therefore use at least the upper control chart limit. We use a normal approximation to the binomial distribution when it is appropriate; otherwise, we use the binomial distribution for computations for this chart.

• *Nonconformities per unit (c chart)*

This chart is called a *c chart* in statistical quality control references. Nonconformities are generally less serious matters than a nonconforming unit. A unit can have one or more nonconformities, but still function for its intended use. An example of a nonconformity is a visual defect. Tire companies sometimes sell *factory blems* which are tires that have some visual defect (a letter that didn't come out right), but are functionally just fine. Computations for this chart are based on the normal distribution.

1.2 The Out-of-Control Criteria

Many criteria have been suggested to determine when a process is operating in a nonrandom fashion. STORM provides you with a broad array of such criteria from which you may select. However, a word of caution is in order. The more of these criteria you *turn on*, the more likely that you will receive a *false* out-of-control signal. That is, one of the criteria will be flagged, but the process is still operating in control. You must take this into account when you review the plots. The more criteria you have turned on, the stronger the signals should be to cause you to launch an assignable cause search for your process.

Another critical point to make is that all but one of the out-of-control criteria are based on runs in the data. Runs can be checked only if the data are entered in the data base in the same order they were produced. *You must enter the data in the exact order of production if you use any runs criteria to interpret your control charts.* If the data are not entered in this order, the only criterion which may properly be used is a point outside a control limit.

You should also be aware that STORM ignores all data points with assignable cause indicators in the data base when determining runs. Thus, you may see a run flagged that starts on one side of an assignable cause point and ends on the other side. Even though they do not appear to be consecutive at first glance, they should be so interpreted.

The criteria may be broadly classified as rules of thumb versus statistical criteria. Prior to the widespread availability of computing devices, it was necessary to use rules of thumb to interpret control charts, since it would be prohibitive to do statistical tests by hand. In new product or process situations where little historical data are available, these rules are still appropriate today. The simple criteria supported by STORM include:

- A run of two or more points outside two standard deviation limits
- A run of three or more points outside one standard deviation limits
- A run of seven or more points above or below the center line
- A run of seven or more points up or down

The statistical criteria supported by STORM include:

- A point outside a control limit
- The number of runs above/below the center line
- The length of the longest run above/below the center line
- The number of runs up or down
- The length of the longest run up or down

These criteria have been coded with values from zero to eight for listing on STORM reports. Below we will list the code and the name of each of these criteria, along with a brief description.

0: A point outside a control limit

This criterion is always automatically on. We use the conventional three standard deviation limits for the charts. This results in a risk of 0.0027 for a double limit mean chart for a normal variable. That is, the probability is only 0.0027 that points outside the control limits would occur due to random chance, rather than an assignable cause. This is 0.00135 for each side of a double limit chart, or for a single limit chart. This 0.00135 value is where quality control texts frequently use the *1 in 1000 chance* phrase to describe the risk. These probabilities assume that the limits are computed based on *history* (see the introductory paragraphs in Section 1 for elaboration on this point). If standards are used, many false "trips" of the control signal could occur due to an incapable process.

1: A run of two or more points outside two standard deviation limits

The concept underlying this criterion is not to wait until the process moves outside the control limits, but try to catch it while it is degrading. This is a rule of thumb criterion, and may not be meaningful if a large amount of data is available. *This criterion should only be used if samples are submitted in their exact order of production.* It will trip whether the points are on the same side or different sides of the center line.

2: A run of three or more points outside one standard deviation limits

The concept underlying this criterion is analogous to criterion 1. Namely, we do not want to wait until the process moves outside the control limits, but try to catch it before then. This is a rule of thumb criterion, and may not be meaningful if a large amount of data is available. *This criterion should only be used if samples are submitted in their exact order of production.* It will trip whether the points are on the same side or different sides of the center line.

3: A run of seven or more points above/below the center line

This is the famous engineering *rule of seven*. It is a rule of thumb criterion, and may not be meaningful if a large number of samples are available. *This criterion should only be used if samples are submitted in their exact order of production.*

4: A run of seven or more points up or down

This is analogous to criterion 3, except it applies to runs up or down rather than above or below the center line. A *run up* is a series of nondecreasing points and a *run down* is a series of nonincreasing points. It is a rule of thumb criterion, and may not be meaningful if a large number of samples are available. *This criterion should only be used if samples are submitted in their exact order of production.*

5: The number of runs above/below the center line

The theory of runs in random data suggests that there should be a *lot* of runs in the data if only random behavior is occurring. The exact number of such runs depends on the amount of data you have; the larger the amount, the larger the number of runs expected. If your control chart plot indicates this criterion has tripped, the probability is 0.05 or less that the number of runs observed would occur by random chance. Every sample in your plot will be flagged if this criterion trips. *This criterion should only be used if samples are submitted in their exact order of production.*

6: The length of the longest run above/below the center line

The greater the number of samples in your data base, the longer a run can be without raising suspicion. If your control chart plot indicates this criterion has tripped, the probability is less than 0.01 that the run would occur by random chance. Each sample in the run will be flagged if this criterion trips, and all runs longer than the critical value will be flagged. *This criterion should only be used if samples are submitted in their exact order of production.*

7: The number of runs up or down

Just as we should have a lot of runs above/below the mean in random data, we should also have a lot of runs up or down. The exact number of such runs depends on the amount of data you have; the larger the amount, the larger the number of runs expected. If your control chart plot indicates this criterion has tripped, the probability is 0.05 or less that the number of runs observed would occur by random chance. Every sample in your plot will be flagged if this criterion trips. *This criterion should only be used if samples are submitted in their exact order of production.*

8: The length of the longest run up or down

The greater the number of samples in your data base, the longer a run can be without raising suspicion. If your control chart plot indicates this criterion has tripped, the probability is less than or equal to 0.0567 that the run would occur by random chance. Each sample in any run which is longer than the statistical critical value will be flagged if this criterion trips, and all runs longer than the critical value will be flagged. *This criterion should only be used if samples are submitted in their exact order of production.*

2. Problem Sizes

Problem sizes in this module are affected by four values which describe your data set. These are:

- Number of variables
- Variables sample size
- Number of attributes
- Number of samples

The *number of variables* is the number of characteristics you are measuring which have continuous values for measurements. For example, you may measure length, width, temperature, etc., as *continuous* measurements. The number of variables partially determines the width of your STORM file for the SPC module.

You will have two choices for entering your variables data in STORM: *raw or summarized*. *Raw* data means you enter the measurements that you took in each sample directly into STORM and it will compute any statistics it needs such as the mean, range and standard deviation. *Summarized* data means that you have already computed these statistics outside of STORM and you will enter the summarized measures rather than the raw data. If you choose summarized, you will enter a constant three columns of information for each variable, corresponding to the three statistics listed above (see Section 4 for the details of data entry). If you choose raw data, you must also tell STORM the *variables sample size,* and you will enter that many columns of data per variable. In this latter case, the variables sample size will partially determine the width of the file.

The *number of attributes* is the number of characteristics which you measure only as categorical variables to reflect the number of nonconforming units in a sample and/or the number of nonconformities in the sample. You will enter a constant two columns of data for each attribute in your data set. The number of attributes partially determines the width of your file.

The final determinant of your file size is the *number of samples* in your data set. Many firms would number their samples corresponding to the production *lot number* from which the sample was drawn. This entry determines the length of your file.

Because there are so many parameters which influence file size, we have prepared Table 1 which shows several sets of values for these parameters and the maximal problem sizes which the *professional version* of STORM supports. The table starts with a column which lists the row numbers for your convenience in following our discussion. Then the type of variables data is listed, which may be raw or summarized *(N/A* is listed for *not applicable* if no variables are included for a particular line in the table). Then the number of variables in the data set is listed, followed by the variable sample size. An entry of *N/A* in this column means either there are no variables in the data set, or that summarized data are entered (which means a constant three columns per variable). The number of attributes is the next column, and the number of samples terminates the table entries.

Row Number	Type of Variables Data	Number of Variables	Variable Sample Size	Number of Attributes	Number of Samples
1	Raw	1	1	0	3650
2	Sum	1	N/A	0	3325
3	N/A	0	N/A	1	3475
4	Raw	1	4	0	3175
5	Raw	1	5	0	3050
6	Raw	5	5	0	1525
7	Raw	5	10	0	1000
8	Raw	5	25	0	490
9	Raw	100	5	0	105
10	Sum	5	N/A	0	1925
11	Sum	100	N/A	0	165
12	N/A	0	N/A	5	2225
13	N/A	0	N/A	100	220
14	Sum	1	N/A	1	2925
15	Sum	5	N/A	5	1390
16	Sum	100	N/A	100	90
17	Raw	1	1	1	3175
18	Raw	1	4	1	2800
19	Raw	1	5	1	2700
20	Raw	1	25	1	1550
21	Raw	5	1	5	1700
22	Raw	5	4	5	1250
23	Raw	5	5	5	1150
24	Raw	5	25	5	445
25	Raw	100	1	100	130
26	Raw	100	4	100	75
27	Raw	100	5	100	65

Table 1: SPC Problem Sizes for Professional STORM with 500K Memory

The first three rows in the table illustrate the maximal number of samples you could enter for a single variable or attribute. Rows 4 through 9 illustrate data sets with only variables data entered as *raw* data. Rows 10 and 11 illustrate only variables data with summarized data entry. Then data sets with only attributes measurements are listed in rows 12 and 13.

The remainder of the entries in Table 1 are for mixed data sets with an equal number of variables and attributes. Rows 14 through 16 illustrate summarized variables data examples, while the last 11 rows list raw data examples.

3. A Sample Problem

The Sparky Electric Company manufactures components used in personal computers. One such electronic device had been giving the company trouble for some time, so an SPC analyst was given the task of studying the process to determine how it was performing. One characteristic of particular concern was the highest voltage with which the device would operate properly. The device should be able to operate with voltages ranging from 110 to 130. The analyst decided the best way to study this voltage problem was as a variable.

Another characteristic of interest was a mechanical dipswitch which the computer user could toggle on or off. The dipswitch either worked or it didn't. If it didn't, the device was rejected and scrapped. This characteristic is an attribute which determines if the unit is conforming or not, so a fraction nonconforming chart seemed appropriate.

A final aspect of this device of interest was a visual inspection for nonconformities (defects). It should not have scratches or nicks so as to appear shoddy. Since this is an attribute measure, we use nonconformities per unit analysis. The results of these measurements are shown in Table 2.

The analyst took a random sample of 25 devices from the process once every hour until 25 samples (of 25 devices each) had been checked. (Although this is not enough history to properly perform analysis, we limited it so the reports which appear later would not be too long.) The voltage test required that the voltage be increased until the device no longer operated properly, and the voltage value which caused the dysfunction was recorded. Since this was time consuming and could damage the units tested, the analyst chose to only measure five of the 25 devices drawn in the sample. These five were drawn at random from the 25.

Sparky Electric Company

Sample Number	Value 1	Value 2	Value 3	Value 4	Value 5
1	121	122	132	112	120
2	115	113	109	119	117
3	125	115	111	119	123
4	134	117	130	117	116
5	128	120	124	117	121
6	121	120	116	119	122
7	108	106	127	120	116
8	123	110	123	124	124
9	124	135	118	113	107
10	110	119	135	118	124
11	127	106	117	126	119
12	117	112	129	121	106
13	116	114	133	111	117
14	123	124	123	121	126
15	130	120	128	116	130
16	115	112	135	119	121
17	125	119	118	135	116
18	134	119	123	110	123
19	128	117	127	106	117
20	121	117	116	120	120
21	108	119	124	120	124
22	123	120	130	117	107
23	124	124	111	115	124
24	110	113	109	113	116
25	127	118	132	122	122

Table 2: Voltage Measurements

For the mechanical test, all 25 devices in each sample were checked, and a count of the units which were defective was recorded. At the same time, the devices were checked for nonconformities (defects) and the total number of them in the sample was recorded. Table 3 has both the number nonconforming and the number of nonconformities which resulted from these counts.

Sample Number	Nonconforming	Nonconformities
1	1	6
2	7	0
3	2	0
4	1	3
5	0	6
6	1	3
7	2	0
8	6	18
9	0	6
10	1	3
11	2	0
12	1	3
13	0	6
14	0	21
15	2	3
16	2	0
17	1	0
18	0	15
19	1	12
20	2	9
21	3	6
22	4	3
23	5	0
24	0	3
25	0	6

Table 3: Mechanical/Visual Measurements

4. Data Entry Using STORM

Due to the large amount of data to be entered in our sample problem, we will need two figures to display aspects of the data entry process. Figure 1 shows the first six columns of data, where we enter the variables (voltage) measurements. Let's start with the entries in the Problem Description area in that figure.

After entering the title, we next enter the number of samples. This determines the number of *rows* in the data set. There were 25 sets of measurements for both variables and attributes in Tables 1 and 2, so we have entered that in STORM. Note that Figures 1 and 2 show only the first 15. To the right of that entry, we have entered a value of 1 for the number of variables, corresponding to the voltage measurements. Next we entered 1 for the number of attributes. We actually have both a mechanical and a visual attribute, but STORM allows us to run both a fraction nonconforming as well as a nonconformities per unit chart on each attribute listed, so we only need to declare one in this case. We could, at our option, declare two, but then only use one of the two capabilities for each in the data set.

```
┌──────────────┤ STORM EDITOR : Statistical Process Control Module ├──────────┐
│ Title : Sparky Electric Company                                             │
│ Number of samples        :      25 │ Number of variables        :        1  │
│ Number of attributes     :       1 │ Raw or summarized data      :      RAW  │
│ Sample size (variables)  :       5 │ Sample size (attributes)  :       25    │
│                                                                             │
│ R15 : C5         VOLTAGE  VR 1/OB 1  VR 1/OB 2  VR 1/OB 3  VR 1/OB 4  VR 1/OB 5 │
│ SAMPLE    1       XXXX      121.      122.       132.       112.       120.  │
│ SAMPLE    2       XXXX      115.      113.       109.       119.       117.  │
│ SAMPLE    3       XXXX      125.      115.       111.       119.       123.  │
│ SAMPLE    4       XXXX      134.      117.       130.       117.       116.  │
│ SAMPLE    5       XXXX      128.      120.       124.       117.       121.  │
│ SAMPLE    6       XXXX      121.      120.       116.       119.       122.  │
│ SAMPLE    7       XXXX      108.      106.       127.       120.       116.  │
│ SAMPLE    8       XXXX      123.      110.       123.       124.       124.  │
│ SAMPLE    9       XXXX      124.      135.       118.       113.       107.  │
│ SAMPLE   10       XXXX      110.      119.       135.       118.       124.  │
│ SAMPLE   11       XXXX      127.      106.       117.       126.       119.  │
│ SAMPLE   12       XXXX      117.      112.       129.       121.       106.  │
│ SAMPLE   13       XXXX      116.      114.       133.       111.       117.  │
│ SAMPLE   14       XXXX      123.      124.       123.       121.       126.  │
│ SAMPLE   15       XXXX      130.      120.       128.       116.       130.  │
└──────────────┤ Enter value for observation              |->|         |──────┘
```

Figure 1: STORM Editor With Variables Data

The next entry refers to whether we are entering raw or summarized data. Raw data means the original measurements are entered before any statistical processing has taken place (as in our example). Summarized means that the data have already been summarized into statistics. If you choose summarized, the values to be entered for each variable include the sample mean, range and standard deviation. If you enter all three of these values, you can implement any or all of the variables control charts available in STORM. If one or more are missing, your choices are correspondingly reduced. Table 4 shows the data required in your data set to plot each variables control chart if you choose summarized data (an "x" in the body of Table 4 means the historical values are required).

Chart Type	----- Historical Data Required -----		
	Mean	Range	Standard Deviation
Mean (x-bar)	x	x	
Range (R)		x	
Standard deviation (s)			x
Variance (s-squared)			x

Table 4: Historical Data Needed for Charts - Summarized Data

The last two entries in the description area are the sample size for variables and for attributes. These two values are not required to be the same, since in practice they typically would not be (attributes charts generally require larger sample sizes). When you have previously chosen raw data as the method for entering variables data, the variables sample size influences the width of the data area. As you can see in Figure 1, we have five columns in the data area labeled OBS 1-1 to OBS 1-5 to allow entry of the five measurements per sample of the voltage. If we had a second variable, the labels would be OBS 2-1, etc. The sample size for the attributes does not influence the size of the data area, since we have a constant two columns to enter nonconforming (DEFECTIVES) and nonconformities (# DEFECTS), respectively. The attributes sample size is necessary, however, to compute control chart parameters for the attributes charts.

Moving now to the Detailed Data area, we see that each row represents a set of sample results. STORM defaults the row labels to SAMPLE 1, SAMPLE 2, etc., up to the total number you entered. You may edit these to assign your own names. The first column of data, headed VOLTAGE in Figure 1, is the variable naming column for the first variable (we have edited it from the default name). Then the columns labeled OBS 1-1 through OBS 1-5 are where we enter the sample measurements for observations one through five of each sample for this variable.

Figure 2 shows the analogous data for the attributes being analyzed. Again, the first column shown in this display is a naming column which we have edited to read MECH/VIS. The column following that, which is labeled DEFECTIVES, contains the count of nonconforming units in each sample of 25 (we reverted back to the old terminology because it fits better in the display!). The next column, which is labeled # DEFECTS, contains the count of the nonconformities in each sample of 25 units.

```
|————————————| STORM EDITOR : Statistical Process Control Module |————————————|
| Title : Sparky Electric Company
| Number of samples        :      25   Number of variables      :       1
| Number of attributes     :       1   Raw or summarized data   :     RAW
| Sample size (variables)  :       5   Sample size (attributes) :      25

  R1  : C9       MECH/VIS DEFECTIVES  # DEFECTS ASIGN CAUS   OPERATOR   MACHINE
  SAMPLE    1        XXXX          1       6       .            .          .
  SAMPLE    2        XXXX          7       0       .            .          .
  SAMPLE    3        XXXX          2       0       .            .          .
  SAMPLE    4        XXXX          1       3       .            .          .
  SAMPLE    5        XXXX          0       6       .            .          .
  SAMPLE    6        XXXX          1       3       .            .          .
  SAMPLE    7        XXXX          2       0       .            .          .
  SAMPLE    8        XXXX          6      18       .            .          .
  SAMPLE    9        XXXX          0       6       .            .          .
  SAMPLE   10        XXXX          1       3       .            .          .
  SAMPLE   11        XXXX          2       0       .            .          .
  SAMPLE   12        XXXX          1       3       .            .          .
  SAMPLE   13        XXXX          0       6       .            .          .
  SAMPLE   14        XXXX          0      21       .            .          .
  SAMPLE   15        XXXX          2       3       .            .          .
        |————| No entry in this position                  |->|        |————
```

Figure 2: STORM Editor With Attributes Data

The next column is labeled ASIGN CAUS and it allows you to *flag* a sample result in the data base to tell STORM to ignore it during computations. The sample result will still be plotted on control charts, but *if you choose to set limits based on history, all sample results which have a value other than a dot (.) in this column will be ignored.* You may put any code you like in this column to remind you of the reason the sample result was flagged. For example, you could enter MATL to indicate the material was the problem. STORM will simply list an *A* to the right of the control chart plot to indicate that you had some code in this field in your data.

The next several columns in the data set (not all are shown) allow you to document information about each sample to help you perform an assignable cause search if needed. The labels OPERATOR and MACHINE are shown in Figure 2. Not shown are columns labeled VENDOR, USER 1 and USER 2. You may change any or all of these labels to potential assignable cause names for your particular situation. In our example, we could enter the machine number in the column headed MACHINE. Then if out-of-control points showed up in a control chart plot, we could see if most of them were associated with a particular machine. If so, perhaps it needs to be adjusted or overhauled. STORM does not use any of these columns except the assignable cause column; the rest are for your use in documentation.

Although not shown in either Figure, there will be a column in the Detailed Data area filled with *XXXX* to separate all the variables in the left area from the attributes to the right.

5. Execution of the Module

The first time you execute the module, there are many specific decisions which you must make. Once you have made them, you can save the results to the data set so as to simplify the process next time. We will first describe the more difficult situation of original execution, and then point out the differences.

5.1 Executing the Module with a New Data Set

STORM needs a lot of information from you concerning exactly what you want it to do for each variable and attribute in your data base. This is what makes the first time use so involved. To help explain this process, Figure 3 lists the steps necessary to initially design our control charts. In the paragraphs that follow, we will explain each step of the process in detail. If you are going to simultaneously read the manual and execute the module, you may want to use the F6 (Config) key and route output reports to your printer so you can review them later.

Step 1: Individual or common choices

Figure 4 shows the menu used to record your decision. If you choose option 1, *Common choices,* then you will complete steps 2 and following only one time for variables and one time for attributes, regardless of the number of each in your data set. Thus, if you want to use the same control charts for every variable, the same history for plots and/or plan design, etc., the common choices option will save you a lot of time since you don't have to answer the same questions over and over. If, on the other hand, some of these choices cannot be the same for every variable (or attribute), you will have to choose option 2, *Individual choices*. This will require that you go through steps 3 and following *individually for each* variable and/or attribute selected in step 2. We chose common choices to obtain the displays in the following figures.

Step 1: Choose individual or common choices for plans

Step 2: Choose variables and/or attributes for which plans are to be designed

Step 3: Choose whether history or standards will be used to define control limits; and which charts are to be used

Step 4: Select history on which charts will be based, if history was chosen at step 3; otherwise, enter standard values to be used

Step 5: Select out-of-control criteria to be applied to each chart selected in step 3

Step 6: Choose the history for which you want the control chart to be plotted in the report

Step 7: Review the control charts (this is easy!)

Step 8: Decide whether to save the plan, redesign it or abandon it

Figure 3: Steps in the Initial Execution of the Module

```
            PROCESS CONTROL OPTIONS

        1)    Design plans - common choices
        2)    Design plans - individual choices
```

Figure 4: Making the Common or Individual Choices Decision

Step 2: Select variables/attributes

An exhaustive list of all variable and attribute names will be presented in a Candidate Selection screen for this step. None of them will have been preselected when you first enter the screen. If you want all of them, you will simply press the F1 key to select them all (we did). If you want most, but not all, you can toggle off the ones you do not want with the space bar. Finally, if you only want to work with a few, you can press the F3 key to toggle them all off, and then toggle the select few back on with the space bar.

Step 3: Choose History or Standards, and Charts

Figure 5 shows the screen used to make this selection, with the STORM default choices displayed. The default choice is to use history to define the control chart limits, which is our selection for Sparky. None of the plans are preselected, so you must turn on the ones you want. You can use the space bar to toggle the *no* to *yes* on the STORM form. If you want a double limit chart, you will need to change both the LCL (Lower Control Limit) and the UCL (Upper Control Limit) entries to *y* for *yes*. Otherwise, just change the *n* to *y* for the single limit chart you desire. In this screen, the x-bar chart stands for the mean chart, the s chart for the standard deviation chart, the s-squared chart for the variance chart, the p chart for the fraction nonconforming chart, and the c chart for the nonconformities per unit chart. These labels correspond to the standard terminology used for these charts in statistical quality control texts. Although not shown in Figure 5, we selected all the charts for Sparky, and made them all double sided charts.

Step 4: Select history for charts; or enter standard values

If you selected history in Figure 5 as the basis for computing control chart limits, you will specify which part of the history to use in this step. Figure 6 illustrates the screen used to make this selection. The default entries specify that the entire data base of samples is to be used. However, if there are any missing values or assignable causes for any samples within this range, those samples will be ignored in the computations. If you desire some other range, one choice is to type in the label name for the first and last sample to include, *exactly as they appear in the data set*. If you cannot remember their names, press the F8 key and the labels will be listed for you. Then all you have to do is move the Pointer to the label you want and press Enter. The F8 option is indicated on this screen when you are executing STORM.

```
        Common choices : Chart selection

        Basis for limits
          (H: History, S: Standards) : h

                                      LCL  UCL

        X-bar chart               : n    n

        Range chart               : n    n

        S chart                   : n    n

        S-squared chart           : n    n

        p chart                   : n    n

        c chart                   : n    n
```

Figure 5: History and Chart Selection Screen

```
     Common choices : Range of samples for history

   Beginning sample name              : SAMPLE   1

   Ending sample name                 : SAMPLE  25
```

Figure 6: Select History for Computing Charts

If we had chosen standards in Figure 5, then STORM would have asked us for the standard values to use. Figure 7 shows the screen with which this is done. STORM will only ask you for the values it needs to determine limits for the charts you have selected. *STORM assumes that the standard deviation value entered is for an individual observation.* The standard deviation of the sample mean, needed in determining control limits, is computed by dividing the value entered by the square root of the sample size.

```
Common choices: Standard values

Mean                               : 0

Standard deviation                 : 0

p (fraction defective)             : 0

c (number of defects)              : 0
```

Figure 7: Specify Standard Values

Step 5: Select out-of-control criteria for each chart

For each control chart you selected in Figure 5, you will be asked to choose the out-of-control criteria for STORM to apply in interpreting the chart. Figure 8 shows this STORM form for the mean (X-BAR) chart. The criteria listed in the figure were explained in Section 1.2 of this chapter. As illustrated, none of the criteria are defaulted to *on*. You can toggle the ones you want using the space bar. A point outside a control limit is not listed since that criterion is automatically on for all charts. The word *sigma* is used in the figure to mean standard deviation, since the Greek letter sigma is commonly used for this purpose. If a criterion is not appropriate for a chart, it will not be listed in the screen analogous to Figure 8 for the chart in question. We will not repeat all the other displays for the other charts in this chapter, but you may review them by executing the module with the sample data set. We changed all criteria to *y* for *yes* to obtain any reports shown later.

```
Common choices : Out-of-control criteria for X-bar chart

Code       Description
0     Points outside control limits (preselected)
1     Run of 2 or more points outside two sigma limits    : n
2     Run of 3 or more points outside one sigma limits    : n
3     Run of 7 or more above/below the centerline         : n
4     Run of 7 or more up or down                         : n
5     Number of runs above/below the centerline           : n
6     Length of longest run above/below the centerline    : n
7     Number of runs up or down                           : n
8     Length of longest run up or down                    : n
```

Figure 8: Selecting Out-of-control Criteria

Step 6: Specify samples for plots

The last step in the process before reviewing the control chart plot is to define the samples you want in the plot. The screen used to do this is like Figure 6, explained in step 4.

Step 7: Review the control chart plots

We have included the mean chart (Figure 9), the variance chart (Figure 10) and the fraction nonconforming chart (Figure 11) to illustrate the results for Sparky, and to explain the basic setup for these charts. Figure 9 shows that the report header includes the data set title, the name of the variable or attribute and the chart type, and the control limits which STORM has determined in this case.

Moving down to the body of the report, the leftmost column lists the names of the samples which are included in the plot. The next column to the right lists the sample value. If raw data were entered for a variable chart, STORM computed this value. Otherwise, it is the value you entered in the data set. STORM also computes the fraction nonconforming values for that chart.

In the central portion of the report is the plot of the sample value versus the control chart limits. For a double sided chart, there are five vertical lines of importance in this section of the plot. The one in the center is the center line for the control chart (indicated as | in the figure). The dotted lines (.) on either side of it are the two standard deviation limits. Finally, the extreme vertical lines (|) are the control chart limits. Values are shown as asterisks (*) in the plot. The values which are inside the control limits are scaled to reflect their values versus the limits. This is not done, however, for points which fall outside a limit. Such points are merely displayed on the limit as a "+". You will have to refer to the value column to the left of the plot to see how far away from the limit such a value was. This is done so that the central display would not be compressed in scaling the plot.

The rightmost column in the figure is where we report any out-of-control criteria situations. Since we chose all of them for Sparky, the numbers *012345678* appear at the head of the column. At the bottom of the report there is a legend which explains what each number means. This legend is the same as that listed in section 1.2 of the chapter. If any of these are *not* chosen, that column is simply left blank in the display. If a sample value is detected as out-of-control for any one or more of these reasons, the number corresponding to the reason is repeated in the column next to the sample value.

```
                     VOLTAGE : X-BAR CHART
        LCL = 110.1647    Center = 119.8080    UCL = 129.4513

   Sample          Value LCL              C           UCL 012345678

SAMPLE    1   121.4000   |    .         |   *      .      |
SAMPLE    2   114.6000   |    .*        |          .      |
SAMPLE    3   118.6000   |    .       * |          .      |
SAMPLE    4   122.8000   |    .         |   *      .      |
SAMPLE    5   122.0000   |    .         |  *       .      |
SAMPLE    6   119.6000   |    .       * |          .      |
SAMPLE    7   115.4000   |  . *         |          .      |
SAMPLE    8   120.8000   |    .         |*         .      |
SAMPLE    9   119.4000   |    .       * |          .      |
SAMPLE   10   121.2000   |    .         |*         .      |
SAMPLE   11   119.0000   |    .       * |          .      |
SAMPLE   12   117.0000   |    .     *   |          .      |
SAMPLE   13   118.2000   |    .      *  |          .      |
SAMPLE   14   123.4000   |    .         |    *     .      |
SAMPLE   15   124.8000   |    .         |      *.         |
SAMPLE   16   120.4000   |    .       | *           .     |
SAMPLE   17   122.6000   |    .         |   *      .      |
SAMPLE   18   121.8000   |    .         | *        .      |
SAMPLE   19   119.0000   |    .      * |           .      |
SAMPLE   20   118.8000   |    .     *  |           .      |
SAMPLE   21   119.0000   |    .      * |           .      |
SAMPLE   22   119.4000   |    .      * |           .      |
SAMPLE   23   119.6000   |    .      * |           .      |
SAMPLE   24   112.2000   | *  .         |          .      |
SAMPLE   25   124.2000   |    .         |      *   .      |
```

Plan based on 25 valid samples from SAMPLE   1 to SAMPLE 25

Sig. Prob. for Chi-Squared test on history range = 0.8187

0   Points outside control limits
1   Run of 2 or more points outside two sigma limits
2   Run of 3 or more points outside one sigma limits
3   Run of 7 or more above/below the centerline

Figure 9: The Mean (X-BAR) Chart Plot

4	Run of 7 or more up or down
5	Number of runs above/below the centerline
6	Length of longest run above/below the centerline
7	Number of runs up or down
8	Length of longest run up or down
A	Assignable cause
M	Missing value

Figure 9 (continued): The Mean (X-BAR) Chart Plot

Some additional information appears at the bottom of the plot. STORM tells us that there were 25 valid samples within the history we selected. For Sparky, that means there were no missing values or assignable cause samples. We are also informed that these were used to estimate both the mean and standard deviation for the process.

Next STORM reports the chi-squared normality test results for any chart for which it is appropriate. There must be a minimum of 25 samples in your data set for this test to be performed. The significance probability is the key value to consider. If it is small (generally less than or equal to 0.05) it means that the assumption of normality *is not a good one.* Thus, control charts based on this assumption may yield misleading or erroneous results in such instances. Values above this threshold mean we cannot reject the hypothesis of normality, but the higher the value the better. It is a very comfortable 0.8187 in Figure 9, given that the highest value possible is 1.0.

After the legend explaining the out-of-control criteria codes, the last two lines in the figure inform us that an "A" is used to signify an assignable cause point and an "M" for a missing value in the data set.

Figure 10 shows the plot of the variance (S-squared) chart for voltage for Sparky. Notice that this chart is not symmetrical, since the squaring operation causes the upper limit to be further to the right. Based on Figures 9 and 10, Sparky's process appears to be acceptable with respect to the voltage variable, but just barely so. Recall that values from 110 to 130 were deemed acceptable, and the control limits on the mean chart are very close to those values.

```
                      VOLTAGE : S-SQUARED CHART
          LCL = 1.1674      Center = 44.1496      UCL = 196.4708

     Sample           Value  LCL    C                    UCL O  345678

     ─────────────────────────────────────────────────────────────────
     SAMPLE   1       50.8000  |     |*                        |
     SAMPLE   2       14.8000  |  *  |                          |
     SAMPLE   3       32.8000  |    * |                          |
     SAMPLE   4       72.7000  |     |   *                      |
     SAMPLE   5       17.5000  |  *  |                          |
     SAMPLE   6        5.3000  |*    |                          |
     SAMPLE   7       74.8000  |     |    *                     |
     SAMPLE   8       36.7000  |     *|                          |
     SAMPLE   9      115.3000  |     |          *               |
     SAMPLE  10       84.7000  |     |      *                   |
     SAMPLE  11       71.5000  |     |   *                      |
     SAMPLE  12       76.5000  |     |    *                     |
     SAMPLE  13       73.7000  |     |   *                      |
     SAMPLE  14        3.3000  *     |                          |
     SAMPLE  15       41.2000  |    * |                          |
     SAMPLE  16       78.8000  |     |    *                     |
     SAMPLE  17       59.3000  |     | *                        |
     SAMPLE  18       74.7000  |     |   *                      |
     SAMPLE  19       80.5000  |     |    *                     |
     SAMPLE  20        4.7000  *     |                          |
     SAMPLE  21       43.0000  |    * |                          |
     SAMPLE  22       71.3000  |     |   *                      |
     SAMPLE  23       38.3000  |    *|                          |
     SAMPLE  24        7.7000  |*    |                          |
     SAMPLE  25       29.2000  |    * |                          |
     ─────────────────────────────────────────────────────────────────
```

Plan based on 25 valid samples from SAMPLE   1 to SAMPLE   25

0   Points outside control limits
3   Run of 7 or more above/below the centerline
4   Run of 7 or more up or down
5   Number of runs above/below the centerline

Figure 10: The Variance Chart Plot

```
6    Length of longest run above/below the centerline
7    Number of runs up or down
8    Length of longest run up or down

A    Assignable cause
M    Missing value
```

Figure 10 (continued): The Variance Chart Plot

Figure 11 shows the plot of the fraction nonconforming for the mechanical dipswitch. Since the lower limit on this chart is 0.0, it is not symmetrical in this case. You may also notice that there is no report of the normality test, since in this instance the chart was not based on that assumption. For large sample sizes, the normal approximation to the binomial will be used, and the normality test performed.

Sparky is in trouble with this dipswitch. An average of seven per cent of the devices are being rejected due to the failure of this switch. This is far in excess of what could reasonably be tolerated. We also observe that sample 2 was above the upper control chart limit, which suggests that an assignable cause search be launched. Even though no out-of-control criteria were flagged, samples 19 through 23 look suspicious because of the run up, given that we have only 25 samples. This might be a case where Sparky would want to set standard limits, rather than limits based on history. The standards would present a visual goal which the process engineers would try to achieve.

Step 8: Decide what to do with the plan

Figure 12 shows the menu used to make this decision. A menu like the one in the figure will be presented to you on the screen after the last control chart plot for a particular variable or attribute. There are three choices available as to the disposition of the plan. First, you may save the plan and proceed to the next variable or attribute, if more are to be considered. In this case, you will be informed that you must save your data file to disk before exiting STORM to save the plan. If you save the plan, *any previously saved plan for a variable or attribute will be lost.* If you expect to add more samples to your history, and want to keep applying the same control chart to the new samples, you should save the plan. Otherwise, you will have to go through the new design process described above every time you want a plot.

```
                         MECH/VIS : P CHART
               LCL = 0.0000      Center = 0.0704      UCL = 0.2400


    Sample            Value  LCL    C                    UCL O  345678

  ──────────────────────────────────────────────────────────────────
  SAMPLE   1         0.0400  |    *  |                          |
  SAMPLE   2         0.2800  |       |                       *  |
  SAMPLE   3         0.0800  |       |*                         |
  SAMPLE   4         0.0400  |    *  |                          |
  SAMPLE   5         0.0000  *       |                          |
  SAMPLE   6         0.0400  |    *  |                          |
  SAMPLE   7         0.0800  |       |*                         |
  SAMPLE   8         0.2400  |       |                     *    |
  SAMPLE   9         0.0000  *       |                          |
  SAMPLE  10         0.0400  |    *  |                          |
  SAMPLE  11         0.0800  |       |*                         |
  SAMPLE  12         0.0400  |    *  |                          |
  SAMPLE  13         0.0000  *       |                          |
  SAMPLE  14         0.0000  *       |                          |
  SAMPLE  15         0.0800  |       |*                         |
  SAMPLE  16         0.0800  |       |*                         |
  SAMPLE  17         0.0400  |    *  |                          |
  SAMPLE  18         0.0000  *       |                          |
  SAMPLE  19         0.0400  |    *  |                          |
  SAMPLE  20         0.0800  |       |*                         |
  SAMPLE  21         0.1200  |       |      *                   |
  SAMPLE  22         0.1600  |       |           *              |
  SAMPLE  23         0.2000  |       |                *         |
  SAMPLE  24         0.0000  *       |                          |
  SAMPLE  25         0.0000  *       |                          |
  ──────────────────────────────────────────────────────────────────
```

Plan based on 25 valid samples from SAMPLE   1 to SAMPLE 25

```
  O    Points outside control limits
  3    Run of 7 or more above/below the centerline
  4    Run of 7 or more up or down
  5    Number of runs above/below the centerline
```

Figure 11: The Fraction Nonconforming Plot

```
6    Length of longest run above/below the centerline
7    Number of runs up or down
8    Length of longest run up or down

A    Assignable cause
M    Missing value
```

Figure 11 (continued): The Fraction Nonconforming Plot


```
                    VARIABLE VOLTAGE

1)    Save plan and go to next variable/attribute
2)    Redesign plan for current variable/attribute
3)    Abandon plan and go to next variable/attribute
```

Figure 12: Decide What To Do With Plan

If you save the plan, it will be appended to your data set at the bottom of the columns which contain the variable or attribute. *It will not be visible to you in the editor, however.* It is essentially encoded for storage, and would be very difficult to interpret stored in this manner. If you exit STORM after saving a data file to disk with a plan in it, and then list the file, you will see a lot of numbers at the bottom of the file. These are the numbers which communicate the plan to STORM. You may obtain a readable listing of any saved plan directly from STORM from a menu described in the next section and illustrated in Figure 13.

If you are not satisfied with the plot you receive for a variable or attribute, *and you can correct it by one of the choices listed in the steps above,* you may choose option 2 from the menu in Figure 12. An example of such a situation is that you want to replot the chart with fewer samples in it, or you want to change the out-of-control criteria you selected, etc.

The last choice in Figure 12 is to abandon the plan and go on to the next variable or attribute. This may be the preferred choice when the plan must be redesigned and the choices available in the steps above cannot fix the problem. The most obvious example of this is one or more points flagged for out-of-control criteria necessitating an assignable cause search. *You may still want to save this plan, however, since the next time you redesign it all your __saved__ choices will be the defaults.* This may save you a lot of time in answering the questions in steps 3 through 6 of the design process.

After you have completed the design process for a variable or attribute and proceed to the next one, the choices you made for the first will be the default choices for the next. This generally saves you time in the design process.

5.2 Executing the Module with Saved Plans

If you have previously executed the module and saved one or more plans to the data set, then the process control options menu will appear as in Figure 13 (it originally appears as in Figure 4). The top two choices are the same as before, and were explained in section 5.1. The last three choices are new, so let's consider each of them.

```
            PROCESS CONTROL OPTIONS

      1)    Design plans - common choices
      2)    Design plans - individual choices
      3)    Operate plans saved to data set
      4)    List plans saved to data set
      5)    Delete plans saved to data set
```

Figure 13: Executing the Module with Saved Plans

If you choose option 3, you will receive a Candidate Selection screen which lists all variables and/or attributes which have saved plans. All of them will have been preselected by STORM as indicated by the asterisk (*) to the left of the names. You may modify these choices as you see fit by the normal process. After completing this screen, you will receive a screen similar to that in Figure 6 where you will specify the range of samples to be included in the plots you selected. Then you will receive the plots of the charts. That's all there is to it!

If you choose option 4 to list the plans, a one-step process occurs. You select the variables and/or attributes for which you wish to see the plans via a Candidate Selection screen. Again, all the variables and/or attributes for which plans have been saved are preselected for the listing. After finalizing your selections, a listing of all the plans chosen will be presented. If you are routing output to your printer or a disk file, these plans will be sent there so you may document them if desired. Figure 14 illustrates such a listing for the variable in our example.

```
                    PLAN FOR VOLTAGE

Plan based on 25 valid samples from SAMPLE   1 TO SAMPLE   25

Mean              = 119.8080
Range             = 16.7200
Standard deviation = 6.6445

25 valid values used in estimating Mean
25 valid values used in estimating Range
25 valid values used in estimating Standard deviation


Out-of-control Criteria Selection

                   0   1   2   3   4   5   6   7   8
X-bar chart        X   X   X   X   X   X   X   X   X
Range chart        X   X   X   X   X   X   X   X   X
S chart            X   X   X   X   X   X   X   X   X
S-squared chart    X           X   X   X   X   X   X

0     Points outside control limits
1     Run of 2 or more points outside two sigma limits
2     Run of 3 or more points outside one sigma limits
3     Run of 7 or more above/below the centerline
4     Run of 7 or more up or down
5     Number of runs above/below the centerline
6     Length of longest run above/below the centerline
7     Number of runs up or down
8     Length of longest run up or down
```

Figure 14: Sample Plan Listing

After the title line, the samples used to design the plan are identified. This is followed by a listing of the statistics which STORM computed in order to design the plans. These statistics would be replaced with the standard values if the plan were based on standards. The number of valid samples available to compute each statistic are the next items reported (these are not listed if the plans are based on standard values). Then the charts are listed which were included in the saved plan for the variable or attribute. To the right of these there is a matrix indicating the out-of-control criteria selected for each chart. The 0 through 8 listing at the top of the matrix are the codes which STORM uses on the plots for each criterion. For your convenience, these are also listed at the bottom of the listing of the plan. An X in the matrix indicates this criterion is on, whereas a blank means it is not.

If you choose option 5 from the Figure 13 menu, you may delete any saved plans from your data set. The process uses a Candidate Selection screen which lists all variables and/or attributes for which saved plans exist. *None* of these will have been preselected. You simply indicate your choices and the plans are instantly deleted.

6. Tips for Using this Module

Most of our tips deal with the substance of using this module, rather than the mechanics. First, try to enter the information for potential assignable causes (machine, operator, vendor, etc.) in the extreme right of your data set. Having it may be a tremendous aid in assignable cause searches. You can print the data set, take the pages on which this information appears and line it up beside the control chart plots which have flagged out-of-control criteria. Then scan the rows for such flagged points to see if some value of a potential assignable cause occurs frequently for the out-of-control points.

The second suggestion is for the selection of out-of-control criteria. We recommend that you use the rule-of-thumb criteria only when you have a small number of samples in your data set (less than 30). After that, use the statistical runs tests which consider how many samples you have in deciding whether to flag a point.

Another point related to the out-of-control criteria has to do with how many you select. If you select all of them, the chances of a false signal are increased. That is, a point will be flagged when the process is still in control. Thus, if you turn a lot of the criteria on, you will have to interpret them accordingly. In such situations, a single out-of-control point for a rule-of-thumb criterion may not be verymeaningful. Conversely, if you only allow the default criterion of a point outside a control limit to be on, you should perform a rigorous assignable cause search anytime it trips.

As indicated earlier in the chapter, we favor the use of history rather than standards for establishing control chart limits. However, we noted examples of conditions where standards may appropriately be used.

For variables in your data set, we recommend using the mean chart and one of the three charts which measure variability. The range chart is the most commonly used in industry, but it ignores many of the data points in the sample if the sample size is very large (12 or more). We prefer the standard deviation or variance chart, in general, to the range chart because these are more powerful statistics. We mentioned earlier than the standard deviation is a biased statistic, but easy to interpret. The variance is unbiased, but more difficult to interpret. Thus, we leave the selection up to you. You may, of course, choose more than one of the three charts which measure variability. However, you are likely to receive a lot of overlapping information on your reports if you do.

There are a couple of hints we wish to reemphasize about the mechanics of using the module. First, if you have many variables and/or attributes in your data set, try to use the *common choices* option in the execute process the first time through, *even if you need different plans in some cases.* You can design common plans based on the one plan which you need most often, and then edit the others later to differentiate them from the common one. This can be done by saving the common plan, and then restarting the design process by choosing the *individual choices* option.

A second point is to save a plan to the data set for each variable or attribute after the initial design process, even if you are not entirely happy with the plan. Any such saved plan will be the default when you redesign it. This is more likely to be close to your final desired plan than the STORM default selections. If so, it will save you time and effort to achieve your final plan.

7. Altering Problem Data Dimensions

This can be a rather intricate process for this module. The only items which can be changed (after original entry) in the Problem Description area are the title and the sample size for attributes. The raw or summarized choice for variables data cannot be changed in any way in STORM once set. The other entries in the Description area may be changed through the routines to insert/delete rows/columns. STORM will automatically update the Description entries to reflect your changes. The insertion and/or deletion of rows is independent of any other choices made in the description area, so we will list and discuss it only once. Other insertion/deletion operations depend on whether attributes or variables entries are being edited. Within variables, there are some differences depending on whether raw or summarized data was entered. We will list the situation below and describe the insert/delete operations allowed.

Rows

The number of samples (rows) can be increased to the maximum allowed or decreased to the minimum of one using the usual insert/delete operations. You may add new samples at the bottom of the data set as new information becomes available. Similarly, if you have some data that are too old to be useful, you may delete these from the top of the data set. STORM allows you to enter/delete rows in the middle of the data set. Remember, however, that you should not use any runs tests if the samples in your data set are not in the exact order of production. If there is an assignable cause for a sample, simply flag it in the assignable cause column, but leave it in the data set.

Variable Columns: Raw data entered

This is the most complex case for changing problem dimensions. There are two situations to consider: inserting/deleting variables and changing the sample size for each variable.

If you want to add a new variable into the data set, position the Pointer on the variable *name* column which you wish to immediately precede the new one. It is critically important that you position the Pointer in this manner. *If you position it on any other column within a variable area, you will change the sample size for all variables, rather than adding a new variable.* If you wish the new variable to be the first in the data set, position the Pointer on the row label column. After positioning the Pointer and pressing the F5 Function key, all the columns needed for the new variable will have been added to the data set with the default column labels. You may add variables until the maximal number allowed has been reached.

The process is similar for deleting a variable. Place the Pointer on the column where the variable *name* of the variable to be deleted appears and press the F6 Function key. *If you position it on any other column within a variable area, you will delete one of the values for every variable in the data set.* Such a deletion could only be restored if you had a saved file with these data in it. You may delete variables until all of them have been deleted, provided you have at least one attribute remaining in your data base. Otherwise, you may delete all but one variable.

If you want to increase the sample size *for every variable in the data set* (they are all required to be the same), position the Pointer on any *observation* column within any variable data area and press the F5 Insert Column key. A new observation column will be inserted immediately to the right of the column where the Pointer was located with the default column label. This new column will appear *for every variable in the data set.* You cannot enter a new column as the first column, since STORM could not distinguish this from a desire to add a new variable. You may increase the sample size for variables until the maximum allowed has been reached.

To decrease the sample size *for every variable in the data set,* position the Pointer on the observation to be deleted and press the F6 Delete Column key. After you confirm this entry, this observation will be deleted *for every variable in the data set.* You can only recover it if you have saved it in a file, so be careful. You may delete observations in this manner until the minimal sample size of one is reached.

Variable Columns: Summarized data entered

This process operates analogously to that described above for raw data entered, except that the sample size cannot be changed in this case. Only operations that deal with a complete variable are permitted. Once the sample size is entered in the Problem Description area, it cannot be changed. STORM could not interpret your sample data entries if this entry could be changed. Thus, you should be careful when entering it.

Attribute Columns

Attribute insertions and/or deletions operate exactly as variables when summarized data are entered. Thus, you may review the paragraphs above to understand how to add or delete complete attributes. You may add them until the maximal number is reached, and delete them as long as at least one attribute or one variable remains in the data set.

You may change the sample size for attributes directly in the Problem Description area. Unless you made an error when you originally entered this value, however, you are responsible for "cleaning up" your data set if you change the sample size. All samples which used the old sample size should be deleted from the data set if it contains only attributes data (no variables). Otherwise, you should flag all samples with the old sample size with assignable cause indicators. *It is statistically incorrect to interpret attributes data determined from one sample size by use of another.*

Columns for Assignable Cause and Potential Assignable Causes

These columns are at the extreme right of the data base. No insertions nor deletions are allowed in this area.

- NOTES -

STATISTICS CAPABILITIES

PROBLEM FORMULATION OPTIONS
- Quantitative and qualitative variables
- Transformation of variables
- Recoding of variables
- Handling of missing values

OUTPUT OPTIONS AND OTHER FEATURES
- Descriptive statistics
  - Mean, variance, correlation matrix, and other statistics
  - Scatter plots and histograms
- Multiple regression
  - Interactive and batch modes
  - Prioritized variables in stepwise regression
  - Forward, backward, forward/backward stepwise, or any combination of procedures
  - Forced entry or removal of variables at any step
  - Summary or detailed output at each step
  - Confidence and prediction intervals
  - Residual plots
  - Residuals can be added to data set
  - Model validation using part of data
  - Durbin-Watson and PRESS statistics

MAXIMAL PROBLEM SIZES (VARIABLES, CASES)
- Personal version: (10, 100)

- Professional version
  Representative sizes, with 500K of net memory for STORM:
  - (10, 3400)
  - (25, 2000)
  - (50, 1100)
  - (100, 475)
  - (150, 150)

FILE NAME FOR THE SAMPLE PROBLEM DATA
- ST.DAT

Chapter 21

STATISTICS

The Statistics module in STORM provides you with a number of widely used procedures, centering on multiple linear regression. The principal categories are as follows:

Data Modification   Numerous variable transformations and recoding facilities are available for modifying your data set or creating new variables, to accommodate polynomial or more complex regression models, as long as they remain intrinsically linear in the coefficients being estimated.

Descriptive statistics   A variety of summary statistics are calculated for variables in the data set. The results are presented in tables, and as charts such as histograms and scatter plots.

Regression Analysis Linear regression is a procedure for estimating a linear relationship between a dependent variable, Y, and one or more independent variables, X_i, $i = 1, 2, ..., k$. The general form of a multiple regression model is

$$Y = B_0 + B_1 X_1 + ... + B_k X_k + e,$$

where e is a random error. It is assumed to have a normal distribution with a mean of zero and a constant variance for all values of the independent variables.

Regression analysis estimates the coefficients B_i, $i = 0, 1, ..., k$, based on a user-supplied set of observations, $\{Y_i, X_{1i}, X_{2i}, ..., X_{ki}\}$, $i = 1, 2, ..., n$. A sample point $\{Y_i, X_{1i}, ..., X_{ki}\}$ is referred to as a *case* hereafter. The module allows several variations of the stepwise regression procedure (forward, backward, and forward-backward), as well as user-directed search, to obtain a satisfactory regression equation.

Although this chapter provides brief explanations of many of the available output statistics, it assumes that the reader is familiar with statistical concepts including multiple regression. Basic statistics texts present this material if you are not familiar with it or need to review it.

1. A Sample Problem

A chain of retail drug stores is interested in developing a model to assist them in setting the price of their merchandise as a function of product characteristics. The qualities believed to be most important in price determination are:

The cost of the product (COST)
The product sales volume (VOLUME)
Whether or not the product needs refrigeration (REFRIG)

Based on data compiled for sixteen current products, management hopes to develop a model relating these variables to the prices that were eventually set, as an aid to setting prices for new products.

2. Data Entry Using STORM

Data entry for the given problem should terminate with a display like that in Figure 1, where the monitor screen has been lengthened to accommodate all the data. Two extra products have been added, as cases 17 and 18. These products do not yet exist, but are under consideration. Under the given assumptions, management wishes to estimate the appropriate price range for each (note that prices have not been entered).

The first row in the data area, labeled VAR TYPE, will allow you to specify whether the variable is qualitative (QUAL) or quantitative (QUAN). Quantitative variables take on numerical values, while qualitative or nonnumeric ones may be used to indicate categories. For example, they may represent the religion or sex of subjects in a demographic study, or the presence or absence of some characteristic. The categories of a qualitative variable may be encoded using any four or fewer characters. In our example, the perishability of a product has been coded as "R" (needs refrigeration) or "NR" (no refrigeration required).

It often happens that the values of certain variables cannot be determined for some of the cases. In the next two rows of the Data area, you can specify how such *missing values* are to be handled. For each variable, you have three options:

- Ignore any case with a missing value (OMIT);
- Replace the missing value with the sample mean for that variable (MEAN);
- Replace the missing value with a user-supplied constant (CNST).

```
|——————————————————| STORM EDITOR : Statistics Module |——————————————
Title : DRUG STORE PRICING MODEL
Number of variables in data set            :        4
Maximal number of cases for any variable :         18


R20 : C4            COST      VOLUME     REFRIG      PRICE
VAR TYPE            QUAN       QUAN       QUAL       QUAN
MV OPTION           OMIT       OMIT       OMIT       OMIT
MV CONST              .          .          .          .
CASE    1            1.2        2.1         R         2.25
CASE    2            5.69       7.75        NR        8.9
CASE    3            2.95       2.05        NR        5.
CASE    4           10.2       10.21        NR       14.55
CASE    5            4.19       6.23        NR        6.5
CASE    6            7.25       8.52        NR       10.75
CASE    7            1.75       1.95        R         3.
CASE    8            2.21       1.75        NR        3.75
CASE    9            9.95       8.25        R        14.75
CASE   10            8.05       9.75        R        12.4
CASE   11            2.15       4.52        NR        3.5
CASE   12            6.75       5.82        NR        9.95
CASE   13            4.35       4.5         NR        7.
CASE   14            7.35       6.75        R        10.95
CASE   15           11.05       8.73        R        16.85
CASE   16            2.23       4.17        NR        3.75
CASE   17            5.38       2.45        NR          .
CASE   18            8.73       9.67        R           .
|——————————| Enter datum value (. for missing value)        |->    |——
```

Figure 1: Data Entry Display

Make your choice in the MV OPTION row. If you select the CNST option, you will have to supply the constant for each variable that has any missing values. These constants must be entered in the row labeled MV CONST. If you fail to enter the default value after having chosen the CNST option, the module will treat that variable as though you had specified the OMIT option. In any case, when entering the data, a missing value should be indicated by a dot (.). You will find the entire Data area initially defaulted to dots, so no action need be taken where a datum is missing. In Figure 1, cases 17 and 18 have no values entered for the variable PRICE. Since the missing value option chosen for that variable is OMIT, any statistical procedure involving the variable PRICE will use only the first 16 cases.

If a variable column has no entries (every case left at the dot default), or if every entry is the same so that the variance of that variable is zero, the regression procedure will automatically drop it from further consideration. However, as we will discuss later, if a variable has some missing values and all other entries are identical, and if the MV OPTION chosen is OMIT, that variable will be used to eliminate cases before being discarded. Such a variable can be used to select a subset of cases to be included in a particular study.

3. Execution of the Module

After creating the data file and instructing the program to execute the module, you will be presented with the menu displayed in Figure 2. The three options lead to an extensive array of capabilities. We will provide rather detailed explanations for each.

```
STATISTICS : PROCEDURES

1)    Data modifications
2)    Descriptive statistics
3)    Regression analysis
```

Figure 2: Menu of Statistics Options

3.1 Data Modifications

Choice of *Data modifications* leads to a menu with two options: *Variable transformations* and *Recode variables.*

3.1.1 Variable Transformations

This feature allows you to create additional variables as a function of already-existing variables. Having chosen it, you will be presented with a list of the eleven transformations offered by the module, as shown in Figure 3. Keep in mind while reading the formulas that "*" denotes multiplication, and "**" exponentiation. Also, *log* refers to logarithm to the base ten, while *ln* stands for the natural logarithm (log to the base e). Options 10 and 11, with parameters A and B set to 1, can be used to take the sum and product of two variables, respectively.

STATISTICS : VARIABLE TRANSFORMATION OPTIONS

1)	New_var =	A + B * Case Number
2)	=	Old_var lagged N periods
3)	=	A + B * Old_var
4)	=	A * log(B * Old_var)
5)	=	A * ln(B * Old_var)
6)	=	A * (Old_var ** B)
7)	=	A * exp(B * Old_var)
8)	=	A * sin(B * Old_var)
9)	=	A * cos(B * Old_var)
10)	=	A * Old_var_1 + B * Old_var_2
11)	=	(Old_var_1 ** A) * (Old_var_2 ** B)

Figure 3: Menu of Variable Transformation Options

By successively using the appropriate transformation function, you can combine more than two variables to form a new one. For example, the product transformation (option 11 in Figure 3) can be used twice to create the new variable $X_4 = X_1 X_2 X_3$.

After selecting a transformation function, you must specify the values of N, or A and B, and indicate which of the variables are to be used for the old variables *(old_var,* or *old_var_1* and *old_var_2)*. This is done by entering your choices on a STORM form, as shown in Figure 4 for the transformation option 11. Note that default values have been preset for the exponents A and B and for the new variable name. The Candidates column will not be present at first; we will discuss that in a moment.

As discussed in Chapter 3, it is now an easy matter to enter the variables and constants using the movable Pointer. In an *Old variable* field, where you must input the name of an existing variable, you may type in the exact name if you remember it. Otherwise, by pressing the F8 Function key you can obtain the list of all the current variables in a Candidate Selection list on the right side of the screen (see Figure 4), with another Pointer. By positioning the List Pointer at the desired variable and pressing the Enter key, you will cause the variable name to be transferred into the Form Pointer, which will immediately advance to the next entry.

```
              PARAMETER SPECIFICATION FOR           CANDIDATES
          New_var = (Old_var_1 ** A) * (Old_var_2 ** B)
                                                     ░░COST░░░
                                                     VOLUME
          Old Variable 1  :░░░░░░░░░░░░░              REFRIG
                                                     PRICE
          Old Variable 2  :  _____

          Constant A      : 1

          Constant B      : 1

          New Variable    : X5
```

Figure 4: Specifying Parameters of a Variable Transformation

Thus, if you press Enter with the situation as shown in Figure 4, the variable COST will be selected as *Old Variable 1*. The *New Variable* default name can be altered to anything you like, including the name of an existing variable. In the latter case, the newly created variable will overwrite the existing variable, which will be lost. When you have made the appropriate entries, the End key will terminate the variable definition and the new variable will be added to your data set. Note that *the new variable will be assigned the missing value code for a case where any old variable has a missing value,* regardless of the treatment prescribed for the old variable's missing values in the MV OPTION row.

We illustrate the use of variable transformation by creating a new dependent variable:

$$\text{GROSS MARG} = (\text{PRICE} - \text{COST}) / \text{PRICE} = 1 - (\text{COST} / \text{PRICE})$$

We argue that gross margin is a more appropriate variable to predict than price, because an error of so many cents is a more significant deviation for a low cost item than for a high cost one. How, then, do we define this new variable? We will do it in two steps, as shown in Figures 5 and 6. Using the transformation shown in Figure 5, we define the variable GROSS MARG = COST/PRICE. This is not in fact the gross margin, but an intermediate variable which we will subsequently overwrite. Using transformation 3, as in Figure 6, the new GROSS MARG becomes one minus the old, which is the desired result. If you now return to the Editor screen, you will find the new variable added to the data set as shown in Figure 7.

```
                PARAMETER SPECIFICATION FOR
    New_var = (Old_var_1 ** A) * (Old_var_2 ** B)

        Old Variable 1  : COST

        Old Variable 2  : PRICE

        Constant A      : 1

        Constant B      : -1

        New Variable    : GROSS MARG
```

Figure 5: Defining a Variable GROSS MARG = COST/PRICE

```
                PARAMETER SPECIFICATION FOR
            New_var = A + B * Old_var

        Old Variable    : GROSS MARG

        Constant A      : 1

        Constant B      : -1

        New Variable    : GROSS MARG
```

Figure 6: Defining a Variable GROSS MARG = 1 - GROSS MARG

3.1.2 Variable Recoding

It is often desirable to reorder, merge, or in some way reinterpret the values of a variable, as when we wish to group cases into several classes. For instance, if the variable is the precise length of a manufactured steel bar, we may want to categorize each bar as being *too short, within tolerance,* or *too long.* If we intend to make ten foot poles, for example, we might recode all values under 9'11" as -1, all those between 9'11" and 10'1" as 0, and all greater than 10'1" as +1.

```
|---------------------------| STORM EDITOR : Statistics Module |----------------|
  Title : DRUG STORE PRICING MODEL
  Number of variables in data set          :      5
  Maximal number of cases for any variable :      18


  R1  : C1            COST     VOLUME     REFRIG     PRICE GROSS MARG
  VAR TYPE            QUAN      QUAN       QUAL       QUAN     QUAN
  MV OPTION           OMIT      OMIT       OMIT       OMIT     OMIT
  MV CONST             .         .          .          .        .
  CASE    1           1.2       2.1         R        2.25   0.466667
  CASE    2           5.69      7.75        NR        8.9   0.360674
  CASE    3           2.95      2.05        NR        5.    0.41
  CASE    4          10.2      10.21        NR       14.55  0.298969
  CASE    5           4.19      6.23        NR        6.5   0.355385
  CASE    6           7.25      8.52        NR       10.75  0.325581
  CASE    7           1.75      1.95         R        3.    0.416667
  CASE    8           2.21      1.75        NR        3.75  0.410667
  CASE    9           9.95      8.25         R       14.75  0.325424
  CASE   10           8.05      9.75         R       12.4   0.350806
  CASE   11           2.15      4.52        NR        3.5   0.385714
  CASE   12           6.75      5.82        NR        9.95  0.321608
  CASE   13           4.35      4.5         NR        7.    0.378571
  CASE   14           7.35      6.74         R       10.95  0.328767
  CASE   15          11.05      8.73         R       16.85  0.344214
  CASE   16           2.23      4.17        NR        3.75  0.405333
  CASE   17           5.38      2.45        NR         .        .
  CASE   18           8.73      9.67         R         .        .
  |----| This entry cannot be changed                   |->|         |----
```

Figure 7: Data File With New Variable Added

Variable recoding is also used to convert a qualitative or nonnumeric variable to one or more quantitative variables. This is necessary because qualitative variables cannot be included in a regression, nor used to generate any output except a histogram. Frequently, given a nonnumeric variable with n categories, we will want to represent it by n-1 zero-one *indicator variables,* as discussed in Section 5.2. We illustrate this by creating a new quantitative variable, NUMB, to replace the categorical variable REFRIG. As its name suggests, NUMB indicates with a number 1 the requirement for refrigeration, the number 0 representing the absence of this requirement.

Choosing the recode option takes you to a STORM form to specify the old variable name (REFRIG), the new variable name (NUMB), and the new variable type (QUAN). Then a second form appears, which looks like Figure 8 in case the old variable is nonnumeric. In the first column, headed OLD CODE, you list the categories of the old variable that you want to recode, and beside each you enter the new code that is to represent it. All existing categories that you do not list will be assigned the default code to be entered at the top of the form. If a default code is not specified, and unless you explicitly define new codes for every category of the old variable, STORM will stop you with an error message. In case you cannot remember all the category names, press F8 to get a Candidate Selection list. Figure 8 shows this form after you have made the appropriate entries to recode *R* as 1 and all else (namely, *NR*) as 0. Again, as soon as you press the End key the new variable NUMB will take its place beside the others.

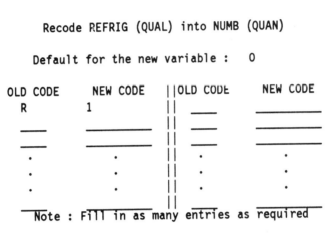

Figure 8: Entry Form for Variable Recoding

If the original variable is quantitative, the column OLD CODE will be replaced by two columns headed LOWR LIMIT and UPPR LIMIT. Use these to specify the range of numeric values of the old variable to convert to the new code entered beside it. The overall range of the old variable is given at the top of the form, for your convenience. Any interval for which you leave LOWR LIMIT (UPPR LIMIT) unfilled will be interpreted as having a lower limit of minus infinity (upper limit of plus infinity). The recoding forms in STORM accommodate up to 30 new code definitions.

If there are missing values in your old variable, they may be explicitly recoded to any other legitimate code. To do so for qualitative variables, you should enter the missing value code (.) like any other old code. For quantitative variables, you must enter "." in both LOWR LIMIT and UPPR LIMIT columns. *If you do not explicitly recode missing values, they will remain as missing values in the new variable,* regardless of the missing value option and whether or not a default value for the new variable is specified.

3.2 Descriptive Statistics

If you select the second option from the Statistics Procedures menu, you will be offered the menu of Figure 9. The four alternatives are explained below.

```
                    DESCRIPTIVE STATISTICS

        1)   Scatter plots
        2)   Frequency tables and histograms
        3)   Means, variances, and other statistics
        4)   Correlation matrix
```

Figure 9: Descriptive Statistics Menu

3.2.1 Scatter Plots

If you choose scatter plots, a Candidate Selection form will appear on which to specify the names of the variables to be plotted along the horizontal (X) and vertical (Y) axes. As before, the names of all the candidates (all the quantitative variables in your data set) will be displayed in a column on the right side of the screen, with a Pointer to position at the chosen label. When you are located at the top of a long list, keep in mind that an Up Arrow will jump you all the way to the bottom. Figure 10 shows this screen after the first variable label has been chosen. Note that the qualitative variable REFRIG is not available, as its codes have no inherent order. If we choose GROSS MARG as the second variable in Figure 10, we obtain the scatter plot illustrated in Figure 11.

```
VARIABLE SELECTION FOR SCATTER PLOT              CANDIDATES

Variable selected for X axis : COST                VOLUME
                                                   PRICE
Select variable for Y axis                         GROSS MARG
                                                   NUMB
```

Figure 10: Selection of Scatter Plot Variables

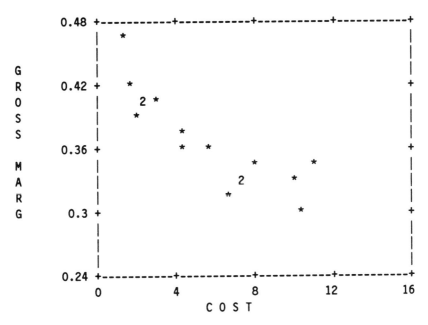

Figure 11: Sample Scatter Plot

In all such plots, the following coding scheme is used to indicate multiple points at the same location:

*	indicates a single case
2 - 9	indicates 2 to 9 cases at that location
A - Z	indicates 10 to 35 cases at that location
#	indicates over 35 cases at that location

Of course, with a small data set like ours, coincident points are rare.

3.2.2 Frequency Tables and Histograms

This option permits you to display the distribution of the values of any variable, both in tabular form and graphically in a histogram. Again, a Candidate Selection form facilitates your choice. If you select a quantitative variable, you will use a STORM form to specify the number and width of the intervals to be used for grouping the values into classes, and the starting point. For example, if you specify 10 intervals each of width 2 starting at 0, then the chart will show the number of observations with values between 0 and 2, the number between 2 and 4, and so on up to the 18-to-20 class of cases. There will always be two extra classes: the low field (all values less than 0) and the high field (over 20).

We illustrate with the variable GROSS MARG. The STORM form tells you the range of values (0.299 to 0.467) and suggests some default values for the starting point (0.3), interval width (0.02) and number of intervals (10). These may be useful to suggest the appropriate orders of magnitude. We changed the starting point to 0.28, and selected 5 intervals each of width 0.04 to obtain the outputs shown in Figure 12 (tabular) and Figure 13 (graphical). As you can see, the table gives the number of observations in each interval, and the corresponding percentage, both individual and cumulative. The histogram shows the same percentages pictorially. The asterisks give the frequency of the class, each asterisk denoting 2%. The last increment is an asterisk if it is between 1% and 2%, and a plus sign if less than 1%. The row of hyphens extending to the right shows the cumulative frequency, each hyphen adding another 2%.

If you want the frequency distribution of a qualitative variable, the output will be as shown in Figure 14 for the variable REFRIG. The class intervals are replaced by the variable categories. Also, since qualitative variables have no logical ordering, cumulative frequencies are not computed.

```
              FREQUENCY TABLE FOR GROSS MARG
      Class Width = 0.0400          Number of Classes = 5
     ----- Class Limits ----    ---------- Frequency ---------
       Lower      Upper      Count      Per cent Cumulative %
     -Infinity     0.2800      0        0.0000      0.0000
       0.2800      0.3200      1        6.2500      6.2500
       0.3200      0.3600      7       43.7500     50.0000
       0.3600      0.4000      3       18.7500     68.7500
       0.4000      0.4400      4       25.0000     93.7500
       0.4400      0.4800      1        6.2500    100.0000
       0.4800    Infinity      0        0.0000    100.0000
```

Figure 12: Table of Frequencies for a Quantitative Variable

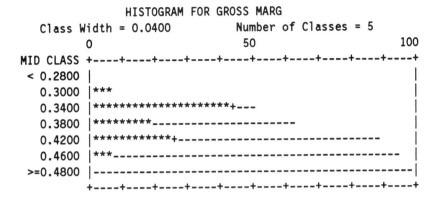

Figure 13: Frequency Histogram for a Quantitative Variable

Figure 14: Frequency Distribution for a Qualitative Variable

3.2.3 Other Statistics

The other options on the Descriptive Statistics menu produce standard statistical measures for any quantitative variables you select. For each variable, the third option produces the mean, standard deviation, skewness, and kurtosis, as well as the percentile values for the 0th, 5th, 25th, 50th, 75th, 95th, and 100th percentiles.

The final option gives the correlation matrix for the chosen variables. STORM gives separately for each entry the sample size on which it is based. This is potentially different for each pair of variables because cases are omitted if *either* variable has a missing value and uses the OMIT option.

We will not present these outputs here, but you may wish to run the sample data file and review them.

3.3 Regression Analysis

Having completed the preliminaries, we are now ready to investigate how the variables are interrelated, using regression analysis. If you choose regression on the Procedures menu (see Figure 2), the Regression Analysis menu shown in Figure 15 will be displayed. The second option, *batch mode,* will quickly provide you with a regression model using the entire data set and based on conventional parameter values. If this is desired, you may skip directly to Section 3.3.7. If you wish to exercise greater control or experiment with different models, the intervening sections explain the features and options available to you.

```
                    REGRESSION ANALYSIS

          1)   Set regression control parameters
          2)   Multiple regression : batch mode
          3)   Multiple regression : interactive mode
          4)   Multiple regression with priorities
```

Figure 15: Available Options for Regression

3.3.1 Control parameters for Stepwise Regression

The first option on the Regression Analysis menu offers you the chance to modify the criteria that will be used to guide STORM in entering or deleting variables, if you intend to use an automatic search procedure to develop the regression equation. Figure 16 presents the form used to enter the parameter values, with the default values shown. As usual, you can change them simply by positioning the Pointer using the Up and Down Arrows and then typing in the desired values.

The six parameters are:

(1) *Maximal number of variables in regression*

This parameter puts an upper limit on the number of independent variables to be included in the final regression equation. The default value is the total number of variables in your data set minus one (for the dependent variable).

REGRESSION CONTROL PARAMETERS

```
Maximal number of variables in regression : 5

Significance level for entering variables : 0.05

Significance level for leaving variables  : 0.1

Cutoff value for tolerance                : 0.001

Confidence level for prediction           : 0.95

Number of cases for validation            : 0
```

Figure 16: Form for modifying stepwise criteria

(2) *Significance level for entering variables*

In a forward step of the stepwise process, a variable will enter only if its significance level (that is, its probability of F-to-enter) is less than this value.

(3) *Significance level for leaving variables*

A variable will be deleted from the equation in a backward step of stepwise regression only if its significance level has risen to a value greater than this parameter. To avoid cycling (the same variable entering and leaving at successive steps), STORM will not allow you to specify a value for this criterion that is less than the criterion for entry specified in (2).

(4) *Cutoff value for tolerance*

The tolerance of a variable, X, not yet in the regression equation is defined as the proportion of the variability of X that is not explained by the other independent variables already in the equation. Thus, a very small tolerance indicates that X is almost a linear combination of the other variables. Any variable with tolerance less than the specified cutoff value will not be considered as a candidate for entering the model. By choosing an appropriate value for this parameter, you can control the *multicollinearity* of the selected variables. To avoid roundoff problems, STORM does not accept tolerance values smaller than 10^{-6}.

(5) *Confidence level for prediction*

This is the degree of assurance you want when constructing confidence and prediction intervals if the regression model is used for prediction.

(6) *Number of cases for validation*

If you have many cases in your data set, you may want to use only part of the data in a *model fitting* phase to develop the regression model. The model can then be used to predict the dependent variable values for the remaining cases, and the accuracy of the predictions can be assessed. Such a process is called *model validation*. The number you enter here determines how many cases are to be used for model validation, counting back from the end of the data set (leaving out cases with missing values for variables using the OMIT option). There are 16 eligible cases in the example (cases 17 and 18 are omitted), and we will opt to use the last four for validation. That is, cases 1 through 12 will be used to develop the regression model, and cases 13 through 16 to validate it. Thus, the last entry on the STORM form should be changed to 4. We will leave all other parameters at their default settings.

3.3.2 Defining the Regression Function

Suppose you select the third option, *Multiple regression: interactive mode,* on the Regression Analysis menu. You will then be presented with the form shown in Figure 17, on which you can choose the variables you wish to include. First you will be asked to specify the dependent variable from the list of all the quantitative variable labels displayed at the right of the screen. Note that the qualitative variable, REFRIG, is not a candidate. To include qualitative variables in the regression equation, you must replace them with the appropriate number of *quantitative* indicator variables, as discussed in Section 5.2. In our case, NUMB is the surrogate for REFRIG.

Position the Pointer with the Arrow keys and press Enter. The chosen variable label will be transferred to the left. From the remaining labels in the list, you can now select the potential independent variables for inclusion in the regression study by marking them with an asterisk (*). You can position the Pointer and use the Space bar as a toggle for the asterisk, or use the F1 key and switch all variables at once.

```
REGRESSION MODEL SELECTION                      CANDIDATES

Select the dependent variable                   COST
                                                VOLUME
                                                PRICE
                                                GROSS MARG
                                                NUMB
```

Figure 17: Dependent Variable Selection

Figure 18 shows that GROSS MARG is to be regressed on COST, VOLUME, and NUMB, while PRICE is not to be considered for inclusion.

```
REGRESSION MODEL SELECTION                      CANDIDATES

Dependent variable selected : GROSS MARG        * COST
                                                * VOLUME
Select independent variables                      PRICE
                                                * NUMB
Note : * marks selected variables
```

Figure 18: Independent Variable Selection

After you have chosen the variables to be included, you will be offered the Beginning Options menu as shown in Figure 19.

```
        REGRESSION ANALYSIS : BEGINNING OPTIONS

   1)   Mean, standard deviation, and correlation
   2)   Start with null regression
   3)   Start with maximal regression
```

Figure 19: Preliminaries to Regression

3.3.3 Descriptive Statistics

The first item on the Beginning Options menu provides you with an output of the correlation matrix of all the variables selected for this study, as well as their means and standard deviations. If you want this information, you should obtain it before going on to option 2 or 3. Once the regression procedure is initiated, the descriptive statistics are lost. In Figure 20, this output is presented for our example.

DESCRIPTIVE STATISTICS FOR REGRESSION VARIABLES
(Based on 12 cases used for model fitting)

	COST	VOLUME	NUMB	GROSS MARG
Average	5.1950	5.7417	0.3333	0.3690
Std Dev	3.2299	3.2053	0.4924	0.0496

Correlation matrix

COST	1.0000	0.9097	9.7179E-03	-0.8998
VOLUME	0.9097	1.0000	-0.0528	-0.8682
NUMB	9.7179E-03	-0.0528	1.0000	0.3111
GROSS MARG	-0.8998	-0.8682	0.3111	1.0000

Figure 20: Means, Standard Deviations, and Correlation Matrix

3.3.4 Specifying the Starting Equation

The next two items on the Beginning Options menu provide you with two starting points from which to begin developing your model. The *maximal regression* option initializes the equation by including as many variables as possible. Only variables which create excessive multicollinearity, as measured by tolerance, are excluded. The *null regression* option starts you off with no variables at all in the model. Let's choose it.

3.3.5 Developing the Regression Equation

Once the initial equation has been chosen, the menu shown in Figure 21 offers you various ways to search for better models. Some of them take you right from the starting point to a final regression equation. Others advance you only one step, and give you the chance to consider the results before deciding on the next step. You may wish to follow the built-in logic of the stepwise procedure, allowing the module to make the decisions for you, or you may want to take your fate into your own hands and enter or delete a variable for your own reasons. You can switch from one strategy to the other at any time.

```
                    REGRESSION CONTROL

        1)   Perform stepwise procedure to end
        2)   Perform one step of stepwise procedure
        3)   Review current regression
        4)   Enter all significant variables
        5)   Delete all insignificant variables
        6)   Enter a specified variable in regression
        7)   Delete a specified variable from regression
```

Figure 21: Alternative Ways to Develop the Regression Equation

The following alternatives are available to you:

(1) *Perform stepwise procedure to end*

The forward-backward stepwise selection process is followed to completion. You can obtain output only for the final model.

(2) *Perform one step of stepwise procedure*

This is the option to choose if you want to obtain intermediate output, since it will only take you one step in the forward-backward stepwise process, stopping then to let you study the resulting model if you choose.

(3) *Review current regression*

Here you can examine the results to date. You may then return to this menu to develop the model further. The reports available at this time are discussed in Section 3.3.6.

(4) *Enter all significant variables*

Starting with the current equation, a forward selection procedure is performed to conclusion. Variables are only added, never deleted. Output is available only at the end.

(5) *Delete all insignificant variables*

Here, only backward elimination steps are taken, with the stepwise control parameters dictating which variables are deleted and how many. Again, the intermediate models are not available for output.

(6,7) *Enter/Delete a variable to be specified*

These options allow you to decide which variable will be added to or removed from the equation. When you choose either one, you will be given an opportunity to select which variable it will be.

3.3.6 Output Reports

For our sample problem, suppose we start from a null regression and follow the stepwise procedure to completion. Whatever way we choose to advance the regression analysis, we will generally want to observe the results by choosing option 3, *Review current regression.* The STORM form displayed in Figure 22 shows the selection of output reports available. You can choose any desired set of reports by entering *y* in the appropriate boxes. As illustrated, you will get only the first and fourth by default, but we shall present all the reports.

```
                REGRESSION OUTPUT SELECTION

     Regression function and ANOVA table      :  y
     Detailed output                          :  n
     Standardized residuals report            :  n
     Validation report                        :  y
     Prediction report                        :  n
     Residual analysis                        :  n
```

Figure 22: Available Outputs for Regression Analysis

(1) *Regression function and ANOVA table*

This report, shown in Figure 23, gives the current regression equation, and provides the following basic information about the model presently under study: R-squared, adjusted R-squared, the standard error of the estimate, and the *analysis of variance (ANOVA)* table.

We see that the stepwise procedure has chosen two of the three candidate variables, COST and NUMB, to include in the model, thereby explaining about 89% of the variance of GROSS MARG *(Adjusted R-Squared* = 0.8924). There are other indications that the regression model is useful. Without the explanatory power of the model, the standard deviation of GROSS MARG is 0.0496 (see Figure 20) whereas the standard error of the estimate, measuring its variation about the regression line, is only 0.0163. Finally, the ANOVA table gives a negligible significance probability *(Sig Prob* = 0.000018) that the model could have produced such consistent results purely by chance.

```
          REGRESSION FUNCTION & ANOVA FOR GROSS MARG

 GROSS MARG = 0.430267 - 0.013857 COST + 0.0322 NUMB

 R-Squared                    = 0.911972
 Adjusted R-Squared           = 0.89241
 Standard error of estimate = 0.016259
 Number of cases used         = 12

                   Analysis of Variance
```

Source	SS	df	MS	F Value	Sig Prob
Regression	0.02465	2	0.01232	46.62022	0.000018
Residual	0.00238	9	2.64353E-04		
Total	0.02703	11			

Figure 23: Summary Statistics of the Current Regression

(2) Detailed Output

This option provides you with information about each of the independent variables separately, including both those which are in and those which are out of the present equation. As we see in Figure 24, STORM gives the values of the coefficients of the variables in the equation, along with the usual measures of our confidence in them. For the variables not included, we list the indicators of their potential value. Also included is the Durbin-Watson statistic, which is discussed below in conjunction with the Residual report.

We may take satisfaction in the values of the significance probabilities for the individual variables, which are very low for the included variables and high for the excluded one *(Sig Prob* = 0.494513 for VOLUME), as they should be.

REGRESSION COEFFICIENTS FOR GROSS MARG

Variable	Coefficient	Std Error	t Value	Two-Sided Sig Prob
Constant	0.43027	0.00973	44.21166	0.000000
COST	-0.01386	0.00152	-9.12949	0.000007
NUMB	0.03220	0.00996	3.23387	0.010259

Standard error of estimate = 0.016259
Durbin-Watson statistic   = 1.233959

VARIABLES NOT IN REGRESSION FOR GROSS MARG

Variable	Partial R-sq	Tolerance	F Value	Sig Prob
VOLUME	0.06018	0.16858	0.51228	0.494513

Figure 24: Detailed Regression Output

(3) *Standardized residuals report*

This report consists of three parts. First, a table lists, for each case, the actual and predicted values of the dependent variable, the *error* or *residual* value (the difference between the actual and predicted values), the estimated standard deviation at that point, and the *standardized residual* value (the residual divided by the standard deviation). Figure 25 shows this table for the sample problem. Any residuals lying outside two sigma and three sigma limits (standardized residuals with magnitudes over 2 or 3) will be marked by a "+" or an "#", respectively, appearing in the right margin.

At the bottom of the table, the Durbin-Watson statistic is repeated and the PRESS statistic is reported. Regression analysis is based on an assumption that all residual values are independent. The Durbin-Watson statistic is an indicator of the validity of this assumption. A small value (generally less than one) suggests that successive residual values are positively correlated, whereas too large a value (generally more than three) may indicate the presence of negative correlation. Most standard statistics texts include a table of critical values for this statistic.

STANDARDIZED RESIDUALS TABLE FOR GROSS MARGIN

Case		Actual GROSS MARG	Predicted GROSS MARG	Residual	Std Dev	Std Residual
CASE	1	0.4667	0.4458	0.0208	0.0127	1.6430
CASE	2	0.3607	0.3514	9.2529E-03	0.0152	0.6092
CASE	3	0.4100	0.3894	0.0206	0.0148	1.3898
CASE	4	0.2990	0.2889	0.0100	0.0132	0.7633
CASE	5	0.3554	0.3722	-1.682E-02	0.0151	-1.111
CASE	6	0.3256	0.3298	-4.223E-03	0.0149	-0.284
CASE	7	0.4167	0.4382	-2.155E-02	0.0130	-1.652
CASE	8	0.4107	0.3996	0.0110	0.0145	0.7588
CASE	9	0.3254	0.3246	8.3405E-04	0.0121	0.0688
CASE	10	0.3508	0.3509	-1.122E-04	0.0134	-8.363E-03
CASE	11	0.3857	0.4005	-1.476E-02	0.0145	-1.018
CASE	12	0.3216	0.3367	-1.512E-02	0.0150	-1.007

Durbin-Watson statistic   = 1.233959
PRESS statistic   = 0.004509

Figure 25: Table of Standardized Residuals

The PRESS statistic is an attempt to measure the predictive accuracy of the model, using only the data that was used to develop it. A case is removed from the data set and a regression model is fitted to the remaining cases. We can now compute the error (or residual) for the omitted case. This calculation is performed for each of the cases. The PRESS statistic is the sum of the squared errors. A good model should have a PRESS statistic close to its own residual sum of squares, given in the ANOVA table. In our example, we find the PRESS value of 0.0045 somewhat larger than the error sum of squares, 0.0024: a small danger signal.

The second part of the Standardized Residuals report gives what we call summary statistics. We report them as in Figure 26 for residuals and standardized residuals, chiefly for comparison with the corresponding measures for the validation data (see the discussion of the validation report in (4), below). Briefly described, they are:

- *Mean error* This is simply the sum of the residuals (standardized residuals), as listed in Figure 25, divided by the number of cases. Not surprisingly, the average residual is zero; this must always be so.

- *Mean per cent error* The per cent error for a case is 100 times the residual or error divided by the actual value. This is a recognition of the idea that an error of 0.1 is more significant if the observation is 0.5 than if it is 50. Thus, we report the average of the residuals as proportions of the observed values. We do not report this statistic for the standardized residuals, because viewing the error as a fraction of the observed value loses its significance once residuals have already been scaled a different way.

```
SUMMARY STATISTICS
                                  Residual   Std Residual
Mean error                         0.0000         0.0127
Mean per cent error               -0.1174           N/A
Mean absolute error                0.0121         0.8594
Mean absolute per cent error       3.1766           N/A
Root mean squared error *          0.0141         1.0108

* Not corrected for degrees of freedom
```

Figure 26: Summary Residual Statistics

- *Mean absolute error* Here, we take the absolute value of the residuals (standardized residuals) before averaging.

- *Mean absolute per cent error* Now we average the absolute values of the per cent errors.

- *Root mean squared error* Each residual (standardized residual) value is squared before being averaged. We then take the square root to rescale the statistic. Note the difference between the root mean squared error (RMSE) and the standard error of the estimate (SEE) reported with the ANOVA table (see Figure 23). For the RMSE, we divide by the full sample size (here, 12 cases), while for the SEE we correct for degrees of freedom and use a smaller divisor (9, as shown in the ANOVA table under *df*).

We cannot learn much from these figures in isolation. The mean error will always be zero, and remains negligible when residuals are taken as a per cent of actual values (0.1174%) or as a per cent of the standard deviation (1.27%). These are averages of *signed* values. Since such statistics will be close to zero when positive values cancel negative, they are good indicators of *lack of bias*. Thus, our model is totally unbiased. However, this is to be expected, since the model was chosen precisely to fit this data.

By averaging *absolute* values, we measure *magnitude*. We see that the residuals, in magnitude, are 3.18% of actual values and 85.94% of sigma, on the average.

The third part of the report is a plot, illustrated in Figure 27, giving a visual display of the standardized residuals. Since the plotted range extends from -2 to +2, any standardized residual whose value falls outside this two sigma interval will be displayed on the boundary. As before a "+" shows a point between two and three sigma, and a "#" denotes a point more that three sigma from the mean.

```
           STANDARDIZED RESIDUALS PLOT FOR GROSS MARG

   Case      -2.0              0.0              2.0
             +---------+---------+---------+---------+
   CASE   1  |                   |              *    |
   CASE   2  |                   |    *              |
   CASE   3  |                   |         *         |
   CASE   4  |                   |     *             |
   CASE   5  |          *        |                   |
   CASE   6  |               *   |                   |
   CASE   7  |   *               |                   |
   CASE   8  |                   |    *              |
   CASE   9  |                   |*                  |
   CASE  10  |                 * |                   |
   CASE  11  |         *         |                   |
   CASE  12  |         *         |                   |
             +---------+---------+---------+---------+
```

Figure 27: Plot of Standardized Residuals

(4) Validation Report

This report becomes relevant in case you decided to use *data splitting* or *cross-validation*, in which a portion of the data, the *estimation data*, is used to estimate the model coefficients (model fitting). The remainder, the *validation data*, is used to measure the prediction accuracy of the model (model validation), by having it make verifiable predictions of the dependent variable for *fresh* cases. This procedure simulates the collection of new data, the preferred validation method when possible.

If data are collected sequentially in time, it is reasonable to pick a point in time to divide the data into the earlier estimation set and the later prediction set. In any case, STORM uses the cases that you enter first for fitting and the later ones for validation. You should keep this in mind when entering the data. If there is no time dependency, the cases should be entered *in a random order* for validation purposes. Once you have completed your validation study and are satisfied with the model, you should conduct a final regression run using all the data for model fitting, to get the best possible estimates of the model parameters.

In the STORM form for setting control parameters (see Figure 16), we set aside 4 cases for validation. Figure 28 displays the various error statistics which are used to show how well the model we have developed fits these additional independent observations. The first part of the report exactly parallels the Standardized Residuals report shown in Figure 25, comparing the observed value of the dependent variable to the predicted value for each case. Of course, the predictions come from a model that is based on other data, and we are interested to see how well it fits this data. We note that for two out of four cases the fit is bad, as flagged in the right margin with "+" and "#". If there were a natural ordering of the data, we might suspect that conditions are changing. If the four cases set aside for validation were a random selection from the 16 total cases, we might look for an assignable cause such as a recording mistake.

The second part gives summary error statistics for the validation data collectively. First, we must explain the statistic marked *"R-Squared" for validation*. This is computed as 1 - SSE/SST, where SSE is the error sum of squares and SST is the total sum of squares. Thus, it is the proportion of the variance of the validation cases from their own mean that is explained by the model. Since this data was not involved in the development of the model, there is no guarantee that the errors are small. It is even possible that SSE > SST, which would make "R-Squared" negative! In such a case, STORM will not report it. On the other hand, if (as we hope) the model fits this data as well as it fits the data used to create it, the value of "R-Squared" should equal the original R-Squared reported with the ANOVA table (see Figure 23).

For your model to be valid and generalizable, the magnitude of the error statistics in this report should be comparable with the corresponding figures for the estimation data. In our case, this would be surprising since two of the four cases are very badly fitted. We see that "R-Squared" is only 0.34 (34% of the variance is explained by the model) as compared to R-Squared = 0.91 for the original regression, as shown in Figure 23. Comparing the other summary statistics in Figures 26 and 28, we see that the measures of bias *(Mean error* and *Mean per cent error),* while still a small fraction of the actual values, are much larger than before. The measures of magnitude of error *(Mean absolute error, Mean absolute per cent error,* and *Root mean squared error)* are roughly double.

```
                   VALIDATION REPORT FOR GROSS MARG

                  Actual  Predicted                     Std
        Case      GROSS MARG GROSS MARG  Residual  Std Dev  Residual
        CASE  13    0.3786    0.3700  8.5816E-03   0.0152    0.5662
        CASE  14    0.3288    0.3606 -3.185E-02    0.0137   -2.323 +
        CASE  15    0.3442    0.3093    0.0349     0.0110    3.1772 #
        CASE  16    0.4053    0.3994  5.9667E-03   0.0145    0.4104

        + denotes residual outside 2 sigma limits
        # denotes residual outside 3 sigma limits

        SUMMARY STATISTICS

        Total sum of squares       = 0.003553
        Error sum of squares       = 0.002339
        "R-squared" for validation = 0.341634

                                       Residual  Std Residual
        Mean error                    4.3910E-03     0.4577
        Mean per cent error             1.0451       N/A
        Mean absolute error             0.0203       1.6192
        Mean absolute per cent error    5.8891       N/A
        Root mean squared error *       0.0242       1.9988

        * Not corrected for degrees of freedom
```

Figure 28: Validation Report on the Prediction Data

(5) Prediction Report

This option allows you to obtain prediction and confidence intervals for any cases in the data set that contain no missing values among the *independent* variables included in the present model. A Candidate Selection form will list all such cases, and you can choose the ones for which you want a report. Since the dependent variable can be missing, you can prespecify cases (other than the observed data points) for which you will want forecasts, by including them in your data set with missing values in the dependent variable column, as we did for cases 17 and 18. The Prediction report is given for our example in Figure 29, where we have arbitrarily chosen to look at cases 2, 15, 17, and 18. The following information is included for each case selected:

Predicted value: the value of the dependent variable predicted by the model.

Confidence and prediction intervals: Corresponding to the level of confidence which you specified when setting the control parameters (95% is the default value which we are using), STORM computes intervals for single observations (for example, the gross margin of a particular product) and for means (the average gross margin for any product with the given values of the independent variables).

PREDICTION REPORT FOR GROSS MARG

Case		Predicted GROSS MARG		--- 95.00% Interval --- Lower Limit Upper Limit		Std Dev
CASE	2	0.3514	Conf	0.3383	0.3645	5.8016E-03
			Pred	0.3124	0.3905	0.0173
CASE	15	0.3093	Conf	0.2822	0.3365	0.0120
			Pred	0.2636	0.3551	0.0202
CASE	17	0.3557	Conf	0.3427	0.3687	5.7569E-03
			Pred	0.3167	0.3947	0.0172
CASE	18	0.3415	Conf	0.3195	0.3634	9.7051E-03
			Pred	0.2987	0.3843	0.0189

Figure 29: The Prediction Report

The statistical literature refers to *prediction intervals* for individual cases and *confidence intervals* when estimating the mean. For both these intervals, STORM lists the limits of the interval and the standard deviation of the prediction.

(6) Residual Analysis

Choosing this alternative produces the Residual Analysis menu shown in Figure 30. The first option gives the same report on standardized residuals as appears in Figures 25, 26, and 27. Options 2 and 3 offer you scatter plots of residuals. They will resemble Figure 31, which was obtained using option 2. For option 3, you will first be given an opportunity to select the variable to be plotted against residuals, using the familiar candidate selection process; you will find it easy to display a number of plots in quick succession. Scatter plots are sometimes helpful in identifying a nonlinear relationship that may exist between the dependent and independent variables. Finally, option 4 allows you to add residuals as a part of your data set for future analysis (for example, to obtain a histogram to validate the normality assumption). They will be assigned sequentially the names RESID 1, RESID 2, ...

```
                    RESIDUAL ANALYSIS

    1)    Standardized residuals report
    2)    Scatter plot of residuals versus predicted values
    3)    Scatter plot of residuals versus a variable
    4)    Include residuals in data set
```

Figure 30: Residual Analysis Menu

3.3.7 Multiple Regression: Batch Mode

In the Regression Analysis menu shown in Figure 15, if you pick batch mode instead of interactive mode, you will quickly be brought to the final regression model based on the type of stepwise procedure you select. You will, as usual, be asked to pick the dependent variable and the set of candidate independent variables, as described in Section 3.3.2. Then, in the form shown in Figure 32, you can choose the type of stepwise procedure to be used, the starting regression (null or maximal), and whether you want output at each step or only at the end. Finally, you have only to select the output reports desired, and STORM will generate them for you.

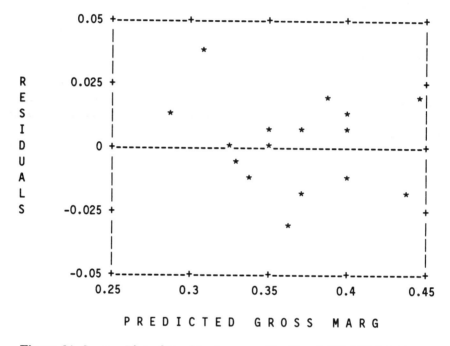

Figure 31: Scatter Plot of Residuals versus Predicted GROSS MARG

```
            BATCH MODE CONTROL OPTIONS

        Regression procedure used
          (F:Forward, B:Backward, S:Stepwise) : S
        Start with maximal regression ?        : n
        Do you want output at every step ?     : n
```

Figure 32: Choice of Stepwise Procedure in Batch Mode

3.3.8 Regression with Priorities

If you choose multiple regression with priorities, the entire procedure will be the same as the interactive option except at the first stage (see Section 3.3.2). There, instead of simply choosing the variables you wish to include, you must assign each independent variable a priority number between zero and nine. These priorities are used in the stepwise regression process, where variables with the highest (lowest) priority value are the first to be considered as candidates to enter (leave) the equation. A priority of zero means that the variable is not included in the regression at all. To assign priorities when in the STORM form for regression model selection, position the Pointer at each variable and type in the appropriate digit. This process will give you more control over the regression model which is developed.

4. Selecting a Subset of Cases

Often we are interested in developing a regression model based on just part of the data set. For example, we may want to conduct a study of only those items which do not need refrigeration and which cost under $5.00. In general, we may need to select cases which have particular values for one or more *selection variables*.

This can be easily accomplished in STORM by creating a new quantitative dummy variable for each selection variable, using the Recode Variable facility. The recoding should assign a value of 1 to the new variable for cases which satisfy the selection criteria and a missing value (.) to all other cases. The way chosen to handle missing values, MV OPTION, should be OMIT.

If you now include the new variables among the independent variables to be considered in the model, STORM will discard all cases for which these variables have missing values. Furthermore, since the remaining cases all have the same value 1, the dummy variables will be ignored thereafter.

5. Tips on Using the Statistics Module

5.1 Treatment of Missing Values

One of the more important features of a statistics package is its facility and flexibility in handling missing values for some variables in some cases. In STORM, the missing value code is the dot default (.). For each variable separately, you can indicate how you want its missing values to be treated. As mentioned in Section 2, you can choose any of three alternatives by making the appropriate entry in the MV OPTION row:

- OMIT: Any case which has a missing value in this column will be omitted from calculations which involve this variable.

- MEAN: The mean value for this variable will be computed, based on the numbers we *do* have, and missing entries will be given this average value. Of course, this option is not available for qualitative variables.

- CNST: All missing entries will be assigned the same value or code, which you must then specify in the next line, MV CONST. For quantitative variables, this must be a real number, while for qualitative variables it can be any string of up to four characters. If you choose this option but then fail to enter the constant value, cases with missing values will be left out of calculations as with the OMIT option.

The OMIT choice is an easy and popular one. However, it may not be appropriate when we have relatively few cases, especially when data for a large number of variables has been gathered. You would not, for example, discard a 50-item questionnaire in which all but one question had been answered.

No matter how they are to be handled, missing values will remain as such in the data set. Nevertheless, they will be treated as acceptable values for purposes of calculation if the MEAN or CNST option is chosen. In this case, we shall call them *acceptable missing values (AMV's)*, while those under the OMIT option will be referred to as *unacceptable missing values (UMV's)*.

Of course, for single-variable statistics (means, variances, etc.), AMV's will be included in the calculation but UMV's will be omitted. For two-variable operations such as correlations or scatter plots, cases will be omitted if either variable has a UMV. Similarly, in regression, we omit cases where *any* selected variable has a UMV. After eliminating cases, STORM removes from consideration any variable with zero variance.

For variable transformations and recodings, missing values are left as missing values, even if they are acceptable. However, in recoding a variable, you can explicitly recode missing values to something else if you want. To recode the missing values of a quantitative variable, you should enter a "." in both the UPPR LIMIT and LOWR LIMIT columns.

5.2 Using Qualitative Variables

Often a variable of interest is nonnumeric. Instead of taking values on an ordered scale, the variable assigns each case to one of a finite number of classes, categories, or types. When entering the data for such a variable in STORM, each class can be symbolized by any string of up to four characters. It is most important to remember that *nonnumeric variables cannot be included in any statistical analysis* except to obtain a histogram of that variable alone. You must identify variables as qualitative by entering QUAL in the VAR TYPE row, or you will only be allowed to enter numbers for the class codes. Note, however, that if you do enter QUAL for a variable, *the data entries will be identified as category codes even if they are all numbers.*

To use a qualitative variable, especially in regression studies, it must first be encoded into quantitative zero-one *indicator variables*. A nonnumeric variable with n classes may be represented by n-1 indicator variables. Suppose, for example, a quarterly seasonal factor is conjectured in a marketing study. The variable SEASON is entered with four classes, encoded SP, SU, F, and W. Three new zero-one variables must now be defined; call them SPRING, SUMMER, and FALL. In relation to the variable SEASON, their values are specified as in Figure 33. For example, if a set of observations is made in the spring (a case has SP entered in the Season column), variable SPRING should have value 1 and variables SUMMER and FALL should be 0. Now, if the three new variables are included in a regression study, the coefficient of SPRING indicates how much higher (lower) the dependent variable (sales, perhaps) is expected to be, all else being equal, in spring than in winter (the class for which all new variables are zero). Similarly, the other coefficients relate the other seasons to winter.

```
--------- Variable -----------
SEASON    SPRING  SUMMER  FALL

  SP         1       0      0
  SU         0       1      0
  F          0       0      1
  W          0       0      0
```

Figure 33: Definition of Indicator variables

It is not our purpose here to teach the practice of statistics, and the above discussion is necessarily cursory and incomplete. Dependence, interaction effects, and other complications should be understood before you can make the best use of a regression study.

5.3 Validating the Model

When using data splitting, recent publications suggest using one half the data for model fitting and the other half for model validation. You should strive to have thirty or more usable cases for fitting the model. If data are scarce, give a higher proportion of your cases (60% or 70%) to model fitting or skip validation entirely until you can acquire more data. If you have ample data and observe that the error measures for model validation are significantly worse than those for model fitting, it may mean that the relationship implied by the model does not exist, or that the model has been specified incorrectly. The latter situation frequently results when model developers put too many independent variables in the equation. Try removing the last variable that entered the regression and rerunning the validation analysis. You may repeat this process several times to observe the effects on the validation errors. You can feel reasonably confident when the model fitting and model validation errors are approximately equal.

Finally, *once you have completed your validation study and are satisfied with the model, you should conduct a final regression run using all the data for model fitting,* to get the best possible estimates of the model parameters.

6. Altering Problem Data Dimensions

In this module, the first two rows labeled VAR TYPE and DEFAULT are frozen and cannot be deleted. Otherwise, rows and columns can be inserted or deleted at will within the allowable limits for your version of STORM.

- NOTES -

DECISION ANALYSIS CAPABILITIES

PROBLEM FORMULATION OPTIONS
- Analysis with or without state probabilities
- Expected Value of Perfect Information
- Expected value of Sample Information

MAXIMAL PROBLEM SIZES (NUMBER OF ALTERNATIVES, NUMBER OF STATES, NUMBER OF INDICATORS):
- Personal version: (50, 50, 50)

FILE NAME FOR THE SAMPLE PROBLEM DATA
- DA.DAT

Chapter 22

DECISION ANALYSIS

In many situations, a decision maker needs to choose an alternative from a finite number of options so as to optimize an objective. For example, a company may want to decide whether to expand its existing facility, build another plant to supplement the current one, or shut down the current facility and replace it with a large modern one. In situations like this, the value of the objective (for example, the profit or payoff) not only depends on what decision alternative is selected, but also depends on future conditions which are not known with certainty. For instance, in the facility expansion example, the payoff depends on the decision as well as the demand that will be encountered during the planning horizon. We will need to specify the possible levels of demand, either in precise detail (demand = 0,1,2, . . . ,1000000 units), or categorized into as few levels as desired (demand = under 1000, 1000-4999, etc. or demand = low, medium, high). Besides demand, other variables may have to be considered. Any assumption about the future (that is, any choice of levels for the variables) is called a *state* (or sometimes *state of nature*) of the decision problem.

The Decision Analysis module in STORM selects a decision alternative which optimizes one of the various possible decision critera, taking into account the uncertain future state of the system. In many situations, some information about the future can be obtained; for example, through market research. This module also helps the decision maker to evaluate the value of such a market research effort.

1. Sample Problem

Analytic Software Inc. (ASI), a growing software developing company, is considering promotional activity for their new product. The company wishes to compare the following three decision alternatives:

ALTERNATIVE 1 (LOW): A low budget promotional campaign
ALTERNATIVE 2 (MODERATE): A moderate budget regional campaign
ALTERNATIVE 3 (HIGH): Hire a national advertising company to design
                    and implement a major media blitz

For each alternative under consideration, the company's estimated payoff over the life of the product depends on the uncertain future which has the following possible states:

STATE 1 (IMMED): No competing product in the immediate future.
STATE 2 (< 18 MONTHS): No competing product within 18 months.
STATE 3 (LIFE): No competing product during the life of ASI's product.

The research department of ASI has estimated the net payoff for each decision alternative and possible future state as given in Table 1, the payoff table, below (in thousands of dollars). The table also includes ASI's estimates of the probabilities of the occurrence of each state.

	IMMED	< 18 MONTHS	LIFE
State Prob.	.6	.3	.1
LOW	100	300	500
MODERATE	50	450	900
HIGH	-100	650	1200

Table 1: The Payoff Table

(i) As president of ASI, what alternative should you pick?
(ii) ASI also has an option to hire a market research firm which, for a fee of $30,000, can survey the potential software development companies and customers. On the basis of this additional *sample information,* the market research firm is expected to come up with either a favorable or unfavorable recommendation. In general, such outcomes are called *indicators.* Based on ASI's past experience, the following conditional probabilities are estimated.

	IMMED (s1)	< 18 MONTHS (s2)	LIFE (s3)
FAVORABLE (I1)	.2	.5	.9
UNFAVORABLE (I2)	.8	.5	.1

Table 2: Conditional Probabilities for Sample Information

For example, the entry in row I1 and columns s2 of Table 2 denotes the probability $P(I1|s2)$.

Should ASI hire this research firm ?

2. Data Entry Using STORM

Figure 1 displays the Editor screen for the decision analysis problem of ASI. For a particular problem, however, certain entries may not be required and hence can be ignored as we will explain below.

2.1 The Problem Description Area

Besides the title, the problem description requires several other entries as shown in Figure 1.

- *Number of Alternatives:* This is the total number of decision alternatives you have to select from.

- *Number of states:* The total number of possible future states.

- *Objective Type (MAX/MIN):* This entry should be MAX or MIN depending on whether objective involves payoffs or costs, respectively.

- *Number of Indicators:* This is the total number of indicators possible in case sample information is acquired. In our example, the possible indicators from the market research are FAVORABLE and UNFAVORABLE; hence, this value is 2. If there is to be no consideration of acquiring additional information, enter 0.

- *Sample Information Cost:* The cost of obtaining sample information. In the ASI problem, this cost is $30,000. Since we are using $1,000 units, we enter "30."

2.2 The Detailed Data Area

The detailed data layout depends on whether the problem includes analysis of sample information or not. The columns of the data set correspond to the future states of the problem. The description of rows is as follows.

```
|---------------------| STORM EDITOR : Decision Analysis Module |-------------------|
| Title : ANALYTIC SOFTWARE INC.: PRODUCT PROMOTION                                |
| Number of Alternatives    :      3  | Number of Indicators    :       2          |
| Number of States          :      3  | Sample Information Cost :      30.         |
| Objective Type (MAX/MIN) :      MAX  |                                            |
|                                                                                  |
| R1 : C3              IMMED < 18 MONTH      LIFE                                   |
| STATE PROB            0.6        0.3       0.1                                    |
| LOW                   100.       300.      500.                                  |
| MODERATE              50.        450.      900.                                  |
| HIGH                  -100.      650.      1200.                                 |
| XXXXXXXXXX            XXXX       XXXX      XXXX                                   |
| FAVORABLE             0.2        0.5       0.9                                    |
| UNFAVORBLE            0.8        0.5       0.1                                    |
|                                                                                  |
|                                                                                  |
|---------| Enter the prior probability of LIFE                    |->|-------------|
```

Figure 1: The Editor Screen After Data Entry

The State Probabilities

The first row of detailed data is labelled STATE PROB. Enter here the prior probabilities for the occurrence of each state defined by the corresponding column label, if known. This information is needed only for the probabilistic analysis and can be left at its default value of "." in case only the analysis without probabilities is required.

The Decision Alternatives

Each of the next several rows represents one of the decision alternatives available to us. For a given alternative, we enter in each column the payoff or cost for the corresponding future state. After the Alternatives rows, there appears a row labelled "XXXXXXXXXX" with all other entries as "XXXX". This row is included only as a separator and does not require any entry from you.

The Sample Indicators

These rows appear only if the sample information is available (that is, if you have entered an nonzero value for the entry "Number of Indicators" in the Problem Description area). In each Indicator row, we enter the conditional probability of that indicator given a future state. For example, the entry in the row labelled FAVORABLE and column labelled < 18 MONTHS is P(FAVORABLE | < 18 MONTHS). That is, if the future is "no competing product within 18 months," then there is a 50% chance that the market research indicator will be FAVORABLE.

3. Executing the module

After entering the problem data as described in Section 2, if you now select the "Execute" option from the Process menu, you will be presented with a STORM form as displayed in Figure 2. In this form, you select the output reports you need for your analysis as well as specifying the coefficient of optimism for the Hurwicz criterion which is explained in the next section. In case your data set does not include sample information data, the STORM Form will not include the list of reports corresponding to the analysis of sample information. Also, if any reports corresponding to the probabilistic analysis are selected, STORM will check for the prior probabilities for each state in the data set and will give an error message if they are not provided.

4. Output Reports

Figures 3 through 6 include all the detailed reports. The summary reports are abridged versions of the corresponding detailed reports and are not presented here. They generally do not include the computational details, but contain the information necessary to make a decision. In this section we discuss the computational details and explain all the detailed reports. Whenever detailed reports are requested, a summary report is included as well.

4.1 Analysis Without Probabilities

The answer to the first part of the sample problem generally depends on the criterion to be optimized. The report titled "Analysis without State Probabilities" as illustrated in Figure 3 gives you the reports based on the criteria that follow. This discussion assumes a maximization objective.

```
                    SELECTION OF OUTPUT REPORTS


        Deterministic Analysis
                Detailed Report                    : n
                Summary Report                     : n
                Optimism Parameter (alpha)         : 0.50


        Probabilistic Analysis
                Expected Value
                        Detailed Report            : n
                        Summary Report             : n


                Expected Value of Perfect Information   : n


                Expected Value of Sample Information
                        Detailed Report            : n
                        Summary Report             : n


        All Summary Reports                        : y
```

Figure 2: Output Options

Optimistic Approach: The Maximax Criterion

In this approach, for each decision alternative, we compute the maximal possible payoff, and then pick the alternative with the maximal value. It is an optimistic approach as it provides the possibility for highest reward with no consideration of potential downside risk. Based on this criterion, the table in Figure 3A shows that the decision alternative HIGH is the optimal strategy.

Conservative Approach: The Maximin Criterion

In this approach, for each decision alternative, you compute the minimal possible payoff, and then pick the alternative with the largest value. This is a conservative approach as the decision is based solely on the downside risk with no consideration to potential for high rewards. Based on this criterion, the table in Figure 3B shows that the decision alternative LOW is the optimal strategy.

```
ANALYTIC SOFTWARE INC.: PRODUCT PROMOTION
DETERMINISTIC ANALYSIS - DETAILED REPORT
              MAXIMAX CRITERION


   Alternative              Payoff


   LOW                      500.00
   MODERATE                 900.00
   HIGH                    1200.00 *
```

Figure 3A: Analysis Without State Probabilities - Maximax Criterion

```
ANALYTIC SOFTWARE INC.: PRODUCT PROMOTION
DETERMINISTIC ANALYSIS - DETAILED REPORT
              MAXIMIN CRITERION


   Alternative              Payoff


   LOW                      100.00 *
   MODERATE                  50.00
   HIGH                    -100.00
```

Figure 3B: Analysis Without State Probabilities - Maximin Criterion

Minimax Regret Criterion

This criterion tries to minimize potential opportunity loss. For each state, first identify the maximal payoff. For a given alternative, the regret (or opportunity loss) is then the difference between this value and the payoff realized. Table 3 below gives the regret values for each state for a given alternative.

	IMMED	< 18 MONTHS	LIFE	Maximal Regret
LOW	0	350	700	700
MODERATE	50	200	300	300
HIGH	200	0	0	200

Table 3: Regret Values for Each State

As shown above (and in Figure 3C), having identified the maximal regret for each decision alternative, we can select the one for which this is least. Based on this criterion, alternative HIGH is the optimal decision.

```
    ANALYTIC SOFTWARE INC.: PRODUCT PROMOTION
     DETERMINISTIC ANALYSIS - DETAILED REPORT
            MINIMAX REGRET CRITERION


      Alternative      Payoff Regret

      LOW                 700.00
      MODERATE            300.00
      HIGH                200.00 *
```

Figure 3C: Analysis Without State Probabilities - Minimax Regret Criterion

Equally Likely Criterion

This criterion assumes that each state has equal probability (1/number of states) of occurrence. Based on this assumption, the decision alternative with largest expected return is selected. As illustrated in Table 4 below (see Figure 3D also), alternative HIGH is optimal.

	Expected Payoff
LOW	$(1/3)(100) + (1/3)(300) + (1/3)(500) = 300$
MODERATE	$(1/3)(50) + (1/3)(450) + (1/3)(900) = 466\ 2/3$
HIGH	$(1/3)(-100) + (1/3)(650) + (1/3)(1200) = 583\ 1/3$

Table 4: Expected Payoffs for Equally Likely Criterion

```
ANALYTIC SOFTWARE INC.: PRODUCT PROMOTION
DETERMINISTIC ANALYSIS - DETAILED REPORT
        EQUALLY LIKELY CRITERION


    Alternative        Mean Payoff

    LOW                  300.00
    MODERATE             466.67
    HIGH                 583.33 *
```

Figure 3D: Analysis Without State Probabilities - Equally Likely Criterion

Hurwicz Criterion

This decision criterion is a compromise between optimistic and conservative approaches. Here, for each alternative, you first compute

Weighted Payoff = alpha • Maximal Payoff + (1 - alpha) • Minimal Payoff

and then select the alternative with the greatest weighted payoff. The weight alpha is called the coefficient of optimism. Note that this criterion is the same as maximax or maximin for alpha = 1 or alpha = 0, respectively. For example, if alpha = 0.2, based on this criterion, alternative MODERATE is the optimal strategy as illustrated below in Table 5 (see Figure 3E also).

```
    Alternative            Weighted Payoff
    LOW              0.2(500) + 0.8(100) = 180
    MODERATE         0.2(900) + 0.8(50)  = 220
    HIGH             0.2(1200)+ 0.8(-100)= 160
```

Table 5: Weighted Payoffs for Hurwicz Criterion

4.2 Analysis with Probabilities: The Expected Payoff Criterion

This analysis is applicable when the decision maker has prior information regarding the probability of occurrence of each state. In ASI's problem, these probabilities are given in

```
ANALYTIC SOFTWARE INC.: PRODUCT PROMOTION
DETERMINISTIC ANALYSIS - DETAILED REPORT
             HURWICZ CRITERION
OPTIMISM PARAMETER (ALPHA) :0.50
    Alternative    Hurwicz Payoff

    LOW                  300.00
    MODERATE             475.00
    HIGH                 550.00 *
```

Figure 3E: Analysis Without State Probabilities - Hurwicz Criterion

Table 1 above. In such situations, we can compute the expected payoff for each decision alternative and then select the one with the maximal value. Based on this criterion, we see in Table 6 below (also see Figures 4A and 4B) that alternatives MODERATE and HIGH are optimal.

```
                                Expected Payoff
LOW         (0.6)(100)  + (0.3)(300) + (0.1)(500)  = 200
MODERATE    (0.6)(50)   + (0.3)(450) + (0.1)(900)  = 255
HIGH        (0.6)(-100) + (0.3)(650) + (0.1)(1200) = 255
```

Table 6: Expected Payoff Criterion

4.3 Analysis With Probabilities: EVPI and EVSI

The decision analysis module in STORM also gives you an ability to evaluate the value of sample information (the market research information in our example) and answer related questions. To that end, this module performs the following additional computations.

```
        ANALYTIC SOFTWARE INC.: PRODUCT PROMOTION
                PROBABILISTIC ANALYSIS
            EXPECTED VALUE - SUMMARY REPORT
            Decision     Expected Payoff

            LOW               200.00
            MODERATE          255.00 *
            HIGH              255.00 *


            Optimal Decision:    MODERATE
            Expected Payoff :     255.00

    Note: Alternative optima exist (marked with *)
```

Figure 4A: Analysis With Probabilities - Expected Payoff Criteria Summary Report

```
        ANALYTIC SOFTWARE INC.: PRODUCT PROMOTION
                PROBABILISTIC ANALYSIS
            EXPECTED VALUE - DETAILED REPORT
    Decision    State       Prob        Payoff    Prob*Payoff

    LOW         IMMED       0.6000      100.00       60.00
                < 18 MONTH  0.3000      300.00       90.00
                LIFE        0.1000      500.00       50.00
                            Expected Payoff          200.00


    MODERATE    IMMED       0.6000       50.00       30.00
                < 18 MONTH  0.3000      450.00      135.00
                LIFE        0.1000      900.00       90.00
                            Expected Payoff          255.00


    HIGH        IMMED       0.6000     -100.00      -60.00
                < 18 MONTH  0.3000      650.00      195.00
                LIFE        0.1000     1200.00      120.00
                            Expected Payoff          255.00
```

Figure 4B: Analysis With Probabilities - Expected Payoff Criteria Detailed Report

Expected Value of Perfect Information (EVPI)

Suppose there is a market research firm which can conduct research and tell you with certainty the state of the future. If such a service is available, how much should you be willing to pay for this information? To answer this question, Figure 5 illustrates the computation of the expected payoff with this information. It shows that the expected payoff with perfect information is 375. Note from the previous discussion that the expected payoff without perfect information is 255. Hence:

Expected Value of Perfect Information (EVPI) = 375 - 255 = 120.

Thus, for market research which can give you perfect information about the future, you will be willing to pay up to $120,000.

```
            ANALYTIC SOFTWARE INC.: PRODUCT PROMOTION
                     PROBABILISTIC ANALYSIS
              EXPECTED VALUE OF PERFECT INFORMATION
       State       Prob   Decision      Payoff   Prob*Payoff

       IMMED       0.6000  LOW           100.00         60.00
       < 18 MONTH 0.3000   HIGH          650.00        195.00
       LIFE        0.1000  HIGH         1200.00        120.00

       Expected Payoff With Perfect Information ..     375.00
       Expected Payoff Without Perfect Information     255.00
       Expected Value of Perfect Information......     120.00
```

Figure 5: Analysis With Probabilities - Expected Value of Perfect Information

Expected Value of Sample Information (EVSI)

In reality, market research or test marketing cannot provide you with perfect information, but gives some information in the form of indicators (for instance, a FAVORABLE or UNFAVORABLE recommendation in the ASI example). To evaluate the value of such information, STORM performs the following computations.

$P(\text{FAVORABLE}) = P(I1|s1) \cdot p(s1) + P(I1|s2) \cdot p(s2) + P(I1|s3) \cdot p(s3)$
$= 0.2 \cdot 0.6 + 0.5 \cdot 0.3 + 0.9 \cdot 0.1 = 0.36$

Now if the market research firm gives a FAVORABLE recommendation (which has a probability of 0.36), the probabilities for each state to occur are

$P(s1|I1) = P(I1|s1) \cdot p(s1) / P(I1) = 0.12 / 0.36 = 1/3$
$P(s2|I1) = P(I1|s2) \cdot p(s2) / P(I1) = 0.15 / 0.36 = 5/12$
$P(s3|I1) = P(I1|s3) \cdot p(s3) / P(I1) = 0.09 / 0.36 = 1/4$

Using these conditional probabilities, Figure 6A shows that if the market research firm's recommendation is FAVORABLE (or indicator I1), then the expected payoffs for decision alternatives LOW, MODERATE, and HIGH are 283.33, 429.17, and 537.50, respectively. Hence if the market research firm's recommendation is FAVORABLE, the optimal decision is to select alternative HIGH. A similar analysis can be performed if the recommendation is UNFAVORABLE (indicator I2) as shown in the bottom half of Figure 6A.

Figure 6B summarizes the detailed computations of Figure 6A. It shows that there is 36% chance that the market research firm will come up with a FAVORABLE recommendation, in which case we will select the decision alternative HIGH resulting in the expected payoff of 537.50. Similarly, with 64% probability, the market research firm will return with an UNFAVORABLE recommendation. This will result in the expected payoff of 157.03 corresponding to decision alternative MODERATE. Multiplying these expected payoffs by their corresponding probability of occurrence and adding them together yields the expected payoff (with sample information) of 294.

Since the expected payoff without the sample information (that is, market research) was 255,

The Expected Value of the Sample Information = 294 - 255 = 39

Also, the expected value of sample information (EVSI) expressed as a percent of the expected value of perfect information (EVPI) represents the effectiveness of the sample information, and is termed the *efficiency of sample information.*

The efficiency of the sample information $= (\text{EVSI} / \text{EVPI}) \cdot 100\ \%$
$= (39 / 120) \cdot 100\ \% = 32.5\ \%$

```
          ANALYTIC SOFTWARE INC.: PRODUCT PROMOTION
                   PROBABILISTIC ANALYSIS
          EXPECTED VALUE OF SAMPLE INFORMATION - DETAILED REPORT
                                           --Conditional-----
   Indicator  Decision  State        Payoff   Prob   Prob*Payoff

   FAVORABLE  LOW       IMMED        100.00  0.3333        33.33
   Prob= 0.36           < 18 MONTH   300.00  0.4167       125.00
                        LIFE         500.00  0.2500       125.00
                        Expected Payoff                   283.33

              MODERATE  IMMED         50.00  0.3333        16.67
                        < 18 MONTH    50.00  0.4167       187.50
                        LIFE         900.00  0.2500       225.00
                        Expected Payoff                   429.17

              HIGH      IMMED       -100.00  0.3333       -33.33
                        < 18 MONTH   650.00  0.4167       270.83
                        LIFE        1200.00  0.2500       300.00
                        Expected Payoff                   537.50

   UNFAVORBLE LOW       IMMED        100.00  0.7500        75.00
   Prob= 0.64           < 18 MONTH   300.00  0.2344        70.31
                        LIFE         500.00  0.0156         7.81
                        Expected Payoff                   153.12

              MODERATE  IMMED         50.00  0.7500        37.50
                        < 18 MONTH   450.00  0.2344       105.47
                        LIFE         900.00  0.0156        14.06
                        Expected Payoff                   157.03

              HIGH      IMMED       -100.00  0.7500       -75.00
                        < 18 MONTH   650.00  0.2344       152.34
                        LIFE        1200.00  0.0156        18.75
                        Expected Payoff                    96.09
```

Figure 6A: Analysis With Probabilities - Expected Value of Sample Information

```
           ANALYTIC SOFTWARE INC.: PRODUCT PROMOTION
                     PROBABILISTIC ANALYSIS
           EXPECTED VALUE OF SAMPLE INFORMATION - SUMMARY REPORT
           Indicator    Prob    Decision      Payoff   Prob*Payoff

           FAVORABLE   0.3600   HIGH          537.50       193.50
           UNFAVORBLE  0.6400   MODERATE      157.03       100.50


           Expected Payoff...........................    294.00
           Expected Payoff Without Sample Information..  255.00
           Expected Value of Sample Information........   39.00
           Efficiency of Sample Information (%)........   32.50
           Expected Net Gain from Sampling.............    9.00
```

Figure 6B: Analysis With Probabilities - Expected Value of Sample Information

Based on this analysis, ASI should invest $30,000 in the market research as it will result in a net expected gain of 39000 - 30000 = $9000.

5. Altering Problem Data Dimensions

The columns in the Data area can be inserted or deleted at will using F5 and F6 keys, respectively. Likewise, Alternative rows and Indicator rows can be inserted and deleted by using F3 and F4 keys, respectively. However, you cannot delete the first row containing state probabilities, nor can you insert another row before it. Of course, the number of Alternative rows, Indicator rows and columns (the number of states) should not exceed the allowable maximal limits for your version of the software, and there should always be at least one Alternative row. Each time a column or row is added or deleted, STORM will automatically update the corresponding problem description value.

DECISION TREES CAPABILITIES

PROBLEM FORMULATION OPTIONS
- No limit on number of decision levels
- Expected value analysis
- Allows payoffs at intermediate as well as end nodes

OUTPUT OPTIONS AND OTHER FEATURES
- Sorted decision tree report
- Optimal decisions report
- Detailed decisions report
- Detects and reports cycles

MAXIMAL PROBLEM SIZES (NUMBER OF BRANCHES)
- Personal version: (250)

FILE NAME FOR THE SAMPLE PROBLEM DATA
- DT.DAT

Chapter 23

DECISION TREES

The Decision Analysis module discussed in the previous chapter (Chapter 22) helps us select a decision alternative (from a finite number of options) which optimizes a decision criterion, taking into account the uncertain future state of the system. As an example, recall the decision problem of Analytic Software Inc. (ASI) discussed in the previous chapter. ASI wishes to decide the level of promotional activity for their new product. The company is considering three decision alternatives, namely, a low budget local promotion (LOW), a moderate budget regional campaign (MODERATE), or a high budget media blitz (HIGH). For each alternative under consideration, the company's estimated payoff over the life of the product depends on the uncertain future which has the following possible states: no competing product in the immediate future (IMMED), no competing product within 18 months (< 18 MONTHS), or no competing product during the life of ASI's product (LIFE). ASI needs to make a decision based on its research department's estimate of the net payoff for each alternative and possible state of the future (see Table 1 in Chapter 22, which also include ASI's estimates of the probabilities of the occurrence of each future state).

This problem can be viewed as a *decision tree* as shown in Figure 1. In this diagram, the square node labelled begin (BEG) is a decision node and the branches emanating from it are the possible decision alternatives. The circled nodes are called *probabilistic* or *chance* nodes, and the branches from them correspond to the possible future (uncertain) states. The value next to such a branch indicates the probability of occurrence of that particular state. The octagonal end nodes at the extreme right of the tree are the 9 possible final outcomes and the value next to each is the corresponding payoff. This representation of the decision analysis problem illustrates the following restrictions of the Decision Analysis module.

> 1. It allows a decision to be made only at the beginning. However, in many situations the decision maker needs to take sequential decisions at different points in time. For example, after two years and depending on the conditions (state) at that time, ASI may want to reassess the situation, with the options of terminating production or enhancing the product and continuing the promotion.

2. It inherently assumes that the probability of occurrence of each state does not depend on the decision taken. However, it is possible that if ASI opts to go for a media blitz (HIGH), it may discourage other developers from producing a competing product, thereby increasing the probability of no competition.

The Decision Tree module allows these generalizations. When viewed as a tree as shown in Figure 1, the problem can have a sequence of decision nodes at various times in the future, and the probabilities associated with state branches can depend on all the previous states and decisions taken. This module analyzes such trees and gives the decision maker the optimal sequential decisions based on the expected payoff at each decision node. As an illustration, consider the following variation of the decision analysis example considered in Chapter 22.

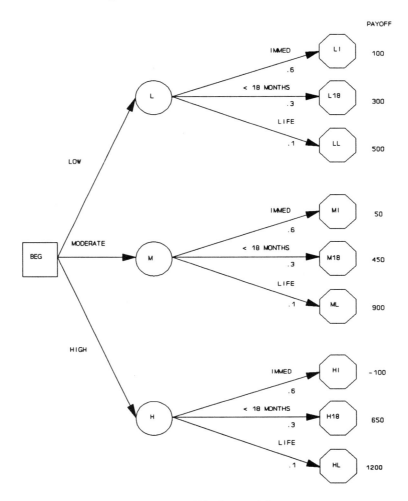

Figure 1: Probabilistic Decision Tree

1. A Sample Problem

Analytic Software Inc. (ASI), a growing software development company is considering promotional activity over the coming year for their new product. The company has narrowed down its decision alternatives to three: undertake a low budget local promotion (LOW), launch a moderate budget regional campaign (MOD), or hire a major advertising company to design and implement a national media blitz (HIGH).

For each alternative, the company's expected returns depend on future conditions. These have been reduced to two possibilities: a competing product is introduced during the year (C), or not (N).

The research department of ASI has estimated the net payoff for each decision alternative and possible state of the future. Based on past experience and current published reports, they have also estimated the conditional probabilities. All of these numbers are shown in Figure 2 and Table 1.

For example, the first branch payoff of -$20,000 gives the cost of the low budget local promotion. As another example, .4 in the probabilistic branch from LOW to LN (LN signifies Low, No competing product) indicates that if ASI opts for a low budget local promotion, there is a 40% chance that there will be no competing product during the first year. The payoff of $35,000 for this branch represents the first year's profit anticipated, given a low budget promotion and no competition. This figure does not include the $20,000 cost of the promotion, which was already assigned at the preceding branch.

After one year, depending on the conditions observed at that time, ASI must decide whether to terminate production or to use the experience gained in the first year to improve the product and continue to promote it. The decision tree in Figure 2 shows the sequence of decisions to be taken, and the possible future states, and also includes the branch probabilities and payoffs (in thousands of dollars) wherever appropriate. Table 1 gives the detailed description of the branches in the tree.

As president of ASI, what decision alternatives will you pick at each decision point?

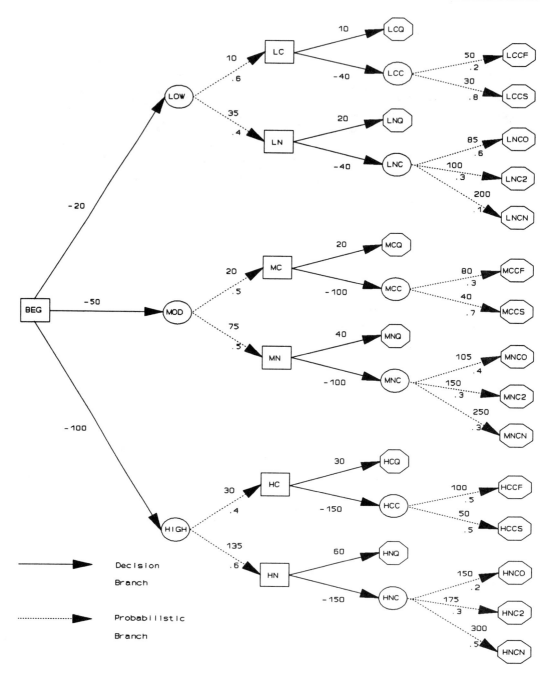

Figure 2: Decision Tree for ASI Example

```
---BRANCH---                                        Branch      Branch
From    To    Description                           Payoff      Prob.

Decisions at the beginning:
BEG     LOW   Use low budget campaign               -20000        .
BEG     MOD   Use moderate budget campaign          -50000        .
BEG     HIGH  Use high budget campaign             -100000        .

Probabilistic branches if low budget campaign is used:
LOW     LC    A competing product within a year     10000        0.6
LOW     LN    No competing product within a year    35000        0.4

Probabilistic branches if moderate budget campaign is used:
MOD     MC    A competing product within a year     20000        0.5
MOD     MN    No competing product within a year    75000        0.5

Probabilistic branches if high budget campaign is used:
HIGH    HC    A competing product within a year     30000        0.4
HIGH    HN    No competing product within a year   135000        0.6


Decisions after one year:

Low budget promotion and a competing product in market
LC      LCQ   Abandon the product                   10000        .
LC      LCC   Enhance and continue promotion       -40000        .

Low budget promotion and no competing product in market
LN      LNQ   Abandon the product                   20000        .
LN      LNC   Enhance and continue promotion       -40000        .

Moderate budget promotion and a competing product in market
MC      MCQ   Abandon the product                   20000        .
MC      MCC   Enhance and continue promotion      -100000        .

Moderate budget promotion and no competing product in market
MN      MNQ   Abandon the product                   40000        .
MN      MNC   Enhance and continue promotion      -100000        .
```

Table 1A: Description of Branches of the Decision Tree

```
High budget promotion and a competing product in market
HC     HCQ     Abandon the product              30000      .
HC     HCC     Enhance and continue promotion   -150000    .

High budget promotion and no competing product in market
HN     HNQ     Abandon the product              60000      .
HN     HNC     Enhance and continue promotion   -150000    .


Probabilistic Branches after second decision:
LCC    LCCF    Competing product a failure      50000      0.2
LCC    LCCS    Competing product is a success   30000      0.8
LNC    LNCO    No immediate competing product   85000      0.6
LNC    LNC2    No competing product w/in 2 years 100000     0.3
LNC    LNCN    No competing product during life 200000     0.1

MCC    MCCF    Competing product a failure      80000      0.3
MCC    MCCS    Competing product is a success   40000      0.7
MNC    MNCO    No immediate competing product   105000     0.4
MNC    MNC2    No competing product w/in 2 years 150000     0.3
MNC    MNCN    No competing product during life 250000     0.3

HCC    HCCF    Competing product a failure      100000     0.5
HCC    HCCS    Competing product is a success   50000      0.5
HNC    HNCO    No immediate competing product   150000     0.2
HNC    HNC2    No competing product w/in 2 years 175000     0.3
HNC    HNCN    No competing product during life 300000     0.5
```

Table 1B: Description of Branches of the Decision Tree

2. Data Entry Using STORM

Figure 3 displays the Editor screen for the decision tree problem of ASI. The entries in the Problem Description area and the Detailed Data area are described below.

```
┌─────────────────────────────────────────────────────────────────────┐
│                  ┤ STORM EDITOR : Decision Trees Module ├             │
│  Title : ANALYTIC SOFTWARE INC.: Promotional Decision                │
│  Number of branches          :          36                           │
│  Objective type (MAX/MIN)     :          MAX                          │
│                                                                       │
│  R1  : C4       FROM NODE    TO NODE     PAYOFF BRANCHPROB            │
│  BRANCH  1         BEG         LOW       -20000.         .            │
│  BRANCH  2         BEG         MOD       -50000.         .            │
│  BRANCH  3         BEG         HIGH     -100000.         .            │
│  BRANCH  4         LOW         LC        10000.        0.6            │
│  BRANCH  5         LOW         LN        35000.        0.4            │
│  BRANCH  6         MOD         MC        20000.        0.5            │
│  BRANCH  7         MOD         MN        75000.        0.5            │
│  BRANCH  8         HIGH        HC        30000.        0.4            │
│  BRANCH  9         HIGH        HN       135000.        0.6            │
│  BRANCH 10         LC          LCQ       10000.         .            │
│  BRANCH 11         LC          LCC      -40000.         .            │
│  BRANCH 12         LN          LNQ       20000.         .            │
│  BRANCH 13         LN          LNC      -40000.         .            │
│  BRANCH 14         MC          MCQ       20000.         .            │
│  BRANCH 15         MC          MCC     -100000.         .            │
│  BRANCH 16         MN          MNQ       40000.         .            │
│  BRANCH 17         MN          MNC     -100000.         .            │
│  BRANCH 18         HC          HCQ       30000.         .            │
│  BRANCH 19         HC          HCC     -150000.         .            │
│  BRANCH 20         HN          HNQ       60000.         .            │
│  BRANCH 21         HN          HNC     -150000.         .            │
│  BRANCH 22         LCC         LCCF      50000.        0.2            │
│  BRANCH 23         LCC         LCCS      30000.        0.8            │
│  BRANCH 24         LNC         LNCO      85000.        0.6            │
│  BRANCH 25         LNC         LNC2     100000.        0.3            │
│  BRANCH 26         LNC         LNCN     200000.        0.1            │
│  BRANCH 27         MCC         MCCF      80000.        0.3            │
│  BRANCH 28         MCC         MCCS      40000.        0.7            │
│  BRANCH 29         MNC         MNCO     105000.        0.4            │
│  BRANCH 30         MNC         MNC2     150000.        0.3            │
│  BRANCH 31         MNC         MNCN     250000.        0.3            │
│  BRANCH 32         HCC         HCCF     100000.        0.5            │
│  BRANCH 33         HCC         HCCS      50000.        0.5            │
│  BRANCH 34         HNC         HNCO     150000.        0.2            │
│  BRANCH 35         HNC         HNC2     175000.        0.3            │
│  BRANCH 36         HNC         HNCN     300000.        0.5            │
│          ┤ Probability associated with BRANCH 1 (. if none) ├─→├      │
└─────────────────────────────────────────────────────────────────────┘
```

Figure 3: Editor Screen for ASI Example

2.1 The Problem Description Area

In addition to the title, only two entries are needed for problem description:

> Number of Branches: The total number of branches in the decision tree. It should always be one less than the number of nodes you have in the tree.

> Objective Type (MAX/MIN): This entry should be MAX or MIN depending on whether the objective involves Payoffs or Costs, respectively.

2.2 The Detailed Data Area

The Data area includes one row for each branch of the tree. For each branch the columns of the data set have fixed labels "FROM NODE," "TO NODE," "PAYOFF" (or "COST" if objective type is "MIN"), and "BRANCH PROB." For each branch, the following information should be entered:

> FROM NODE: An up-to-four-character code for the starting node for this branch.

> TO NODE: An up-to-four-character code for the ending node for this branch.

> PAYOFF (or COST): This value is the payoff or cost associated with this branch. For a decision branch, it can be interpreted as the payoff obtained (or cost incurred) if the decision corresponding to this branch is chosen. If the branch is probabilistic, it represents the immediate payoff if the corresponding to state occurs.

> BRANCH PROB: If the branch corresponds to a decision alternative, this value should be left as a dot ("."), the default value. For the probabilistic or chance branch, this should be the corresponding probability.

3. Executing The Module

After entering the problem data, select the "Execute" option from the Process Menu. Your data will then be checked for consistency and accuracy. If a mistake in data entry is identified, STORM will give you an error report. Otherwise, you will be presented with a

STORM Form as displayed in Figure 4. In this form, you select the output reports you need for your analysis.

```
          SELECTION OF OUTPUT REPORTS

      Sorted Decision Tree Report    : n
      Optimal Decisions Report       : y
      Detailed Decisions Report      : n
```

Figure 4: Output Options

4. Output Reports

The first option, Sorted Decision Tree Report, gives the input data by decision tree level in tabular form. Figure 5 shows the output for our sample problem. The first node, at level zero, is the beginning node, BEG. From it, we have three branches emanating to nodes LOW, MOD, and HIGH, which are represented by the first three rows. Each of those level-one nodes are then listed with their successors, and so on. Nodes are classified into three categories: decision nodes (Dec), probabilistic or chance nodes (Prob), and terminal nodes (End).

```
     ANALYTIC SOFTWARE INC.: Promotional Decision
            DECISION TREE SORTED BY LEVEL
  -- From Node --  ---------- Emanating Branch ----------
  Name Type Level  Name       To Node    Payoff      Prob

  BEG  Dec     0   BRANCH  1   LOW     -20000.0000      .
                   BRANCH  2   MOD     -50000.0000      .
                   BRANCH  3   HIGH -100000.0000        .

  LOW  Prob    1   BRANCH  4   LC       10000.0000   0.6000
                   BRANCH  5   LN       35000.0000   0.4000
```

Figure 5A: Decision Tree Sorted By Level

```
      ANALYTIC SOFTWARE INC.: Promotional Decision
                DECISION TREE SORTED BY LEVEL
      -- From Node --  ---------- Emanating Branch ----------
      Name Type Level  Name        To Node      Payoff      Prob

      MOD  Prob    1   BRANCH  6   MC        20000.0000    0.5000
                       BRANCH  7   MN        75000.0000    0.5000

      HIGH Prob    1   BRANCH  8   HC        30000.0000    0.4000
                       BRANCH  9   HN       135000.0000    0.6000

      LC   Dec     2   BRANCH 10   LCQ       10000.0000       .
                       BRANCH 11   LCC      -40000.0000       .

      LN   Dec     2   BRANCH 12   LNQ       20000.0000       .
                       BRANCH 13   LNC      -40000.0000       .

      MC   Dec     2   BRANCH 14   MCQ       20000.0000       .
                       BRANCH 15   MCC     -100000.0000       .

      MN   Dec     2   BRANCH 16   MNQ       40000.0000       .
                       BRANCH 17   MNC     -100000.0000       .

      HC   Dec     2   BRANCH 18   HCQ       30000.0000       .
                       BRANCH 19   HCC     -150000.0000       .

      HN   Dec     2   BRANCH 20   HNQ       60000.0000       .
                       BRANCH 21   HNC     -150000.0000       .

      LCQ  End     3

      LCC  Prob    3   BRANCH 22   LCCF      50000.0000    0.2000
                       BRANCH 23   LCCS      30000.0000    0.8000

      LNQ  End     3
```

Figure 5B: Decision Tree Sorted By Level

```
        ANALYTIC SOFTWARE INC.: Promotional Decision
               DECISION TREE SORTED BY LEVEL
   -- From Node --  ---------- Emanating Branch ----------
   Name Type Level  Name       To Node    Payoff      Prob

   LNC  Prob    3   BRANCH 24   LNCO    85000.0000   0.6000
                    BRANCH 25   LNC2   100000.0000   0.3000
                    BRANCH 26   LNCN   200000.0000   0.1000

   MCQ  End     3

   MCC  Prob    3   BRANCH 27   MCCF    80000.0000   0.3000
                    BRANCH 28   MCCS    40000.0000   0.7000

   MNQ  End     3

   MNC  Prob    3   BRANCH 29   MNCO   105000.0000   0.4000
                    BRANCH 30   MNC2   150000.0000   0.3000
                    BRANCH 31   MNCN   250000.0000   0.3000

   HCQ  End     3

   HCC  Prob    3   BRANCH 32   HCCF   100000.0000   0.5000
                    BRANCH 33   HCCS    50000.0000   0.5000

   HNQ  End     3

   HNC  Prob    3   BRANCH 34   HNCO   150000.0000   0.2000
                    BRANCH 35   HNC2   175000.0000   0.3000
                    BRANCH 36   HNCN   300000.0000   0.5000

   LCCF End     4

   LCCS End     4

   LNCO End     4
```

Figure 5C: Decision Tree Sorted By Level

```
        ANALYTIC SOFTWARE INC.: Promotional Decision
              DECISION TREE SORTED BY LEVEL
   -- From Node --  ---------- Emanating Branch ----------
   Name Type Level  Name        To Node      Payoff    Prob

   LNC2 End     4

   LNCN End     4

   MCCF End     4

   MCCS End     4

   MNCO End     4

   MNC2 End     4

   MNCN End     4

   HCCF End     4

   HCCS End     4

   HNCO End     4

   HNC2 End     4

   HNCN End     4
```

Figure 5D: Decision Tree Sorted By Level

This report will help you check your data entry, especially if the branches were entered in the Editor screen without any particular order.

The second output option, the Optimal Decisions Report, shows the sequence of optimal choices and the corresponding expected payoffs. As shown in Figure 6, the optimal initial decision is to undertake the national campaign (HIGH), with total expected payoff of $54,500. That payoff is achieved as follows.

```
           ANALYTIC SOFTWARE INC.: Promotional Decision
                     OPTIMAL DECISIONS REPORT
  ----- From Node -----   ----- Emanating Branch -----   ---- To Node ---
  Name Type  Exp Payoff  Name          Prob      Payoff  Name  Exp Payoff

  BEG  Dec    54500.000  BRANCH  3       .   -100000.000  HIGH  154500.000

  HIGH Prob  154500.000  BRANCH  8     0.400   30000.000  HC     30000.000
                         BRANCH  9     0.600  135000.000  HN     82500.000

  HC   Dec    30000.000  BRANCH 18       .     30000.000  HCQ        0.000

  HN   Dec    82500.000  BRANCH 21       .   -150000.000  HNC   232500.000

  HCQ  End        0.000

  HNC  Prob  232500.000  BRANCH 34     0.200  150000.000  HNCO       0.000
                         BRANCH 35     0.300  175000.000  HNC2       0.000
                         BRANCH 36     0.500  300000.000  HNCN       0.000

  HNCO End        0.000

  HNC2 End        0.000

  HNCN End        0.000
```

Figure 6: Optimal Decisions Report

1. The initial promotional cost of $100,000 is offset by subsequent profits of $154,000.

2. The figure of $154,000 is obtained by making the right decisions a year hence, depending on whether or not competition develops.

3. If after a year there is a competitive product in the market (HC), then ASI should quit (HCQ), getting $30,000 payoff for the first year and $30,000 payoff for subsequent phase-out sales. Thus with probability 0.4 we receive $60,000.

4. If no competition arises within a year (HN), then ASI should enhance the product and continue promotion (HNC), resulting in $135,000 payoff in the first year plus net revenue of $82,500 in subsequent years, yielding a total of $217,500 with probability 0.6.

5. The $154,000 in step 2 is the weighted average of the figures in Steps 3. and 4.: (.4)(60000) + (.6)(217,500).

6. The figure of $82,500 for node HN is the expected revenue for the subsequent years: (0.2)(150000) + (0.3)(175000) + (0.5)(300000) = 232,500, less the investment of $150,000 for the enhancement/promotion.

The final output available, Detailed Decisions Report, gives all the computations needed to arrive at the optimum in the same format as the Optimal Decisions report. Asterisks are used to indicate optimal choices at a decision node.

5. Altering Problem Data Dimensions

The columns in the Data area cannot be inserted or deleted. However, the rows (branches in the tree) can be inserted and deleted by using F3 and F4 keys, respectively. Of course, the number of rows should not exceed the allowable maximal limits for your version of the software, and there should always be at least one row. Each time a row is added or deleted, STORM will automatically update the corresponding problem description value.

Appendix A

RUNNING STORM

1. Introduction

Running STORM is slightly different depending on your disk drive configuration. You may have a system with:

- One Floppy Disk Drive
- Two Floppy Disk Drives
- One Fixed Disk Drive and One Floppy Disk Drive

Each of these is discussed below, but you should review only the section dealing with your system configuration. In general, we have tried to make it as easy as possible to run STORM by minimizing the number of diskette exchanges you must make on systems without a fixed disk drive.

If you are a new user of microcomputers and are not familiar with how to start your computer and enter DOS, you may want to review your DOS manual or get help from a more experienced friend. In the following sections, we assume that you have carried out the instructions in Chapter 1 and made working copies of your STORM diskettes on diskettes or the fixed disk where you plan to run STORM. If you have not done so, you should do it at this time.

2. Running STORM on a System with One Floppy Disk Drive

This is the most demanding system for you to run because it requires more diskette exchanges than the other systems. The STORM1 diskette has the sections of STORM which are common to all modules (such as the Editor) and as many modules as can be fitted. The remaining modules reside on the other STORM diskettes. However, you should not be concerned with the assignments of modules to disks, as STORM will always prompt you for the diskette it needs.

We shall assume that you have an "A>" prompt on your monitor. Then the following sequence would be typical of a STORM session:

Step 1.   Insert the working copy of STORM1 into your disk drive.

Step 2.   Type STORM and press the Enter key. The STORM logo should appear. Press any key to continue.

Step 3.   The Main Menu (see Figure 1 in Chapter 2) should appear; select the desired module and press the Enter key.

Step 4.   If the requested module is not on the diskette currently in your disk drive, STORM will prompt you to enter the other STORM diskette and press any key to continue.

Step 5.   You wish to read a previously saved data file from a diskette, so you follow the STORM procedures to specify the file name. If STORM cannot find that file on the inserted diskette, it will tell you so. You can then insert the data diskette and read the file.

Step 6.   You ask STORM to execute a part of the module procedures using the current data, and it needs a part of the program on a STORM diskette that is not in the disk drive. You will again be prompted to enter the proper diskette and press any key to continue.

Step 7.   You complete your analysis and wish to save the results on a data diskette. Be careful! If your working copy diskettes for STORM are not write protected, your report files might be written to one of those diskettes. What you should do is insert the data diskette into your drive and then instruct STORM to write the file on it. Don't worry if you forget, however, since STORM will only write the file if there is adequate space on your diskette. Otherwise, it will simply tell you there's not enough room.

Step 8.   You may exit STORM or return to work with other data sets and/or modules.

From the above discussion, it should be clear that the times you will most likely need to exchange diskettes in your drive are:

- When choosing a new module.
- When reading a data file or writing a report file.
- When returning to execute STORM after other file
  read or write operations.

You may now wish to proceed to Chapter 2 of this manual and complete the introductory exercise.

3. Running STORM on a System with Two Floppy Disk Drives

The STORM1 diskette has the sections of STORM which are common to all modules (such as the Editor) and as many modules as can be fitted. The remaining modules reside on the other STORM diskettes. However, you should not be concerned with the assignments of modules to disks, as STORM will always prompt you for the diskette it needs.

With two floppy disk drives, you could put STORM1 in drive A and STORM2 in drive B, and the package would then run without interruption. However, you should generally run STORM from one drive, leaving the other free to read/write data or report files. We shall assume you have an "A>" prompt on your monitor. Then the following steps would be typical of a STORM session:

Step 1. Insert the working copy of STORM1 into drive A.

Step 2. Type STORM and press the Enter key. The STORM logo should appear. Press any key to continue.

Step 3. The Main Menu (see Figure 1 in Chapter 2) should appear; select the module you wish to use and press the Enter key.

Step 4. If the requested module is not available on either disk drive, STORM will prompt you to enter the needed STORM diskette and press any key to continue. If there is an open drive (no diskette inserted), the diskette may be placed in that drive. Otherwise, you should replace one STORM diskette with the other. This will allow you to leave your data diskette (if applicable) in drive B and your STORM diskette in drive A.

Step 5. You wish to read a previously saved data file from a diskette, so you follow the STORM procedures to specify the file name. You should specify the drive name as the one which is not currently needed for the STORM diskette. Left to its own devices, this is the one STORM will specify as the default.

Step 6. You ask STORM to execute a part of the module procedures using the current data, and it needs a part of the program on a STORM diskette that is not in either disk drive. You will be prompted to enter the proper diskette. You should enter it into the drive which you do not expect to need for any other purpose in your next process step.

Step 7. You complete your analysis and wish to save the results on a data diskette. Be careful! If your working copy diskettes for STORM are not write protected, your report files might be written to one of those diskettes. What you should do is insert the data diskette into the desired drive and then instruct STORM to write the file on it. Don't worry if you forget, however, since STORM will only write the file if there is adequate space on your diskette. Otherwise, it will simply tell you there's not enough room. Again, we recommend that you reserve drive B for data input/output.

Step 8. You may exit STORM or return to work with other data sets and/or modules.

From the above discussion, it should be clear that the times you will most likely need to exchange diskettes in your drives are:

• When choosing a new module
• When reading a data file or writing a report file
• When returning to execute STORM after other file read and/or write operations

You may now wish to proceed to Chapter 2 of this manual and complete the introductory exercise.

4. Running STORM on a System with a Fixed Disk

This is by far the easiest and most desirable method for running STORM. However, if you plan to run STORM from diskettes, you should read sections 2 or 3 of this appendix. If your data files are on the fixed disk, the exchanges described in those sections for data diskettes will not be necessary.

Once you have completed the installation procedures, you should be connected to the directory which contains the STORM files each time you want to run STORM. Otherwise, for advanced DOS users, there is an alternative available. If you wish to be connected to a directory (presumably your data directory) other than the directory where STORM resides, you should include the name of the STORM directory in your PATH statement. That will enable DOS initially to find the STORM main program, and the overlay loader subsequently to find the overlays as they are needed. Consult your DOS manual for further information concerning directories and the PATH command.

Once you are in the proper directory, type STORM and press the Enter key. The logo screen will be displayed on your monitor. Press any key to continue. You are now ready to proceed with the introductory exercise in Chapter 2.

Appendix B

DATA FILES FOR
THE SAMPLE PROBLEMS

For your convenience, we have stored on the STORM diskettes the data for all of the sample problems used in this manual. Thus, once you feel comfortable with the process of data entry, there is no further need to type in all the data when you wish to solve a problem in the course of reviewing a new module. Instead, you can simply read an existing file, choosing the appropriate one for the module at hand. The data files reside on the same diskette as the module they belong to.

Listed below are the names of the data files for each module.

Module	File Name
Linear & Integer Programming	LP.DAT, IP.DAT
Assignment	ASN.DAT
Transportation	
Uncapacitated	TR.DAT
Capacitated	TRC.DAT
Distance Networks	DNET.DAT
Flow Networks	
Maximal flow	FNET.DAT
Transshipment	SHIP.DAT
Project Management	
Deterministic	PM.DAT
Probabilistic	PERT.DAT
Queueing Analysis	QUE.DAT
Inventory	INV.DAT
Assembly Line Balancing	ALB.DAT

Module	File Name
Layout	LAY.DAT
Investment	FIN.DAT
Forecasting	FC.DAT
Production Scheduling	PS.DAT
Material Requirements Planning	
Bill of Material file	BOM.DAT
Master Schedule file	MAST.DAT
Inventory Status file	MRPINV.DAT
Item Master file	ITEM.DAT
Capacity file	CAP.DAT
Statistical Process Control	SPC.DAT
Statistics	ST.DAT
Decision Analysis	DA.DAT
Decision Trees	DT.DAT

Appendix C

THE STORM FORMAT FOR PROBLEM DATA FILES

We present here a brief description of the format and conventions used by STORM when storing the data for a problem in a disk file. This may be useful to the more knowledgeable users of our package who wish to create data files outside of the STORM Editor. Although we do not recommend this practice, it may become necessary. For example, you may have large data sets already prepared in another format, such as the MPS format for linear programming, and want to write your own program to convert those files to run on STORM. Otherwise, you may simply want to be able to look over a data file occasionally and interpret its contents. However, the latter should not be necessary. Instead, read the file into STORM and use the print option on the Process menu to obtain hard copy in the more readable Editor format.

All data files created by STORM are plain, free-format ASCII files. The data entries are laid out in the file, row by row, in the same order in which it is presented on the screen by the data Editor. Therefore, you must be familiar with the data layout for the particular module you are interested in.

When preparing a data file on your own, you can use the Tab character as a delimiter between entries; that is, to signal that you have completed entry of one datum and are moving to the next cell to the right. A blank or space is also interpreted as a delimiter except where blanks are acceptable characters in the entry. A new line must be signalled by the appropriate end-of-line (EOL) characters. It is not necessary to enter an EOL marker each time a new line would start on the Editor screen. However, no line should exceed eighty characters in length.

In the Detailed Data area, an asterisk alone in a data field is interpreted as a signal to retain the default entry for that item and skip to the next field. Two asterisks in a data field are a signal to skip to the next row, retaining the default values in that cell and for all the remaining cells in the current row. If the pair of asterisks occur in the row of column labels, they are interpreted as a signal to skip to the first row of the detailed data. Note that if you use the two asterisks, STORM will expect to find the row label for the following row next in your data file. The sole exception to the above is the MRP module. Since that module makes use of five files (rather than the customary one), an asterisk will cause an error message if you choose the "Execute" branch (see Chapter 19). To overcome this problem, you should first read the file(s) in using the "Prepare Data Files" branch, and then save them to disk. The saved files should then work fine.

It is very important that the Problem Description items be correctly entered. If STORM encounters any infeasible or illegal data in that area, the file read process will terminate fatally. However, once the Problem Description data have been successfully read into core, the Editor can allocate memory for the Detailed Data area. It then proceeds to initialize all the labels and cells in the Data area to the proper defaults. Thereafter, any erroneous entries found while reading the rest of the data file will not terminate the file read process. If such an error is encountered, the default value will be retained and you will be informed of the fact.

We will now discuss the various items in the order they should appear:

Title

This should be entered on the first line of the file. STORM will read to the end of the first line (the first EOL marker) for the title. The title can be at most sixty characters long. There can be embedded blanks in it, and Tabs are also taken as delimiters.

Problem Description Items

These must appear after the title line, in the same order they are visited when you are creating a new data set. Any errors in the entries in this area will terminate the file read process. Since the individual entries cannot have embedded blanks in them, you can use blanks, Tabs, and EOL characters as delimiters.

Column Labels

Column headers should be entered in the file next. There should be one label for each column, in the order they appear on the Editor screen. The labels can be at most ten characters long and can have embedded blanks. Tabs and EOL's will act as delimiters. Because blanks could be embedded, STORM will read ten characters or to the next Tab/EOL character, whichever is shorter. You can put seven to ten labels on one line, delimited by Tabs.

Row Labels and Detailed Data

Enter next the rows of the detailed data, each preceded by its row label, one row at a time. The row labels can be at most ten characters in length and can have embedded blanks. The comments made above about the column labels are valid here, too, and we delimit the row label by a Tab character. The remaining items in the row are entered (left to right) in the order they appear on the Editor screen. In this part of the data set, blanks, Tabs, and EOL's all act as delimiters. The process continues through all the rows of the Detailed Data, or until an end-of-file (EOF) mark is reached.

To summarize, the data files are in a free format and all we really look for is the correct order of the data items and proper delimiters between them.

Appendix D

IMPORTING AND EXPORTING DATA

1. Introduction

In many situations you will be faced with a need to either read into (import) or extract from (export) a STORM data set. Importing refers to reading in a block of information and positioning it at a certain place in a data set already created, whereas by exporting we mean extracting a block of data and storing it in a disk file.

Importing data is necessary whenever some information required as a part of a STORM data set already exists in a machine-readable form. If the volume of such information is tiny, it can be easily entered at the keyboard, using the STORM Editor. However, in case of large volumes of data, it may be wiser to import it directly from a disk file, thus avoiding a lot of unnecessary keystrokes and, more importantly, eliminating any data entry or typographical errors. Importing is thus useful when the information exists on a mainframe or a minicomputer and is to be downloaded to the microcomputer, or when it exists in a database or a spreadsheet and can be extracted easily as a disk file.

Exporting a block of a STORM data set can be useful in case you want to use a part of the data to create some plots or graphs. You may also need to include a part of the data in a report that describes your analysis, for purposes of documentation.

In addition to the situations mentioned above, there can be innumerable needs to use the import/export facilities within STORM. For example, after analyzing a time series using the forecasting module, you may want to build an economic model for it using the statistics module. The column of data can then be exported out of the forecasting data set and imported later into a statistics data set. At the end of this appendix, we offer several suggestions on other situations wherein you may find the import/export facility handy.

2. Description of the Import/Export Process

The import/export facility in any module of STORM is available as a block operation in the Editor. The block operation is invoked with the F1 key and is described in section 7 of chapter 4. The import/export process consists of the following steps, taken after you have selected either the *Import ASCII file* or the *Export ASCII file* option.

- Marking the block of data
- Specifying some parameters associated with it
- Specifying a name for the disk file

Of these steps, marking of a block is discussed in section 4.7, and is accomplished by pressing the F1 key after positioning the cell pointer at each of the two corners that define the block. The file specification is done on a form similar to the one used for data and report files. The only difference is that the default extension for import/export files is EXT, since they contain extracts from the data set. Like the data and report files, the extract files are ASCII files, for your convenience.

2.1 Parameters for Import/Export Blocks

Because of the nature of the import/export files and the way they are intended to be used, it is necessary to get more input from you after the block has been identified. Therefore, once you have defined the block, you will be presented with the form shown in Figure 1.

```
            IMPORT/EXPORT BLOCK PARAMETERS


        Include column labels in the block ?   :  n

        Include row labels in the block ?      :  n

        Number of columns in a group           :  .
```

Figure 1: Specification form for block parameters

The first two parameters are needed because the row and column labels cannot be marked as a part of the block during the marking process. Particularly for import operations, it may be essential to include some meaningful names for the variables, time series, etc. in the extract files and have them read into the STORM data set so that interpretation of the reports created by STORM will be easier. Whether to include both types of labels or only one will depend on the module and the problem you are working on. For example, in a forecasting problem, you are likely to want to import both the time series names and the labels for the periods, whereas in an inventory problem, only the row labels need to be imported. Our default for both these parameters is "n" for no. Note that inclusion of the row labels increments the number of columns in the block to be read/written by one. Similarly, including the column labels affects the number of rows processed.

The *Number of columns in a group* parameter provides you with some flexibility that may be necessary for a smooth import/export operation. However, its main purpose is to help you when you are importing files created outside STORM or when you are exporting files to be fed into some other program. Whenever you are exporting blocks to be imported into a STORM data set, it may be best to leave the parameter at its default, a missing value. STORM will then assume that the parameter is equal to the number of columns in a block, plus one if row labels are included.

As we said earlier, the last parameter is most useful when the extract files are acting as a bridge between STORM and some other program. For example, suppose you want to import a block of twenty columns from a spreadsheet. When you direct the spreadsheet to export the block, it may only write the block out in lines that are at most eighty characters long. If each column of data takes nine characters, with an additional space separating two adjacent columns, the spreadsheet program will be able to fit only eight columns in one line. In such circumstances, many programs will write the block of twenty columns out in groups of eight columns. So the spreadsheet will write the first eight columns completely, stretching over as many lines as the number of rows in the block being written out. In our example, it will then write out the next eight columns completely, and then finish the job by writing the last four columns. If you were to then consider importing that file into a STORM data set, the grouping parameter should be set equal to eight.

Similarly, for export operations, the value of the group parameter can be set correctly only when you know something about the program that will be ultimately reading in the extracted block. It may have some restrictions on the length of each record or line in the extract file and the order in which the data in the block must be presented in the extract file in order for it to be able to read the information properly. Once you study these requirements, you will be able to specify the correct value of the group parameter.

To summarize, the group parameter can take any value between one and the number of columns in the block being imported/exported. In either case, you must have the correct value for this parameter for the operation to be successful.

3. Reading of Import Files

The import files are read by the STORM file read function that is also employed in reading whole data files. While reading the import files, this function does not expect to read the data set title, the problem description items, and any other data which is not a part of the marked block. One other difference between the ordinary read process and the import process is the order in which the data are expected to be read. During data set read operations, we expect to read an entire row of data, before proceeding to the next row. During the import operation, we are guided by the group parameter specified. For example, if the group parameter is seven, we expect to read the first seven columns of the block completely, and then the next seven columns, and so on until all the columns of the block are read in.

Apart from these differences, the file read process for whole data sets and importing of blocks is identical. The conventions laid out in Appendix C for the format to be used for the labels, numeric data, and character or alphanumeric data are also observed during the reading of the import files. For example, we expect to read all data in a free format, with spaces, tabs, and end-of-line markers acting as delimiters for all data items except the labels. Only tabs and end-of-line markers act as delimiters for the labels, and we read at most ten characters for any label. Similarly, we will read at most four characters for nonnumeric data items. In addition, as each entry is being read in, error checks will be performed to determine if it is acceptable in the cell it is intended for. Any errors will result in warning messages.

4. Writing of Export Files

Export files are plain ASCII files, which are formatted. Each column of data is written with a fixed field width of ten characters, with a space separating two adjacent columns. We will write as many columns on one line as the group parameter specified by you. For example, if you mark a block with ten columns, and specify the group parameter to be five, we will write out five columns on each line and the total length of each line or record will be fifty four. The first five columns will be completely written out, followed by the next group of five columns. The number of lines in the extract file written out will be twice the number of rows in the marked block.

While writing out, all numeric data will be right-justified in the field of ten characters, while labels and other nonnumeric data will be left-justified.

5. Tips and Suggestions

There are other uses for the import/export facility in addition to moving data between STORM modules. Some of these are listed below, but the list is by no means exhaustive. It should give you a flavor of what can be accomplished with import/export operations.

Copy and move operations: With the import/export facility, you can copy blocks of data in the Editor. This can be accomplished by first exporting the source block and then importing it as many times as necessary. This can come in handy in linear programming, if you have block-diagonal coefficient matrices with identical blocks. The move operation can also be accomplished by first copying the block to its new destination and later deleting it from its old place.

Correcting data entry omissions: Sometimes you might omit entering one cell's data. If you are entering data by columns, you might realize the mistake when you have reached the end of the column. If you have already entered a few columns, the insert/delete operations are of no help to you. Luckily, you can move a part of the column by the approach described above and then insert the omitted entry in its cell.

Transposing a square block: While you may never need to do this, we will describe how this can be done just to leave you with some ideas that may come in handy in other situations. Suppose you want to transpose a block of ten columns and ten rows. As a first step you can mark the block and export it with a group parameter of one. Each column will then be written entirely before the next column is written to the disk file. As a second step, you should mark the same block again and import the extract file just written out, this time with a group parameter of ten. The result will be a transpose of the original block.

Getting around problem description entries that cannot be altered: In some STORM modules, there are some problem description entries that determine the layout and dimensions of the detailed data matrix. Therefore, these entries cannot be altered in the Editor. Using the import/export operations, you can get around this difficulty. For example, in the transportation module, if you declared your problem to be uncapacitated and later wanted to make it capacitated, here is how you could do it. First you should create another data set that is declared to be capacitated and is of the same dimensions as the first data set. Then you could export all the information from the first data set which is common to the capacitated data set, like the labels, the cost matrix, the supply and demand arrays, to a disk file and import it in the new data set. You now have a capacitated data set and can go ahead and enter the capacities on the routes. A similar situation arises if you have created a project management data set with deterministic activity times and would like to convert it to one with probabilistic activity times. In general, you can export all the common information from the old data set and import it into the new data set.

We hope with these few tips, you will have become aware of the utility and versatility of the import/export operations in STORM. Once you have experimented with it, we think you will find it to be useful.

INDEX

STORM: PERSONAL VERSION 3.0
SOFTWARE LICENSE AGREEMENT

OPENING THIS PACKAGE MEANS THAT YOU ACCEPT THESE TERMS AND CONDITIONS. IF YOU DO NOT AGREE TO THEM, RETURN THE UNOPENED PACKAGE TO YOUR DEALER FOR A REFUND.

1. The software remains the property of Storm Software, Inc. Storm Software, Inc. grants you a nonexclusive license to use it subject to this Agreement. The software involves valuable copyright, trade secret, trademark and other proprietary rights of Storm Software, Inc. Storm Software, Inc. reserves all such rights. You agree not to infringe, and agree to take appropriate steps for the protection of such rights.

2. You may use the software on a single computer or move it and use on another computer, but the software may not be used on more than one computer at the same time under any circumstance. You may make one copy of the software solely for back-up purposes. You must reproduce and include the copyright notice on such back-up copy. Any such back-up copy of the software will be the property of Storm Software, Inc. and will be subject to this Agreement.

3. You agree not to (i) copy (except as permitted herein), disassemble, change or modify the software of the accompanying materials, (ii) assign, transfer, or grant sublicenses or other rights to the software, (iii) install the software on a local area network, or (iv) provide use of the software in any multiple user arrangement to users who are not individually licensed by Storm Software, Inc.

4. DISCLAIMER: THE SOFTWARE IS SUPPLIED "AS IS" WITHOUT WARRANTY OF ANY KIND, EITHER EXPRESS OR IMPLIED. YOU ASSUME THE ENTIRE RISK AS TO THE PERFORMANCE AND RESULTS OF THE SOFTWARE. SHOULD THE SOFTWARE PROVE DEFECTIVE, YOU (AND NOT STORM SOFTWARE, INC. OR ITS DEALERS) ASSUME THE ENTIRE COST OF ALL NECESSARY SERVICING, REPAIR OR CORRECTION.

STORM SOFTWARE, INC. EXPRESSLY DISCLAIMS AND SHALL HAVE NO LIABILITY FOR ANY IMPLIED WARRANTIES, INCLUDING BUT NOT LIMITED TO IMPLIED WARRANTIES OF MERCHANTABILITY, OR FITNESS FOR A PARTICULAR PURPOSE. SOME STATES DO NOT ALLOW THE EXCLUSION OF IMPLIED WARRANTIES, SO THE ABOVE EXCLUSION MAY NOT APPLY TO YOU. THIS WARRANTY GIVES YOU SPECIFIC LEGAL RIGHTS WHICH VARY FROM STATE TO STATE.

WE HAVE NO LIABILITY TO YOU OR ANY OTHER PERSON OR ENTITY FOR (i) ANY DAMAGE OR LOSS, INCLUDING SPECIAL, INCIDENTAL OR CONSEQUENTIAL DAMAGES, CAUSED BY USE OF, OR INABILITY TO USE,

/ARE, DIRECTLY OR INDIRECTLY, EVEN IF STORM
.E, INC. HAS BEEN ADVISED OF THE POSSIBILITY OF SUCH
ES; (ii) CLAIM OF INFRINGEMENT; OR (iii) CLAIM IN TORT,
.1ER OR NOT ARISING IN WHOLE OR PART FROM STORM
WARE, INC.'S NEGLIGENCE, STRICT LIABILITY OR PRODUCT
BILITY. SOME STATES DO NOT ALLOW THE LIMITATION OR
.CLUSION OF LIABILITY FOR INCIDENTAL OR CONSEQUENTIAL
JAMAGES, SO THE ABOVE LIMITATION OR EXCLUSION MAY NOT
APPLY TO YOU.

Prentice Hall warrants that the diskettes on which the software is recorded are free
from defects in materials and workmanship under normal use for a period of ninety
(90) days from the date of delivery as evidenced by a copy of your receipt.

5. Storm Software Inc.'s liability (whether in tort, contract or otherwise, and
notwithstanding any fault, negligence, strict liability or product liability of Storm
Software, Inc.) with regard to the software or this Agreement will not in any event
exceed the compensation paid by you for the software.

6. If you violate this Agreement, we may terminate your license to use the software and
take other action against you. Upon such termination, you agree either to destroy
your copy of the software or to return your copy of the software to us at our request.

7. This agreement will be governed by the laws of Ohio.

8. Should any part of this Agreement be held invalid, the remainder of the Agreement
will still be in effect.

9. As used in this Agreement (i) "you" and "your" refer to any person or entity that
acquires or uses this package; (ii) "we" and "our" means Storm Software, Inc.; (ii)
"package" means the software, the user's manual(s) and other items accompanying this
Agreement; (iv) "software" means the computer program contained in this package,
together with any and all codes, techniques, software tools, formats, designs, concepts,
methods, processes, know-how and ideas associated with that computer program, any
and all copies of all or any part of the software and any and all manuals and other
printed material contained in this package relating to the software.

10. YOU ACKNOWLEDGE THAT YOU HAVE READ THIS AGREEMENT,
UNDERSTAND IT AND AGREE TO BE BOUND BY ITS TERMS AND
CONDITIONS. YOU ALSO AGREE THAT THIS AGREEMENT IS THE
COMPLETE AND EXCLUSIVE STATEMENT OF THE AGREEMENT
BETWEEN US.

11. Should you have any questions concerning this agreement, please write to: Storm
Software, Inc., P.O. Box 22658, Cleveland, OH 44122-9998.